D1106750

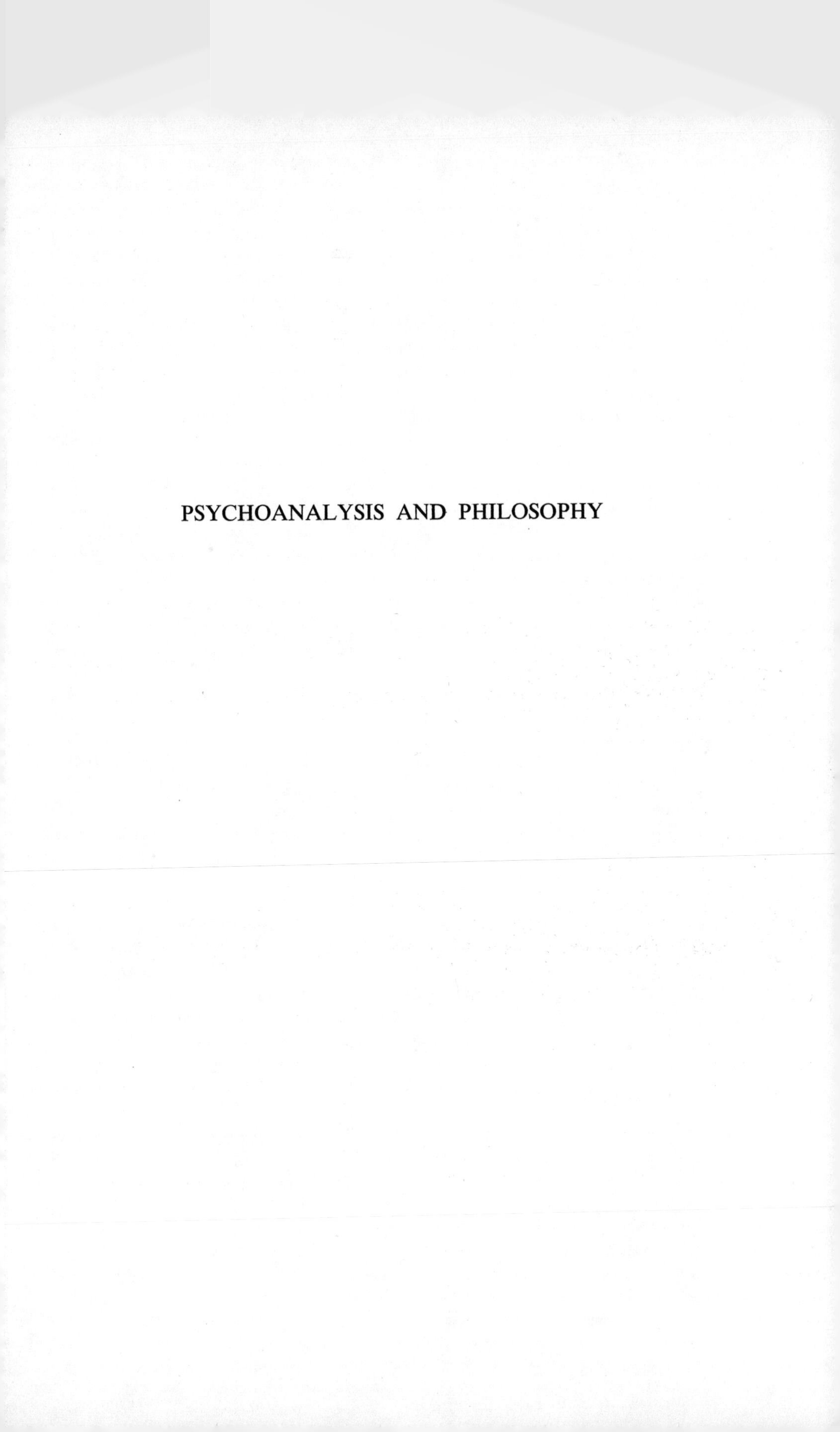

PSYCHOANALYSIS AND PHILOSOPHY

Psychoanalysis and Philosophy

Edited by

CHARLES HANLY
and MORRIS LAZEROWITZ

INTERNATIONAL UNIVERSITIES PRESS, INC.
New York New York

Library of Congress Catalog Card Number: 77-138247

Manufactured in the United States of America

CONTENTS

EDITORS' INTRODUCTION

Psychoanalysis is among the latest in the series of significant scientific discoveries that have made basic improvements in our understanding of nature, history, and man. Although it is still unclear what the full range of the influence of psychoanalysis on the different branches of philosophy will be, it is certain that the influence should be very great. This collection of original papers is an exploration of a variety of relationships between philosophy and psychoanalysis by members of both disciplines who share a common reciprocal interest. It constitutes an attempt to clear the air and dispel misunderstandings, with the aim of improving our understanding of both disciplines and achieving a rapproachement between them. The studies fall into the following categories: applied psychoanalysis, scientific method in psychoanalysis and other sciences, Freudian theory and recent rival theories, the nature of philosophy and the application of psychoanalytic concepts to philosophy.

This work does not attempt to forge any systematic, logical unification ot psychoanalysis with philosophy. Professor Putnam of Harvard University wished, in the words of Jones, to "bring about a union of science with philosophy." Freud was unsympathetic to any sort of attempt to blend psychoanalysis with philosophy; Freud's often quoted observation was: "Putnam's philosophy is like a beautiful centre piece; everyone admires it but nobody touches it." A number of remarks Jones makes in his writing leaves it an open question whether he was opposed to any attempt to bring the two subjects together into some sort of unity. Two observations he made in his posthumously published *Free Associations* (1959) will perhaps suffice to show his ambivalent attitude toward philosophy. About Jung, who postulated a psychic toxin by which the mind poisoned the brain, he wrote: "His grasp of philosophical principles was so insecure that it was little wonder that they later degenerated into mystical obscurantism" (p. 165). But about Greek science he wrote: "It is no chance that when the Greek genius faltered at the threshold of scientific thought by disdaining the experimental method and enmeshing itself in the quandaries of philosophy, it was medical study alone which forced it into some relationship, however strained, with reality" (p. 15). The opposing implications regarding philosophy embedded in these statements cannot fail to reflect a conflict in his opinion of philosophy, and other of his remarks strengthen the impression that he was both drawn to it and repelled by it. Despite this underlying ambivalence, however, his interest in philosophy was sustained, and there can be no doubt that he was eager for mutual understanding among psychoanalysts and philosophers.

The collection of essays is dedicated to the memory of Ernest Jones who was one of the most important and original followers of Freud, and who has made an impressive personal contribution to human understanding. With a fearlessness of thought and action that matched Freud's courage, Jones brought psychoanalysis to Canada and the United States, where it has flourished and steadily expanded ever since. He gave distinction to the University of Toronto on whose Faculty of Medicine he taught for four years. During this time, which he described as his "most prolific years in respect of literary output," he wrote his famous analytical study on *Hamlet, The Nightmare,* and many other well-known contributions. His interests extended in many directions beyond psychoanalysis to literature, art, and music. His special interest in philosophy was, in some measure, responsible for these studies.

CHARLES HANLY
MORRIS LAZEROWITZ

REFERENCE

Jones, E. (1959), *Free Associations: Memoirs of a Psychoanalyst.* New York: Basic Books.

INTRODUCTION

Elizabeth R. Zetzel, M.D.

> The doctrine of repression is the foundation stone upon which the whole structure of psychoanalysis rests, the most essential part of it. Yet it is nothing but a theoretical formulation of a phenomenon which may be observed as often as one undertakes the analysis of a neurotic. One notices a resistance then making itself evident in opposition to the work of analysis and inducing a failure to recall memories in order to frustrate it. . . . Considered theoretically, the fact that this resistance coincides with an amnesia leads inevitably to that view of the unconscious which is peculiar to psychoanalysis and which after all distinguishes it quite clearly from philosophical speculations about the unconscious [Freud, 1914, p. 16].

Freud made this statement in 1914. The title of this volume bears evidence to a continuing interest in the relationship between philosophy and psychoanalysis. Despite significant developments in both disciplines, about only one of which I am qualified to write, the crucial problem area remains the same. It concerns the significance, both qualitative and quantitative, of that part of mental life which exists outside the range of conscious introspection. How far is conscious thought, the instrument on which Descartes based his fundamental premise, an independent vari-

Dr. Zetzel is Director, Psychotherapy Study Center, Massachusetts Mental Health Center; Associate Clinical Professor of Psychiatry, Harvard Medical School; and Training Analyst, Boston Psychoanalytic Society.

able? How far, conversely, is it comparable to the part of an iceberg which is visible above the waterline? —the complex end product of multidetermined unconscious physical and mental activities.

Philosophers had introduced the concept of unconscious processes before Freud made his pioneer discoveries. The empirical phenomenon, resistance, led to theoretical formulation of repression. The dynamically repressed unconscious, as Freud understood it, was not synonymous with the nonconscious. It comprised, first, the significant memories which had been purposively forgotten. Of equal, if not greater importance, however, were the alien, unwanted wishes which he first described in *The Interpretation of Dreams* (1900-1901). Dreams, which he described as "the royal road to the unconscious" had, as we now know, played an important role in the development of Descartes' thought. Indeed, Lewin (1958) suggests that Descartes' "res cogitans" more closely resembles the subjective experience of the successful dreamer than it does the thought processes of our conscious waking life. One may thus raise some question as to the definition of thought implicit to the famous axiom, "I think, therefore I am." The differentiation between primitive primary-process thinking and acquired reality-oriented secondary-process logical thought remains a central area of common interest to the philosopher and the psychoanalyst. This also is one of the areas in which Ernest Jones made significant and important contributions.

Before considering Jones' *Essays in Applied Psycho-Analysis,* (1964) certain general questions must be raised as to the areas in which we may best approach the relationship between psychoanalysis and philosophy. Are these areas actually those explicitly directed toward subjects outside the range of clinical psychoanalysis? Must we not in addition always bear in mind the close interrelationship between clinical findings and their application, thus seeking the more general implications of contributions not explicitly defined as pertaining to applied psychoanalysis? This general question is ably dealt with by Roazen (1969). He makes it abundantly clear that the Freudian contributions most relevant to his subjects are not the essays whose titles suggest that they are most relevant. It is, rather, the consistent approach to the unconscious roots of mental life which adds to our understanding of the nature of man both as an individual and as a member of society.

The same general approach is necessary in considering those of Jones' contributions relevant to the title of this volume. These are by no means confined to his *Essays in Applied Psycho-Analysis* (1911-1922). His papers on anxiety illustrate his general biological approach to the nature of man. His papers on female sexuality bear evidence to his unwillingness to accept a one-sided approach to the nature of human intrapsychic conflict. His open-mindedness in respect to some of the disturbing implications of Melanie Klein's contributions bear evidence to his attitude toward the expansion of knowledge. In "The Future of Psychoanalysis" (1936), he stated:

> . . . we must brace ourselves to welcome such changes, fortifying ourselves with the reflection that we face new truth and to hold truth above all other considerations was Freud's greatest lesson to us and his most precious legacy to psychological science [p. 276].

It is appropriate that this volume, dedicated to his memory, be introduced by specific emphasis on internal consistency and steadiness of Jones' point of view from 1908, when he made his first analytic contribution, up to the time of his death.

Very few contemporary philosophers, psychologists, or psychiatrists would deny the enormous importance and continued impact of many of Freud's pioneer discoveries. Verbal acceptance and acknowledgement of his genius is often, however, highly deceptive. Ernest Jones was one of the pioneer analysts who remained most alert to the manifold expressions of all that may be included under the simple heading, "resistance." The philosopher, Nietzsche, made the following statement: " 'I have done this,' says my memory; 'I cannot have done this,' says my pride. Finally, memory gives way." This statement was cited by Freud (1901, p. 147) in a discussion of repression touching on the relationship between psychoanalysis and philosophy. It might be described as one of the basic cornerstones of Ernest Jones' personal philosophy. Genuine search for truth involves willingness to confront one's self with certain fundamental aspects of human nature. These are inevitably, and often increasingly, painfully unwelcome to pride, to consciousness, and above all to the unconscious. This fundamental attitude determined Jones' relative lack of enthusiasm for developments within the discipline of traditional psychoanalysis which tended to make the profession more widely accepted as respectable and scientific. It was not that he minimized the importance or the philosophical implications of psychoanalysis as a general psychology which included understanding of the nature of consciousness, the links between psychoanalysis and literature, mythology, anthropology and linguistics. Quite the contrary; it was Jones who coined the term "so-called normal" to indicate the depth of pathology which may be consistent with external adaptation. It was Jones who wrote the first definitive article on the psychoanalytic theory of symbolism and its relation to other forms of indirect representation and the development of language. It was Jones who made some of the most scholarly efforts to investigate the history and the prehistory in both language and tribal customs of certain superstitions, of the nightmare, of the basic oedipal triangle and its manifold variations in folklore, myth, and poetic drama.

Jones' most important contributions to applied psychoanalysis antedated those developments comprised under the heading of contemporary ego psychology. These, as is well known, have added much to our knowledge of the ego's modes of defense and adaptation. The impact of environment and culture on the developing child has provided many areas in which contemporary psychoanalysis has found new lines of communication with other disciplines. Jones was not only a psychiatrist and a physician, but also a highly erudite scholar. He brought these gifts to bear in the area of unconscious mental content and its basic homogeneity. He sought such evidence in the taboos of the primitive, in the roots of language, in the superstitions of civilized man, in the rituals of different religions, in the dreams and symptoms of the adult neurotic, and in the slips and errors of the ordinary civilized adult. Freud had been the pioneer in all of these areas. Jones was less speculative, possibly less impatient with the tedium of bibliographical research, and more satisfied with certain of Freud's basic findings than Freud himself. In his writings on applied psychoanalysis, he set himself a goal which can only be appreciated fully with the perspective gained by time, distance, and the added knowledge which has been accumulated since.

This goal might be summarized as follows: In *The Interpretation of Dreams,* Freud first described and documented the qualitative differences between primary- and secondary-process thinking. The unconscious part of the mind, whatever its sources and meaning, is only capable of the first. It can only wish. It cannot test reality, it knows no opposites, and it cannot distinguish part from whole. It can and must accept any available path of discharge. In this context, Freud described condensation, reversal, and the other forms of substitution and shift of emphasis comprised under the general concept of displacement. These, in summary, characterize unconscious, i.e., primary mental processes.

In interpreting dreams and the symptoms of adult neurotic patients, Freud demonstrated the means by which unconscious mental processes regressively modify familiar, essentially logical thoughts. Thoughts, memories, and wishes subject to such processes continue throughout life to dominate that part of the mind which, for whatever reason, is inaccessible to the corrections imposed by the perception of external reality. By applying to mental life the principle of determinism then dominant in the physical sciences, Freud then found it possible to deduce much of the latent meaning expressed by the manifest façade of the dream or the neurotic symptom. He discovered exceptions to the general statement that the meaning of the dream or the symptom cannot be understood in terms of its manifest content. Certain dream elements, for example, elicited no significant personal associations or memories. These elements are, moreover, frequently found in very similar forms, not only in different dreams of the same dreamer, but also in the dreams of others. They often closely resemble figures or objects familiar in legend, myth, and fairy story. In dreams they can often best be understood in relation to the latent meaning of the rest of the manifest dream, increasingly recognized as the disguised gratification of a repressed infantile sexual wish. In briefest terms, this describes some of the findings which initiated the psychoanalytic theory of symbolism.

It would be outside the scope of this Introduction to enter into a detailed discussion of the theory of symbolism. Certain of Jones' (1916) statements in his important paper on the subject may be subject to some modification in the light of contemporary knowledge. Basically, however, his concept of the fundamental nature of that which he described as true symbolism retains its nucleus of significance and importance. I would, in this context, like to consider mainly what I believe to be the basic orientation and goal which determined Jones' approach not only to symbolism, but to the other topics discussed in his *Essays in Applied Psycho-Analysis*.

If, one might state, primitive mental life (whether phylogenetic or ontogenetic) is governed by primary-process thinking with the emergence of characteristic symbols, how can this discovery be demonstrated by scholarly, organized research? *The Interpretation of Dreams* (Freud, 1900-1901) has shown that this very process involves the displacements which determine gross shifts of value, bizarre substitutions, and even complete reversals. In this case, it is indeed possible that black may appear not only as white, but simultaneously, consecutively, or in reversal as green, blue, or red. Hate may, as Freud demonstrated in the interpretation of one of his own dreams, parade under the guise of great affection or love. Here, in a general form, we are confronted with one of the problems which has understandably proved most provocative to the critics of psychoanalysis. How can one deal with a theory of current life which is determined by a concept of mental processes which, by their very nature, stubbornly refuse to conform to all the rules of reason and logic? These, after all, remain the major equipment of the scientist and philosopher.

Ernest Jones was almost uniquely sensitive to this problem. As early as 1908, he indicated his awareness of the hidden resistance which could be implicit to verbal, rational acceptance of Freud's findings. It is not only the sexual or aggressive content of unconscious fantasy which determines the strength of negative reactions; it is also the mode of thought, its irrationality and absurdity which must deeply offend our usual conception of ourselves as logical, reasonable, sensible human beings. But suppose, one might imagine Jones thinking to himself, one were to use one's reason, one's learning, and one's patient curiosity to investigate some of these symbols recognized in dreams. If, as suggested, they are universal, produced independently by human beings living in all parts of the world, in all ages, then there should be some available evidence. Let us take a common substance like salt, for example, and find out what it has meant and continues to mean to mankind over and above its significance as a necessity to life.

The contemporary reader of some of Jones' (1911-1922) essays, for example, "On the Symbolic Significance of Salt" (Vol. 2, pp. 22-109), "The Madonna's Conception Through the Ear" (Vol. 2, pp. 266-357), or on "Beliefs Concerning the Nightmare" (Vol. 2, pp. 110-113), may at times feel that Jones is belaboring the obvious. The detailed enumeration of superstitions and the investigation of the common roots of words do not always make for very interesting reading. The skeptical reader might, moreover, wonder whether Jones proves his point. Salt has had very different meanings in different cultures at different periods of history. Here it may be a dangerous taboo; there it may be used as a good luck amulet. To be seated *above the salt* has a well-established traditional meaning. The ominous implication of spilled salt is equally familiar.

But we now know that some of the most common symbols may have different, even opposite meanings. There is a rich literature on many symbols—the bridge, for example. Does this confound the theory of symbolism? Does it not rather mean that in order to understand symbols we have to remember that, since they are unconsciously produced, they are subject to the same distortions attributable to the very nature of primary-process thinking which determines the disguises which characterize the manifest dream? Though I do not believe he made this point quite explicit, Jones' (1911-1922) essays richly demonstrate the ubiquity and importance of primary-process thinking in determining not only the mores and the superstitions but also the symbols and rituals which express some of the religious and moral values of mankind. With rare exceptions, this work was not undertaken in a spirit of controversy or polemics. It was not, on the whole, directly imaginative or creative. It was rather investigative and cumulative. Its major permanent significance does not derive primarily from its actual subject matter or content. Other writers have made and are making at least equally valuable contributions to our understanding of both specific symbols and to the relation between psychoanalysis and other disciplines. Jones' method and his contributions do, however, bear closely on the topic included within the title of this volume, namely the relationship between psychoanalysis and philosophy. Whether or not the contemporary philosopher or psychologist accepts Freudian instinct theory is essentially irrelevant to the crucial issues. These concern the qualitative differences between conscious and unconscious mental life and the possible methods by means of which a philosophy or a psychology can include the irrational and the concrete within its horizons.

One of the popular contemporary answers to this problem

concerns attempts to expand the field of conscious experience. The dangers this entails are becoming increasingly familiar with, for example, the spread of the hallucinogenic drugs. The experiences in question may nevertheless be seen as further confirmation of the continued importance of the concrete and primary, under the surface of our conscious, often restricted mental life. The readiness of unconscious material to emerge as dream, fantasy, or hallucination during the creative process, sleep, psychosis, or the influence of drugs concerns the role, both positive and negative, of direct concrete experience as compared with abstract logical thought. Jones' approach to this same area involved the search for evidence of the concrete and primary in folklore, myth, and literature. He achieved his goal to a significant degree, posing the basic problems which confront both philosopher and psychoanalyst. I concluded an earlier tribute to Ernest Jones (Zetzel, 1958) with a statement equally appropriate to this Introduction:

> We can recognize a man endowed with the highest intellectual gifts and an outstanding capacity for secondary-process thought, directing his interest to the expansion of a theory of mental life which stresses the continued activity and power of the instinctual, the concrete and the primary. This dichotomy characterized both his own contributions and his attitude towards controversial issues. . . . It is therefore appropriate to remind ourselves that Ernest Jones, dean of psycho-analysts and the biographer of Freud, emphasized to the end of his life the permanent significance and validity of the fundamental concepts so clearly described in the original Freudian model [p. 317].

REFERENCES

Freud, S. (1900-1901), The Interpretation of Dreams. *Standard Edition,* 4 & 5. London: Hogarth Press, 1953.

——— (1901), The Psychopathology of Everyday Life. *Standard Edition,* 6. London: Hogarth Press, 1960.

——— (1914), On the History of the Psychoanalytic Movement. *Standard Edition,* 14:7-66. London: Hogarth Press (1957).

Jones, E. (1911-1922), *Essays in Applied Psycho-Analysis.* New York: International Universities Press, 1964.
——— (1916), The Theory of Symbolism. *Brit. J. Psychol.,* 9:181-229.
——— (1936), The Future of Psychoanalysis. *Internat. J. Psycho-Anal.,* 17:269-277.
Lewin, B. D. (1958), *Dreams and the Uses of Regression.* New York: International Universities Press.
Roazen, P. (1969), *Freud and Political and Social Thought.* New York: Alfred A. Knopf.
Zetzel, E. (1958), Ernest Jones: His Contribution to Psychoanalytic Theory. *Internat. J. Psycho-Anal.,* 39:311-317.

PHILOSOPHY, LANGUAGE AND ILLUSION

ALICE AMBROSE, PH.D., LL.D.

"What is your aim in philosophy?—To show the fly the way out of the fly-bottle."—*Philosophical Investigations,* Wittgenstein

"What has once been thought can never be unthought." *The Physicists,* Duerrenmatt

Anyone who reads the post-*Tractatus* writings of Wittgenstein cannot fail to be struck by the psychoanalytic atmosphere with which he surrounds a good deal of his philosophical work. It is therefore interesting to learn that Wittgenstein once described himself as "a disciple of Freud" (Rhees, 1942-1946), that his first reaction to reading Freud, presumably sometime after 1919, was one of admiration. ". . . I sat up in surprise," he said, "here was someone who had something to say" (p. 41). It is known that he later rejected psychoanalysis, its theory, and what he took to be its practice. But he continued to admire Freud for his observations and suggestions, and apparently psychoanalytic theory kept sufficient hold on his mind to prompt him to discuss it in the

---

Dr. Ambrose is Sophia and Austin Smith Professor of Philosophy at Smith College. She has published widely in the field of philosophy and was Editor of the *Journal of Symbolic Logic* from 1954 to 1968.

course of several lectures during his years at Cambridge University. Moore (1959), to whose chair he succeeded, reports on criticisms made in lectures he gave in the academic year 1932-1933 (pp. 316-317).[1] By 1946 he had so far renounced his discipleship as to characterize psychoanalysis, in private conversation, as offering or imposing upon one a mythology (Rhees, 1942-1946, p. 52). What was rejected, however, seems to have left a residue which deeply influenced his thinking about philosophy during the 1930's and 1940's, and in my opinion psychoanalytic ideas which colored his thought were the natural medium in which to present his new and illuminating conception of the nature of philosophical problems. They belong together. The conception he came to is not unadulterated by other, more conventional conceptions, and only infrequently was expressed in nonmetaphorical language. But it is there, and not too difficult to see. In this paper I shall try to show that, despite his rejection of Freudian theory, what was most original about Wittgenstein's conception of philosophical problems derives in part from certain likenesses between psychoanalytic insight into the workings of the mind and his understanding of philosophy. I shall try to make clear, from his general observations, what these likenesses are, starting from his remark that a philosophical problem is a mental cramp, and proceed to a concrete problem for illustration of the general view which his work led to.

The hold psychoanalysis retained on the mind of Wittgenstein is apparent from his language, which is similar in some respects to that used by psychoanalysts in the description of mental disturbance and its cure. Traditional philosophical activity was described by him as one might appropriately describe psychologically aberrant behavior, as something requiring treatment. He often remarked on the extraordinary incongruity between the philosopher's talk and his ordinary talk and behavior, as if it indicated a mental split or at least an impoverished sense of real-

[1] Notes which I took on these same lectures agree with Moore's report.

ity. Imagine, for example, a typical dispute between sceptic and nonsceptic over whether physical objects and other minds exist, which is carried on in the presence of each other and of chairs, desk, and blackboard, occurring *outside* philosophy. In connection with the not wholly imaginary discussion between two philosophers, one of whom protested, while pointing at a tree or while looking at his opponent, "I know that that's a tree," or "I've known it was you all the time," Wittgenstein (1951) is reported to have observed that it would be appropriate to say to an onlooker who was dumbfounded by what he had overheard: "They're not mad; they are only philosophizing." The features of the philosopher's talk which prompt this reaction have also been remarked by Professor John Wisdom (1953) as follows: "If when you are seeking water in the desert someone gazes at what looks like water in the distance and says, 'I doubt whether there's really water there,' you don't think him absurd. But the philosopher says 'I'm not sure' while he's drinking the water; he says it when no one would, or when no one but a madman would, or when no one but a madman or a philosopher would. And then also he is queer in that he doesn't act, doesn't feel, doesn't anticipate the future in the way his words suggest" (p. 173). And Moore, the philosopher of common sense, once observed (1966) that ". . . the view that nature is not real has really been held not merely by madmen but by able philosophers. . ." (p. 13). The tone of Wittgenstein's remarks about a philosopher who treats philosophical problems in the usual way has made itself felt sufficiently to elicit the following summing up in a recent history of philosophy (Maurer et al., 1962): "In short, a man disturbed by a philosophical problem is intellectually sick" (p. 544). Some things Wittgenstein (1956) has said might seem to justify this summing up: "The philosopher is the man who has to cure himself of many sicknesses of the understanding before he can arrive at the notions of the sound human understanding" (p. 157). For Wittgenstein (1953), treatment of philosophical questions was "like the treatment of an illness" (p. 91) whose cure is effected by reaching a correct understanding of the problem, uncovering its actual nature. A philosophical question when rightly understood ceases to pose a problem: clear understanding of its nature should make the problem aspect of the question "*completely* disappear" (p. 51).

The extremely unorthodox conception of a philosophical problem as one not requiring solution but, to use Wittgenstein's word, dissolution, a problem which, like a neurotic symptom, is dissolved by insight into what produces it, can only be appreciated if seen in historical perspective. Throughout the history of philosophy the common conception has been that a philosophical question has a true answer which the philosopher endeavors to find. Many philosophers—Descartes and Kant very explicitly—have been aware of the fact that for centuries controversy in philosophy has taken the path of anarchy. Indeed, the history of philosophy gives us a succession of metaphysical Messiahs, and we can expect the number to multiply. Firm results, established propositions, solved problems are like the fruits for which Tantalus reached. To use Kant's metaphor, a philosophical problem is a Sisyphian stone. The curious thing is that the failure to resolve a dispute is not owing to lack of any sort of relevant information. The philosopher does not need to wait on fact, and what is especially curious is that argument can continue in the presence of all the facts required to settle the dispute, *if* the dispute is factual. Elsewhere I have argued (Ambrose, 1966)[2] that philosophical disputes will not be terminated by any new fact, and that a philosopher who comes to a decision does not do so in consequence of any new information. As in the case of the William James puzzle about whether the man goes round the squirrel when he goes round the tree, all the facts, linguistic and material, which might be relevant to the solution of a philosophical problem, are known and thus cannot really be at issue. Wittgenstein (1953) stated flatly that philosophical problems "are,

[2] See especially chapters 5 and 13 of *Essays in Analysis.*

of course, not empirical problems" (p. 47). If we examine carefully the kind of evidence a philosopher produces for his view, which invariably takes the form of a demonstrative argument, we can see that the view is not empirical. Yet it is puzzling that without any logical flaw in the demonstration being made evident by either side, argument and counterargument hold the field like two armies neither of which loses but neither of which wins. It is hardly an exaggeration to say that in a philosophical debate, taken in its historical setting, we witness the meeting of two irresistible forces, neither of which can give way to the other and neither of which can be stopped.

This sort of situation has often prompted thoughtful people to move away from philosophy as being nothing more than playing with words. However earnest the pursuit of truth is pictured as being, rhapsodic praise of philosophy cannot allay the suspicion that a position and its supporting argument are not what they seem. They leave the impression that despite the aura surrounding them, sometimes factual, sometimes logical, they are mere matters of words. It was Wittgenstein's perception into the subterranean workings of language which enabled him to see philosophy in a new way. To anticipate what will be gone into later, a number of things he said indicate clearly that he came to look on the work of philosophers as a kind of verbal activity carried on under the illusion that propositions about the world are being investigated. Thus he said, "When we reject some form of symbolism we're inclined to look at it as though we'd rejected a proposition as false. . . . This confusion pervades all of philosophy."[3] For example, the sentence, "Things are nothing more than aggregates of sense data," has the appearance of stating a fact about the constitution of things, but according to him it is instead a grammatical statement, in his special sense of "grammatical."

[3] From notes taken by Margaret Masterman and Alice Ambrose in the intervals between dictation of *The Blue Book,* 1933-1934. Hereafter to be referred to as *The Yellow Book.*

Wittgenstein's insight into the workings of philosophy had its immediate antecedents in the growing attention to language found in the work of G. E. Moore. Primarily and quite explicitly Moore conceived of himself as defending the truth of common-sense beliefs against attacks which, from the time of Parmenides through F. H. Bradley, his contemporary, have been directed against them. The standard conception of a philosophical view as having one or another truth-value was presupposed in Moore's defense.[4] But in the course of analyzing a view's implications for common sense, Moore found himself increasingly involved in examination of the language used by philosophers in the expression of their views. For example, his investigation of the claim that existence is a predicate became an investigation of the uses of the word "exists." His critique of the Bradleian view that time is unreal but nevertheless exists became an examination of the question whether, as the words "real" and "exists" are ordinarily used, Bradley could escape the charge of inconsistency. "We might naturally think," he wrote (1922) "that to say 'Time exists . . .' is equivalent to saying that it is real. What more, we might ask, can a man who says that Time *is* real mean to maintain about it than that it exists . . . ?" (p. 199). "What . . . *ought* Mr. Bradley to mean by 'Time is unreal'? What would most people mean by this proposition?" (p. 209).

It is plain from these questions that Moore takes the use of these words in ordinary language as the touchstone by which the philosopher's use of them is to be tested. And this made it look to some philosophers as if Moore were defending ordinary language against its misuse by metaphysicians. As Malcolm (1942) once put it, "The essence of Moore's technique of refuting philosophical statements consists in pointing out that these statements *go against ordinary language*" (p. 349). He argued that the linguistic consequences associated with views Moore took as

[4] In connection with one philosophical view he states unambiguously that it is a false empirical statement and his own counterposition a true one (Moore, 1942, p. 672).

going against common sense *a fortiori* constituted a *reductio ad absurdum* of those views. For example, Bradley's dismissing causal occurrences as mere appearance on the ground that the concept *cause* is self-contradictory has a quite unacceptable consequence for ordinary language. This is that the word "cause" and its correlate "effect" will be self-contradictory, which is to say they will have no use for referring to anything; nor will specific causal words such as "make," "create," "build," "mend," etc. They will be on a footing with such phrases as "female brother" and "cubical sphere." That is, if what Bradley argues is correct, then as a corollary, language, which as a matter of fact is in constant use to describe situations of various kinds, would be shown to lack use. This consequence shows Bradley's claim, not the language of common sense, to be at fault.

Some of Wittgenstein's work also seems to be directed to the defense of ordinary language against its abuse by philosophers. He writes (1953): "When philosophers use a word—'knowledge,' 'being,' 'object,' . . . one must always ask oneself: is the word ever actually used in this way in the language-game which is its original home?—What *we* do is to bring words back from their metaphysical to their everyday usage" (p. 48). It is of course clear that the defense of the language of the common-sense man is very different from defense of the truth of the beliefs a common-sense philosopher like Moore attributes to him. Wittgenstein differed from Moore in an important way: it was not part of his purpose to defend such beliefs. He saw the work of the philosopher differently. Thus he wrote (1958): "There is no common-sense answer to a philosophical problem. . . . Nor is a philosopher's disagreement with common sense that of the scientist disagreeing with the coarse views of the man in the street" (pp. 58-59). The implication is that a philosophical problem is in a different category from that to which a practical problem, or for that matter, a scientific problem belongs. His finding the source of such a problem in the failure "to command a clear view of the use of our words" (1953, p. 49), his disavowal of any need to reform ordinary language, made it natural to understand Wittgenstein to be protecting the language of common sense, that is, ordinary language, against its misuse by philosophers.

The two interpretations of Moore's work, as defending basic common-sense beliefs and as defending the propriety of common language, carry with them corresponding interpretations of the metaphysical pronouncements against which they are directed. One is that they represent mistaken ideas about fact on the part of the metaphysician, the other that they represent mistaken ideas about correct language. But each interpretation has paradoxical implications. Bradley's behavior is out of joint with his assertion that causation is unreal, taken as an assertion of fact: his expectations regarding the effect of a flame on wax are the same as anyone else's. And his ordinary verbal behavior goes against supposing that he makes his assertion through ignorance of usage or with the idea of correcting usage: his causal language is the causal language of Everyman. Wittgenstein made another and different interpretation of the pronouncements of the metaphysician, which does not represent him as laboring under either a mistaken idea about fact or a mistaken idea about what constitutes correct language. According to him, his mistake lies in what he supposes himself to be doing with language—using it to describe reality.

Wittgenstein and the logical positivists questioned whether philosophers use language in such a way as to express something true or false. Their dramatic charge that the statements of metaphysics express nothing whatever forced upon philosophers' attention the peculiar status of metaphysical statements within language, so that their use of words came under scrutiny as it had not hitherto. But the application of their general criterion that a sentence is nonsense if it expresses neither an *a priori* proposition nor one testable in sense experience, aside from being inadequate to its task of eliminating metaphysics, was not accompanied by an inquiry into the linguistic connection between a view and the argument, or line of reasoning, which led to it. Clearly, argument and view are bound up with each other in such a way that if the argument is intelligible and leads to the view, the view cannot itself be a piece of literal nonsense. In fact we often feel ourselves placed in a dilemma by the view in conjunction with its argument. The view strikes us as unacceptable, while supported by reasoning in which we can find no flaw. Recall Zeno's claim that motion is impossible, and the 2000-year-old piece of reasoning on which it rests. This situation prompted Wittgenstein (1953) to say of such a claim, "This is not how it is!"—and in view of the argument—"Yet this is how it has to be!" (p. 47). The question arises whether either a view or the argument on which it rests has the kind of content we are inclined to attribute to it. According to Wittgenstein (1958), the problem is actually a verbal muddle, felt as a problem concerning matter of fact (p. 6). "The character of a metaphysical question [e. g., can physical objects exist unperceived, is] that we express an unclarity about the grammar of words in the *form* of a scientific question" (p. 35). The philosopher is not mistaken about fact nor about what ordinary usage is; his mistake consists in misconceiving what he is doing with language. He supposes himself to use it in order to raise a question about fact, and to give a reasoned answer which conveys information. But this is an illusion, created by the philosopher's use of words; and he himself is held captive by it. According to Wittgenstein (1953) the temptation to this kind of use is fed by our ordinary language. ". . . Certain analogies between the forms of expression in different regions of language" (p. 43) hold us obsessively, and this obsession is not recognized or even recognizable as such.[5] "A simile that has been absorbed into the forms of our language produces a false appearance . . ." (Wittgenstein, 1953, p. 47), so that questions arise which seem to concern a fact of the world instead of a matter of expression.[6] The language the philosopher uses in raising a question, in giving

[5] From my notes on Wittgenstein's lectures, 1934-1935.
[6] *The Yellow Book*

an answer, and in supporting the answer with a piece of reasoning all conspire to produce the illusion that a problem with a true or false answer exists. Instead, the puzzlement felt represents a verbal confusion, and to clear it up we have to see into "[our] entanglement in our own rules" (p. 50). By understanding the verbal nature of the problem, that is, by laying bare its linguistic morphology, we shall cease to be entangled in the problem and cease putting forward either position or counterposition. Insight will make it disappear. That is, it will not be solved; it will dissolve. This description by Wittgenstein of his conception of his task is reminiscent of psychoanalytic descriptions of the treatment of neurotic symptoms. Just as insight into their determinants effects their cure, so insight into the linguistic structure of a philosophical problem eliminates the pathological entanglement with words.

Now if something in the philosopher's use of language creates the appearance of a factual problem whereas there is only a verbal muddle, then it is essential to make clear how his use of words differs from their use to state fact. One of Wittgenstein's procedures was to place it alongside ordinary usage. Like Moore, he made ordinary language the standard. This is by no means to say that he did not recognize how readily ordinary language can give rise to philosophical puzzlement. What Moore (1922) said could very well have been said by Wittgenstein: "It seems to me very curious that language . . . should have grown up just as if it were expressly designed to mislead philosophers . . ." (p. 217). Nevertheless, Wittgenstein made it quite clear that he did not see linguistic reform as in any way his task, an attitude vastly different from that of a good many logical positivists. An understanding of the nature of problems framed in everyday language is not to be gained by reforming language. A reform might yield a language in which some problems would not arise. But avoiding a problem is not a way of understanding it. Nor would a reformed language be itself problem-free. If problems are to be understood rather than circumvented, then one must see how in the case of each problem ordinary language "has gone on holiday" (Wittgenstein, 1953, p. 19).

Dissatisfaction with ordinary language, according to Wittgenstein (1953), has been a goad to philosophers. "We disapprove of the expressions of ordinary language," he wrote, "and are tempted to say our way of speaking does not describe the facts as they really are" (pp. 121-122). And again (1958), "There is puzzlement and mental discomfort, not only when our curiosity about certain facts is not satisfied . . . but also when a notation dissatisfies us—perhaps because of various associations which it calls up. Our ordinary language, which of all possible notations is the one which pervades all our life, holds our mind rigidly in one position, as it were, and in this position sometimes it feels cramped, having a desire for other positions as well. Thus we sometimes wish for a notation which stresses a difference more strongly, makes it more obvious, than ordinary language does, or one which in a particular case uses more closely similar forms of expression than our ordinary language. Our mental cramp is loosened when we are shown the notations which fulfill these needs" (p. 59). However, the philosopher's discontent with language because it hushes up a difference he would like to see stressed or stresses one he would like to minimize[7] is, according to Wittgenstein, not recognized as a linguistic discontent at all—the philosopher is "not aware that he is objecting to a convention" (p. 57). He therefore expresses his objection in words which create the impression that he is stating an incontestable fact rather than, as Wittgenstein puts it, "recommending a notation" (p. 60). In a philosophical dispute "the one party attack the normal form of expression as if they were attacking a statement; the others defend it, as if they were stating facts recognized by every reasonable human being" (Wittgenstein, 1953, p. 122). The Hobbesian cynic who says all desires are selfish cer-

[7] *The Yellow Book*

tainly appears to be generalizing about human nature, as though he were exposing an ordinary belief as naïve. But this is an example of a confusion which according to Wittgenstein pervades all of philosophy: the confusion of looking at the rejection of a form of symbolism as though it were the rejection of a proposition as false.[8] The first rule of procedure then is "to destroy the outward similarity between a metaphysical proposition and an experiential one," to "show that this proposition hides a grammatical rule" (Wittgenstein, 1958, p. 55). What one needs to see is that the boundaries of a word's use are being redrawn, e. g., that Hobbes urges that the word "selfish" cover all conceivable desires, rather than assert a true-or-false position about man's actual desires. This insight constitutes the therapy for removing the temptation to put forward a philosophical position.

But something remains opaque in Wittgenstein's description of the philosopher as recommending a notation under the guise of asserting a fact. The nature of the recommendation, and hence its purpose, is unclear. Until it is clarified the role of argumentation in relation to the philosophical position remains a mystery. What is the function of Hobbes' supporting argument if his conclusion concerns the *word* "selfish" rather than the nature of desires? Wittgenstein leads us nearly to the promised land, nearly to the point of understanding philosophy, but not quite. He tells us that the philosopher objects to current linguistic conventions, and that in a fact-stating idiom he is recommending a notation, presumably an alteration of ordinary language. When this is joined with his assertion that in philosophy language is "like an engine idling, not when it is doing work" (1953, p. 51), one can conclude that any alteration proposed is idle, that it is not for the usual practical purposes served by a new notation nor for the purpose of reforming language now in use. Berkeley's well-known advice to philosophers to speak with the vulgar and think with the learned is actually consonant with this, despite the

[8] *The Yellow Book*

superficial invidious comparison between the philosopher's talk and ordinary speech.

Two things, the idleness of the alteration and its concealment by language seemingly used to support a factual position, call for explanation. The explanation of the philosopher's activity which I wish to suggest is consonant with but goes beyond anything Wittgenstein explicitly said. It is as follows: first of all, that the reasoning the philosopher engages in with the ostensible purpose of demonstrating his position is a justification for the linguistic alteration which the factual-appearing position conceals, and second, that his reasoning has as its purpose the creation of the illusion that an important truth is being established. If the philosopher gave explicit notice that he was introducing a change in current usage, the spell cast over our minds by his pronouncement would lose its power. His pronouncement fascinates us because of the illusion that it expresses a proposition about a phenomenon. One can explain the maneuvering with terminology as a game played *for the sake of* the illusion created. This is its purpose, to permit the philosopher the comfort of the idea that he is providing a solution to a scientific problem. Concealment of what he is doing with words, from himself as well as others, creates and sustains the illusion. Wittgenstein (1953) said that we have an urge to misunderstand the workings of our language (p. 47). This is different, however, from saying that the philosopher is playing an unconscious game with words in the interests of an illusion. It is one thing to say, for example, that in the startling form of words "all desires are selfish," Hobbes unwittingly conceals an objection to a convention and an extension of the scope of the word "selfish." It is another thing to say that the concealment of the innovation by the fact-stating idiom is a means used to create the illusion that a theory about human kind is being supported. John Wisdom (1955) said of Wittgenstein's listeners and readers that they often "found it difficult to get a steady light giving an ordered view of what they wished to see" (p. x). The present thesis makes intelligible the philosopher's channelizing his dissatisfaction with language into verbal innovations. It provides the framework for understanding what a philosopher is doing with language, by asking, in the case of each problem: By what means does he create the illusion of producing a theory? This thesis has been worked out and applied to a number of philosophical problems by Professor Morris Lazerowitz, and in some measure by Wisdom.

I want now to illustrate it by a brief account of a metaphysical view about the nature of things which Lazerowitz has subjected to this kind of semantic analysis (1955, pp. 144-163; 1964, pp. 231-235). This is the view that the things constituting the physical world are composed of attributes and the substance which supports them, or in which they inhere, and that this substance is unknowable. What it is that possesses attributes is forever beyond the reach of our minds—as Locke put it, this component of things is an "I know not what." The nature of things is thus hidden from us, for a thing is more than the sum of its attributes. The latter are knowable, whereas their support is beyond discovery by any conceivable science, and as inaccessible to God as to us. Consider the following experiment, conducted in imagination on some common object, such as an orange. If, one by one, we strip away its attributes, its color, shape, solidity, taste, etc., what remains is something of which we can form no conception other than that it supports attributes. What it itself is is impenetrable to our understanding. Strip Croesus of his possessions—his houses, money, garments, and a bare Croesus remains, something which only modesty would prevent us from apprehending. But strip him of his every attribute and what is left is a mere *x,* beyond describing and beyond knowing. As Kant (1783) said in the *Prolegomena,* ". . . in all substance the proper subject, that which remains after all accidents (as predicates) are abstracted, consequently that which forms the substance of things, remains unknown" (Sec. 46). We are everywhere surrounded by the unknowable.

We seem to have here a theory about the ultimate structure of things, and a kind of experiment to demonstrate it. But if we realize that the existence of the putative component of things in which properties inhere cannot be made probable by any conceivable test in the laboratory, and that it is really being argued for nonempirically, we begin to dispel the empirical mists which veil the theory from our understanding. It is important also to realize that a contrary theory exists which has its convinced adherents in the philosophical world. Hume conducted what appeared to be a careful observation of things, and finding only the solidity, shape, color disclosed to his senses, and no conceivable remainder, concluded that substance was a fiction, a myth of the intellect. According to him a thing is nothing more than a bundle of qualities. Now there is no way of deciding the issue between Hume and a substratum philosopher like Locke either by observation or an experiment. It is hardly necessary to point out that Locke and Hume give precisely the same consideration for their opposite conclusions. The nature of the theory and of the countertheory becomes the more puzzling in view of Russell's (1940) comment that "The introduction of an unknowable can generally . . . be avoided by suitable technical devices. . ." (p. 122). As it turns out, the device he proposes is a linguistic one. He writes: "I wish to suggest that wherever there is, for common sense, a 'thing' having the quality C, we should say instead that C itself exists in that place, and that the 'thing' is to be replaced by the collection of qualities existing in the place in question. Thus 'C' becomes a name, not a predicate" (pp. 121-122). Lazerowitz points out that if an unknowable can be eliminated by the device of altering a current mode of speech, then neither Locke's theory nor the Russell-Hume countertheory can be anything more than the verbal imitation of a scientific view. Maneuvering with terminology cannot banish from existence or bring into existence a matter of fact, any more than altering the meaning of the word "dollar" will change the amount in my bank account. Nor will it reveal to us the nature of things, for example, that things are no more than bundles of qualities.

Russell (1945) places the responsibility for substratum theory on ordinary language. "Substance," he says, "is a metaphysical mistake, due to transference to the world-structure of the structure of sentences composed of a subject and a predicate" (p. 202). Lazerowitz places it instead on the hidden things metaphysicians have done to language.

Proceeding on the hypothesis that the metaphysician produces the illusion of a theory by revising ordinary usage, Lazerowitz asks what the substratum philosopher does with general names and adjectives, used in ordinary English to denote things and their attributes, which enables him to say what attributes a thing has but not what it is. Of course, ordinary English presents no obstacle to saying what a thing is: Some things are mice, some things are chairs, some things are inkwells—there is no non-philosophical difficulty about saying what a thing is as against saying what properties it has. Ordinary language is not the source of the philosophical idea of unknowable substratum; it is what the philosopher does with ordinary language that produces this idea. If we construe the intellectual "experiment" of stripping a thing down to an unknowable residue as supplanting a general noun like "mouse" by "that which has the attribute of being a mouse," the linguistic import of the experiment begins to show through. Unlike the noun "mouse," the new noun referred to by the phrase "subject of attribution" is devoid of descriptive content. The new noun has the syntactic function which "mouse" has in the sentence, "This mouse is grey," that is, as grammatical subject; but it is a dummy noun, an "*x*." "This mouse is grey" gives way to "This *x* has the property of being a mouse and grey," where "*x*" has no semantic function. It has been given no meaning. The dissimilarity between "*x*" and a noun such as "mouse" could not be given its correct linguistic explanation without destroying a piece of metaphysics. The fact that the symbol "*x*" has been assigned a syntactical use but no meaning is reported in a camouflaged way by the empirical-sounding form of words, "Substratum is unknowable."

The linguistic mechanics by which the noun "mouse" is displaced from its role of subject in the sentence "This mouse is grey" by a bare "*x*" is effected by artificially reducing the noun to adjectival status. Nouns and adjectives clearly differ in their grammatical functioning but it is important to notice their semantic similarity. The descriptive content of general nouns is identifiable with that of a loose and indeterminate set of adjectives. A substantive deprived of its adjectival sense is shorn of its descriptive content. This is what the stripping experiment shows. In ordinary English the difference in syntactic role of nouns and adjectives overshadows the semantic dependence of nouns upon adjectives. The metaphysician who wishes to recompose grammar so as to stress this semantic dependence can effect it by the seemingly experimental procedure of taking away a thing's properties. The identity between nouns and adjectives which is covered up by their syntactic difference can be brought into prominence by artificially reclassifying nouns with adjectives. He changes the syntactic function of nouns and in this way highlights a similarity which for some reason is important to him. To be concrete, if in a sentence such as "This mouse is grey" the noun is reduced to adjectival status by transferring it to the predicate, and if at the same time the subject-predicate structure of the sentence is retained by replacing the subject by an *x*, we have as a result, "This *x* is a mouse and grey." The new subject of predication, "this *x*," is one to which no meaning has been assigned—it is merely a syntactic hook on which to hang adjectives, including the noun "mouse" which has been turned into an adjective. The recomposed sentence creates the idea that an attribute, "being a mouse and grey," is being predicated on a subject which eludes observation. The grammatical recategorization brings into existence a metaphysical theory. As Lazerowitz (1964) puts it, the substratum philosopher "separates the grammatical work a noun does in subject-predicate sentences from its use to name things, and he turns over its grammatical work to an *ersatz* subject. This he does in such a way, typically, as to create an illusion so vivid that its fraudulent nature can go undetected for a truly remarkable period of time. The substratum theory can now be seen as a two-layer structure which consists, at the preconscious level, of a statement embodying a linguistic innovation designed to heighten a fact minimized in the language of everyday speech, and the vivacious illusion, at the conscious level of our minds, that the philosophical words make a deep factual claim about the ultimate nature of things" (p. 234). The illusion is bolstered by a fact, remarked on by Wittgenstein (1958) as a general feature of metaphysical assertions, that words which, as he says, "express discontentment with our grammar . . . can also be used to state a fact of experience" (pp. 56-57). It is obvious that at a certain stage of scientific investigation a substance might be described as having an unknowable component.

But an illusion produced by a covert linguistic innovation would certainly be dispelled if there were only its fact-claiming appearance to protect it. For example, everyone can see through the transparent factual idiom to the verbal revision the following words seek to introduce: "You cannot go fishing for pleasure since pleasure is not one of the things you can catch." But an illusion which has persisted from the time of Aristotle must find its support in deeper sources than discontent with ordinary language. Wittgenstein (1953) indicated that he took this to be the case when he said that philosophical problems "have the character of *depth*. They are deep disquietudes . . ." (p. 47). Dreams, and thoughts we describe as coming from nowhere, are constant reminders that a part of our mind is shut off from conscious awareness. I suggest that it is from these deeper recesses of the mind that the strength and durability of the verbally staged illusions derive. The suggestion gains plausibility if we couple the common resistance felt to Freud's claim that an important part of our own mind is sealed off from us with the fact that many philosophers have been at pains to deny, directly or obliquely, the existence of that hidden unconscious activity.

Locke, for example, held that consciousness was an accompaniment of all thought, Descartes that the essence of mind is thinking, where thinking specifies into a series of wholly conscious activities. Freud and Descartes present the superficial appearance of saying the same thing when the one says that "internal objects are less unknowable than the external world" (Freud, 1915, p. 171) and the other that "the Mind is more easily known than the Body" (Descartes, 1641, Meditation 2). But Freud was referring to a technique for exploring the unconscious part of the mind, whereas Descartes' philosophical view of mind as a wholly conscious entity in effect denied the existence of any such dark chamber. It is by no means out of the question that Descartes was using the denial to fend off a disconcerting self-perception which it was necessary to deflect. One way of coping with the uneasy perception of something hidden within ourselves is to project this perception upon things outside us. By an unconscious mechanism, the unwelcome perception is turned away from oneself and superimposed on physical objects. The consciously enjoyed illusion of a matter of fact created by the words, "A thing is an unknowable substance in which experienceable attributes inhere," has as its latent content—its unconscious counterpart—the dim recognition of the unknowable in oneself. As Lazerowitz (1964) put it, the substratum metaphysician "finds it easier to live in a world of unknowables than to live with an unknowable within himself" (p. 235). The words by which he appears to express a view about the constitution of things "is a means, via the introduced syntactical subject [of attribution], of enabling us to project an inner state onto outer things" (p. 235). A novelist has different devices. Kafka, for example, could project his quest for the unknown into a narrative, *The Castle,* in which the Land Surveyor K, evidently himself, sought obsessionally and in vain to get to Klamm, who in some way was also himself. Philosopher and novelist, each to his own artistry. Sturge Moore described the poetry of Yeats as "dream-soaked." If it is correct to characterize philosophical theories as illusions of theories, it is a possible explanation of the illusions' centuries-long hold on us to describe them as soaked with unconscious thought.

REFERENCES

Ambrose, A. (1966), *Essays in Analysis.* London: Allen & Unwin.

Descartes, R. (1641), *Meditations.* Indianapolis, Ind.: Bobbs-Merrill, 1960.

Freud, S. (1915), The Unconscious. *Standard Edition,* 14:159-215. London: Hogarth Press, 1957.

Hume, D. (1739), *A Treatise of Human Nature,* ed., L. A. Selby-Bigge. Oxford: Clarendon Press, 1941.

Kant, I. (1783), *Prolegomena to Any Future Metaphysics,* ed. Paul Carus. Chicago: Open Court Publishing Co., 1929.

Lazerowitz, M. (1955), *The Structure of Metaphysics.* London: Routledge & Kegan Paul.

——— (1964), *Studies in Metaphilosophy.* London: Routledge & Kegan Paul.

Locke, J. (1690), *Essay Concerning Human Understanding,* ed. A. S. Pringle-Pattison. Oxford: Clarendon Press, 1928. Book II, Chapt. 23, Section 2.

Malcolm, N. (1942), Moore and Ordinary Language. In: *The Philosophy of G. E. Moore,* ed. P. A. Schilpp. LaSalle, Ill.: Open Court Publishing Co., pp. 343-368.

Maurer, A. A. et al. (eds.) (1962), *Recent Philosophy, Hegel to the Present.* New York: Random House.

Moore, G. E. (1922), The Conception of Reality. *Philosophical Studies.* London: Routledge & Kegan Paul, pp. 197-219.

——— (1942), A Reply to My Critics. In: *The Philosophy of G. E. Moore,* ed. P. A. Schilpp. La Salle, Ill.: Open Court Publishing Co., pp. 533-677.

——— (1959), Wittgenstein's Lectures in 1930-33. In: *Philosophical Papers.* London: George Allen & Unwin, pp. 252-324.

——— (1966), *Lectures on Philosophy,* ed. C. Lewy. New York: Humanities Press.

Rhees, R. (1942-1946), Conversations on Freud. In: *L. Wittgenstein. Lectures and Conversations on Aesthetics, Psychology and Religious Belief.* Berkeley: University of California Press, 1966, pp. 41-52.

Russell, B. (1940), *An Inquiry Into Meaning and Truth.* New York: Norton.

——— (1945), *A History of Western Philosophy.* New York: Simon & Schuster.

Wisdom, John (1953), *Philosophy and Psychoanalysis.* Oxford: Blackwell.

——— (1955), Foreword. *The Structure of Metaphysics,* by M. Lazerowitz. London: Routledge & Kegan Paul, pp. vii-xii.

Wittgenstein, L. (1922), *Tractatus Logico-Philosophicus*. London: Routledge & Kegan Paul, 1961.

——— (1942-1946), *L. Wittgenstein. Lectures and Conversation on Aesthetics, Psychology and Religious Belief,* ed. Cyril Barrett. Berkeley: University of California Press, 1966.

——— (1951), Last philosophical notes, on knowledge and certainty. (unpublished).

——— (1953), *Philosophical Investigations,* ed. R. Rhees & G. E. M. Anscombe. Oxford: Blackwell.

——— (1956), *Remarks on the Foundations of Mathematics,* ed. G. H. von Wright, R. Rhees & G. E. M. Anscombe. New York: Macmillan.

——— (1958), *The Blue and Brown Books*. New York: Harper.

PSYCHOANALYSIS: PHILOSOPHY OR SCIENCE?

CHARLES BRENNER, M.D.

The aim of the present chapter is to eliminate one possible area of misunderstanding which philosophers may have in approaching the field of psychoanalysis. It may appear to the inquisitive philosopher that psychoanalysis is one more among the considerable list of introspective psychologies that have appeared over the centuries, and that Freud's theories about the development and functioning of the human mind are speculations based on roughly the same range of data as that which has been available to everyone who has been interested in the mind of man from Socrates to Sartre.

The fact that Freud (1915) often referred to his psychological theories as "metapsychology" (p. 181) has doubtless contributed to the notion that psychoanalysis is speculative rather than empirical, and that it bears somewhat the same relationship to other branches of psychology that metaphysics does to physics. The truth of the matter is that Freud meant by "metapsychology" merely the empirically based psychological theories of psycho-

---

Dr. Brenner is on the faculty of the New York Psychoanalytic Institute; Lecturer in Psychiatry, Yale University Medical School; and past President, American Psychoanalytic Association.

analysis. The similarity between metapsychology and metaphysics is one of spelling,[1] not of meaning.

If it were true that psychoanalysis is one among many speculative systems of psychology which are based primarily on introspection, Freud's theories would deserve no different consideration from those of any of his fellow observers of the nature of man. Psychoanalysis as a method of treating the mentally ill, according to this view, would have its chance successes, depending on how lucky Freud's guesses were. As a systematic method of investigating human psychology, it would be assumed to be of little value, since presumably it is based on Freud's preconceptions and is only suited to confirm these preconceptions.[2]

I shall endeavor to show that this view is in error on several counts. In the first place, Freud did not base his theories on introspective data, but on observation, and in particular, on the close and extended observation of mentally ill (neurotic) patients who came to him for treatment. Self-observation played no significant role in the development of his ideas except at the start, and its principal role then was to convince him of the considerable similarity between many aspects of the mental functioning of those who are seriously neurotic (his patients) and one who is not (himself). In the second place, the method of psychoanalysis, which Freud devised, was not intended to prove anything, nor was it constructed on the basis of any speculations about the mind. It developed from an attempt to help patients to remember what they had forgotten, without recourse to hypnosis. Finally, and this is of principal importance, Freud had access to a vastly wider range of data than did any of his prede-

[1] Metapsychology is correctly defined as the study of the relationship between body and mind. There is some suggestion that Freud had the dictionary definition of the word in mind when he introduced it into psychoanalytic terminology, since its first use was in connection with a discussion of the energies of the instinctual drives, the latter representing the demands made on the mind by the body.

[2] For examples of this view among contemporary philosophers, see Hook, 1959.

cessors. He did *not* theorize on the basis of the same data as others before him had observed. On the contrary, it is neither speculative brilliance nor the sheer force of a superior intellectual capacity that account for the pre-eminence of Freud's contributions to human psychology. There have been other men, many of them philosophers, who were as brilliant and as profound as he, who have tried with far less success to plumb man's mind. The fact is that the psychoanalytic method, applied in a therapeutic situation, gives the psychoanalyst who applies it access to data previously unknown and largely unsuspected. It is this which is the principal reason for Freud's unparalleled achievements and for the fruitfulness of the investigations of those who followed his lead in using the psychoanalytic method. A brief historical survey of the early development of psychoanalysis may afford some documentation for these assertions.

Freud came to psychology quite indirectly—by the back door, one might say (Freud, 1925; Jones, 1953; Brenner, 1955; Arlow, 1956). He began his scientific career as a neuroanatomist, physiologist, and embryologist in the physiological laboratory of Brücke. His early contributions included studies of spinal ganglia, of new staining methods for microscopy, and of the action of cocaine on the nervous system, including its anesthetic properties. His desire was to continue in the laboratory, but a career in academic medicine was closed to him because he was a Jew. On Brücke's advice, he became a practicing neurologist instead, as a compromise between his scientific interests and his need to be self-supporting. He worked for years in the neurological clinic of the University of Vienna and published a number of papers in the field of clinical neurology during the years from 1884 to 1900, among them a monograph on aphasia in 1891 and one on cerebral diplegia in 1893. Indeed, when he was finally appointed to the faculty, as a clinical professor, it was in neurology, not in psychiatry. Nevertheless, when he began to practice neurology, he discovered, as every practicing neurologist has discovered both before and since, that the majority of his patients were psychiatric ones. Willy-nilly, he became a psychiatrist.

In an autobiographical sketch which he wrote in 1925, Freud has described the steps in the development of the method of treating mentally ill patients which he eventually called psychoanalysis. Even before he embarked on that road, he had convinced himself of the uselessness, or ineffectiveness, of the various methods of physical therapy which were popular and highly recommended by the best medical authorities of the time: electrotherapy, hydrotherapy, bed rest, high fat diets, and the like. He had been impressed, during a stay in Paris, by the ability of the French neuropathologist, Charcot, to produce and to dissipate hysterical symptoms by hypnosis. Under the influence of Charcot's findings, he employed hypnosis as widely as possible in treating those of his patients with hysterical symptoms, despite the fact that hypnosis, and those who made use of it, were looked on somewhat askance by the Francophobe majority in Viennese medical circles. In skillful hands hypnosis can give good results in many cases of hysteria, though improvement, even when striking, is usually only temporary. Thus Freud continued to use it as his best method of treatment despite its limitations, but with a certain individual modification, a modification which it is necessary to discuss in some detail, since the subsequent development of the psychoanalytic method hinges upon it.

An older colleague of Freud's, Josef Breuer, told him of an experience he had had in treating a young woman with hysterical symptoms by means of hypnosis some years earlier. Breuer and the patient together had discovered that if, with the help of hypnosis, she was able to recall the thoughts and re-experience the emotions connected with the onset of one of her symptoms, that symptom promptly disappeared. The patient herself compared this sort of talking cure to chimney-sweeping. Breuer and Freud called it the cathartic method, their assumption being that its therapeutic effect was due chiefly to the release of emotions that it produced. Their first assumption about the pathogenesis of hysterical symptoms was that they were due to pent-up emotion that had never been adequately discharged by conscious expression. If the traumatic episode could be remembered and the emotion discharged, the hysterical symptom would disappear.

As Freud accumulated experience in the use of his and Breuer's hypnotic technique, he became progressively dissatisfied with it. First, he was too often unable to induce a deep hypnotic trance in his patients; second, patients became too dependent on being hypnotized; and third, some of his female patients fell in love with him. At this juncture he had what turned out to be a brilliant idea. He recalled some demonstrations by the famous French hypnotist, Bernheim, which he had witnessed at Nancy. Bernheim showed that it was possible to lift the veil of posthypnotic amnesia by insisting that the subject could, did, and must remember what had happened to him while he had been in the hypnotic trance from which he had just been awakened with the admonition (suggestion) that he would remember nothing of what had gone on during the trance. Freud reasoned that since the symptoms of hysteria and those produced by hypnotic suggestion are indistinguishable, the fact that a posthypnotic amnesia could be undone by suggestion *without* hypnosis might be taken as evidence that a hysterical amnesia could be undone in the same way. Possibly, he thought, he would be able, with Bernheim's technique, to get his patients to remember the forgotten events and emotions that underlay their hysterical symptoms without having to rely on hypnosis, with its attendant disadvantages.

In his first attempts in this direction, Freud retained some of the techniques of the hypnotist. For example, the patient lay on a couch with his eyes closed. When he complained of being unable to think of anything to say, Freud would place his hand on the patient's forehead and say, "When I remove my hand, a thought will come to you." Rather soon, however, these remnants of hypnosis were discarded, and the patient was instructed simply to lie on the couch and to say whatever came to his mind, without consciously selecting or editing his thoughts.

These historical remarks, it will be recalled, are intended to substantiate the view that psychoanalysis is empirical rather than speculative, and based on observation rather than on introspection. Freud had no special *Weltanschauung* which he tried to prove, except that of empirical science in general, as he himself emphasized (Freud, 1932). He developed the psychoanalytic method because he was searching for a way to help his neurotic patients remember forgotten events related to the onset of their symptoms. No one could have anticipated how far the application of the psychoanalytic method would lead, how rich a harvest of new knowledge concerning the mind of man it would reap, any more than anyone could have predicted the fruitfulness of Pasteur's application of the method of microscopy to biology, or of Galileo's use of the telescope in astronomy. Unlikely as it seems that great, new discoveries in the field of psychology could be made by instructing a subject to say *everything* that comes to mind, and to relax conscious control of his thoughts as much as possible, yet the fact is that the view one gains of the mind by this apparently simple maneuver is unparalleled. Just as Galileo learned previously unsuspected facts about the moons of Jupiter by looking through his newly invented telescope, just as Pasteur revealed a whole new area of biology by applying to it the use of the compound microscope, so Freud, by devising and developing the psychoanalytic method, made possible the most important discoveries in the field of human psychology in the recorded history of science.

To be sure, psychoanalysis has its special problems as a science. A statement of their nature and a brief discussion of each may be of interest here. For one thing, the data which psychoanalysts observe are, in the main, verbal communications. Behavioral manifestations which are accessible to the analyst's observation (i.e., the patient's behavior during an analytic session) are by no means ignored; quite the contrary. Nevertheless, verbal communications comprise the overwhelming majority of psychoanalytic data. The problem of the validity of such data is a special, though not a unique concern in psychoanalysis.

Another difficulty which is inherent in the subject matter of psychoanalysis is that it does not lend itself to the experimental method. On this ground alone some philosophers of science refuse it the very name "scientific." Their view appears to be, "If it is not experimental, it is not scientific." However correct this judgment may be, the fact remains that psychoanalysis is an observational, rather than an experimental science. In this respect it resembles such other branches of natural science as astronomy and paleontology. Whatever significant experiments ingenuity might devise in the area of human psychology with which psychoanalysis deals, common humanity would forbid (Brenner, 1962). Certainly psychoanalysts, whose professional orientation is basically therapeutic, do not even think in such directions.

Still another difficulty with which psychoanalysts are faced has to do with the fact that psychoanalytic data do not permit ready quantification. It has not yet been possible to measure, in any reliable or useful way, the strength of an impulse, the intensity of a fear, or the severity of a conflict.

Finally, one may mention that psychoanalysis deals with psychopathology. Psychoanalytic subjects are patients, that is, mentally ill people. The question has been raised whether conclusions drawn from the study of mentally abnormal persons have relevance for psychology as such.

First, a few words about the nature of the data which are observable by the psychoanalytic method. Reports of thoughts, feelings, physical sensations, dreams, daydreams, etc., deal with what are usually termed subjective or introspective phenomena. Introspective psychologists use such data just as psychoanalysts do, but with one difference. The introspective psychologist or philosopher is concerned with his own thoughts and feelings; the psychoanalyst is concerned with the thoughts and feelings of another, who reports them to him. *A priori,* the difference seems unimportant. One might argue, indeed, that the introspectionist has an advantage over the psychoanalyst, since a description of a mental event can never convey precisely the quality and vividness of the event (experience) itself. The difference is of great importance, great enough to justify the distinction we have made between introspection and observational science. What makes the difference so great is the fact that in every individual there are psychological factors at work *unconsciously,* i.e., unknown to the individual himself, which play a major role in his mental life. More than this, among these unconscious factors are many which the individual is at pains not to recognize, which would cause him shame, remorse, guilt, or fear, were he to admit them to himself. Such wishes, needs, memories, and fantasies must be forgotten, denied, even vigorously disproved. It is no wonder, therefore, that introspection gives such a limited, warped, and individually distorted view of mental functioning. It is no wonder that "subjectivity" is so nearly synonymous with "inaccuracy." An independent observer, particularly one with experience, can gain a far more accurate and useful view of mental functioning from a patient's verbal communications than anyone can from introspection.

One of the virtues of introspection over so-called academic or scientific psychology has always been that the former dealt, however subjectively, with the emotionally important factors in man's mental life: with his passions, his ambitions, in a word, with his major motivations. Academic psychology, on the other hand, while conforming to high standards of statistical and experimental validity, could study only what was trivial and unimportant emotionally. The psychoanalytic method is the only method so far available which has made possible the scientific observation of the major motivational forces of man's mental life. It has the virtue of including in its scope the whole area of mental functioning that academic psychology could never compass and at the same time of avoiding the gross distortions which are an ever-present danger, if not an inevitable concomitant of introspection, with its strong, subjective bias.

So much for the nature of the data which are accessible to the psychoanalytic method, and the question of their reliability. We have mentioned as additional special problems of psychoanalysis that it is not experimental, and that the problem of quantification has yet to be solved. As for the first of these, it may be remarked that the importance of the experimental method in natural science has become so great in recent years as to cause some to overlook or to forget that many great advances have been made in various fields of science on the basis of observational data too. An obvious example is Darwin's theory of evolution. Indeed, in the generation following the publication of *The Origin of Species,* the experimental scientists, led by Lord Kelvin, conclusively proved, to their own satisfaction, that Darwin's theories were impossible (Ritvo, 1965). Observation should not be underrated as a scientific tool, nor must experiment be overrated. Each has its place; *a priori,* one cannot say in which situation the one will be more useful than the other. The history of science contains enough examples of wrong guesses by the greatest scientists to make all of us cautious about categorical assertions, however apodictic they may seem to us. The view that, "If it is not experimental, it is not scientific," would seem to be an excellent example of a rash and incautious assertion.

It may be of interest to note that psychoanalysts have devoted considerable attention to the particular aspect of the technique of observation that astronomers have called "the personal equation." In psychoanalytic observations "the personal equation" is both more complex and more difficult to deal with than it is in astronomy. Severe mental conflicts of the sort that are associated with grave neurotic symptoms will ordinarily make it difficult or impossible to practice psychoanalysis successfully, just as color-blindness incapacitates one from piloting a vessel or from matching colors. For this reason, prospective psychoanalysts must be relatively healthy, psychologically speaking, and each should undertake, as part of his training, a personal psychoanalysis. In this way the adverse influence of personal bias and incapacity on the use of the psychoanalytic method can be kept to a minimum.

Finally, a word on the propriety of basing psychological theories on observations made upon mentally sick persons. Experience has shown that, provided the brain is not malformed, injured, or destroyed by disease, there are far-reaching similarities between the mentally ill and the mentally sound. As he explained in *The Interpretation of Dreams,* Freud (1900) was first convinced of these similarities with respect to certain limited aspects of normal mental functioning, namely, dreams, jokes, and the slips, errors, and lapses of memory that he lumped together under the heading, "everyday psychopathology." It was only when he had come to recognize the similarity that these *normal* mental phenomena show to neurotic symptoms that Freud proposed his first general psychological theories, which inaugurated a new epoch in human psychology. Subsequent experience with the psychoanalytic method has substantiated and extended Freud's original conclusion concerning the relevance of the study of pathology to an understanding of the normal in mental life. The same mental conflicts which, though largely unconscious, give rise to neurotic symptoms, are as intimately connected with normal character traits, personal and professional interests, and the like. In this connection, the epigram of Kris (1947), that psychoanalysis is human behavior viewed as conflict, deserves much greater attention than it has as yet generally received. The central significance of conflict in mental life and development is among the most important insights that the application of the psychoanalytic method has enabled psychoanalysts to attain in their study of human psychology.

Moreover, experience has shown that it is no easy matter for an individual to communicate to a stranger an unedited version of his thoughts, emotions, and physical sensations for any extended period of time. For a subject to co-operate in the use of the psychoanalytic method, he must be strongly enough motivated to overcome at least the initial resistance to complete candor that he will invariably experience. In the vast majority of cases, this motivation must derive from the suffering or incapacity which the subject experiences as part of his neurotic illness. In a word, the subject must be a patient in the usual run of things. It is difficult to conceive how the psychoanalytic method could have been either devised or first applied except in a therapeutic context. The method grew out of Freud's needs as a physician caring for neurotic patients, as we have seen. It is, therefore, no accident that it is as much a method of treatment as of scientific observation.

REFERENCES

Arlow, J. A. (1956), *The Legacy of Sigmund Freud.* New York: International Universities Press.

Brenner, C. (1955), *An Elementary Textbook of Psychoanalysis.* New York: International Universities Press.

——— (1962), Review of "Freud's Concept of Repression and Defense," by P. Madison, *Psychoanal Quart.*, 31:562-563.

Freud, S. (1900), The Interpretation of Dreams. *Standard Edition,* 5:509-621. London: Hogarth Press, 1953.

——— (1915), The Unconscious. *Standard Edition,* 14:166-204. London: Hogarth Press, 1957.

——— (1925), An Autobiographical Study. *Standard Edition,* 20:7-74. London: Hogarth Press, 1959.

——— (1932), New Introductory Lectures on Psychoanalysis. Lecture 35. *Standard Edition,* 22:158-182. London: Hogarth Press, 1964.

Hook, S., ed. (1959), *Psychoanalysis, Scientific Method, and Philosophy.* New York: New York University Press.

Jones, E. (1953), *Sigmund Freud: Life and Work,* Vol. 1. New York: Basic Books.

Kris, E. (1947), The Nature of Psychoanalytic Propositions and Their Validation. In: *Freedom and Experience,* ed. S. Hook & M. R. Konvitz. Ithaca: Cornell University Press.

Ritvo, L. B. (1965), Darwin as the Source of Freud's Neo-Lamarckism, *J. Amer. Psychoanal. Assn.,* 13:499-517.

THE STRUCTURE OF TRAGEDY AND THE STRUCTURE OF THE PSYCHE IN ARISTOTLE'S *POETICS*

GEORGE DEVEREUX, PH.D.

It is my purpose to attempt a drastic reorientation of the psychoanalytic study of art, which has hitherto been limited to the exploration of one or more of the following problems: (1) Sublimation and the process of sublimation.[1] (2) The suitableness of artistic creativity for the implementation of sublimation. (3) The projection of psychic content—be it conscious, preconscious, or unconscious—into the work of art. (4) The interaction between the psychological material to be projected, and the suitability of the artist's raw material for the implementation of this

---

Dr. Devereux is Professor of Research in Ethnopsychiatry, Temple University School of Medicine (on leave); currently, Visiting Professor in Paris.

[1] Existing discussions of this problem are unsatisfactory. The capacity to sublimate is a special characteristic of man. The process of psychosexual maturation and the process of sublimation are equally "natural"; moreover, they overlap in every significant respect. Genitality and sublimation represent the normal culmination of these two convergent processes. In the Aristotelian frame of reference, each of the two is an *arete*.

projection.[2] (5) The need to adapt the material to be expressed to certain sociocultural conventions—to the "rules of the art."[3] In adhering to these conventions, the artist also signals that his product is artistic (Devereux, 1961a). (6) The range of the "consumer's" perceptiveness.[4] (7) The relationship between the active, creative experience of producing a work of art, the mediation of this experience by the performing artist, and the receptive, creative experience of the ultimate "consumer"—of the public.

While these topics play a major role in the psychoanalytic exploration of art,[5] they only bracket the pivotal element on which the very possibility of the existence of art depends: the duplication of the structure of the psyche by the structure of the work of art, and the manner in which this duplication is brought about, albeit in a modified manner. This problem is entirely distinct from the transformation of the content of the psyche into art or from the artistic representation of psychic mechanisms.

Indeed, no matter what the psyche may contemplate, imitate, or create, the one thing it invariably does is replicate itself. This implies that an "artistic" product of a "mind" whose structure is not identical with that of the human mind, could not be apprehended as art at all, any more than ground meat can be apprehended as an ox. Though the fundamental structure of the human psyche—as distinct from the contingent (time-, place-,

[2] I refer here to such basic facts as the limited capacity of marble to stand stress, the range of the human voice and the length of time a human being can sing, etc. Great artists exploit these limitations; mediocre ones are handicapped by them (Devereux, 1961a).

[3] The rules of counterpoint lend wings to the fugal movement of Mozart's "Jupiter Symphony"; they shackle the feet of musical clod-hoppers.

[4] Fugues for 24 voices have been composed, though no human ear, not even that of Mozart, is capable of apprehending such a mass of sound as polyphonic in structure. Such fugues are "polyphonic" for the eye only. Cf. also Lycophron's *Alexandra* and its twentieth-century equivalent, James Joyce's *Finnegan's Wake,* both of which require a "key." The problem of such works is completely disposed of by the distinction between metaphor and riddle in Aristotle's *Poetics* (1458a, 23ff.)

[5] See Freud (1906), Kris (1952), Kubie (1958), Sachs (1951), Waelder (1965).

culture- and experience-bound) mind of the artist—has not changed since prehistoric man painted the great frescoes of the Altamira cave, it took man a long time to learn to transcend the limitations of his culture-bound tastes, to learn to appreciate these paintings, or the sculpture of the Marquesans, as art.[6] Yet, the obstacle was purely a quasi-quantitative one. The difficulty confronting the consumer of "exotic" art was no different in essence from that which confronts a navigator accustomed to a Mercator's projection map, when he tries to use a polyconic projection map:[7] he must—and can—simply learn to detect the elements which remain invariant in a series of continuous ("topological") transformations, representing different projections of the structure of the psychic apparatus. If, however, his familiar Mercator's projection map is cut up into small equal squares, scrambled, and then pasted back on a sheet of paper in an arbitrary order, orientation becomes impossible.

The problem of the replication *(Mimesis)* of the structure of the psyche in the work of art will be studied here with special reference to its replication in Greek tragedy, as analyzed by Aristotle in his *Poetics*. I hold that Aristotle's deceptively simple concept of *mimesis* is essentially psychological: the main "thing" that is imitated (called hereafter: the *Imitandum*) is the *structure* of the human psyche. Aristotle analyzed and formulated the practices of the Greek tragic poets in psychological terms, or in terms readily convertible into psychological ones.[8] Thus, he lists as means of imitation at the poet's disposal: scenery, gesture, dance, metrical speech, song, and music. One notices at once that all of these means are directed at those senses whose experi-

[6] The problem of cross-cultural art appreciation has been analyzed elsewhere (Devereux, 1961a). Needless to say, I speak here of genuine art appreciation and not of snobbish, arty pretenses.

[7] For this problem see Devereux (1967a, pp. 121-128).

[8] The nonhellenist is reminded that, contrary to what the theoreticians of neoclassical tragedy thought, Aristotle's *Poetics* is not nomothetic. It does not legislate; it generalizes the practices of Greek dramatists. Its counterpart is not J. J. Fux's (1725) *Gradus ad Parnassum,* but W. Piston's, (1948) *Harmony* or *Counterpoint* (1947).

ences are sublimable.[9] This implies that even this dry enumeration of means is psychoanalytically exploitable.

On another level, the fascination which Aeschylus, Sophocles, and Euripides continue to exert, even after a lapse of nearly two and a half millennia, has important implications. It proves Aristotle right in defining tragedy as the imitation of something, which, on closer scrutiny, turns out to be psychological in nature. This psychological "something" is, moreover, not primarily the content (e.g., "Oedipus complex") but the structure of the psyche. The "imitation" of both content and structure is, necessarily, a stylized ("transformed") replica of the *Imitandum*. This was, I believe, fully understood by Aristotle. He defines in nearly identical ways the dream—a distorted reflection which can be intuitively decoded, as one may recognize ("decode") the distorted reflection of an object in moving water by seeing through the distortion (*On Divination by Dreams,* 464b, 5)—and the metaphor, which the audience must be able to decode, and which he calls the greatest, most highly individualized and least teachable of the great poet's skills (*Poetics,* 1458a, 24).

The congruence of these two definitions shows that Aristotle's seemingly naïve and pedantic definition of tragedy, as an imitation of "great deeds," has unsuspected depths. In the simplest possible sense, it implies that even though the "real" Oedipus must have awkwardly staggered out of the Palace after he blinded himself, on stage his gait must be imitated by means of a stylized and perhaps almost danced stagger, more—and differently—expressive than was the "real" Oedipus' painful advance. The actor who plays Oedipus must project, through a gesture-gait metacommunication, the inner meaning of this gait—the psychological experience of blind stumbling. He must do more than incarnate the "historical present"; his performance must be "located" at the confluence of Oedipus' past triumphant tribula-

[9] For the crucial distinction between sublimable and nonsublimable spheres of the senses, see Devereux (1961a, 1966a).

tions and of his future wanderings, which culminated in his translation to the world of Heroes. Like an analysand's utterance, the performance must impinge on the audience's senses and conscious, but only the better to bypass both, reserving its full impact for the audience's unconscious, which alone is able to apprehend self-resonantly (= Aristotle's concept of *philanthropos*), and therefore to decode this stylized (distorted) imitation of a psychological model, i.e., of a familiar psychic content poured into a mould identical in structure with the human psyche. This decoding process was accurately described by Aristotle himself, in connection with dreams.

The topic of the replication of the structure of the psyche in the structure of tragedy cannot be dealt with here in its entirety. Inquiry is limited to a consideration of two complementary structures only, both intimately related to the problem of so-called "boundaries" within the psyche—to temporal and spatial structures. The coherence of the former is accounted for by what Petzoldt (1923) calls "succedaneous causality," the coherence of the latter by what he calls "simultaneous causality." Though the very concept of structure is a singularly complex one and the existence of a structure of the psyche manifestly a self-imputation (Devereux, 1940, 1945, 1961b, 1966b, 1967a), I will analyze here only the replication of intrapsychic "boundaries" in the temporal dimension ("before" and "after" the tragedy, as understood by Aristotle) and in the spatial dimension ("on stage" vs. "off stage," also as defined by that author). I will show in particular that that which is "before" (the first verse) and "after" (the last one) is identical in nature with that which is off stage. I will similarly show that that which is the (Aristotelian) tragedy (first to last verse) and that which is on stage are also identical in nature.

This finding is not unexpected. A temporal structure can be converted into a spatial one, by subjecting it to a 90° "rotation," and vice versa (Devereux, 1967a). The structures, as explanatory frames of references, stand, moreover, in a complementarity relationship, *stricto sensu,* to each other.[10] Psychologically, this implies that the traditional "spatial" structure, the Freudian Ego, has a counterpart in a "temporal Ego," (Devereux, 1966a, 1966b, 1967b). The structure and the reach of the two is much the same. Hence, the application of the Freudian "spatial" ego to Greek material having proved to be fruitful,[11] it stands to reason that the analysis of Greek data in terms of the "temporal" ego is likely to be equally productive.

The replication of these two psychic structures in Greek tragedy can best be analyzed in terms of two Aristotelian distinctions: (1) between that which is "within" the tragedy (the unified plot) and that which is "without" it, in that it precedes or follows the tragedy proper (temporal structure); (2) between that which happens on stage and that which occurs concurrently off stage (spatial structure).

Before tackling Aristotle's analysis of these matters, a general problem must be clarified. Though Aristotle had certainly not discovered the Freudian model of the psyche, he operated at times as though he had done so, simply because he projected his own, remarkably normal,[12] mind almost without distortion

[10] In the same sense, range can be converted into depth, and vice versa, by a 90° "rotation" (Devereux, 1955, pp. 74-76). Underlying this theory is the ergodic hypothesis of the calculus of probabilities. If the ergodic hypothesis is blended with the Heisenberg-Bohr-Jordan principle of complementarity, the two nonsimultaneous statements: "the organ creates the function," and "the function creates the organ" are both equivalent and complementary.

[11] See E. R. Dodds (1951, 1965). These are the only works which satisfy both the psychoanalyst and the hellenist. In his most creative periods, Freud thought like a Greek. I have already indicated (fn. 1) that his concept of genitality is an Aristotelian *arete.* The continued influence of unconscious material on behavior is accounted for by Aristotle's handling of the concept of potentiality in "On Remembering and Forgetting" (*Parva Naturalia*). Plato (*Republic,* Bk. viii) foreshadows the struggle between psychic instances. The Greek concept of the *nous* resembles, in many ways, the concept of the ego. The difference between superego and ego ideal is analogous to the distinction F. M. Cornford (1912) makes between *horkos* (oath = fence) and *nomos* (positive law).

[12] When reading Aristotle—though not Plato—I am at times almost haunted by Musset's line, in praise of Molière: *"et comme le bon sens fait parler le génie."*

on the object of his analysis. He had the singular capacity of seeing the self-evident intelligently. Hence, Aristotelian analyses can be so readily translated into psychoanalytic terms, not because he had "anticipated" Freud, but because the Freudian model of the psyche is congruent with the structure of Aristotle's extraordinarily *human* mind.

I propose to show that two of Aristotle's seemingly trivial remarks: that one must differentiate between the tragedy itself and that which precedes and follows it, and also between what happens on stage and that which goes on concurrently off stage, are profoundly meaningful. They help us realize that much of the incredible effectiveness of Greek tragedy is a direct result of the invariance of the psyche in the group of transformations which constitutes the plot. Methodologically, the study of these invariants parallels, on the psychological level, the analysis of structural invariants in the various transformations of a myth, as revealed by Levi-Strauss' mythological researches.[13]

BEFORE THE BEGINNING—AFTER THE END

Though stressing that that which is located between the first and the last verse of a tragedy forms a unified whole—what we would now call a *Gestalt*—Aristotle also analyzed its relationship to what preceded and succeeded it. He drew a distinction between that which happens on stage and that which happens, at times concurrently, off stage. In theory, it would be best to discuss these two matters simultaneously. In practice, the predicament of the scholar is much the same as that of Aristotle

[13] Levi-Strauss (1958, 1964) has provided studies of extraordinary importance for the student of Greek tragedy. Levi-Strauss' "structuralism" and my own "complementarism" (Devereux, 1940) are both focused on the problem of invariants in groups of transformations. He emphasizes the logic of these transformations; I emphasize their complementarity. It is my thesis that structuralism and complementarism presuppose each other (Devereux, 1970).

and also of the tragic poet: only one event can be presented on stage at any given time.[14]

It is self-evident that whenever Aristotle speaks of the plot of a tragedy, or simply of a tragedy, he means a particular tragedy and not a trilogy, and especially not a trilogy followed by a satyr play, or by a satyr-play equivalent, such as Euripides' *Alcestis.*[15]

Aristotle insists that a tragedy must be a whole; it must have a beginning (first verse), a middle, and an end (last verse). The manner in which he defines both the beginning (*arche*) and the end (*teleute*) is extremely sophisticated. The *arche* is that which, by itself, does not necessarily follow upon something else, but is followed by something which necessarily derives from it. The *teleute* is that which, of itself, must necessarily follow upon something else, but is not necessarily followed by something deriving from it (Aristotle, *Poetics,* 1450b, 27f.).

These definitions have, at times, been considered trivial or even pedantic. They might be merely pedantic, had they been written by a medieval scholar in Latin. Written by Aristotle, and

[14] As Levi-Strauss (1964) pointed out, only the polyphonic composer does not labor under this handicap. We must bow to the limitations of the essentially homophonic nature of language.

[15] From this, quite as much as from the fact that (judging by the surviving fragments, records of performances—didaskalia—and miscellaneous traditions) post-Aeschylean trilogies seldom dealt with the same personage, or even with the same myth cycle, it has been concluded that post-Aeschylean trilogy arbitrarily juxtaposed three disparate plays. (This is, more or less, the view expressed by Pickard-Cambridge [1962] and in other authoritative works.) The one trilogy which did survive—Aeschylus' *Oresteia*—is certainly so organic a whole that it resisted even the onslaughts of compilers of "selected plays" in antiquity. This does not facilitate inquiry into the internal coherence of lost post-Aeschylean trilogies. My own view is that such late trilogies, no matter how disparate their respective plots of the component tragedies were, did form a *psychological* whole or *Gestalt.* A Beethoven sonata, each of whose movements has its own theme, or themes, is not a grab-bag; it is quite as much a coherent *Gestalt* as a so-called "cyclic" sonata, each of whose movements is built upon transformations of the same basic theme. The *Oresteia* is of the cyclic sonata type; Euripidean trilogies were, I believe, of the Beethoven sonata type.

in Greek, there is much depth behind their deceptively simple façades. To begin with, the Greek word *arche* is singularly rich and nuanced; it implies beginning or origin, but also the concept of directing or ruling. It is not just a way of denoting a point in time. What is denoted is a point-event, which, in mathematics, would be the point at which not simply a line—a scalar—but, specifically, a vector begins. In Aristotle's thought, an origin already implies a direction and also a force propelling the system in the direction of a *teleute;* of a specific, terminal point-event, which is at once the last point of a vector and the closure-element of a *Gestalt. Arche* and *teleute* are, thus, the boundaries of a temporal structure.[16] If one translates *arche* and *teleute,* respectively, as "beginning" and "end," disregarding the other implications of these words in the Greek language and in the context of Aristotle's philosophy of temporal structures, nearly all of what he thought and sought to express is lost.

Indeed, were Aristotle's definitions taken literally, one would be led to the manifestly absurd conclusion that Aeschylus' *Libation Bearers (Choephorae)* neither presupposes his *Agamemnon,* nor necessarily leads to his *Eumenides.* What is more, one would be forced to question whether a tragedy's prologue (which informs the audience of the antecedent events which lead up to the tragedy's plot) and the final prophecies of the deity from the *theologeion,* in a Euripidean drama (which predict the events deriving from the enacted plot), really "belong" to the tragedy.

Now, as Aristotle knew better than anyone else, everything presupposes something antecedent and has, in turn, both immediate and remote consequences. This obvious point can hardly have escaped him while writing his *Poetics.* Correctly seen, what Aristotle implies is that it is the audience which perceives some-

[16] I do not mean to imply that, despite his manifestly teleological conceptions, Aristotle did not distinguish between a *teleute* and an *arete.* In the first approximation, *teleute* is the completion of a Gestalt; *arete* is, specifically, its *system-adequate* completion which, in Aristotle's thought, is at once a biological and a moral (ethical) concept/event/state/end.

thing as an *arche* and something else as a *teleute,*[17] thereby creating or contriving a temporal structure—a *Gestalt* or configuration in time. The plot of a tragedy has a beginning, a middle, and an end, simply because, persuaded by the tragic poet, we so experience it. Beginning, middle, and end exist, so to speak, on the psychological level only. It is the audience which declares that everything it can, for all practical purposes, dispense with, when seeking to understand and to respond to the plot configuration in a particular, coherent way, lies "outside" (before or after) the unitary plot.

This is not an anachronistic imputation, since much the same is true also of Greek law. The beginning of a murder, viewed as a legal temporal configuration, was the murderous act. The presence or absence of the intention to kill, or, for that matter, its possible justification, were, for a long time, not only chronologically before, but functionally outside the boundaries of the configuration that formed the object of the legal mind's contemplation (Adkins, 1960). Later on, about the time the Greek tragic poets produced their masterpieces, this configuration was broadened to bring intention and justification within the boundaries of the legally relevant configuration.[18]

In Aristotle's definition of the tragic plot's *arche* and *teleute,* these entities (modes of experiencing) are the psychologically

[17] The same is true of the scholar or literary critic: Witness the debate, which rages since antiquity, over whether the *Odyssey* once ended, or really ends, or should end, not where it does, in fact, but with verse 23:296. For the psychologist this simply means that different persons see different point-events as the *teleute* of an action—as the point where, in their apperception, "it is all over but for the shouting."

[18] In some of Antiphon's forensic *Tetralogies,* the crux of the matter is precisely the definition of these boundaries, under the guise of an attempt to determine who is "really" the "cause" of a homicide. The history of modern criminal law is largely a history of the gradual expansion of the boundaries of the legally relevant configuration. Its *arche* increasingly includes also the psychiatric status of the "criminal." One wonders whether the *arche* will ever be pushed back far enough to consider as the "cause" not the criminal, but those who warped his character in childhood to the point where he practically had to become a criminal. On this chain of remoter causes and attributions of responsibility, cf. G. Devereux (1956).

determined boundaries of the configuration. The unity of the plot is thus not that of an abstractly conceived sequence of events, i.e., of a slice of time[19] inherently *ausgegliedert* from a continuum, at points which form "natural" articulations;[20] it is the unity—and reach—of a particular mode of experiencing. Only in terms of this configuration of the experience is something felt, and therefore made to lie "before" or "after," by not being experienced as directly relevant. It is a matter of the reach of what I have called the temporal ego. Logically expressed, the *arche* and the *teleute* are, respectively, the points beyond which the tracing of causes and the pursuit of consequences become uneconomical and increasingly subject to the law of diminishing returns.[21] All this is largely a matter of coherent ways of experiencing slices of time, in function of the reach of one's temporal ego.[22]

All this was stated, in so many words, by Aristotle himself (*Poetics,* 1450b, 35f.). The plot may not be of such magnitude (length) as to make an overview impossible, i.e., it must not overtax memory, or the reach of the psychic apparatus. This insight leads in a straight line to my concept of the temporal ego, which enables the individual to experience himself as continuous and invariant in time. This capacity depends, in turn, on the possibility of organizing each and every segment of one's path through time into a coherent event-experience—into a plot.[23]

Once initiated, a psychological or physiological process must

[19] Conceived, in Leibnizian terms, as "the order of events."

[20] On such "natural" points, cf. Angyal (1941).

[21] The same law also helps one determine the point at which one must shift from one type of explanation to another, cf. Devereux (1945, 1961b).

[22] Both scotomata and obsessions can influence the manner in which an *arche* or a *teleute* is determined. For a discussion of the antipsychoanalytic psychiatrist's premature assertion: "This is all I need to know," see Devereux (1967a), especially chapters xxi-xxiv. For an example of the indefinite postponement of the *teleute* experience, cf. the case of an analysand who obsessively worried over what happened to used matches (information furnished by a colleague). This analysand simply refused to close the temporal structure.

[23] Limitations of space preclude a detailed analysis of this process at the present time.

follow a set course from its *arche* to its *teleute* at a strictly defined rate. The whole progression closely resembles the *Gestalt* psychologist's concept of a push toward closure, which, incidentally, is indispensable for a logical formulation of the theory of psychoanalytic technique (Devereux, 1951). Interferences with this normal progression create states of tension; repeated interferences may cause neuroses.[24] These considerations must be taken into account in appraising the meaning and scope of Aristotle's insistence that, both as regards the internal unity of its plot and as regards its absolute duration in time,[25] the drama must respect the reach of the human psyche.

His analysis of the dynamics of the tragic plot shows the same awareness of basic psychological structures and processes. The matter is best approached in terms of Aristotle's notions about the role of the irrational in the dynamics of the plot, since this manner of tackling the problem will eventually lead us directly to the problem of on stage and off stage.

Aristotelian boundaries of tragedy

1. That which is most rational (secondary process), i.e., that in which the cause-and-effect nexus is most readily discernible, is within the boundaries of tragedy. Thus, Aristotle insists that whenever something can be brought about either by rational or by irrational (primary-process) means, it is best to bring it about by rational means (*Poetics,* 1460b, 27f.).[26] I do not see

24 In physiology: *coitus interruptus,* abortion, and (inferably) the habit of Roman gourmets of making themselves vomit so as to be able to begin eating some more. In psychology: the Zeigarnik experiment (interruption of a task before completion [Zeigarnik, 1927]) and perhaps the Pötzl (1917) experiments. Neurosis is unfinished business, a "hot penny."

25 Needless to say, I speak here mainly of the length of the performance, rather than of the so-called "unity of time," preached not by Aristotle, but by the theoreticians of neoclassical drama. Aristotle simply noted, as a fact, that the plot of many Greek dramas unfolds in the course of a single revolution of the sun (one day).

26 Cf. the dictum of the Aristotelian St. Thomas Aquinas: A supernatural explanation should not be resorted to until after all natural explanations have been exhausted. The key word is "all"; nearly all parapsychological reasoning disregards this clause, cf. Devereux (1953).

how one could speak more clearly of sublimation. The very indication of the availability of two means for bringing about a given situation anticipates Freud's maxim: "Where id was, there shall ego be."[27] Hence, Aristotle feels that the irrational should not be within the material boundaries of the tragedy, but outside it (*Poetics,* 1454b, 6). He echoes this thesis again with respect to spatial structures: That which is presented on stage should contain nothing irrational; if something irrational is necessary, let it occur off stage (*Poetics,* 1460a, 26f.). That, psychologically at least, "before and after" mean the same thing as "off stage" is shown by his remark that the gods should intervene only in order to reveal antecedent events, which man (the spectator?) cannot know, and for the purpose of prophesying future events, this being possible for the gods, who see all (*Poetics,* 1454b, 2ff.).

2. That which not only is rational—or at least plausibly and necessarily interconnected—but is also so perceived, i.e., is responded to as if it were a causal sequence, by the audience, is within the Aristotelian boundaries of tragedy. The plot must induce not only a *post hoc* but also, and indeed above all, a *propter hoc* feeling (*Poetics,* 1452a, 16f.). How realistic Aristotle is even about this alleged rule is shown by his admission (*Poetics,* 1455b, 24) that some of the elements of the plot's "knot" can lie outside the events presented on stage.

Underlying these specifications, when they are examined in the light of psychoanalysis, is the deep and novel insight that the length of the plot—i.e., of the essence of the tragedy—is decisively limited by the reach of the spectator's temporal ego. The magnitude of this temporal configuration—the distance between *arche* and *teleute*—is determined by the spectator's ego-reach-

[27] This, incidentally, underlines once more the consistently ignored implication that the best and most stable sublimation is that whose manifestations most closely approximate the behavior that would result from the unsublimated acting out of an impulse: A body-destruction fantasy is better sublimated by the surgeon, who cuts up people, than by the butcher, who cuts up meat, cf. Devereux (1961a).

linked ability to perceive this slice of time as a structured whole.[28] Whatever lies outside the boundaries of this ego-capacity-limited configuration either is, or is perceived as, "the irrational." Though the existence of the irrational, viewed as a force impinging upon the configuration, is recognized, it does not belong to the configuration itself; it is clearly felt to come from "elsewhere." In psychoanalytic terms, it is experienced as ego-alien, exactly the way an erupting unconscious impulse is experienced as ego-alien.[29]

Thus, what is within the tragedy can only be what—and as much as—the ego can effectively master and concomitantly abreact (catharsis). Whatever cannot be handled in this way is experienced as "outside" the tragedy, even if a bad playwright assigns to it a central position in his plot.[30] The actual plot of Greek tragedy, both as it is and as Aristotle defines it, has boundaries set by, and coinciding with, both the poet's and the audience's temporal ego-reach. Whatever is outside this series of

[28] If this inference is admitted, it is just possible that during the troubled years of the Peloponnesian War and the period of decline which followed it, there occurred a diminution of the attention span, reflecting an impairment of the ego. (Cf. Callimachus: "A big book is a big mess.") The surviving tragedies of the three great poets are fairly long (averaging about 1300 vv.). Now, the so-called "Suidas" (s.v. Aristarchos Tegeates) says that Aristarchus gave tragedy its "present" (*nun*) length. H. J. Rose (1934) thinks that this means that tragedy became increasingly shorter. Rose's inference seems valid, though I cannot agree that he is right in citing the *Rhesus* (996 vv.) as a sample of late, short tragedy. The *Rhesus* is an authentic play by Euripides and has, moreover, probably lost its prologue (Ritchie, 1964). Ritchie's conclusions are supported by my findings. The structure of the dreams in the *Rhesus,* the *Hecuba,* and the *Iphigenia amongst the Taurians,* of Euripides, is absolutely the same, and so is the latent content. This makes the hypothesis of a different authorship of the *Rhesus* psychologically implausible.

[29] Ego-dystonic acts are at times performed in a dissociated or amnesic (fugue) state, accompanied by a feeling of "drivenness" (Devereux, 1956). At times the dissociation leads to multiple personalities: when Dr. Jekyll is on stage, Mr. Hyde is off stage, and *vice versa.* Cf. Euripides, *Medea,* 1019ff.

[30] This may explain why mediocre ghost and horror stories elicit feelings of indifference and implausibility. It may even explain why most good stories of this kind are short stories, rather than novels. The few really good ghost novels treat the irrational ("uncanny," [Freud, 1919]) allusively, and always as something external. In the most gripping scene of James' *The Turn of the Screw,* the children pretend to be unaware of the uncanny things going on around them.

happenings, which is perceived as forming a configuration, is either inherently irrational, or, if not irrational in itself, is so perceived.[31]

ON STAGE—OFF STAGE

One can proceed from the analysis of the *arche* and the *teleute* directly to that of the psychological import of Aristotle's—again deceptively simple—distinction between events occurring on stage and events occurring concurrently off stage. What precedes the *arche* or follows the *teleute* is, in every important respect, identical in nature with what the Greek tragic poet habitually relegates off stage. What he causes to precede or to follow his tragedy is understandable in terms of, and determined by the reach of, the temporal ego; what he causes to happen off stage is understandable in terms of, and determined by the reach of, the (traditional Freudian) structural ego. This, as will be shown, is made obvious by the manner in which Aristotle defines both types of material. That which lies either without the temporal bounds of the tragedy, or else takes place off stage, is clearly not rational; it is not material usually manipulated by either the temporal or the spatial ego. It is, as Aristotle plainly states, irrational material. This has a curious implication for the trilogy. It means that, when viewed from *within* the *Libation Bearers* of Aeschylus, the contents of the antecedent play, *Agamemnon,* and

[31] Since Freud's work, and as a result of it, the irrational has become accessible to rational understanding. Unfortunately, those whom Rabelais called "abstractors of quintessence" have unwarrantably extrapolated from the possibility of studying the irrational rationally, a kind of metaphysical game which implicitly denies the irrationality of the irrational; they condescendingly pity Freud for his "obsolete" nineteenth-century positivism (Devereux, 1966c). Does the fact that we have learned to study the behavior of gas models thermodynamically (i.e., in terms of statistical mechanics) abolish the basic fact that the individual molecule continues to obey the laws of classical (celestial) mechanics? For a further critique of this deterioration of psychoanalytic theory into a Platonic ballet of ideas, see Devereux (1967a). The present trend can only lead to a pseudo psychoanalysis, without Freud.

of the succeeding play, *Eumenides,* are irrational, and vice versa of course. In this frame of reference, "rational" and "irrational" are thus clearly complementary entities,[32] when these terms are intended as explanatory. Even though they may pertain to exactly the same object or event, they cannot be offered simultaneously, just as psychological and sociological explanations cannot be advanced simultaneously, because they stand in a complementary relationship to each other (Devereux, 1945, 1961b, 1961c). That which, in the tragedy's temporal structure, is before or after is, in its spatial structure, off stage. That which, in the time dimension, is the plot is, in space, that which is on stage. This theoretical and methodological position is perfectly congruent with Aristotle's distinction between on stage and off stage.

Aristotle says that tragedy is about[33] great deeds which, in contradistinction to the epic, are not narrated but performed; tragedy is directed at spectators rather than at audiences *stricto sensu*. Let us now see how this applies to the *Oedipus Tyrannus* of Sophocles, which Aristotle seemed to consider the most typical of all Greek dramas. What are Oedipus' great deeds? His exposure, his parricide, his solving of the riddle of the Sphinx, his incest, and his self-blinding. Yet, *not one* of these great deeds actually occurs on stage. This means either that Aristotle was talking nonsense, or that what he meant by "great deeds" is not what some commentators think he meant.

Now, the fact is that very few great deeds (motor behavior) occur on stage in any Greek tragedy. Those that do occur physically on stage may be made invisible to the spectators. In Euripides' *Hecuba,* Polymestor is blinded and his children are killed not on the open stage itself, but inside a tent placed on the stage.

[32] Jordan (1947) clearly shows that Freud sensed this fact. The translation of the relevant passage in the *Standard Edition* omits the crucial word, *Vertretung* (Freud, 1916-1917, p. 279). It took a nuclear physicist to understand Freud.

[33] I.e., it is an imitation pertaining to an original; it is not the original itself, nor even a fully equivalent duplication (*eidolon*) of that original. This point is crucial.

Some great deeds were performed before the tragedy begins and are *talked about* in the prologue; others occur off stage and are *reported by* Messengers. Regardless of whether the tragic poet takes recourse to a prologue, a Messenger's report, or a tent, he causes great and violent deeds (rawly instinctual acting out) to reach his audiences only after they have undergone a preliminary filtering or processing—e.g., in the rational and conscious mind of the personage who recites the prologue, or of the Messenger who is, at times, not even an active participant in these events, but simply a bystander, or even a purveyor of second-hand information.[34] When he is an active participant in the events he reports, he may, as in the *Oedipus Tyrannus,* admit that he had disobeyed "great" orders, by not exposing the infant Oedipus. The Messenger in Euripides' *Iphigenia amongst the Taurians* (vv. 260 ff.), though he had been forced to participate in certain violent acts, files a minority report: He agrees with the one pious man who believed Orestes and Pylades to be supernatural beings. In short, the great deeds (raw acting out) reach the audience in an already purified and even intellectualized form, which attenuates their direct impact upon the emotions. This represents a sublimation (art).

Aristotle not only described the practice of removing violence from the stage and of mediating it both to the personages on stage and to the audience by means of verbal reports, but approved of this way of dealing with raw violence. Yet, he specifically defined tragedy as the presentation of great deeds and events on stage. This can only mean that, for him, the great deed was not the raw act *per se,* not Polynices' and Eteocles' reciprocal fratricide, not the sexual embrace of Oedipus and Jocasta. Rather, it was the impact of these deeds upon those who performed them or were affected by them, or beheld them in one way or another,

[34] In Euripides' *Children of Heracles,* the Messenger explains that he did not witness the events he reports (vv. 847ff). This has given rise to inferences which I believe to be unwarranted.

as the Messengers and at times even the Chorus did.[35] The great deed is not the short and brutal act of Oedipus' self-blinding, off stage, but his reaction to it, on stage. Once this point is firmly grasped, the extravagant views of Tycho von Wilamowitz-Moellendorff (1917) on the absence of real psychology in the plays of Sophocles, and of Walter Zürcher (1947)[36] on its absence in Euripides' plays, collapse under the weight of their own scientific nihilism.

Greek tragedy simply takes place on two levels: the raw event occurs off stage; its psychological consequences are shown on stage. The two are, as Aristotle has shown, effectively compartmentalized. As the personages move on and off stage—be it at the beginning or at the end of the drama, or in the course of the play itself—they pass from one psychological world to another. Before, after, and off stage is the world of instinctual acting out in great deeds. In that world there is neither unity of time nor of place, because there is none in the world of the unconscious instinct representatives. Neither is there decorum, lofty seemliness *(semnos),* or ego control. When coming on stage, the dramatic personage passes from the world of actualized instincts and fantasms into the world of conscious ego functions; going off stage, he plunges back into the depths of the unconscious and acts in accordance with its dictates.

One of the most conclusive proofs of this interpretation is the convention that the Choral Ode can bridge any span of time, can represent any duration in time. Even if the Ode lasts only a few minutes (as measured by a real clock), it represents psychologically a length of time which permits the unfolding (off stage) of

[35] The role of the Chorus as quasi-Messenger—as a source of information, rather than of comment—should not be minimized. The Chorus gives much information, e.g., in Euripides' *Heracles the Madman.* In Aeschylus' *Libation Bearers,* it is not Clytaemnestra who narrates her dream; it is the Chorus (vv. 527ff.).

[36] Both Zürcher and the younger Wilamowitz-Moellendorff operate in terms of a purely literary and aprioristic conception of what men are like and of what psychology is about.

events which, in reality, would require many days. This is, undeniably, a technical convention, but it is also something else and infinitely more than just that. Unwittingly, but with a somnambulistic sureness of touch, it also reflects the characteristic timelessness of the unconscious. It therefore utterly disregards the distinction between simultaneousness and successiveness. In so doing, it practically abolishes the categories: past, present, and future, which are among the most important acquisitions of the ego. Hence, in Euripides' *Suppliant Women,* the Athenian army can march to Thebes, give battle, win it, and send back a Messenger during the time it takes for the Chorus and the actors on stage to sing and recite a total of 38 verses (598-633) only, and requiring, at the most, a very few minutes. By verse 634 the Messenger is back with news of an Athenian victory; by verse 794, Theseus himself returns on stage.

Objectively speaking, this much simply cannot happen in a matter of two to four minutes in reality; it can, however, happen in dreams (Devereux, 1967c). Seen externally, this convention is utterly unrealistic: the clock of reality, ticking off minutes on stage, is hopelessly fast. When, however, one views matters psychologically, the clock of reality on stage accurately measures the time it takes one to dream what happens off stage. Brilliantly conceived and executed experimental work shows the objective duration of even a very long dream (corresponding to Theseus' expedition against Thebes) to be very short. A long dream can be dreamed in the course of some four minutes (corresponding to the length of the time it takes the personages on stage to sing 38 verses).[37] Such "absurd" conventions can come into being and be accepted only if corresponding phenomena exist in the human psyche. In this case, the duality of time is represented by two "clocks": one, with hands, which measures the duration of the actual dream, and a handless imaginary clock, which

[37] The duration of dreaming is determined by means of electroencephalograms. The literature on the subject is, by now, considerable and conclusive. For a relatively recent summary of findings, see Dement (1966).

measures the time needed for the dreamed events to occur in reality. The Choral Ode in Greek tragedy fills this *dual* time span effectively and, therefore, makes the convention psychologically believable.

The antithesis between on stage and off stage parallels and perhaps echoes a peculiarity of Greek religion and cult. The *agalma*—the beautiful marble, bronze or chryselephantine statue, perhaps the work of a Phidias, shown in the nave (*naos*) open to the public in Greek temples—was not the real statue of the deity. There was often a second and real statue, which was originally not simply a representation of the deity, but the deity itself. It was a (usually wooden and rough-hewn) *xoanon*. In a sense, this *xoanon* was the *Imitandum* hidden behind or under, and represented (imitated) by the *agalma*. In another sense, the nave and its *agalma* correspond to on stage in Greek tragedy, while the hidden chamber (sometimes called *abaton* or *adyton*), with its *xoanon*, corresponds to off stage. Unfortunately, we know much more about the public cult performed in the *naos* than of that performed in the hidden recesses of the temple. That there was a difference is suggested by the existence of mystery cults, such as that of Eleusis and of certain highly individualized and subjective cult actions, or quasi cult actions, represented, e.g., by the descent into the cave of Trophonius, from which one emerged unable to laugh. Moreover, this descent was obligatorily combined with the drinking of the waters of Lethe: of the waters of forgetting but also of remembrance. This descent into the cave was, thus, a visible symbol of a descent into the timeless unconscious (Kouretas, 1960). Nothing like it is found in the cult actions performed, e.g., before Phidias' statue of Athena in the Parthenon.

In relation to Greek tragedy, the problem can be formulated either psychologically or sociologically. The relationship between the *xoanon* and the *agalma* cults, between before and after and the main plot, between off stage and on stage, and between acting out (even in dream, where the acting out is symbolic) and the impact of impulse-triggered acts upon the individual, is, in a psychological frame of reference, dynamically and functionally the same.[38]

Sociologically, we must content ourselves with plausibilities. We know that archaic and crude cult actions involved the *xoanon* and not the *agalma*. It was Hera's hoary *xoanon,* and not her classically beautiful *agalma,* which was annually "revirginated." It would be sacrilege, in Wilamowitz-Moellendorff's sense, to imagine that either Euripides or his audience visualized Artemis' cult statue, before which the Taurians performed human sacrifices, as a statue by Phidias. It must have been a crude *xoanon,* before which such a brutal cult action was imaginable. The statue of Athena, which Odysseus and Diomedes stole from the Trojans, was also an archaic, magic-laden image: the goddess herself, and not the kind of "empty" statue some late Greek authors mention. It was certainly not even the kind of statue which simply mediates the deity to man's limited imagination, in ways which Maximus of Tyre (Oration 8, fin.) poeticized with great and moving eloquence. I deal here, admittedly, with probabilities, but they are great probabilities.[39]

Psychologically, tragedy deals with two separate universes of discourse: the world of the on-stage *agalma* and that of the off-stage *xoanon*. This unfolding of the plot on two levels duplicates, on the outside, the two-level inner functioning of the psyche. Moreover, this manner of presenting rawly instinctual material—which Aristotle does not wish to be tampered with or eliminated (*Poetics,* 1453b ff.)—reduces to a manageable, catharsis-susceptible and sublimable level the impact of potentially explosive material on the spectator's psyche. The enactment, on stage, of

[38] a/b = c/d = e/f, where a, b, c, d, e, f are objective data and the fraction lines and equal signs only constructs. Cf. Kronecker's dictum: "God made the integers; man made all the rest."

[39] Let those who doubt this, ask themselves whether they could imagine even the most pious monk or nun going into an ecstatic trance before Van Dyck's painting of Christ on the Cross. A similar ecstasy elicited by Matthias Grünewald's painting is believable.

tragic "great deeds" would have been intolerably stimulating and anxiety-arousing. The spectacle of Oedipus cohabiting with Jocasta, or the rending asunder of Pentheus by his mother and the Maenads, could only have elicited a shock-reaction of revulsion (*miaros*). Had this taken place on stage, even the civilized Athenian audiences could have coped with it only in the manner in which the brutish Romans coped with their bestial circus games: by means of an immediate and violent acting out in adjacent brothels. Such scenes could not have led to a beneficial and pleasurable catharsis, simply because Athenian audiences were not made up of psychotic sadists and jaded decadents, and also because the tragic personages themselves were, despite their flaw (*hamartia*), neither freaks nor psychotics, but only men and women built on a heroic scale.

This specification is important in that it refutes in advance the possible objection that nowadays dramatists (?) project criminal, perverted, or psychotic acting out upon the stage itself. These sophisticated—or is it decadent?—horror-comics can afford to drag out into the open violently Ego-dystonic material only because the still half-way normal portions of their audiences' psyches—hardened by the horrors of our century—are defensively numbed and have, moreover, only a limited capacity to empathize with the private nightmares of grossly warped *dramatis personae*. It seems self-evident that Euripides' epileptic Heracles[40] and Sophocles' Ajax, who—like Aeschylus' and Euripides' Orestes—experience transitory psychotic seizures,[41] are

[40] That this Heracles was an epileptic was conclusively proven by Blaiklock (1952). He might have added that Heracles' traditional life history is that of an epileptic.

[41] The *bouffée délirante,* rapidly followed by a temporary social remission but not a cure (Devereux, 1956b) is common in primitive and archaic societies. Such crises are recurrent. Orestes had at least three such crises, of variable duration. Briefly relieved by Apollo's purifying intervention and by the verdict of the Athenian Areopagus, relieved a second time by the expiatory theft of the *xoanon* of Artemis from the Taurians, the seizures kept recurring until he bit off his finger. It is probable that Stesichorus had at least two bouts of hysterical blindness, since he wrote two *Palinodes* (expiatory retractions), cf. Chamaeleon in Papyrus Oxyrhynchus, 29 (fr. 16). Page (1962, p. 106) writes:

men who "have" an illness; they are not disease entities which "have" a human being as a thing to perch upon. The Athenian audiences could therefore empathize with them better than I at least can empathize with the clinical entities—not even genuine case histories[42]—masquerading as human beings on the modern stage.

This point is so important that it deserves further discussion. Aelian preserves an ancient Greek story about a man who saved an eagle attacked by a serpent, because he felt the eagle to be the more natural beast of the two; Percival saves a lion from a dragon for the same reason (*Natura Animalium* 17:37). This means that they could empathize better with a warm-blooded creature than with a reptile. It is a matter of gradations of empathy. Xenophon (*Symposium* 9, 2ff.) describes how the banqueteers—amongst whom was Socrates—were aroused by a beautifully danced imitation of Dionysus' courtship of Ariadne. By contrast, Aelian reports an episode which suggests that only a manifestly neurotic athlete was sufficiently stimulated by the coupling of dogs to be shocked by it (*Varia Historia* 3:30). One assumes that only a psychotic would be aroused by the coupling of two praying mantes, which culminates in the female's devouring of her mate.

This implies that one could tolerate on stage the sexual coupling of Cocteau's "trapped-rat" Oedipus with his mother, while the sight of Sophocles' Oedipus simply kissing Jocasta might arouse intolerable anxiety. The more authentically human, the more *suo iure*, the more empathizable a dramatic personage is, the less rawly instinctual and fantasmatic his behavior on

---

"duas esse palinodias ignorabamus." There is evidence that more than one Stesichorean *Palinode* was known to the ancients. Both Hippolytus (= pseudo-Origen, *contra haer.* 6.14) and Irenaeus (*adv. haer.* 1.23.2) speak of Stesichorean *Palinodes* in the plural.

[42] Greene's (1944) remark that Euripides' Electra is only a "case history" reflects so abysmal an ignorance of psychiatry that it does not even deserve to be refuted. By contrast, it is easy to agree with Arnott (1959, p. 229), that the Oedipus in Jean Cocteau's *La Machine Infernale* is simply a "trapped rat," with whom one cannot empathize. See further comments on this point below.

stage can be.[43] By contrast, since Frankenstein is, by definition, a monster, he must outdo himself in monstrousness to be even mildly interesting. I can listen with detachment to a Sedang Moi (South Vietnam) tale about the ghost who moans: "Ouch! It hurts!" while he compulsively devours his liver, but am shaken by the off-stage self-blinding of Oedipus or by accounts of how Iphigenia and Polyxena were sacrificed off stage.

The same subtle distinction between off stage and on stage also manifests itself in the manner in which heroes die in Greek tragedy. The brutal or fantasmatic slaying of Agamemnon, Clytaemnestra, Aegisthus, Medea's children, and so forth, invariably occurs off stage, as do archaic human sacrifices. Deaths that are held to be ethically seemly—those of Ajax, of Alcestis, of Euadne—occur on stage.[44] This finding disposes of the assertion of some commentators that, since in the Greek theatre only three actors played (in succession) the total of half a dozen or more speaking roles found in a given drama, the author could not afford to have them lying about idly as corpses, when they should be up and about their business of playing another personage. Like any other technical limitation inherent in one's material or prescribed by the rules of the craft, the three-actor rule was creatively exploited—so as to achieve a high "density"—by the great tragic poets, though it probably handicapped the lesser ones.[45]

All that is off stage in Greek tragedy is, of course, not invariably rawly instinctual or fantasmatic; when it is not, it is at least handled in a dreamlike manner.[46]

[43] Cf. footnote 20. Anatole France makes the Devil completely credible, by attributing to him a diabolically subtle and allusive remark: "Why should you fear me, when you know that I do not exist?"

[44] Hippolytus' death is a special case. His fantasmatic accident occurs off stage; he dies on stage. This hardly proves that he is the pure and noble hero commentators old and new believe him to be. In Euripides, he is an offensive, hostile, arrogant and sex-phobic prig. "Kann man denn nicht lesen?" (Wilamowitz-Moellendorff, 1917).

[45] See the brilliantly contrived exit in Euripides: *Bacchae,* 1148f.

[46] What Hippolytus says of his off-stage relationship with Artemis, is much like an "ethereal" (schizoid) dream, or daydream.

The large range of means at the disposal of the tragic poet: speech, song, music, drama, scenery, also played a role in determining what was to be presented on stage, and how.[47] Once more, a basic artistic problem must be considered first. Infinitely greater depth, intensity, and intimacy of emotion are tolerable in a string quartet than in a Wagnerian *Gesammtkunstwerk*, where a combination of extreme raw material with elaborate resources for mediating it to the audience can make a good work intolerable and a bad one nauseating.[48] By relegating a number of affectively intense "great deeds" off stage, Greek tragedy managed to achieve the sublimated affective intensity of a Mozart string quartet—a feat of dramaturgy probably unparalleled before or since. In a sense, the epic teaches the same lesson. Being, like a messenger's report or (at times) like a choral ode, "about" things, it had to be accompanied on the lyre,[49] in order to mobilize the whole range of the audience's affects.

There is actually good evidence that the Athenian audience's capacity to tolerate affect—while undoubtedly great—had definite limits. The horrible appearance of Aeschylus' Erinyes is said to have frightened women into miscarrying in the theatre. Athens fined Phrynichus because his *Capture of Miletus* caused the audi-

[47] The technical competence of Greek stage setting, machinery, etc., is no longer underestimated (Webster, 1956).

[48] A concrete example will show this. Though Wagner's taste was far from perfect, he had sense enough to mediate the erotic element in *Tristan* almost exclusively by means of orchestral passages, whose pulsations closely approximate those of the coital rhythm. Moreover, these passages rely, both for basic inspiration and for the handling of technical means, on the infinitely more sensual—and, in my estimate, also infinitely greater—music of Berlioz' *Romeo and Juliet,* which Berlioz—wisely—did not intend to be presented as an opera. By eliminating in advance all optical stimulation, Berlioz could raise the erotic intensity of his music one notch higher than could Wagner, who was encumbered at those points by the additional visual stimuli emanating from the stage. The occasional performing of *Romeo and Juliet* as an opera is a senseless gilding of the lily.

[49] Already in Homer's *Odyssey* (Bk. 8) Demodocus sings his lays to the accompaniment of a lyre, as Achilles, in the *Iliad* accompanies himself on the lyre while singing of the great deeds of heroes (*Iliad,* 9:185ff.).

ence to sob and to grieve. I do not consider it impossible that Sophocles' failure to win the first prize with the trilogy, of which *Oedipus Tyrannus* was a part, may have been due to his (extremely restrained) reference to the Theban plague, at a time when the grievous memory of the Athenian plague was still very much alive.[50] Some such consideration may also help one understand why Euripides was so unpopular in Athens, where his dramas were played on the stage, while he enjoyed an immense popularity in (enemy) Syracuse, where they were apparently mainly read. Possibly, he went too far—that is, too deep—in his consciously psychological approach to characterization, and perhaps also with such devices as causing Pentheus' head to be brought (believably) on stage.[51] As regards characterization, there is, in terms of objective psychology, a world of difference between his literally clinical accounts of Heracles' madness or of the transformation of his Hecuba into a savage bitch (which are clinical precisely because Euripides does *not* turn either Heracles or Hecuba into a phantom or into a monster) and the psychologically interpretable and psychologically convincing—but not psychologically *treated*—madness of Ajax in Sophocles' drama, or the tragic fight of the Sophoclean Oedipus against the dawning insight that he, himself, is the (self-) accursed slayer he is looking for. So clinical an approach, especially if, unlike modern drama, it does not dehumanize man into a disease entity, is certainly harder to endure as a play on the stage, than as a dramatic poem read in private. This, I believe, explains why, in his lifetime, Euripides was more popular with readers than with audiences. His immense posthumous fame, second only to that of

[50] If this hypothesis is admissible, it may help one assign an approximate (*post quem*) date to this drama.

[51] This example is, in one sense, badly chosen, in that it is chronologically unsatisfactory. The *Bacchae* was written after Euripides exiled himself to Macedonia. There is, however, no reason to assume that he did not go to similar "extremes" in some of his earlier (lost) plays; the realistic rags of Telephus were often held up to ridicule by Aristophanes and by his successors.

Homer,[52] may be due to the fact that later generations had lost their formerly profoundly emotional belief in the basic, archaically "real," actuality of the myths he had dramatized—a belief which formerly made audiences feel that he had gone intolerably far—that is, intolerably deep. It is not the depth of Euripides' probing, but the burning actuality of his myths, which time had attenuated. Because of the slow attrition of literal faith, the average man's response to Euripides' dramatic representation of some bloody and scandalous tradition was probably no longer: "Ye gods!" but: "How interesting."[53] In Periclean Athens the poet had to control and to regulate the impact of the myth's emotional outflow; late mythographers had to put hot air under high pressure to create a semblance of affective significance and relevance.

The analysis of Aristotle's inductively formulated "rules" of tragedy proves that he described the means used by great dramatic poets for regulating the affect triggered off by the plots of their tragedies. He shows that these means were complex, nuanced, tightly interlocking, and meshing sublimatory devices, closely patterned upon the temporal and spatial structure of the mind, only whose content is reflected in the plots themselves.

[52] This is shown, on the one hand, by the fact that Euripidean passages on papyrus and on shards (*ostraka*) outnumber passages from any other Greek author, Homer always excepted, and, on the other hand, by the fact that Euripidean passages cited by other Greek authors are more numerous than passages from Aeschylus and Sophocles combined. Finally, only seven plays by Aeschylus and seven by Sophocles, as against 19 by Euripides, were transmitted to us in their entirety. Scholia on Euripides are, likewise, much richer than those on his rivals.

[53] This may explain why the "gothic horror" mythographers of hellenistic and Roman times had to pile new monstrosities on old ones in an attempt to endow ancient myth once more with the power to elicit *mythical* credibility. This need was particularly acute in an age where both the hellenistic ruling houses and such Roman rulers as the Julio-Claudians, Commodus, Heliogabalus, etc., behaved in reality much like the Atreids do in myth. It is only a slight modification of the views of Bowra (1930) to say that the "heroic age" of the myth, the epic, and the tragedy is a vision of a strong, if brutal, age through the half-muddied nostalgic lenses of a period of decline. A hero is Richard the Lionhearted seen through lenses on which Hitler is painted in translucent colors.

REFERENCES

Aelian, *Natura Animalium.*

——— *Varia Historia.*

Adkins, A. W. H. (1960), *Merit and Responsibility: A Study in Greek Value.* Oxford: Clarendon Press.

Angyal, A. (1941), *Foundations for a Science of Personality.* London: Oxford University Press.

Aristotle, *Poetics.*

——— *On Divination by Dreams.*

Arnott, P. D. (1959), *An Introduction to Greek Theatre.* London: Macmillan.

Blaiklock, E. M. (1952), *The Male Characters of Euripides.* Wellington: New Zealand University Press.

Bowra, C. M. (1930), *Tradition and Design in the Iliad.* Oxford: Clarendon Press, 1958.

Cornford, F. M. (1912), *From Religion to Philosophy.* London: E. Arnold.

Dement, W. (1966), The Dream in Human Cultures. In: *The Dream in Human Societies,* ed. G. E. von Grunebaum and R. Caillos. Berkeley: University of California Press.

Devereux, G. (1940), A Conceptual Scheme of Society. *Amer. J. Sociol.,* 54:687-706.

——— (1945), The Logical Foundations of Culture and Personality Studies. *Trans. N. Y. Acad. Sci.,* 7:110-130.

——— (1951), Some Criteria for the Timing of Confrontations and Interpretations. *Internat. J. Psycho-Anal.,* 32:19-24.

——— (1953), Extrasensory Perception and Psychoanalytic Epistemology. In: *Psychoanalysis and the Occult,* pp. 16-46. New York: International Universities Press.

——— (1955), *A Study of Abortion in Primitive Societies.* New York: Julian Press.

——— (1956a), *Therapeutic Education.* New York: Harper.

——— (1956b), Normal and Abnormal. In: *Some Uses of Anthropology, Theoretical and Applied.* Washington: Anthropology Society of Washington.

——— (1961a), Art and Mythology: A General Theory. In: *Studying Personality Cross-culturally,* ed. B. Kaplan. New York: Harper & Row.

——— (1961b), Two Types of Modal Personality Models. In: *Studying Personality Cross-culturally,* ed. B. Kaplan. New York: Harper & Row.

——— (1961c), Mohave Ethnopsychiatry and Suicide. In: *Studying Personality Cross-culturally,* ed. B. Kaplan. New York: Harper & Row.

——— (1966a), Rapports Cliniques et Phylogénétiques entre les Odeurs et les Emotions dans la Névrose Caractérielle d'un Hottentat Griqua. *Psychopathol. Africaine,* 2:65-76.
——— (1966b), La Nature du Stress. *Rev. Méd. Psychosom.,* 8:103-113.
——— (1966c), Loss of Identity, Impairment of Relationships, Reading Disability. *Psychoanal. Quart.,* 35:18-39.
——— (1966d), Transference, Screen Memory and the Temporal Ego. *J. Nerv. Ment. Dis.,* 143:318-323.
——— (1967a), *From Anxiety to Method.* Paris: Mouton & Co.
——— (1967b), La Renonciation à l'Identité. *Rev. Franç. Psychanal.,* 31:101-142.
——— (1967c), Observation and Belief in Aeschylus' Accounts of Dreams. *Psychother. & Psychosom.,* 15:114-134.
——— (1970), *La Naissance d' Aphrodite, Échanges et Communications.* Paris & The Hague: Mouton.
Dodds, E. R. (1951), *Greeks and the Irrational.* Berkeley: University of California Press.
——— (1965), *Pagan and Christian in an Age of Anxiety.* New York: Cambridge University Press.
Freud, S. (1906), Delusions and Dreams in Jensen's Gradiva. *Standard Edition,* 9:7-93. London: Hogarth Press, 1954.
——— (1916-1917), Fixation to Traumas—The Unconscious. *Standard Edition,* 16:273-285. London: Hogarth Press.
——— (1919), The Uncanny. *Standard Edition,* 17:217-256. London: Hogarth Press, 1955.
Fux, J. J. (1725), *Gradus ad Parnassum.*
Greene, W. C. (1944), *Moira.* Cambridge, Mass.: Harvard University Press.
Jones, E. (1949), *Hamlet and Oedipus.* London: Victor Gollancz.
Jordan, P. (1947), *Verdrängung und Komplementarität.* Hamburg: Stromverl.
Kouretas, D. (1960), Aspects Modernes des Cures Psychothérapiques Appliquées dans les Sanctuaires de la Grèce Antique. *Communications au XVII*[e] *Congrès International d'Histoire de la Médecine,* Athenes-Cos.
Kris, E. (1952), *Psychoanalytic Explorations in Art.* New York: International Universities Press.
Kubie, L. S. (1958), *Neurotic Distortion of the Creative Process.* Lawrence: University of Kansas Press.
Levi-Strauss, C. (1958), *Anthropologie Structurale.* Paris: Plon.
——— (1964), *Le Cru et le Cuit.* Paris: Plon.
Page, D. L. (1962), *Poetae Melici Graeci.* New York: Oxford University Press.
Petzoldt, J. (1923), Kausalität und Wahrscheinlichkeit. *Naturwissenschaft,* 17.

Pickard-Cambridge, A. W. (1962), *Dithyramb, Tragedy and Comedy,* ed. T. B. L. Webster. Oxford: Clarendon Press.

Piston, W. (1947), *Counterpoint.* New York: Norton.

——— (1948), *Harmony.* New York: Norton.

Pötzl, O. (1917), Experimentell erregte Traumbilder in ihren Beziehungen zum indirekten Sehen. *Zschr. gesamt. Neurol. Psychiat.,* 36:278-349.

Ritchie, W. (1964), *The Authenticity of the Rhesus of Euripides.* Cambridge, Mass.: Cambridge University Press.

Rose, H. J. (1934), *A Handbook of Greek Literature.* London: Methuen, 1960.

Sachs, H. (1951), *The Creative Unconscious.* Cambridge, Mass.: Sci-Art Publishers.

Waelder, R. (1965), *Psychoanalytic Avenues to Art.* New York: International Universities Press.

Webster, T. B. L. (1956), *Greek Theatre Production.* London: Methuen.

Wilamowitz-Moellendorff, T. von (1917), *Die dramatische Technik des Sophokles.* Berlin: Weidmann.

Zeigarnik, B. W. (1927), Das Behalten erledigter und unerledigter Handlungen. *Psychol. Forsch.,* 9:1-85.

Zürcher, W. (1947), *Die Darstellung des Menschen im Drama des Euripides.* Basel: Reinhardt.

LAWLESS SENSATIONS AND CATEGORIAL DEFENSES: THE UNCONSCIOUS SOURCES OF KANT'S PHILOSOPHY

LEWIS S. FEUER, PH.D.

Kant has long seemed to be, on the basis of Heine's (1835) celebrated description, the archetype of the pedantic, academic professor, pursuing on a strict schedule his passionless studies. That is only, however, because we have left aside the Kant who has told us of his inner strife (1746b, 1797b, 1798). It is from such documents that we are enabled in part to reconstruct the emotional sources of Kant's philosophy.

Now the basic tenets of a philosopher generally reflect assumptions which are held because they are the ones that best express his emotional standpoint toward reality. Every philosopher has what George Boas (1948) calls a "protophilosophy," the set of his underlying axioms which are not themselves called into question. The protophilosophy issues from the philosopher's decision-base as the projection in propositional form of the philosopher's

Dr. Feuer is Professor of Sociology at the University of Toronto. He has written several books and numerous papers in the fields of psychoanalysis, philosophy, and sociology.

sense of reality, with all its emphases, conflicts, repressions, exaggerations. And Kant's protophilosophy is what we seek to subject to psychoanalytic study, and thereby to ascertain the deepest emotional, nonlogical determinants of his philosophy. The *Critique of Pure Reason* (Kant, 1781) rests on two important propositions: (1) that we do not know things as they are in themselves, but only as they appear to us, as phenomena; and (2) that our mental functioning imposes on our sensations certain necessary and universal forms and structures (Royce, 1919).

Kant's Sensory Life: His Estrangement from Sensation

That we do not know things as they are but only as phenomena is Kant's basic notion. We may describe this notion as the "estrangement" assumption; it asserts that our sensations do not convey information concerning the external world, that we are from the beginning estranged from reality, that sensations are to be mistrusted, that only through naïve common sense do we assume that they tell us something about the external world. There is thus a denigration of the status of sensation, which becomes a phenomenal wall between ourselves and genuine reality. Schopenhauer (1818), indeed, said that Kant's greatest service was to demonstrate the "dreamlike creation of the entire world" (p. 430). The first impression which the *Critique* made on its readers was, as a matter of fact, its destruction of naïve realism. That was why Moses Mendelssohn called Kant the total pulverizer, "Den alles Zermalmenden" (Paulsen, 1902). As against common-sense materialism, Kant (1781) was prepared to entertain the transcendental hypothesis that "our present mode of knowledge hovers before us, and like a dream has no objective reality, . . . that this life is an appearance only" (p. 619).

What type of person is inclined, on emotional grounds, to denigrate the role of sensation? It is the kind of person who, in various ways, is at odds with his own sensuality or sexuality, who seeks to repress or contain his sexuality with various defense mechanisms. It is, above all, the kind of person in whom sensory reception evokes an experience of guilt. It is characteristic of persons engaged in such intense repression of sensation that the world of things in themselves recedes for them as something which has been shorn of its reality. Thus Kant developed an intense dislike for all varieties of sensations, proportionate to the degree that they evoked some sort of sexual association.

To begin with, the sense of smell awoke Kant's resistances. It was too obtrusive and could not be shut out easily; it infringed on freedom more than the other senses. In his *Anthropology,* a work invaluable for his self-portrayal, Kant (1798) tells us: "Smelling is, as it were, a tasting in the distance, and forces others to partake, whether they will or not. . . . Which organic sense is the most ungrateful and also the least useful? That of smelling. It does not pay to cultivate, or perhaps even to refine it; for there are more objects of nausea—especially in populous places—than of enjoyment, which the sense can procure us, and our enjoyment through this sense can at the best be only fleeting and temporary, if it is to give us pleasure" (11:311).

A hostility to the sense of smell, Freud (1930) has noted, is an especial trait of those who are offended by the notion of sexuality. The first "depreciation of his [man's] sense of smell," Freud believed, took place in the course of human evolution when man adopted an erect posture; thereby "the whole of his sexuality" was threatened with an organic repression, "so that since this, the sexual function has been accompanied by a repugnance which cannot be accounted for. . . . All neurotics and many others besides, take exception to the fact that 'inter urinas et faeces nascimur' [we are born between urine and feces]. The genitals, too, give rise to strong sensations of smell which many people cannot tolerate and which spoil sexual intercourse for them" (p. 106).

What is remarkable is that Kant in his speculative anthropology was reaching for a similar explanation of the origin of his own sensory neuroses. Kant, like Freud, believed that the transition to an erect posture was part of a process in which reason became so dominant that it "meshed" man into "discomforts and diseases." He linked the dominance of reason in its physiological consequences to man's assumption of an erect stance. The Italian thinker, Moscati, had proved, wrote Kant in 1771, that "the upright walk of man is forced and unnatural: that . . . if he makes it a necessity and constant habit, he must look forward to discomforts and diseases, which show beyond dispute that he has been misled by reason and imitation to diverge from the original animal arrangement . . ." (Wallace, 1882, p. 112; Lovejoy, 1911; Kant, 1786a, pp. 31-32). Reason, said Kant, had led man to assume the biped posture; thereby, he rose above the animals, but in return, he was "obliged to endure certain disorders that afflict him in consequence of his having raised his head so proudly above his comrades." Reason, in other words, was the agency for the repression of natural man, and inevitably brought illness in its wake.

The sense of vision too could torment Kant with its intrusive sexual suggestion. He complained that when he lectured his thoughts were "interrupted continually because a button was wanting on the coat of one of his hearers. . . . Peculiarities in the appearance of students were apt to disturb him, such as a bare neck, an exposed breast, or long hair carelessly over the neck and brow, which were regarded by some youths as evidences of genius" (Stuckenberg, 1882, p. 81). A missing button on the coat seemed especially to upset his equanimity, for he referred to it explicitly in his *Anthropology* (1798) as making for difficulties in the way of "abstraction" or, as we would call it today, "repression":

"Many men are unhappy because they cannot abstract. The wooer might contract a good marriage if he could only overlook a wart in the face of his sweetheart, or a missing tooth in her mouth. But it is a particularly naughty feature of our power of attention to fasten itself, even involuntarily, upon the very defects of others, to direct one's eye upon a missing button on the coat right opposite to one's eye . . ." (Kant, 1798; 9:21). The missing button with its import of undress would disturb Kant in the course of his lecture with its portent of lawless, uncontrollable sensation; the missing button threatened the stability of the categorial defensive system.

The sense of sight was, to Kant's mind, "the noblest" of the senses, because it was the least "sensory" of the senses. It dephysicalized the physical world, and (we might add) desexualized reality. "It comes nearest to a pure contemplation of the immediate representation of the given object, without any mixture of perceptible sensation," wrote Kant (1798; 10:322). Vision too, the noblest of the senses, could however become ignoble and lowly, and then would have to be repressed for what it brought to mind. And Kant in the course of his life twice sustained a blindness which was evidently neurotic in its origin. "In earlier life," wrote his friend and biographer, Wasianski, "he had two remarkable affections of the eyes: once, on returning from a walk, he saw objects double for a long space of time; and twice he became stone-blind" (De Quincey, 1863, p. 147). Now, as Freud (1910) has illumined, what underlies psychogenic visual disturbances are the retaliatory measures which the ego imposes on "sexual pleasure in looking [scopophilia] . . . so that the ideas in which its desires are expressed succumb to repression and are prevented from becoming conscious . . ." (p. 216). The unconscious self, the transcendental ego, as it were, does not allow the conscious empirical self to see objects of sexual interest. "The ego refuses to see anything at all any more, now that the sexual interest in seeing has made itself so prominent" (p. 216). It is "as though a punishing voice was speaking from within the subject and saying: 'Because you sought to misuse your organ of sight for evil sensual pleasures, it is fitting that you should not see anything at all any more' " (pp. 216-217). We might say that a categorical imperative underlies Kant's epistemology: "Act so that your senses can sense no object which provokes your sexual instinct."

Kant first began to have visual disorders in his fortieth year, the same year in which his interest in mental illness became so great that he wrote his essay (Kant, 1764b), *Versuch über die Krankheiten des Kopfes* ("Essay on the Diseases of the Mind"). The visual disorder would threaten him as he lectured. This was the time when Kant was going through a difficult intellectual and emotional transformation. He was still outwardly the sceptical, Voltairean satirist who, in 1766, published *The Dreams of a Spirit-Seer,* but he was also undergoing those changes which were to lead him to revolt against the psychological method, and embark on the *Critique*. The visual disorders may well have been the first overt reproaches of his conscience against the empirical, psychological method.

Kant (1797b) wrote in later years: "Among the morbid accidents of the eyes (not sicknesses, properly speaking), I experienced one which affected me for the first time in my fortieth year, afterwards, at intervals of a year, and which now happens to me a few times in the same year. Here is what its symptom was: when I was reading on a page, suddenly all the letters became confused, and to that was added a certain feebleness of sight which rendered them entirely unreadable to me" (pp. 430-431, author's translation).

Later in his life, Kant was surprised to discover that he had become blind in one eye. One cannot help observing that a favorite term of ridicule for Kant (1762) was to refer to somebody as "Cyclopean," one-eyed (p. 36). He used this term especially in referring to pedantic scholars: "mere poly-history is a cyclopean learning which lacks one eye—the eye of philosophy" (Kant, 1803, p. 170).[1] But Kant too found himself at last a Cyclopean. Was he, as it were, semi-castrated in self-punishment, rendered like the pedants who had lost contact with reality? In

[1] On the symbolic use of "Cyclopean" as indicative of physical and intellectual one-sideness, see Freud (1900, p. 443).

truly antinomian fashion, he was only semi-incapacitated; half of himself kept an access to physical reality which the other half denied, like thesis and antithesis.

A sensory demand was for Kant a threat to the rational will. He extended this attitude to inordinate lengths. Thirst, with its suggestion of maternity and birth, was particularly threatening. It could be overcome, Kant (1797b) maintained, by the resolution not to yield to it. The imbibing of fluids was associated with shame. Thus, for more than half a century, he refused to have anyone present when he drank tea. Once, when a friend did intrude, Kant asked the friend to sit down in a place where his own tea-drinking would be unobservable.

Sound was equally perturbing to Kant. He resented music on the curious ground that it was "like an odor, which spreads in every direction and must be breathed even when not wanted." He also thought that listening to music tended to make one effeminate (Stuckenberg, 1882, pp. 142-143). This dual anxiety over sensory experience for its sensual suggestion, on the one hand, and the fear for his masculinity, on the other hand, was a prototype for Kant's antitheses. His sensory life was divided against itself. A man of boundless scientific curiosity, he longed to know the richness of the world's varied phenomena, yet he avoided any first-hand contact with its sensory fullness. He could amaze listeners with his meticulous knowledge of the structure of Westminster Bridge or St. Peter's in Rome; he could grow rapturous upon the joys of travel: "To sit upon a piece of the wall of an old Roman theatre (in Verona or Nismes), to have under one's hands the house-furniture of that people, discovered after so many years in Herculaneum . . . to be able to exhibit a coin of the Macedonian kings . . . all this arouses the senses of a connoisseur to profound attention" (Stuckenberg, 1882, pp. 109, 146-147). But then, it turned out (Kant, 1798) that it was all derived from travel books which were his favorite reading for relaxation. He read every important book of this kind which he could find (11:316). "The first academic teacher of physical geography," remarked Paulsen (1902), "never saw a mountain with his own eyes" (p. 45). He could never bring himself to travel more than a few miles from his native city.

Indeed, the ocean remained for Kant a fearful philosophical symbol. "A wide and stormy ocean," he wrote in the *Critique of Pure Reason* (1781), "surrounded the island of truth." He called it, "the native home of illusion, where many a fog bank and many a swiftly melting iceberg give the deceptive appearance of farther shores, deluding the adventurous seafarer ever anew with empty hopes, and engaging him in enterprises which he can never abandon and yet is unable to carry to completion" (p. 257). The ocean's water carried all the valences of an overwhelming feminine enticement; its maternal water brought bewilderment. He would be no adventurous seafarer, and he assured himself that only illusion lay beyond. He was convinced (1798) that simply seeing the sea was enough in his case to bring on seasickness: "Seasickness—of which I myself have had an experience in a voyage from Pillau to Koenigsberg, if, indeed, anyone chooses to call it a sea voyage—with its tendency to vomit, arose in my case, as I believe to have observed, solely through the eyes. For when the ship began to roll, and I looked out of the cabin, my eyes caught now the lowness and in the next moment the highness of the shore"; so that through his "power of imagination" there was stirred up "an antiperistaltic movement on the part of the intestines" (11:358).

Kant preferred to substitute a world of reports for the world of sensations, maintaining a safe distance from what might impinge on his senses. To ascertain the source of this protective self-withdrawal from the world of sense, we must seek more deeply into Kant's unconscious. "Kant," recorded Hippel, the burgomaster of Königsberg, "often says that if a man were to write and say all he thinks, there would be nothing more horrible on God's earth than man" (Stuckenberg, 1882, p. 133). What horrible things would Kant have written had he dared to write all he thought?

The Categorial Defenses: The Psychology of "Transcendental Deduction"

The second of Kant's protophilosophical postulates is that our minds impose on our experience certain necessary forms and categories (Lovejoy, 1907). We may call this the assumption of the "law enforcement" agency of the human mind. Here we are confronted by the imposing argument of the so-called "transcendental deduction of the categories." The so-called "deduction" was, in effect, as we shall see, a concealed, highly personalized psychological statement. Kant was compelled to denigrate the world of sensations, to shut out the sexual suggestions of the senses, to render for himself a desexualized, shadowy version of reality. He had to struggle to hold on to his sanity against the lawless data, the sensations which threatened to emerge with any upheaval. And as a neurotic, intent on preserving order, Kant imposed on the lawless data his *a priori* categories of the understanding. The "transcendental deduction" projected his own introspective experience of controlling what otherwise would be a subversive world. It expressed his own struggle to hold on to rationality in an experiential world which would otherwise break apart. The "transcendental deduction," for all its rejection of the psychological method, is an example of cryptopsychologism.

All his life Kant struggled to master his melancholy and gloom. There is a stereotyped myth of Kant as a purely rational man, always in equilibrium, undisturbed by emotion. To dispel this myth, the noted Kantian scholar, Hans Vaihinger (1898), was once moved to write an essay entitled "Kant als Melancholiker." Kant, indeed, drew abundantly in his writings from his own experiences with neurosis. The opening sentence of his essay on mental therapy (Kant, 1797b) is a frank avowal of self-analysis: "As I cannot illustrate this proposition by examples drawn from the experience of others, I must necessarily consult my own; and when I have made known the result, I may then put the question to others—Whether or not they have made similar observations?" (Colquhoun translation, p. 246).

Kant had gone through a youth without joy, a tormented youth, which had led him to long to quit life. He had, he wrote (1797b), "always had a natural disposition towards hypochondriasis; which, in my earlier years, rendered me even disgusted with life." He tried to attribute this suicidal feeling to his "flat and narrow chest, which leaves little room for the motion of the heart and lungs." But clearly, his youthful suicidal despair had more than a physiological basis, as his own spontaneous comments on the ordeal of adolescence indicate: "Many people," wrote Kant, "think that their youth was the happiest and the most agreeable time of their whole life; but this is certainly not so. It is the hardest period, because one is under discipline, and can seldom have a true friend and less rarely freedom" (1803, p. 196).[2] How strange is this! For youth to almost all people is preeminently the age of friendship, comradeship, and mutual confidence, and if there is a discipline imposed from above, a generational comradeship of protest and evasion usually unites the young. But in Kant, the discipline of curbing himself, coping with his awakened sexual desires, was evidently of such a character that he could confide to no friend. The bed became associated in Kant's mind with the source of morbid illness. Descartes had loved the comfort of his couch, and had enjoyed taking his ease there with books and meditations. Not so Kant (1797b), to

[2] "Moral friendship," wrote Kant, "is the complete confidence of two persons in revealing their secret thoughts and feelings to each other, in so far as such disclosures are consistent with mutual respect for each other." This "need to reveal himself to others is strong," but "hemmed in and cautioned by fear of the misuse others may make of the disclosure of his thoughts, he finds himself constrained to lock up in himself a good part of his opinions . . ." (Kant, 1797a, p. 143). Kant warned: "Even to our best friend we must not reveal ourselves, in our natural state as we know it ourselves. To do so would be loathsome." Friendship, said Kant, was "man's refuge in this world from the distrust of his fellows," but his loathsomeness in his own eyes, always unexplained, made the communion he sought impossible (Kant, posth., 1930, pp. 206-207). Cf. also Paton (1956), pp. 54-55.

whom bed was "the nest of numberless diseases" (p. 249), and for youth especially it was the place for sexual self-abuse: "The impulses to this habit can be escaped by continuous occupation, which keeps one from spending more time in bed and in sleeping than is necessary. Thoughts about it can be banished from the mind by these occupations; for, so long as the subject is even in the imagination, it gnaws at one's vital powers" (Kant, 1803, p. 219).

The *Critique of Pure Reason* (Kant, 1781) abounds with metaphors which depict reason as imposing law on lawless data. Reason is like the "police," preventing the violence of which citizens live in fear; reason is like "an appointed judge who compels the witnesses to answer questions" and secures general order. Without the control of the *a priori* categories, there is the threat of "barbarism" (p. 8). Against this menace of "anarchy" (p. 9), we must "institute a tribunal [to] assure to reason its lawful claims" (pp. 20-21). The lawless sceptics, "a species of nomads, despising all settled modes of life, broke up from time to time all civilized society" (p. 27). The aim of the transcendental deduction is to secure a "clear, legal title" for the categories. Kant likened the senses to the vulgar lawless mob; their domination over the understanding constituted insanity; they were akin to the Freudian id. Kant (1798) warned: "The understanding should rule without weakening sensuousness—which in itself has a mob-characteristic, since it does not reflect . . ." (9:407). The senses had a potential for mad uprising against their superiors: "The senses prefer no claim upon them (the judgments of the understanding), but resemble the common people, who, if they are not a mob (ignobile vulgus), submit readily to their superior, the understanding, though they certainly also want to be heard in the matter. Hence if certain judgments and insights are regarded as proceeding immediately (and not through the mediation of the understanding) from the internal sensuousness, and if the latter is, consequently, presumed to wield a rule of itself, this is mere extravagance of fancy closely allied to insanity" (9:409).[3]

In Kant's own life, the function of the mind was to achieve mastery over the lawless propensities of the body. He felt his will had triumphed in a number of cases. Afflicted by a respiratory cough, he "resolved" to conquer it by closing his mouth completely, and breathing only through his nose. It was hard at first, but the nose triumphed, and he fell asleep. Kant concluded (1797b) that to conquer the cough all that had been required was "an immediate action of the mind . . . for which a firm resolution is highly necessary. . . ." So well did he train himself that if he opened his mouth while asleep, he would awake. He believed likewise that he had overcome nightly thirst by training himself to breathe deeply "with full chest and thus, so to speak, drink in air through the nose" (pp. 424-427, author's translation). The categories of understanding were similarly the means by which the mind imposed order on the disorderly sensations. Where the categories for any reason broke down in a more than temporary way, the person was insane. Underlying Kant's epistemological concern for preserving "the unity of self-consciousness" was a psychological concern, an anxiety lest the lawless data and emotions rend that stability which he maintained with such difficulty. The manifest argument was epistemological; the latent significance was the control of a psychological anxiety.[4]

Evidence of Kant's anxiety concerning the unity and order of his mental processes is to be found in the details of his social and personal habits. Even during his moments of relaxation at social parties, Kant was concerned with the maintenance of the unity

[3] It is noteworthy that the one American philosopher who struggled all his life to retain mastery over his lawless, wayward impulses also had a tremendous emotional fixation on Kant's categorial system. Peirce wrote: "I was a passionate devotee of Kant. . . . I believed more implicitly in the two tables of the Functions of Judgment and the Categories than if they had been brought down from Sinai" (Murphey, 1961, p. 33).

[4] Tillich has interpreted the categories subjectively as the union of anxiety and courage. This view is not unlike the analysis of the Kantian categories which I am presenting. See Thomas (1963, p. 116).

of the mind against centrifugal distractions. A successful social party in his view (1798) had to be controlled by the categorial framework: "such entertainments must not skip abruptly from one thing to another . . . , for, in that case, the social party disperses in a condition of distraction of mind . . . unity of conversation lacking altogether, and the mind thus finding itself utterly confused . . ." (16:48).

All of Kant's personal eccentricities derived from an "overdetermined" preoccupation to exclude "bestial" elements from his experience, that is, whatever was suggestive of sexuality. An object that had a bodily or sexual association tormented him. He went to great lengths never to perspire, wearing thin, silk clothes in the summer. Then, if he did chance to perspire, "he had a singular remedy in reserve. Retiring to some shady place, he stood still and motionless—with the air and attitude of a person listening, or in suspense—until his usual *aridity* was restored. Even in the most sultry night, if the slightest trace of perspiration had sullied his nightdress, he spoke of it with emphasis, as of an accident that perfectly shocked him" (De Quincey, 1863, p. 119). Perspiration was a defiling bodily secretion, too suggestive of sexual secretions. He had to restore his "aridity," that is, to desexualize his bodily life. This was the physical counterpart of categorial control. Kant apparently suffered from an unconscious fear of impotence. For example, he had to see the church tower from his window in order to think. Once, when his neighbor's poplars shut the tower from his view, he found himself unable to think. Measures had to be taken to trim the poplars. The erect church tower sustained him.

Kant went to the most extraordinary lengths to avoid wearing garters, so much so that one might infer that the enclosed leg had a tremendous emotional valence for him—his manhood enveloped in female sexuality. True, he argued that garters obstructed the circulation, but his substitute for them suggested an inordinate reaction. "In a little pocket . . . there was placed a small box, something like a watch-case, but smaller; into this box was introduced a watch-spring in a wheel, round about which wheel was wound an elastic cord, for regulating the force of which there was a separate contrivance. To the two ends of this cord were attached hooks, which hooks were carried through a small aperture in the pockets, and, so, passing down the inner and the outer side of the thigh, caught hold of two loops which were fixed on the off side and the near side of each stocking. As might be expected, so complex an apparatus was liable, like the Ptolemaic system of the heavens, to occasional derangements . . ." (De Quincey, 1863, p. 119). Here was a virtual mechanical analogue of the table of categories and analogies of experience designed at a tremendous expenditure of effort and energy to avoid the garter around the leg.

Kant also took a strong stand in the controversy over vaccination; he opposed it, questioning Jenner's evidence in its favor (De Quincey, 1863). He regarded vaccination as an "inoculation of bestiality," and in response to two queries in 1800, when the subject was being warmly debated, indicated that it was, in his view, morally unjustifiable (Wallace, 1882). Curiously, at this time, opponents of vaccination were arguing that "cowpox inoculation was comparable to incest, introducing into the human body a disease of bestial origin similar to syphilis" (Stern, 1927, p. 22). It was evidently under Kant's influence that his close Jewish friend and former pupil, Dr. Marcus Herz, published in 1801 an open letter entitled, *Über die Brutalimpfung* (On the Inoculation of Bestiality). The "bestial" was denied admission by Kant into his body even as its threatening incursion was held in check by the controls of perception and the categories.

The struggle with sexuality was moreover a theme which provoked Kant to his deepest reflections on history. The basic model of conflict in man, the exemplar of his inner strife, was, according to Kant (1786a), that between his sexuality and the demands of the surrounding culture, "All evils which express human life, and all vices which dishonor it, spring from this unresolved conflict." Like Freud, he traced many human ills to the postponement of marriage which was the outcome of social requirements. "But as society increases in complexity nature does not alter the age of sexual maturity. She stubbornly perseveres in her law. . . . Hence manners and morals, and the aim of nature inevitably come to interfere with each other. . . . The civilized state comes into inevitable conflict with that disposition. . . . But the space of time during which there is still a conflict is as a rule filled with vices and their consequences—the various kinds of human misery." The basic cause of human misery, according to Kant, was in the "inevitable conflict between culture and the human species" (pp. 60-61). He defined the "perfect civil constitution" as the one which would terminate this conflict. In the mechanisms of repression attendant to this conflict we look for the source of Kant's protophilosophical postulates.

With the repression of sexuality, Kant's sense of the reality of the external world diminished. The world which was sexually unknowable became truly unknowable. Indeed, the unknowable world of things in themselves, the abyss in which categories and science foundered, had the aspect for Kant of the "abyss" of sexuality. The mystery of sexuality was a principal example of the unknowable reality from which he drew back in literal fear. When the poet Schiller, in 1795, sent Kant a magazine with an article on sex differences in organic nature, Kant replied that "the natural arrangement that all impregnation in both of the organic kingdoms requires two sexes . . . opens up an abyss for the human reason." If the origin of sex were not simply the playfulness of Providence, but if this arrangement were as reason indicated "the only possible one," then Kant said, "an infinite prospect lies before us, of which we can make simply nothing, about as little as Milton's angel tells Adam of the Creation: 'Male light of distant suns mingles with female for ends unknown.' "[5] Sexuality was, as Kant (1786b) indicated in the *Pro-*

[5] The article, unsigned, was by Wilhelm von Humboldt, and entitled "Über end Geschlechtsunterschied und dessen Einflusz auf die organische Natur."

legomena, the exemplar of the incomprehensible: "It therefore only sounds paradoxical and is really not strange to say that in Nature there is much that is incomprehensible [for instance, the faculty of procreation]" (p. 98).[6]

KANT'S ANALYSIS OF "INSANITY"

According to Kant, insanity[7] is a categorial disorder, the rebellious data of sense having overcome the categories which made a unified experience possible. Kant postulated three specific modes of insanity corresponding to the principles of each of the major divisions of the *Critique of Pure Reason*.

Breakdowns in the operation of the transcendental aesthetic, transcendental analytic, and transcendental dialectic each define a corresponding type of insanity. Kant thus distinguishes between three types of insanity—tumultuous, methodic, and systematic.

The tumultuous insanity, as Kant (1798) explains it, includes that which most clearly exhibits the breakdown of the most basic connections necessary for experience: "Craziness [amentia] is the incapacity to put our representations even into that connection which is necessary for the mere possibility of experience. In the insane asylums the female sex is, by reason of its talkativeness, especially subject to this disease; that is, to intersperse with their narration so many productions of their lively imaginations that nobody can understand what they really wish to say. This first class of insanity is *tumultuous*." Then there are those suffering from a fragmentary methodical insanity in which the power of judgment is disordered. The imagination of such persons "causes a play of the connection of dissimilar things"; they can be "very jolly, rave absurdly, and please themselves in the enjoyment of so

[6] Poet-advocates of sexual revolution have intuitively seized on the Kantian terminology to express their aim: "the barrier of noumenon-phenomenon/ transcended/ the circle momentarily complete/" Kandel (1966, p. 5).

[7] Kant (1798) used the German word, *Verrückung*.

extensive a relation of conceptions which, in their opinion, rhyme together." Less deep-seated a disorder, according to Kant, is *methodic* insanity (dementia) which includes, for instance, those persons afflicted by persecution complexes, "who imagine that they have everywhere enemies." In such cases, everything which the afflicted person says is "conformable to the formal laws of thinking necessary for the possibility of experience." Last, there is *systematic* insanity in which the patient "flies beyond the whole ladder of experience . . . and believes that thus he comprehends the incomprehensible"; he can square the circle, and knows the mystery of the trinity (16:398-399). The last is evidently the metaphysical mode of insanity.

This whole discussion of insanity in the *Anthropology* has a remarkable philosophical consequence which Kant overlooks. For if the causation of insanity, the disruption of the categories of the understanding, is a question of psychological anthropology, if a psychological method would explain the modes of insanity, then likewise one would expect the psychological method to explain the origin and development of the categories of the understanding. We should have a genetic account of the categories rather than a transcendental deduction of them.

Insanity indeed was only the extreme case of categorial disorganization for Kant. The categorial system, the precondition of sanity, evolves from experiences in infancy and childhood. It is threatened by drunkenness, drugs, and dreams. The precategorial stage of childhood is not really experience, according to Kant (1798), because it consists "of scattered perceptions that have not yet been united in the conception of the object" (9:18). Drunkenness disrupts the categorial framework because it makes it impossible "to regulate our sensuous representations in accordance with the laws of experience" (11:353-354). Also, the imbibing of such drugs as the chica of the Peruvians or the ava of the South Sea Islands brings on "mis-states of the senses" (11:356). Then too there is the involuntary play of our imagination which we call dreams, "unloosening" (11:358) in sleep, in which we spend "unconsciously . . . probably one-third part of our life" (11:360). Kant's categorial table, his defense mechanism against sensation, was like a beleaguered fortress, holding in check the lawless, nomadic, barbarian invasions.

The Lawless Element in Kant's Psyche

A chance association of Kant's affords us an initial clue to his sensoriphobia and to the meaning of the categories. All his life, Kant suffered from insomnia. It grew especially bad in later years when it was accompanied by spasmodic attacks. He should have called a doctor, Kant (1797b) stated: "But then, impatient at not being able to sleep, I soon had recourse to my Stoic remedy of occupying my mind intensely with whatever object I chose at will (I concentrated for example, on the numerous associations which the name of Cicero brought to mind), thereby turning my attention from this sensation and making it ineffective" (author's translation). In his insomnia, the name of Cicero brought a curious subsidence. "Cicero," we may reasonably infer, had a most significant valence for Kant's psyche. Its very sound would have suggested directly his mother's breasts which the anxiety-ridden old man still cherished in his unconscious. The word, Cicero, as pronounced in German, is similar to the word *Zitze* (teat). His associations to the first two syllables would have carried Kant to the memory of his mother's softness, and brought him sleep, as his mother did when he was an infant. Thus an oedipal fantasy was disguised as an irreproachable classical allusion which had the unusual property of liberating Kant from anxiety and sleeplessness.

Still another free association of Kant's pointed toward his emotional tie with his mother as the source of his neurosis. Kant felt that his youth was so miserable that he wished to die. He attributed this youthful death-wish to his flat chest. But in his *Pedagogy,* he states that flat chests are caused by leading-strings, in other words, that they are the physiological consequence of over-involvement with one's mother. Kant resented leading-strings strongly; they had bound him, as umbilical cords, to his mother, and brought about his physiological and psychological illness: "Leading-strings are very injurious. A certain author once complained of being narrow-chested, which he attributed entirely to leading-strings. . . . Children do not learn to walk with the same steadiness by the use of such means as when they learn it by their own efforts" (Kant, 1803, p. 143). In other words, Kant's own unsteadiness, his inability to remain erect, were tied to his over-involvement with his mother. An oedipal longing, an impaired sexuality, and a death-wish are all suggested by this passage. Curiously, "leading-strings" (the maternal umbilical cord) remained for Kant the symbol of an emasculating influence on reason. In the Preface to the second edition of the *Critique of Pure Reason,* he (1781) stated that reason "must not allow itself to be kept, as it were, in nature's leading strings," but must constrain nature "to give answer to questions of reason's own determining" (p. 20).[8] There is a suggestion here that his emotional fixation on his mother, who had bound him with leading-strings, had inhibited Kant's intellectual development.

Kant was indeed sexually fixated on his mother. He exhibited a distaste for physical sexuality, which seemed to him out of keeping with a civilized, refined person. There is a section of Kant's essay, *Observations on the Feeling of the Beautiful and Sublime,* which might be subtitled: "Why I Never Married." Kant (1764a) analyzes the cause of bachelorhood, how there "arises the postponement and finally the full abandonment of the marital bond." He confesses that he does not know how noble souls can manage to combine refinement of taste with a natural simplicity of sexual response: "if only I saw how this were possible to achieve. . . . A very refined taste serves to take away the wildness of an impetuous inclination," makes it "modest and

[8] Again, in 1794, Kant referred to "the leading-string of holy tradition" which "becomes bit by bit dispensable, yea, finally, when man enters upon adolescence, it becomes a fetter" (p. 112).

decorous," and limits it to "few objects"; thus refined, "such an inclination usually misses the great goal of nature." A very refined taste, says Kant, "demands or expects more than nature usually offers"; therefore, "it seldom takes care to make the person of such delicate feeling happy." It becomes "oversubtle because actually it is attracted to none"; its sexuality atrophies (pp. 90-91).

Kant seemed to have some awareness that his attachment to his mother was at the basis of his so-called "refinement of taste." In a remarkable discussion of the grounds of men's sexual preferences among women, he tended to agree with Buffon that the mother's traits determine the son's later sexual preferences. "The figure that makes the first impression," wrote Kant (1798), "at the same time when this impulse is still new and is beginning to develop, remains the pattern all feminine figures in the future must more or less follow so as to be able to stir the fanciful ardor, whereby a rather coarse inclination is compelled to choose among the different objects of a sex." Therefore, a woman with "tender feeling and a benevolent heart" was superior to one with "merriment and wit in laughing eyes."[9] As a coy bachelor, he added: "I do not want to engage in too detailed an analysis of this sort, for in doing so the author appears to depict his own inclination" (16:49). That, of course, was precisely what Kant was doing.

Above all, Kant's emotional fixation on his mother gave rise to a passionate resistance to the evolutionary hypothesis. This curious aberration in his thinking deserves a special discussion.

Kant's Emotional Antagonism to the Evolutionary Hypothesis

In studying the psychoanalytic basis of a philosophy, a most important indicator is found in the points of inconsistency in the

[9] Kant always mocked at women for talking too much, for their *übermundigkeit* (verbosity).

given philosophy, i.e., a place where the philosopher's underlying emotion is constrained by his own doctrine. The formal philosophy has then failed to express adequately the informal emotions—the underlying basis of the philosopher's decision. Thereupon, the emotion breaks through and imposes its will on the philosophy with a crude directness, demanding a certain doctrine without any further ado. The point of inconsistency is a place where a quantum of the philosopher's raw emotion has not yet been rationalized into philosophical form. For this reason, it helps us especially to perceive the character of the philosopher's emotion and unconscious. The hypothesis of organic evolution awakened in Kant a resistance which was quite out of keeping with his formal philosophy, and which was evidently based on intense, unresolved oedipal feelings.

Lovejoy (1911) showed most clearly how Kant disapproved of "any attempt to inquire into the origin, the laws of genesis, of organisms in general, or of the original stock 'from' which any species is descended" (p. 47). And Lovejoy observed the significance of certain traits of Kant's character in relation to his concept of nature: ". . . it was because of certain temperamental peculiarities of his mind—a mind with a deep scholastic strain of its own, one that could not quite endure the notion of a nature all fluent and promiscuous and confused, in which a series of organisms are to an indefinite degree capable of losing one set of characters and assuming another set." Why, however, did Kant have such a strong emotional resistance to the notion of a nature "all fluent and promiscuous"? Lovejoy's metaphor indeed grasps at those very elements of the sensory world with which Kant's conscious self was at war—a world lawless, indeed, in a sexual way, which he endeavored to contain with his categories.

The concept of a promiscuous Nature awoke in Kant an anxiety which he called "a not unmanly terror." A promiscuous "Mother Nature" seemed to open her womb to all adventures. She threatened all the defenses which Kant had laboriously constructed against his own sexuality and oedipal longings. The concept of evolution implied a mother whose promiscuity would bring forth what could only be "monstrosities." Kant depicted such a mother as "the earth in travail, giving birth to animals and plants from her pregnant womb, fertilized by the sea-slime." To believe, he wrote, "that one species should originate from another and all from one original species, or that all should spring from the teeming womb of a universal Mother—this would lead to ideas so monstrous that the reason shrinks before them with a shudder." Again, in his review of Herder's *Philosophy of the History of Mankind,* Kant spoke of such hypotheses as "so monstrous that reason recoils from them." He abhorred the idea of a "single primordial womb" (Lovejoy, 1911, pp. 46-47).

There was nothing in Kant's theory of knowledge which forbade a hypothesis of organic evolution.[10] The categorial structure, Kant thus perceived, was not strict enough to exclude all lawless tendencies. Nevertheless, Kant felt compelled to ostracize evolutionary theories as metaphysics and sought to close any opening in the philosophical-defensive system: "A hypothesis of this kind," he wrote (1790) in his *Critique of Teleological Judgment,* is a "daring adventure," and there were "few investigators of Nature, even of the most acute minds, to whom the hypothesis has not at times presented itself. For absurd it is not. . . . *A priori,* in the judgment of reason alone, there is nothing self-contradictory in this. Only, experience shows no example of such a thing" (pp. 79-80).

But Kant's revulsion against the evolutionary hypothesis did not stem from the fact that he could point to no experienced cases of it. A hypothesis of organic evolution was "metaphysics" not because it violated the categories' limits but because it aroused anxiety. "These ideas [Kant wrote inconsistently and

[10] The youthful Kant had united an evolutionary cosmology with an optimistic conception of the rule of a First Cause effectuating "harmonies and beauties." In his student days, when he was in bold revolt, Lucretius, the Roman materialistic evolutionist, was his favorite poet, and he memorized long passages of the *De Rerum Natura,* and delighted in the grandeur of its imagery. Kant (1755, pp. ix, 22, 24, 26, 148-150, 154).

defensively] will not, indeed, cause the investigator of nature to shrink back from before them with a shudder, as from before a monstrosity (for there are many who have played with them for a time, though only to give them up as unprofitable). But the investigator *will* be frightened away from them upon a serious scrutiny, by a fear lest he be lured by them from the fertile fields of natural science to wander in the wilderness of metaphysics. And for my part I confess to a not unmanly terror in the presence of anything which sets the reason loose from its first and fundamental principles and permits it to rove in the boundless realms of imagination" (Lovejoy, 1911, p. 47).

The evolutionary hypothesis, with its evolving Mother Nature, thus filled Kant with disgust. Evolutionary fertility, in Kant's mind, was like that of a mother's which ends with the menopause. Kant conceded that such a theory might well suggest itself to the paleontologist, the "archeologist of nature": "He can suppose the womb of Mother Nature to have given birth at first to creatures of less purposive form," then to better adapted ones, "until finally, Nature's womb, grown torpid and ossified" (Lovejoy, 1911, p. 48), would produce no new species; her "potency" would be at an end. Kant saw Nature as his mother writ large, and he projected the anxiety which she aroused in him on Nature as a whole. From the scientific standpoint, there was no reason why evolution should terminate in a cosmic menopause, why the emergence of novel species should be brought to an end. It was only when Nature was personified as Mother Nature that it seemed natural to say her womb would grow "torpid and ossified." Evolution, genesis, awoke in Kant's mind all the repressed anxieties of his own relationship to his mother. The study of biological origins trespassed on the domain of Kant's repressions, and he preferred to see the problem put aside.

The underlying function of "reason" was thus more than epistemological; it was the censor of lawless emotions. The role of reason indeed was to repress all lawless sexual associations. "The fig leaf," Kant wrote (1786a) "was a far greater manifestation of reason than that shown in the earlier stage of development." It reflected the "consciousness of a certain degree of mastery of reason over impulse" (p. 53). The emergence of the primacy of reason in Kant was thus linked to its origin in the repression of sexuality. Reason represses lawless sexual data: this is the first *a priori* categorial imposition on the sensuous manifold. The categories were based on the repression of the id by the superego.

Why, we may inquire, did the thought of his mother exercise such a tremendous hold on Kant's unconscious? The answer might well lie in the traumatic impact which his mother's death had on the onset of his adolescence. "The thirteenth or fourteenth year," wrote Kant (1803) "is usually the time when the sexual instinct is developed in a boy" (p. 219). Kant's mother, it should be remembered, died in 1737, when Kant was in his thirteenth year. Toward her, he felt a warmth which he did not feel toward his father who lived on until 1746. What would be the effect of the death of his mother on a Pietist boy of thirteen? His first sexual stirrings were concomitant with the death of his mother. Thus, we may surmise, a deep guilt was placed upon Kant's sexuality. In his unconscious, he would associate his own sexual lust with the death it brought his beloved mother. Herein, we may surmise, was the source of that hypochondria which afflicted Kant in his youth so that he hated life itself. And here as well was the basis of his attitudes toward marriage and women. He atoned for his guilt by remaining faithful to his mother's memory, and ridiculed the learned and polite women whom he met. They were compared unfavorably with his own ignorant mother. Kant never, therefore, became a full Voltairean child of the Enlightenment. Instead, he wrote (1803) a diatribe against bluestockings: "A woman who has her head full of Greek, like Mme. Dacier, or who carries on profound discussions in mechanics, like the Marquise de Chastelet, may just as well have a beard beside; for a beard would perhaps express still more unmistakably the air of profoundness which she is trying to acquire. . . . So far as learned women are concerned: they use their books in something like the way they use their watch—namely, carry it, in order to let it be seen that they have one" (p. 86). The pietistic mother whose breasts brought him sleep ruled in Kant's unconscious, and finally prevailed against all the new fashions of the salons.

Kant's Dreams

Persistant oedipal longings and guilt were evident in Kant's dreams, and became a torture for him. During his later years, said his Boswell, Wasianski, "his dreams became continually more appalling: single scenes, or passages in these dreams, were sufficient to compose the whole course of mighty tragedies, the impression from which was so profound as to stretch far into his waking hours. Amongst other phantasmata more shocking and indescribable, his dreams constantly represented to him the forms of murderers advancing to his bedside; and so agitated was he by the awful trains of phantoms that swept past him nightly, that in the first confusion of awaking he generally mistook his servant, who was hurrying to his assistance, for a murderer. In the daytime we often conversed upon the shadowy illusions; and Kant, with his usual sort of stoical contempt for nervous weakness of every sort, laughed at them; and, to fortify his own resolution to contend against them, he wrote down in his memorandum book, 'No surrender now to panics of darkness' " (De Quincey, 1863, p. 142).[11]

Kant became terrified of the dark. He began to burn a light in his room to ward against its powers, "an expression of the great

[11] According to Freud (1900), in every case, "the robbers stood for the sleeper's father. . . . Robbers, burglars, and ghosts, of whom some people feel frightened before going to bed, and who sometimes pursue their victims after they are asleep, all originate from one and the same class of infantile reminiscence" (pp. 403-404). Freud had noted, too, that the moon in the child's consciousness was used to signify the place of its birth. According to Stekel (1935), "The pale moon symbolizes the white rump out of which in the infantile theory of sex, the baby is born" (p. 115). Thus, the moonbeam would have awakened Kant's oedipal feelings and anxieties.

revolution accomplished by this terrific agency of his dreams." Previously, he had barricaded the windows of his room, night and day, to keep out lawless data, like his categorial structure. "If he saw but a moonbeam penetrating a crevice of the shutters, it made him unhappy." Now with darkness a terror, and silence an oppression, he placed a repeater in his room as well as a lamp (De Quincey, 1862, p. 142).

The content of Kant's dreams, we are told, would have provided the scenes of mighty tragedies. He did not wish to be held responsible for the motivations indicated by his dreams. "That was a cruel saying," wrote Kant, "and utterly opposed to experience, which is attributed to the Greek emperor who condemned a man to death that had been reported as having had a dream wherein he murdered the emperor: 'Well, he would not have dreamed it, if he had not thought about it while awake' " (De Quincey, 1862, p. 142). Evidently Kant too was murdering his own emperor, his father, in his dreams (Freud, 1916); and the father as monster would come to Kant every night to wreak his punishment. The themes of Kant's dreams suggest why every night in his life was filled with the reproaches of his conscience. Kant (1798) recorded them in a remarkable passage of the *Anthropology:*

"Thus, I well remember, have I, being a boy, tired out by play, laid me down to sleep, and in the moment of dropping off to sleep was quickly awakened by a dream, as if I had fallen into the water, and near drowning, was being turned around in a circle; but all in order to fall soon asleep again, and more quietly—probably because the activity of the chest muscles in breathing, which depends altogether upon the will, relaxes, and must therefore (the movement of the heart being checked by the stoppage of the breath) be revived by the imagination of the dream. To this we may also count the beneficial effect of dreams in the so-called nightmares (incubus). For without this terrible imagination of a monster that oppresses us, and the exertion of all our muscular power to change our position, the stoppage of the blood would soon put an end to our life. This seems to be the reason why nature has so arranged matters that most of our dreams involve difficulties and dangerous circumstances, since such pictures excite the forces of our soul more than dreams wherein everything happens according to our desire. We often dream that we cannot lift ourselves on our feet, or that we have lost ourselves, or stopped in the middle of a sermon, or through forgetfulness, put on a nightcap instead of a wig on entering a large assembly, or that we can fly in the air like a bird, or burst out in joyful laughter without knowing why. But it will probably remain a mystery forever, how it happens that in our dreams we are often transported back to long vanished times, and speak with people long since dead; and that, although we are tempted to look upon the whole occurrence as a dream, we nevertheless feel ourselves compelled to consider the dream an actuality. But we may probably accept it as certain that there can be no sleep without dreaming, and that a person who thinks he has not dreamed, has only forgotten his dream" (14:162).

From the vantage point of our knowledge of Kant's philosophical writings and biography, what can the themes of Kant's dreams tell us? Without exception, they all involve what we might call "categorial collapses,"—a breakdown in the causal sequence or time-order. We often dream, says Kant, (1) "that we cannot lift ourselves on our feet," (2) "that we have lost ourselves or stopped in the middle of a sermon," (3) "that through forgetfulness we put on a nightcap instead of a wig on entering a large assembly," (4) "that we can fly in the air like a bird," (5) that we "burst out in joyful laughter without knowing why," (6) that "we are . . . transported back to long vanished times," (7) that we "speak with people long since dead."

A certain continuity runs through Kant's dream themes. He can't lift himself on his feet, that is, he has a fear for his capacity for being erect, his masculinity. He is stopped mid-sermon; something disturbs him (we have already learned) as the clothes in disarray, the missing button in his lecture. Some lawless sensation is obtruding. What is the character of that sensation? It is indicated in the next theme; he would inwardly prefer to put on a nightcap rather than the wig. "The bed is the nest of numberless diseases," Kant (1797b) warns. "To sleep much at a time, or at intervals is a method of avoiding those cares to which we are exposed, when awake" (p. 249). The bed is the source of sin, or moral weakness. But in his dream, his unconscious speaks, and he prefers the nightcap to the wig. Next, he flies like a bird —the classical symbol for sexual intercourse. He has overcome his anxieties and achieved orgasm. Then he bursts out in joyful laughter without knowing why. The preceding theme tells us why: He has enjoyed the liberation of sexual experience. Then he is back in vanished times, speaking with persons long since dead—not only his mother, but his father, we may infer, in view of the numerous murderer-robber dreams which Kant had. Indeed, Kant's dreams brought the reassurance that his father was dead—though guilt feelings always remained. Kant's father had died after a palsy-stroke incapacitated him for 18 months (Wallace, 1882). Kant, then not quite 20 years old, was too poor to pay burial dues, and there was no service at the grave. A man who has nursed his father during his last illness, and felt his death keenly, will often dream he is conversing with him as though he were alive. The dreamer, says Freud (1900) may have actually desired that death terminate his father's miseries. But when the father dies, the son bears the unconscious self-reproach that his wish contributed to shorten the dead man's life. The dream then consoles the son that now that his father is dead he is actually free, liberated from discipline.

The flying bird became for the old philosopher, in his last years, a pathetic symbol for the freedom he had never had. He had a "child-like love for birds in general," tells Wasianski, and "he took pains to encourage the sparrows to build above the windows of his study." He would then watch them with delight and tenderness. But one trait in Kant especially impressed his friend: "Of all the changes that spring carries with it, there was one only that now interested Kant; and he longed for it with an eagerness and intensity of expectation, that it became almost painful to witness: this was the return of a little bird (sparrow was it, or robin red-breast?) that sang in his garden, and before his window." The bird, or one like it, had sung there for years, "and Kant grew uneasy when the cold weather, lasting longer than usual, retarded its return" (De Quincey, 1863, p. 138).

Kant's dream as a boy seems to have revolved around his oedipal affection for his mother, his guilt before his father, and resultant potency fears; there was an alternation of fear and joy, like thesis and antithesis. Thus: Kant as a boy dreams of falling into water, nearly drowning, and being turned around in a circle, all in order to fall asleep again more contentedly. Falling into water, of course, is a familiar symbol for birth. In addition, however, the dream curiously identifies Kant with his mother. As Freud (1915-1916) observed, "If one rescues somebody from the water in a dream, one is making oneself into his mother" (p. 161), and Kant himself is being rescued from drowning in his dream. But here the surcease of quiet sleep comes in the aftermath of being turned around in a circle; he has had, as it were, intercourse with his mother, turning around in her watery circle. The dream brings contentment to Kant. He proposes a fanciful explanation for the dream's satisfaction: Its very traumatic aspects, like nightmares generally, serve to excite us and awaken our will to breathe and survive.

Dreams, according to Kant, keep us alive. Without their traumatic stimuli, we would relax into death. Kant's strange theory of dreams is actually a remarkable evidence of his own weariness with life, his longing for death. Unless our will, he says, were revived by the traumatic content of dreams, our chest muscles would relax and we would stop breathing. Just as the categorial understanding polices the sensations, so the will is supposed to stand guard over the chest muscles. An act of will is thus required to keep us breathing and alive. This curious theory that every breath requires an act of will is indicative of a strong underlying death-wish; he breathed as a matter of duty. The tremendous guilt associated with his oedipal fantasies made him long to die, yet he rationalized his dream-anxieties by saying they stirred in him the will to live.

Kant's Attack on the Psychological Method

The distinctive method of Kant is the so-called transcendental method. As always, the "method" that a philosopher adopts constitutes the most important of his protophilosophical postulates. And in Kant's case, what is important about the transcendental method is what it is not. What A. C. Ewing (1938) has called the "anti-psychological side" of Kant's thought is nowhere more evident than in his "transcendental deduction" of the categories. This, Kant insists, has nothing to do with what he calls an "empirical deduction," namely, a genetic account of the categories. The striking fact, however, is that though Kant devotes a huge labor to explaining what he means by a "transcendental deduction," it turns out to be a covert application of the psychological method. Every transcendental demonstration of a category consists of an attempt to show that "experience" would be impossible without it. This appeal is precisely to an experiment in imaginative introspection. What, asks Kant, keeps your experience together and differentiates it from irrational, uncategorized presentations? Uncategorized presentations are, according to Kant, what we have when we are insane, drunk, dreaming, or infants; the categories are the conditions of sanity, the conditions for the possibility of experience. Their "deduction" is an argument that we would be like insane people if we didn't accept them. This is an exploration into the descriptive psychology of sanity.

Experience itself, Kant (1781) acknowledges, could conceivably defy being subsumed under the categories: "Everything might be in such confusion that, for instance, in the series of appearances nothing presented itself which might yield a rule of synthesis and so answer to the concept of cause and effect" (p.

124). Such is presumably the experience of an insane man, or possibly the infant's experience—"the blooming, buzzing confusion" (James, 1890). One might refuse to call it "experience" in Kant's terms, and reserve "experience" only for the categorized contents of consciousness. The insane man's or child's experience would then require another word.

The actual items in Kant's "transcendental deduction" are much the same as those in genetic investigations (e.g., of Jean Piaget) into how the child gradually differentiates between objective and subjective reality. Kant (1781) argues that the workings of causality enable us to distinguish between objective and subjective successions of appearances: "Were it not so, were I to posit the antecedent and the event were not to follow necessarily there-upon, I should have to regard the succession as a merely subjective play of my fancy; and if I still represented it to myself as something objective, I should have to call it a mere dream" (p. 227).[12]

Yet Kant (1781) repeatedly denied that his transcendental undertaking had anything to do with psychological, genetic analysis: "We are indebted to the celebrated Locke for opening out this new line of [psychological] enquiry. But a *deduction* of the pure *a priori* concepts can never be obtained in this manner; it is not to be looked for in any such direction." We must show for the categories, he continues, "a certificate of birth quite other than that of descent from experiences." A "physiological" (psychological) derivation, he stated, would be an empirical enterprise, not a deduction. "Plainly the only deduction that can be given of this knowledge is one that is transcendental, not empirical." And with respect to pure *a priori* concepts, the effort of genetic psychology "is an utterly useless enterprise which can be engaged in only by those who have failed to grasp the quite peculiar nature of these modes of knowledge" (p. 122).

Kant, however, was in a quandary as to just what status to

[12] Also, cf. Ewing (1924), pp. 156-164.

assign the categories with respect to genetic analysis. *A priori* concepts, he argued, cannot have an empirical origin, but, he acknowledged, they did have some sort of origin. Searching for an origin which was not empirical in character, an alternative which would preclude genetic analysis, he seized on an embryological concept; he postulated an "epigenesis of pure reason." The categories were thus exempt from causal law. Their origin was, so to speak, immaculate.

The use of the term, "epigenesis" shows to what desperate straits Kant had been driven. He was trying, on the one hand, to fend off genetic analysis, and, on the other hand, to preserve his "transcendental deduction" from the charge that he was engaged in reading off the decrees of the noumenal ego, an enterprise of rational psychology which was illicit from the standpoint of the *Critique*. Wolff, a young embryologist, had published a booklet, *Theoria generationis,* which introduced the concept of epigenesis. He showed that the organs of plants develop by differentiation from undifferentiated tissue at the tip of the growing shoot or root. The growth of the bud, Wolff wrote, was not an "unfolding" of something already preformed; rather, it was an epigenesis, a novel emergence. Something appeared which was not there before (Singer, 1931). This theory was a landmark in its time. One must remember that the preformationist school held such notions as that Eve's ovary had within it the forms of all subsequent men and women (27 million of them), and that spermatozoa were packages of complete homunculi which could be observed under the microscope. Nevertheless, an epigenetic origin for the categories of the understanding signified a break within the causal order which violated the categories themselves. For an epigenetic origin was a minor creation of something out of nothing, and would have violated Kant's (1781) principles that "in all changes of appearances substance is permanent" (p. 212) and that "all alterations take place in conformity with the law of the connection of cause and effect" (p. 218).

Actually, in every case of transcendental deduction which

Kant adduced, we find that what he did was to try to discover a psychological causal law of rational experience. Then, he attempted to repress the fact that he had been engaged in genetic psychology, and laid claim to a "pure deduction." In a minimal sense, every transcendental deduction is empirical in the sense of being a "deduction" by reference to the possibility of human experience, but Kant denied that this had any relevance to particular psychological causal laws (Ewing, 1938). Then, we may ask: what is this "transcendental deduction" which is empirical without being empirical, which discusses the conditions which make rational human experience possible but which has nothing to do with the causal laws of psychology?

Essentially, what Kant has done is to present in transcendental language the outcome of a long series of experiments commenced in infancy. The infant has to discover the distinction between material and psychic reality, between the objective and subjective. He discovers substance, the enduring, for instance, as he reaches in anxiety for his mother's breast and milk, and finds, at recurrent intervals, the same persisting breast and the same joy of milk.

Kant's antipsychological bent became so strong that in later years he denied that psychology could be a science (Kant, 1786b, p. 141). Yet he himself had studied anthropology, the customs of people, the sexual preferences of men, in the spirit of a psychologist looking for causal explanations. Why then this hostility to psychology? It was part of Kant's fear of the consequences of genetic analysis. Recognize a science of psychology, and the whole pseudopsychological apparatus of the "transcendental deduction," the whole law-enforcement agency of the categories, is endangered. As Ewing (1924) emphasizes, with the denial of a science of psychology, Kant's conception of a creative synthesis was entrapped "in a hopeless contradiction" (p. 66).[13] The creative synthesis can have one of two statuses:

[13] See also Ward (1922), pp. 48, 58, 59, 154, 155, 166.

on the one hand, it can be taken as an event within the phenomenal world, an event of the psychical order, or on the other hand, the synthetic unifying activity may be regarded as noumenal, although operating from the noumenal realm on the sensations. If the first alternative is taken, "it should be the study of psychology not of epistemology"; if the second alternative is taken, "if it is noumenal, it is on Kant's own principles unknowable" (Ewing, 1924, p. 66). Actually, Kant treats synthesis as both phenomenal and noumenal; it is phenomenal when he regards it as a knowable psychical process; it is noumenal when he takes it as a condition for the existence of the phenomenal world. This was what happened when genetic facts were dephysicalized for a transcendental derivation. As William James wrote (1890): "I call this view mythological, because I am conscious of no such Kantian machine-shop in my mind, and feel no call to disparage the powers of poor sensation in this merciless way" (2:275).[14]

We cannot, however, rest with James' statement that he is not "conscious" of a Kantian machine-shop in his mind, for we can imagine Kant replying that James is not conscious of a machine-shop of his categories because they derive from an unconscious source. He would say that James talks about the contents of consciousness in the empirical self, while he was talking about the *a priori* legislation of the transcendental self.

Thus we must shift the gravamen of our analysis to the question of who is misreporting or repressing the contents of his unconscious? Is James repressing from consciousness the evidence for a transcendental mind which legislates *a priori* categories? Or did Kant's own unconscious motives lead to a tremendous reaction against the psychological method and the natural self so that he projected a transcendental self, which like all such projections coexisted inconsistently and precariously with knowledge?

[14] See also Vol. 1, p. 363.

The Antipsychological Revolution in Kant's Life

Kant, in his middle years, came to reject the psychological method of which he had been previously such an enthusiast. In his revulsion lay the basis for the separation of the transcendental from the empirical self. The transcendental self never fitted well into Kant's system. In fact, it was one of those "points of inconsistency" which cast a light on the philosopher's underlying conflicts. It was solely a formal presupposition; you knew the transcendental "I" existed, but you knew nothing more about it. To say that such a noumenal ego existed, without knowing some identifying characteristics about it, contravened Kant's own restriction of knowledge to the phenomenal realm. Yet Kant was convinced that this unknowable transcendental self existed. His transcendental self was a formal equivalent for the unconscious, repressed self. It was the unconscious subject which, as Kant insisted, could never be made object. That is, in psychological language, it could never be brought from the unconscious into consciousness. The theory of the transcendental self, in other words, reflected the tremendous self-repression on Kant's part. The estrangement of the transcendental from the empirical self corresponded to the intensity of the repression of his unconscious. Like the transcendental self, it was reduced in conscious experience to the vague sense of its presence somewhere.

Let us try to trace briefly the circumstances of the antipsychological revolution in Kant's life. The period in Kant's life when the British psychological method most appealed to him was that when, in Wenley's (1910) words, he was "the brilliant young *Docent,* a familiar in the *beau monde,* a frequenter of my lady's *salon,* a witty and courted conversationalist, a great reader of poetry and travels, a fastidious dresser even" (p. 80). Kant at this time, moreover, enjoyed the close friendship of the beautiful and witty Countess Keyserling. She was a young woman when Kant, a few years older, became tutor to her sons. The Countess evidently felt warmly towards her friend; she painted a highly sentimental portrait of Kant. He, on his part, treasured to his old age the wit with which she mocked at stuffed shirts. He called her "the ornament of her sex," and recorded in his *Anthropologie* a joke she had told him about a pompous Grandmaster of the Knights of Malta. Despite their differences in social origin, Kant occupied at table the place of honor next to the young Countess (Fromm, 1898, pp. 144-155).[15]

Kant evidently began to read the British moralists around 1756 (Schilpp, 1939). Under their influence he wrote *Observations on the Feeling of the Beautiful and Sublime* (1764a), and *Dreams of a Spirit-Seer* (1766) which gave him the reputation of a stylist, as a German *La Bruyère*. Kant was in so much of a "social whirl" that his friend, the gifted Hamann, worried that social distractions would interfere with his philosophical labors.[16] He rejected his Pietist upbringing, the church of his father; he refused to go to church even on the university's ceremonial occasions.

At this time, Kant was emphatically a follower of Shaftesbury (1711) according to whom a key philosophical method was ridicule, raillery, and humor: "Truth, 'tis supposed, may bear all Lights: and one of those principal Lights or natural Mediums, by which Things are to be view'd, in order to a thorough recognition, is Ridicule itself, or that Manner of Proof by which we discern whatever is liable to just Raillery in any subject" (p. 61).[17] In a Shaftesburyan vein, Kant stated that he would not

[15] Also, cf. Wallace (1882), p. 21; Paulsen (1902), p. 34; Cassirer (1923), 3:152-153. The exact circumstances, place, and date of Kant's tutorship to the Countess's sons are not clearly known.

[16] It was Hamann who wished to be an Alcibiades to Kant's Socrates (Smith, 1960, p. 238). Kant confessed himself too much a "poor son of the earth" to fathom his friend's "divine language of the intuitive reason" (Smith, 1960, pp. 46-47). On Kant's refusal to attend church, see Wallace (1882, p. 46) and Stuckenberg (1882, p. 354).

[17] Kant wrote: "According to Shaftesbury, it is a valuable touchstone for any truth if it can stand mockery" (Rabel, 1963, p. 291). Kant also greatly admired Lichtenberg who was celebrated for such observations as: "In woman the seat of the *point d'honneur* coincides with the center of gravity. . . . Every-

blame the reader if he were to dispatch spirit-seers as "candidates for the hospital." With excretory sarcasm, Kant declared metaphysics was the outcome of disordered digestions. He thought that perhaps purgatives might be the therapy for metaphysics. Perhaps as "the keen Hudibras" surmised, "visions and holy inspirations are simply caused by a disordered stomach." One passage of Kant's analysis, "the outspokenness of which is hardly bearable in English," according to the translator, was rendered in a censored version. The original (1776) states: "if a hypochondriacal wind rages in the bowels, then it depends on which direction it takes, if it goes downwards, then comes thence a f____, if it rises however upwards, then it is either a vision or a holy inspiration" (p. 84). The reference to the *Hudibras* of Samuel Butler (1612-1680) is noteworthy, for *Hudibras,* "the most memorable burlesque poem in the English language" (according to Sola Pinto), mocks at the militant Puritans, their metaphysics and fanaticism. The peculiarity of insanity, to which metaphysics was akin, said Kant, was "that the confused individual places objects of his imagination outside himself, and considers them to be real and present objects." This confusion of the subjective and objective, of the psychical with the physical, was, in Kant's diagnosis, the defining characteristic of the metaphysical disease.

Metaphysics was regarded by Kant, during his psychological period, as belonging to the pathology of the human mind.[18] "No metaphysician," Kant declared, "could do as much good in the world as Erasmus of Rotterdam and the celebrated Montaigne of France had accomplished" (Stuckenberg, 1882, p. 120). A sense of humor was the surest antidote to metaphysics. Because to Kant, metaphysics was a mental aberration with physiological

---

one should study at least enough philosophy and *belles lettres* to make his sexual experience more delectable" (*The Lichtenberg Reader,* pp. 49, 50; Stuckenberg, 1882, p. 119).

[18] Kant, according to Hamann, regards Mendelssohn's lectures as a system of illusion; "they are to him similar to Mendelssohn's description of a lunatic" (Stuckenberg, 1882, p. 404).

causes, he was interested, throughout his life, in the psychology of crackpots and clairvoyants, from Swedenborg to Cagliostro.[19] "The number of crackpots increases from year to year," Kant (1798) observed. His first essay on this subject, "Versuch über die Krankheiten des Kopfes" (1764b) was called forth by the appearence in Königsberg of a wild prophet from the woods, in nomadic accouter, and bearing a Bible. His name was Jan Pawlikowicz Zdcmonyrskich Komarnicki, and he was accompanied by a herd of cattle and a boy of eight who charmed Kant as a Rousseauan savage who had "none of the bashful awkwardness caused by bondage or compulsory lessons of attention" (Wallace, 1882, p. 111). Kant was much interested in studying the crackpot whom the people called the goat-prophet. Noting that an insane man could still be very intelligent, he classified mental illness into three categories—hallucination, delirium, and mania—and noted that by a common blind spot men do not see what exists but what conforms to their inclinations. A woman looks at the moon through a telescope and thinks she sees the shadow of two lovers, but her pastor sees the two towers of a cathedral. But melancholia, said Kant, was found perhaps in everyone. It was, according to him, accompanied by what we would now call anxiety, and it led people to fear that they were laughable, or to laugh without seeming cause. These very themes (as we have seen) appeared in Kant's dreams. "All sorts of obscure representations excite in him a violent desire to do something evil, by the idea of which he is much tormented, although it never comes to the fact" (Kant, 1764b, p. 310). This was Kant commenting on his own melancholy and distinguishing it from the visionary, exalted fanaticism of those like Mohammed and John of Leyden, whose cult of divine inspiration was truly dangerous.

[19] Cagliostro inspired the essay in 1790, "Über Schwärmerei und die Mittel dagegen." The Fifth Monarchy men provided an example of crackpots in his *Versuch*. Kant referred to the "wonderful sayings" of Holberg that "the number of crackpots grows from day to day," and that they might take it into their heads "to found a Fifth Monarchy." Mohammed and John of Leyden were prototypes of crackpots (Cassirer, 1923, 2:307-311).

As a mature man of the Enlightenment, Kant insisted at this time that mental disorders had physiological causes. Indeed, he housed their etiology, as we have seen, in the digestive system: "I cannot persuade myself," he wrote (1764b), "that the disorders of the mind must result, as is commonly believed, from pride, love, too hard study, and other misuses of the spiritual resources. . . . This confuses the cause and effect." Medicine, with some help from philosophy, could cure these disorders with proper dietetic rules for the spirit. Some intellectual laxative or cathartic could be devised: "For if, according to Swift's observations, a bad poem is simply a purging of the brain . . . why shouldn't the writing of a pitiable chimera have the same virtue? But it would then be prudent to indicate to nature an alternative way of cleansing, so that the sickness could be basically and quietly cured, without everybody else being disturbed by it" (p. 315).[20]

The raillery of Kant in *Dreams of a Spirit-Seer* was part of his own effort at psychological therapy to rid himself of metaphysical tendencies. As he confessed to Moses Mendelssohn, he had to struggle with tendencies in himself much like those of Swedenborgian mysticism: "the attitude of my own mind is inconsistent and, so far as these stories are concerned, I cannot help cherishing an opinion that there is some validity in these experiences in spite of all the absurdities involved in the stories about them. . . ." (Kant, 1766, p. 162).[21] His work was thus in large part, as Kant was aware, one of self-criticism.

His own struggle for liberation from metaphysics had been a hard one: "I have purified my soul from prejudices. . . . [Now] I observe my judgments, together with their most secret causes, from the point of view of others" (pp. 85-86). It was a psychological inquiry into "the most secret causes" of his beliefs which had liberated him from them—accomplished the transition from dogmatism to scepticism. Within a few years, however, Kant's

[20] Author's translation.

[21] Broad (1949-1952, p. 86) has noted the evidence in Kant's correspondence of his unresolved attraction toward Swedenborgian doctrines of the supernatural.

therapy of raillery was confronted with new, far deeper resistances than before (Wallace, 1882).

Kant's lectures on ethics at this time still presented him forthrightly as one working in the method and fashion of the English psychological school. The announcement for his lectures for the winter semester of 1765-1766 stated: "The attempts of Shaftesbury, Hutcheson, and Hume, which although unfinished and deficient, have nonetheless progressed farthest in the search for the first principles of all morality, will receive that precision and supplementation which they now lack. And since in ethics I always consider historically and philosophically what happens before I point out what ought to happen, I shall make clear the method by which one must study man. . . . This method of ethical investigation is a pretty discovery of our times and, if one considers it in its entire plan, was altogether unknown to the ancients" (Schilpp, 1939, p. 8). Thus, at this time, Kant, like his master, Shaftesbury, used the concept of taste to write in a naturalistic fashion concerning such questions as "the relation of the sexes." "The European alone," wrote Kant (1764a), "has found the secret of decorating with so many flowers the sensual charm of a mighty inclination," whereas the Oriental "is of a very false taste," and "thrives on all sorts of amorous grotesqueries" (pp. 112-113). Underlying the principle of justice for Kant at this time was not an emotion-free categorical imperative but the more Humean-Shaftesburyan "universal affection toward the human species" (p. 58).

When Kant wrote that Hume had awakened him from his "dogmatic slumber," what he probably had in mind was that the genetic-psychological method had first put to rout that of the Leibnizian metaphysics.[22] Genetic analysis had undermined the

[22] Kant at different times gave different explanations for what had awakened him from his "dogmatic slumber." To Professor Christian Garve, he wrote in 1798 that it was thinking about the antinomies "that awakened me from my dogmatic slumber and drove me to a critique of Pure Reason, in order to remove the scandal of an apparent contradiction of Reason with itself" (Rabel, 1963, p. 356). Kant's account of the influence of Hume is set forth in his *Prolegomena to any Future Metaphysics* (Kant, 1784, p. 7).

metaphysical tendency. Kant's favorite metaphor for metaphysics became one which characterized it as a desexing activity. In his *Inaugural Dissertation* (1770), he wrote that "it commonly happens that one of the disputants appears as it were to be milking a he-goat and the other to be holding a sieve," and again in the *Critique of Pure Reason* (1781) he averred that the propounding and answering of absurd questions not only brings "shame" on the former but presents one, "as the ancients said, the ludicrous spectacle of one man milking a he-goat and the other holding a sieve underneath" (p. 97). A metaphysical questioner thus brings a "shame" upon himself akin to that of a man who blunders sexually, who mistakes male for female. Rationalistic metaphysics in other words operated to feminize one, to shame one. This was the "dogmatic slumber," i.e., the extinction of one's manhood.

Kant, struggling to rid himself of melancholy and guilt, was assisted by the psychological method of Hume. Here was a method which was bold, clear, masculine, without chimeras. Kant was led to revel in the English novels, in Fielding's *Tom Jones* and *Jonathan Wild,* in Richardson's *Clarissa,* in Laurence Sterne's *Tristram Shandy,* in Jonathan Swift's satires and Butler's *Hudibras.* In the spirit of an anthropological relativist, Kant pondered the cultural variations of the Malays, Peruvians, Jews, American Indians, Otaheite tribe, Connecticut Puritans, Scottish Highlanders, Swedes, Tunguses, Russians, Siberian Shamans, and Tahitians (Kant, 1798, 2:20-24, 32; 9:411; 14:159-165; 15:66).[23]

But in the period around 1769, there took place what Paulsen (1902) refers to as "the revolution of 1769" (p. 311). It was not so much a revolution as a counter-revolution against the psychological method. "The year 1769," wrote Kant, "brought me a great light" (Ward, 1922, p. 8).[24] A year before, he had still

[23] See also Kant (1803), pp. 132, 139, 162.
[24] Cf. Kant (posth.), p. 4 and Stuckenberg (1882).

believed that space was something external to the mind, and he had derived a theory of absolute space from the orientations of the left and right hands; the following year, he believed it was solely a form of intuition (Stuckenberg, 1882; Ward, 1922). In his *Inaugural Dissertation,* Kant (1770) announced his definitive break with the English psychological school. Together with Epicurus, Shaftesbury and his school were to be "quite rightly condemned," for trying to reduce the criteria of morals to the feelings of pleasure or unpleasantness (pp. 60-61). As Paulsen (1902) stated: "Pure reason alone is to be considered. As contrasted with it all empirical principles are 'impure.' " From this time, we may surmise, dates Kant's transformation into a person "in whose heart nature has placed little sympathy, who is naturally cold and indifferent to the sufferings of others; perhaps, being endowed with great patience and endurance, he makes little of his own pains, and presupposes or even demands that every person should do the same" (p. 335).

We are at a loss as to what events during Kant's middle years produced this moral revolution. That he was returning from the Voltairean-Shaftesburyan ethics to the Pietist standpoint is clear when we note that it was precisely the latter which held as Kant did (1803, p. 269; 1794, p. 43), that moral change had to be revolutionary. As Pinson (1934) wrote: "The most characteristic experience and central point in the life of a Pietist was the *Wiedergeburt* or the regeneration. The *Wiedergeburt* became the dominant motif . . ." (p. 115).[25] Furthermore Kant's change of attitude toward lying was indicative of the reinstatement, in his mind, of paternal authority. The Kant of the psychological method was reflected in the tolerant statement: "Many children have a disposition to lie, which has no other cause than a vivacious imagination." The Pietist Kant now added (1803): "It is

25 Pietist nurture of children inculcated an intimate sense of God's Presence. The biographies of Kant's older contemporary, Zinzendorf, give a vivid picture of what Pietism must have meant in Kant's upbringing. See Meyer (1928), pp. 132, 202; Weinlick (1956), p. 28.

the father's affair to see to it that they break off this habit . . ." (pp. 194-195). He wrote that lying was "the really corrupt spot in human nature," though the psychologist in Kant recognized that the inclination to "guileless lying" is always found in children and "now and then in adults, otherwise good" who when telling "alleged adventures" cannot prevent their imagination from "growing like an avalanche . . . with no intention whatsoever than merely to be interesting" (p. 194).[26] Again, we are struck by Kant's reference to the father as the one who has to condition the child, a natural liar, to become a truth-teller. The tremendous importance Kant came to assign to truth-telling, the horror which he came to attach to lying, suggest the reinstatement of his father's authority over that of the psychological culture. However, the source of the crisis of paternal reinstatement, of the restoration of the superego, eludes us. Freud (1913), in studying children's lies, said that they can be designed to conceal reminders of oedipal feelings or hidden incestuous love. Later, he stated that "Kant's Categorical Imperative is thus a direct heir of the Oedipus complex" (Freud, 1924, p. 167).

Kant's expulsion of all feeling from the categorical imperative was the basic characteristic of his moral doctrine; its repressive rigorism was part of the same struggle to contain lawless sensations which was the aim of the controls of the *a priori* categories. Kant's Voltairean, hedonistic tolerance was replaced with the principle that: "To act morally is to do what one does not want to do" (Paulsen, 1902, p. 332). Good acts, as Kant wrote, could be carried out without any feeling: "pardon without sympathy, conjugal faithfulness without love" (Schilpp, p. 115). A world of ethical automata, emasculated from feeling but obedient to principle, became the highest moral projection. One wonders with Freud if an ethic of pure "formal" principle is not one dominated by an underlying castration complex, in which emotion has been extirpated.

[26] Cf. Jean Piaget (1932), pp. 160-165.

Kant himself recognized that he had gone through a series of psychological-intellectual stages, and he believed that his psychological evolution recapitulated the psychological history of mankind. Comte and Freud both proposed laws of psychological evolution, and Kant was their precursor. "The first step in matters of pure reason, marking its infancy, is *dogmatic*. The second is *sceptical:* and indicates that experience has rendered our judgment wiser and more circumspect. But a third step, such as can be taken only by fully matured judgment, is now necessary. . . . This is not censorship but the criticism of reason . . ." (Kant, 1781, p. 607). This law of evolution, from dogmatic to sceptical to critical, Kant believed, was inherent in the nature of the human mind. He wrote in his notes: "Can a history of philosophy be written mathematically (this must mean dogmatically, or from concepts)? Can we show how dogmatism must have arisen; and from it scepticism, and that this necessarily leads to criticism? Yes, if the idea of a metaphysic inevitably presses on human reason, and the latter feels a necessity to develop it; but this science lies entirely in the mind although only outlined there in embryonic form" (Paulsen, 1902, p. 290). Kant's law of intellectual evolution and its three sequential stages was patterned on stages of his emotional development, which he subsequently transposed into logic. We have not, however, been able to unravel the source of the transitional drive, the emotional revolution in Kant's later life.

Perhaps Kant developed resistances to the British psychological method to the degree that it tended to uncover so much of what he found "loathsome" in his own nature. Why, for instance, was his own nature so cold? Why was he so lacking in the benevolent affection that Shaftesbury regarded as natural in human beings (Fowler, 1882)? Shaftesbury had traced the origin of the moral sense to feelings of fellowship and family affections. By analogy, Kant would have had to inquire into the origins and consequences of his own disturbed family life, e.g., his coldness to his sisters and his condescension toward his father. It would have obliged him to look deep within himself to investigate his attitudes toward mother and father, something which he preferred not to do. He must have been aware of the latent threat in Hume's "experimental method" to the very basis of his moral life. Hume (1738) had, for instance, blandly found that a child's murder of its parent was as natural as a sapling destroying its parent tree: "I ask, if, in this instance, there be wanting any relation which is discoverable in parricide or ingratitude? Is not the one tree the cause of the destruction of the former, in the same manner as when a child murders his parent?" And Hume had gone on even further to query the moral turpitude of incest, asking "why incest in the human species is criminal, and why the very same action, and the same relations in animals, have not the smallest moral turpitude and deformity?" (pp. 175-176). These explorations must have seemed as "monstrous" to Kant as did the evolutionary speculations concerning a promiscuous Mother Nature, and would have led to his finally drawing back in horror from the psychological method.

Rousseau, the revolutionary primitivist-populist, symbolized in Kant's mind his emotional revolution against the psychological method. During the latter sixties, what de Vleeschauer (1962) calls a "change in tonality" in Kant's thinking was taking place, and Rousseau came to represent the reinstatement of his father's moral supremacy (p. 41). Kant described this change in himself in an oft-cited passage: "There was a time when I despised the masses who know nothing. Rousseau has shown me my error. This dazzling advantage vanishes, and I should regard myself as of much less use than the common laborers if I did not believe that this speculation (that of the Socratic-critical philosophy) can give a value to all others, and to restore the rights of humanity" (Paulsen, 1902, p. 39; Schilpp, 1939, p. 40).

Kant shared none of Rousseau's optimism, sentimentalism, and worship of feeling. But in Rousseau, Kant found the reverence for the "common laborer," i.e., his own father. The son's pilgrimage was over. His early revolt against his Pietist father had been social as well as philosophical. Kant had found his way into the social life of the Königsberg aristocracy. He had been tutor to their children and a guest at their parties. He had put aside his associations with his humble family. Now, however, he recalled the deep moral character of his father: "I still remember how once disputes arose between the harness-making and saddler trades regarding their privileges, during which my father suffered much. But, nevertheless, this quarrel was treated by my parents, even in family conversation, with such forbearance and love towards their opponents, and with so much trust in Providence, that the memory of it, although I was then a boy, has never left me" (Paulsen, 1902, p. 39). The Voltairean-Shaftesburyan standpoint was essentially that of the enlightened middle classes and aristocracy. Kant partially renounced their genetic-psychological method. The critical philosophy would come to terms with the Pietist-Rousseauan values, with the outlook of the "common laborer." Such was the psychological drama which underlay Kant's revolution of 1769.

In a sense, this essay is written in the tradition of the psychological method which Kant followed in his middle years. Only rarely has any scholar proposed that the psychoanalytic method be applied to Kant's philosophy. Hall (1912), a lonely pioneer, thought that unconscious feelings and motives determined Kant's postulates (p. 414), and Pfister (1923, p. 78) spoke of the *Zwangsneurose des Schematisieren* (the compulsion to schematize).[27] But most philosophers have shared the view of Weldon (1958): "There is no reason to suppose that his [Kant's] experiences, except in the strictly intellectual sphere, were of the slightest interest or importance; and if they were, we shall certainly never know it, since his biographers could discover nothing but the most meagre trivialities to record of him" (p. 1). Actually "trivialities" can be psychologically momentous, and Kant's own psychological writings belie the notion that he was

[27] See also Loewenberg (1953).

a creature of pure intellect. We have tried to unravel the nonlogical, emotional, and unconscious determinants of Kant's philosophy.

REFERENCES

Boas, G. (1948), The Role of Protophilosophies in Intellectual History. *J. Philos.*, 45:673-684.

——— (1957), *Dominant Themes of Modern Philosophy*. New York: Ronald Press.

Broad, C. D. (1949-1952), Immanuel Kant and Psychical Research. *Proc. Soc. Psychical Res.*, 49:79-104.

Cassirer, E., ed. (1918), *Briefe von und an Kant, 1749-1789*. Berlin: Bruno Cassirer.

———, ed. (1921-1923), *Immanuel Kants Werke*. Berlin: Bruno Cassirer.

Clark, R. T., Jr. (1955), *Herder: His Life and Thought*. Berkeley: University of California Press.

De Quincey, T. (1862), The Last Days of Immanuel Kant. In: *De Quincey's Works*, Vol. 3. Edinburgh: Adam & Charles Black.

Ewing, A. C. (1924), *Kant's Treatment of Causality*. London: K. Paul, Trench, Trubner.

——— (1938), *A Short Commentary on Kant's Critique of Pure Reason*. London: Methuen.

Fowler, T. (1882), *Shaftesbury and Hutcheson*. London: S. Low, Marston, Searle and Rivington.

Freud, S. (1900), The Interpretation of Dreams. *Standard Edition*, 4 & 5. London: Hogarth Press, 1953.

——— (1910), The Psycho-Analytical View of Psychogenic Disturbance of Vision. *Standard Edition*, 11:209-218. London: Hogarth Press, 1957.

——— (1913), Infantile Mental Life: Two Lies Told by Children. *Standard Edition*, 12:305-309. London: Hogarth Press, 1950.

——— (1915-1916), Introductory Lectures on Psycho-Analysis. *Standard Edition*, 15 & 16. London: Hogarth Press, 1963.

——— (1924), The Economic Problem in Masochism. *Standard Edition*, 19:159-172. London: Hogarth Press, 1950.

——— (1930), Civilization and Its Discontents. *Standard Edition*, 21:64-145. London: Hogarth Press, 1961.

Fromm, E. (1898). Das Kantbildnis der Gräfin Karoline Charlotte Amalia von Keyserling. In: *Kantstudien*, 2. Cologne: Kölner Universitätsverlag.

Hall, G. S. (1912), Why Kant Is Passing. *Amer. J. Psychol.*, 23:370-426.

Heine, H. (1835), *Religion and Philosophy in Germany*. London: Trübner, 1882.

Herz, M. (1801), In: *Jewish Encyclopedia,* 6:368. New York: Funk & Wagnalls, 1901-1906.

Hume, D. (1738), *A Treatise of Human Nature*. New York: Dutton, 1930.

James, W. (1890), *The Principles of Psychology,* 1 & 2. New York: Holt, 1910.

Kandel, L. (1966), *The Love Book*. San Francisco.

Kant, I. (1755), *Kant's Cosmogony*. Glasgow: J. Maclehose, 1900.

——— (1762), *Kant's Introduction to Logic*. Philadelphia: 1886.

——— (1764a), *Observations on the Feeling of the Beautiful and Sublime*. Berkeley: University of California Press, 1960.

——— (1764b), Versuch über die Krankheiten des Kopfes. In: *Immanuel Kants Werke*. 2:301-311. Berlin: Bruno Cassirer, 1922.

——— (1766), *Dreams of a Spirit-Seer, Illustrated by Dreams of Metaphysics*. London: New-Church Press, 1900.

——— (1770), *Kant's Inaugural Dissertation and Early Writings on Space*. Chicago: Open Court, 1929.

——— (1781), *Immanuel Kant's Critique of Pure Reason* (Second Edition). London: Macmillan, 1963.

——— (1783), *Prolegomena to Any Future Metaphysics*. Chicago: Open Court, 1929.

——— (1786a), Conjectural Beginning of Human History. In: *Kant on History*. Indianapolis: Bobbs-Merrill, 1963, pp. 53-60.

——— (1786b), *Prolegomena and Metaphysical Foundations of Natural Science*. London: G. Bell, 1909.

——— (1790), *Kant's Critique of Teleological Judgement*. Oxford: Clarendon Press, 1928.

——— (1794), *Religion Within the Limits of Reason Alone*. New York: Harper, 1960.

——— (1797a), *The Doctrine of Virtue*. New York: Harper, 1964.

——— (1797b), Von der Macht des Gemüths durch den blossen Vorsatz seiner krankhaften Gefühle Meister zu Sein. In: *Immanuel Kants Werke,* 7:411-431. Berlin: Bruno Cassirer, 1916. On the Power of the Mind in Overcoming Unpleasant Sensations by Mere Resolution. In: J. Sinclair, trans., *The Code of Health and Longevity,* 3:245-259. Edinburgh: 1807.

——— (1798), Anthropology of Immanuel Kant. *J. Speculative Philos.,* 9 (1875):16-27, 239-245, 406-416; 10 (1876):319-323; 11 (1877): 310-317, 353-363; 14 (1880):154-169; 15 (1881):62-66; 16 (1882):47-52, 395-413.

——— (1803), *The Educational Theory of Immanuel Kant*. Philadelphia: Lippincott, 1904.

——— (posth.), *Lectures on Ethics*. London: Methuen, 1930.

——— (posth.), *Reflexionen Kants zur kritischen Philosophie,* 2. Leipzig: Fues's Verlag, 1882-1884.

The Lichtenberg Reader. Boston: Beacon Press, 1959.

Loewenberg, R. D. (1953), From Immanuel Kant's Self-Analysis. *Amer. Imago,* 10:307-322.

Lovejoy, A. O. (1907), Kant's Classification of the Forms of Judgment. *Philos. Rev.,* 16:588-591.

——— (1911), Kant and Evolution. In: *Forerunners of Darwin: 1745-1859.* Baltimore: Johns Hopkins Press, 1959, pp. 173-207.

"Marcus Herz." *Jewish Encyclopedia,* 6:368. New York: Funk & Wagnalls, 1901-1906.

Meyer, H. W. (1928), *Child Nature and Nurture.* New York: Abingdon Press.

Murphey, M. G. (1961), *The Development of Peirce's Philosophy.* Cambridge, Mass.: Harvard University Press.

Paton, H. J. (1956), Kant on Friendship. *Proceedings of the British Academy.* London: Oxford University Press, pp. 45-66.

Paulsen, F. (1902), *Immanuel Kant: His Life and Doctrine.* New York: Scribner.

Peirce, C. S. (1933), *Collected Papers of Charles Sanders Peirce,* 4. Cambridge, Mass.: Harvard University Press.

Pfister, O. (1923), *Zur Psychologie des philosophischen Denkens.* Bern: Bircher.

Piaget, J. (1927), *The Child's Conception of Physical Causality.* New York: Humanities Press, 1930.

——— (1932), *The Moral Judgment of the Child.* Glencoe, Ill.: Free Press, 1948.

Pinson, K. S. (1934), *Pietism as a Factor in the Rise of German Nationalism.* New York: Columbia University Press.

Rabel, G. (1963), *Kant.* Oxford: Clarendon Press.

Royce, J. (1919), *Lectures on Modern Idealism.* New Haven: Yale University Press.

Schilpp, P. A. (1939), *Kant's Pre-Critical Ethics.* Evanston: Northwestern University Press, 1960.

Schopenhauer, A. (1818), *The World as Will and Idea.* New York: Doubleday, 1961.

Shaftesbury, A. (1711), *Characteristicks* (5th ed.). Birmingham, 1773.

Singer, C. (1931), *A Short History of Medicine.* Oxford: Clarendon Press.

Smith, R. G. (1960), *J. G. Hamann; 1730-1788: A Study in Christian Existence.* New York: Harper.

Stekel, W. (1935), *The Interpretation of Dreams.* New York: Grosset, 1962.

Stern, B. J. (1927), *Should We Be Vaccinated? A Survey of the Controversy in its Historical and Scientific Aspects.* New York: Harper.

Stuckenberg, J. H. W. (1882), *The Life of Immanuel Kant*. London: Macmillan.
Thomas, J. H. (1963), *Paul Tillich: An Appraisal*. Philadelphia: Westminster Press.
Vaihinger, H. (1898), Kant als Melancholiker. *Kantstudien*, 2:139-141.
Vleeschauwer, H. J. de (1962), *The Development of Kantian Thought*. London: T. Nelson.
Wallace, W. (1882), *Kant*. Edinburgh: Blackwood.
Ward, J. (1922), *A Study of Kant*. Cambridge: Cambridge University Press.
Weinlick, J. R. (1956), *Count Zinzendorf*. New York: Abingdon Press.
Weldon, T. D. (1945), *Kant's Critique of Pure Reason*. Oxford: Clarendon Press, 1958.
Wenley, R. M. (1910), *Kant and His Philosophical Revolution*. Edinburgh: T. T. Clark.

PSYCHOANALYSIS AND THE PHILOSOPHICAL PROBLEMS OF FREE WILL

ANTHONY GARRARD FLEW, M.A.

Ernest Jones was, for a doctor, and even for a psychoanalyst, unusually interested in philosophy. He wrote an essay on "Free Will and Determinism" (1924). It is, therefore, generally appropriate to present here a philosophical contribution centering on these topics. This paper, like that of Ernest Jones, will suggest wide-ranging implications about the significance of the whole psychoanalytic enterprise. But, since much ground is to be covered, and since some of the things to be said will appear paradoxical, it will surely help if we provide an outline itinerary now, before the journey begins.

Section 1 considers psychoanalysis as concerned with men and their motives. Two points are made: (a) Jones, like Freud, was committed to philosophical materialism; yet psychoanalysis constantly speaks of the conscious and the unconscious mind as if they were incorporeal substances. (b) Psychoanalysis is funda-

Mr. Flew is Professor of Philosophy at the University of Keele, Staffordshire, England. He has taught at colleges and universities both in the United States and abroad, and has published several books.

mentally teleological while being also committed to psychic determinism; yet Jones seems to take teleology to be incompatible with determinism. It is suggested in both cases that the apparent inconsistencies can and must be removed and, in particular, that psychic determinism is not merely compatible with but presupposes teleology.

Section 2 distinguishes two ways in which psychoanalytic discoveries may be relevant to philosophical inquiries about free will: (a) they may be directly relevant to the subject of these philosophical investigations, and (b) they may throw light on the reasons why the investigators see or fail to see what they do. Section 3 notes that the main contribution of Ernest Jones was to the second of these two areas of inquiry, but that in making them he was taking a great deal for granted about the first. This leads very naturally to section 4, a summary statement of what the philosophical problems of free will are. In the light of this, it quickly becomes clear in section 5 that we can find plenty of obvious and exoteric interests involved in these philosophical inquiries before we have to press on to uncover more obscure and esoteric unconscious concerns.

Section 6 can be regarded as a complement to section 3, since it refers to the other of the two kinds of inquiry distinguished in section 2. Certain very important false assumptions about free will and choice are uncovered—assumptions which are common to Ernest Jones and many other psychoanalytic writers. Finally, in section 7, three larger morals are drawn. The first (a) starts from a point made in 6, that psychic determinism presupposes rather than precludes the possibility of choice. Hence, if universal causal determinism really is, as it is so widely assumed to be, incompatible with genuine human choice, then psychic determinism must be not what it has almost universally been mistaken to be—the psychological special case of universal causal determinism—but rather something wholly irreconcilable with that traditional sort of determinism. The second (b) is that Ernest Jones' confidence that the discoveries of atomic physics must be altogether irrelevant to the present questions is only warranted if human choice is indeed compatible with traditional determinism. Jones himself—in my view wrongly—assumed that it is not. The third (c) is that, once granted a full understanding both of the differences between conscious and unconscious desires and of the nature of psychic determination, the role of psychoanalysis must be seen as essentially emancipatory. It is a therapy which can extend the possibilities of human choice rather than a science tending to show that there is, after all, no such thing.

So much for the program. The performance can now begin.

1. Psychoanalysis as Concerned with Men and Their Motives

Psychoanalysis I take to be a discipline, or perhaps only a candidate discipline, concerned with what Flugel (1934) terms, *Men and their Motives*. Flugel's title is apt in two ways. In the first place, it puts the emphasis, where it belongs, on men and not on minds. In his autobiography, Jones (1959) made it emphatically clear that he himself was, without any substantial reservation, a philosophical materialist:

> I should not hesitate, therefore, to describe myself as a philosophical materialist. . . . I would say that in the realms of both thought and action the distinction between men who believe that mental processes, or beings, can exist independently of the physical world and those who reject this belief is to me the most significant of all human classifications; and I should measure any hope of future evolutionary progress by the passage of men from the one class to the other more than by any other single criterion [p. 59].

He thus ranged himself, and indirectly psychoanalysis too, in the tradition of those who see men as corporeal and mortal—in the tradition of Aristotle as opposed to Plato, of Ryle as opposed to Descartes (Flew, 1964).

In this association of psychoanalysis with an Aristotelian rather than with a Platonic-Cartesian view of man, Freud's biographer was, as always, faithful to the spirit and to the fundamental insights of the Master. For Freud surely was an unwavering and lifelong mortalist and, in the last if not the first analysis, a philosophical materialist too. Nevertheless, to balance the picture, one must also notice two things. First, Freud and Jones also constantly insist on talking of "regions of the mind," of "the psychic apparatus," and so on, in ways which must suggest to themselves and to others that the substantives *mind* and *psyche* are to be construed as words for substances and, since there are no suitable corporeal substances available, as words for presumably incorporeal and as such essentially mysterious substances. Yet to precisely the extent that they do this, they are seeing their psychoanalytic work through incongruously Cartesian spectacles, hinting that the mind in general and the unconscious mind in particular is after all something which could significantly be said to exist apart from the person whose mind it is. For to say in this philosophical context that the mind is a substance is to say that it is something which could significantly be said to exist separately, and apart from the person whose mind it is. But if it is once granted that we (or our minds) are incorporeal substances, it begins to seem sensible to propose that we (or our minds) might survive what might otherwise and uninstructedly have been thought of as our deaths and dissolutions.

Consider some examples of these unfortunate and unfortunately typical ways of talking. For instance, in a B.B.C. broadcast, Jones (1956) once asked: "What did Freud really do? That can most shortly be answered by saying that he discovered a previously inaccessible region of the mind we now call the unconscious." Again, Freud (1915-1917) himself insists time and time over that "the unconscious is a special region of the mind" (p. 212); that "we are accustomed to operate with it as though it were something palpable to the senses" (p. 279). He does not accept that ". . . the unconscious is nothing real in the scientific sense, is a mere makeshift, *une façon de parler*. . . . Something not real, which produces effects of such tangible reality as an obsessional action!" (p. 278). Until and unless this way of talking is either abandoned or shown to be interpretable in innocuously un-Cartesian terms, psychoanalysis is bound to be seen as something inconsistent with precisely that philosophical materialism to which both Freud and Jones were ultimately and fundamentally committed.[1]

The second thing to be noticed as at least ostensibly inconsistent with the claim that in his philosophical materialism Jones was true to the spirit of Freud is Freud's several times publicly expressed sympathy with the case for the occurrence of genuine telepathy. Certainly this was a sympathy which his biographer made it quite clear that he could not approve. Nevertheless Freud seems never to have committed himself to what would in the present context be the decisive step of concluding that the power of telepathy is a power of communication between incorporeal substances, which at any particular time may or may not happen to be embodied. For notwithstanding that Freud wrote of telepathy, "Ce n'est que le premier pas qui coûte. Das weiter findet sich" [It is only the first step that counts. The rest follows]. Any following involved here is not a matter of logical necessity but rather of psychological association. It is a point which Freud (1927) had perhaps himself taken when he wrote of the spiritualists, that "Unfortunately they cannot succeed in refuting the fact that the . . . utterances of their spirits are merely the products of their own mental activity" (p. 28).[2]

The second way in which Flugel's title, *Men and their Motives,* is apt is in emphasizing that psychoanalysis is concerned with motives. Psychoanalytic explanation is a sophisticated de-

[1] For a recent essay toward the sort of interpretation required, see Miles (1966).

[2] Jones (1953-1957) provides a convenient secondary source for these quotations (3:405, 436).

velopment of the most familiar sort of explanation of human behavior—an explanation in terms of motives, purposes, intentions, and plans. It is a development made possible by the introduction of the techniques of analytic therapy and by the corresponding systematic extension of the meanings of all these words. One of the two main extensions consists in making it possible to speak consistently of unconscious motives, unconscious purposes, unconscious intentions, unconscious plans, and so on (Flew, 1956). Since it is explanation of this kind which is involved, and since these are its key terms, the world of psychoanalysis is much closer to that of historiography or of literature than to that of classical mechanics or chemistry.

It would be possible, in principle, to explain one and the same set of movements both as the expressions of conscious or unconscious purpose and as the outcome of electrochemical processes in the central nervous system (Flew, 1965). There is no necessary inconsistency between explanations of these two fundamentally different categories. Nor, of course, do the teleological characteristics have to be attributed to any incorporeal substances postulated for the purpose: they can and must be taken to be what they paradigmatically are—attributes of corporeal persons. The rise of psychoanalysis does not, therefore, as such and in this aspect, constitute any threat to philosophical materialism. Jones (1953-1957), in his chapter on Freud "The Medical Student," in order to indicate the ideas and ideals which Freud imbibed in Brücke's Institute, quotes from a manifesto by one of the leaders of the Helmholtz school of physiology:

> No other forces than the common physical and chemical ones are active within the organism. In those cases which cannot at the time be explained by these forces one has either to find the specific way or form of their action . . . or to assume new forces equal in dignity to the chemical-physical forces inherent in matter, reducible to the force of attraction and repulsion. . . . Yet Brücke would have been astonished . . . had he known that one of his favorite

> pupils, one apparently a convert to the strict faith, was later, in his famous wish theory of the mind, to bring back into science the ideas of 'purpose,' 'intention,' and 'aim' which had just been abolished from the universe [1:45].

So far, except perhaps for the final clause, so good. But Jones continues: "We know, however, that when Freud did bring them back he was able to reconcile them with the principles in which he had been brought up; he never abandoned determinism for teleology" (1:50). This further comment is unsatisfactory. By insisting that Freud never abandoned determinism for teleology, and still more by allowing that physiological work such as that done in Brücke's Institute could abolish from the universe "the ideas of 'purpose,' 'intention,' and 'aim,' " Jones appears to suggest what no psychoanalyst can afford to say—that determinism and teleology are incompatible. He cannot afford to say this because psychoanalysis is essentially both teleological and deterministic. It is teleological in as much as it offers explanations ultimately in terms of such notions as purpose, motive, and intention. It is also, insofar as it insists that there always is a motive or a purpose or an intention, deterministic. This is Freud's "psychic determinism," which is, obviously, not incompatible with teleological notions, for it contains them. Yet, as we shall see, it is by no means equally obvious how this psychic determinism relates to the universal, material causal determinism of the school of Brücke.

Two final comments are in order before passing to section 2. First, notice how important it is in any account of psychic determinism to insert a phrase such as "insofar as." The reason is that no one seems to have decided the precise scope of the teleological or psychic determinism presupposed by psychoanalysis. They have not, that is, really decided exactly how much behavior is to be taken as motivated. So long as everyone appreciates that this is what the situation is, the most prudent thing may be to leave the question open to be settled by the progress of the research. But if a provisional and rather indeterminate line has to be drawn, then perhaps this could most suitably be done by urging that psychoanalysis presuppose, and aspire to show, that there is a teleological explanation for all behavior which can be brought under voluntary control, deliberately leaving the precise meaning of *can* still to be specified. This proposal seems to chime with the general practice and aspirations of the more moderate psychoanalysts. It allows them to work both on behavior which already is under voluntary control, and on all such ongoings as "compulsive actions" which may be brought under such control—whether by means of analytic therapy or otherwise. To go further than this would be unwarranted and would, incidentally, require an even greater extension of the ordinary sense of "behavior" than that already usual in psychology (Miles, 1966, pp. 35-36).

Second, it does need firmly to be pointed out that to have expelled teleological notions from the universe of discourse of the physiologists is not at all the same thing as to have abolished from the universe "the ideas of 'purpose,' 'intention,' and 'aim.' " It is one of the many paradoxes of the history of ideas that the long and necessary battles to exclude such notions from physics, chemistry, biology, and physiology, have often misled people into thinking that a total rejection of teleological concepts must be defining characteristics both of any science and of a scientific outlook. Yet that notions like purpose, intention, and aim have no place in the explanations of the sciences not dealing with human beings is no reason for denying that they have proper and indispensable applications on what is, so to speak, their own home ground. What is wrong with animistic projections, and with the Pathetic Fallacy in general, is not any employment of purposive ideas, but their unwarranted imposition onto things which must be constitutionally incapable of the desiring and the planning thus attributed.

2. Two Sorts of Relevance of Psychoanalysis

Psychoanalysis can be relevant to discussions about the freedom of the will in two fundamentally different ways. Or, better, it can be relevant to two different sorts of discussion. It can be relevant insofar as its findings or its presuppositions bear upon those issues of fact and of philosophy with which any such discussions must be primarily concerned. It can also be relevant insofar as there is room for psychoanalytic explanations of why the participants maintain the positions which they do maintain. That there is a fundamental difference here is obvious. Nevertheless, it is extremely difficult, and maybe undesirable or even impossible, completely to insulate the examination of the one sort of question from speculation about the other.

To illustrate the way in which psychoanalysis may be relevant to the former, consider the following remarks made by Jones (1920):

> One of the psychological arguments against the belief in a complete mental determinism is the intense feeling of conviction that we have a perfectly free choice in the performance of many acts. . . . It only means that the person is not aware of any conscious motive. When, however, conscious motivation is distinguished from unconscious motivation, this feeling of conviction teaches us that the former does not extend over all our motor resolutions. What is left free from the one side receives its motive from the other—from the unconscious—and so the psychical determinism is flawlessly carried through. A knowledge of unconscious motivation is indispensable, even for philosophical discussion of determinism (pp. 77-78).

We shall later challenge the common but catastrophic assumption that the presence of motivation, or even the possibility of prediction, must necessarily preclude "a perfectly free choice." For the present it is sufficient to concur with the conclusion. Perhaps some extremely puristic philosopher might want to insist that, since philosophical questions are essentially logical (as opposed to factual), what has (it is thought) in fact been discovered by the psychoanalysts cannot be relevant to a "philosophical discussion of determinism." But purism of this kind would be stilted, narrow-minded, and perverse. For whatever philosophical problems may or may not be, many, though surely not all, derive much of their interest and importance from their origin in the discoveries and presuppositions of other inquiries which are not philosophical (Popper, 1963). More specifically, the supposed discoveries of the particular unconscious motives operating in many cases of the sort which Jones had in mind, and the general psychoanalytic presupposition that such motives are always present, constitute perfect specimens of the kinds of discoveries and presuppositions which generate philosophical problems. They raise and make urgent the questions of how far, if at all, such discoveries, and the presuppositions which they must tend to validate, could be compatible with everyday beliefs and assumptions about responsibility and choice.

To illustrate the way in which psychoanalysis may be relevant to the second sort of question, consider the following statement which Jones (1953-1957) made in his biography of Freud, when his mind was not on general philosophical and theoretical questions but preoccupied with Freud's anti-Americanism: "He was so obviously unfair . . . that one is bound to seek some explanation of his attitude" (2:66). This provides a good example of how we all do naturally and properly raise psychological questions about the sources of beliefs when we feel that those beliefs are so inept as to demand explanation. It is, surely, this general fact which occasioned Ryle's (1949) magisterial ruling: "Let the psychologist tell us why we are deceived; but we can tell ourselves and him why we are not deceived" (p. 326).

Now there certainly is an important truth behind this dismissal —the truth that, typically, the layman asks for a psychological explanation only of behavior which fails to satisfy a norm. It is this fact which provides the main bridges between the two fundamentally different sorts of questions which we have been distinguishing. When, as in the case of Freud's judgements about North America, something seems to be going seriously awry, we move very easily from discussing North America to discussing Freud. We take it as given that it is not the original subject which is defective—or not so defective, or not defective in that way—and we proceed to inquire why the judge himself is out of sorts. Psychological explanation thus comes to be thought to be typically, or even only, concerned with what is deviant. The association is greatly strengthened in and by the particular case of psychoanalytic explanation, since any professional expertise of the psychoanalysts derives almost exclusively from their study of neurotic patients in a therapeutic situation. (Incidentally, this last observation is one which often gives great offense both to analysts and to lay spokesmen for analysis. Yet it would be, to put it no higher, imprudent for friends of the profession to suggest that it is engaged in giving expensive and time-consuming therapy to patients who in fact enjoy rude mental health. Nor will it do to go all metaphysical and to say that we are all neurotic *really*. For then the substance of our original observation simply re-emerges as the point that analytic patients are, presumably, egregiously neurotic!).

However, although there certainly is this important truth behind what Ryle says, it cannot by itself constitute a finally sufficient reason for limiting either psychology in general or psychoanalysis in particular to the explanation only of the untoward. For, as has by now been remarked fairly frequently, the classical sciences have progressed from the putting of questions primarily about the unusual to the pressing of more fundamental inquiries about the usual. In general, there would seem always to be room for explanations of functioning as well as of malfunctioning. In particular—to take the case of most immediate concern—if when confronted by mistakes we postulate, and can often or always discover, unconscious motives so operating as to disarrange the normal functioning, then surely it must be reasonable to presume that similar motives must have been present—albeit not operating to the same ill effect—in some or all the cases where the functioning happens to have been normal. And if this is so, and if psychoanalysis is a genuine area of knowledge, then it becomes equally reasonable to ask the analysts to throw light on the questions of what unconscious motives are in fact present, but not to such dire effect, also in nondeviant cases.

The first and generally crucial points to seize here are that questions why people want to get it right or wrong, or why they would like this to be true or false, are fundamentally different from questions about whether they have got it right or wrong, or whether it is true or false. Furthermore, the justifying reasons which are relevant to the latter are not any sort of rivals to the desires or motives, both conscious or unconscious, which figure in answers to the former. It is therefore entirely possible that a person may have both a fully adequate motive for getting it right and be in a position to know that he has in fact done so; it is equally possible that an overwhelmingly strong desire that things should stand thus and thus should cohabit with decisive justifying reasons for the belief either that they do or that they do not (Flew, 1965).

A further point worth noting here is that the deviations for which psychological explanation may be required can be virtues as well as defects, without such distinctions affecting the need for such explanation. Consider, for instance, the surely legitimate question: "Why does this man stand out against all his mates (colleagues) by insisting on doing a full day's work for his pay (remuneration)?"; or "Why did that man see clearly when all his contemporaries were in a fog?"

3. The Two Sorts of Relevance Applied to Ernest Jones

The distinction made in section 2 can now be applied to Jones' (1924) paper on "Free Will and Determinism," which begins with two questions: "At the outset one might pose the psychological question of how it comes that this problem has possessed such an extraordinary interest for the thinkers of all ages" (p. 178); and, on the following page, "A second consideration that calls for psychological inquiry is the ambivalence so often to be noted among those expressing opinions on the matter" (p. 179). Both these questions are, as he says, psychological, and as such they both belong to the second of the two sorts of discussion distinguished in section 2.

Now, it does not seem to be in principle unsound, or impossible, to raise such psychological questions without taking for granted the correctness of any particular view of the philosophical problems, much less a dim one. But this very essay on "Free Will and Determinism" would be enough to show, if any demonstration were needed, that it must be extremely difficult. We are so habituated both to raising psychological questions about motivation whenever we trip over something that we take to be a deviation, and to assuming that what is in fact statistically abnormal is therefore sinister, that we almost inevitably assume mistakenly that any psychological, and especially perhaps any psychoanalytic, explanation must be of something that has somehow gone wrong. Neither reader nor writer is likely to pay sufficient heed to the caveat: "There are of course philosophical and rational grounds for believing in one or the other. . . ." We are more likely to remember only ". . . that even philosophers may be influenced by unconscious motives . . ." and to mistake this as necessarily discrediting (Jones, p. 186).

In fact, Jones takes for granted some rather depreciatory views on philosophical issues. These assumptions condition his formulations of psychological questions. Thus Jones (1924) writes as if it were obvious and beyond dispute that free will and determinism must be logically incompatible, that we are required to opt for one or the other. He also finds that "the ambivalence so often to be noted among those expressing opinions on the matter" requires psychological inquiry (p. 179). Jones regards "the incompatibility thesis" as a truism while in fact it is quite certainly controversial and, in the opinion of many, false.[3] It is a pity that he did not take more to heart his own autobiographical observation that in philosophy "the questions are mostly not well put; it takes great insight to put a question well or fruitfully. . . . The question of free will . . . is a striking example of this" (Jones, 1959, p. 61).

It is largely because of these unfortunate assumptions, and also because of his failure to state what the philosophical problems are supposed to be, that Jones's account of the overt sources of interest and concern is so unconvincing. He begins, as we have just seen, with two psychological questions. He does not misconstrue the word *psychological* to be a synonym for *psychoanalytic;* nor does he ignore overt interests and concerns in order to excavate unconscious forces. Yet, he does not adequately explain why there is concern about the supposed alternatives of free will and determinism and about the possibility or impossibility of a reconciliation between them. This strong interest seems incongruous in the light of his assertion that "the sociologist makes the curious observation that in practical daily life it does not seem to make any difference whether a given person, community, or religion adopts one or the other belief, in free will or determinism" (Jones, 1924, p. 180).

This alleged observation of the sociologist is one which ought not to pass unchallenged, for it cannot be assumed that the belief

[3] *Editors' Note:* Jones (1924) ventured the opinion that different philosophers have taken antithetical positions on the question of freedom and determinism but that, even in doing so, they made some type of logical accommodation with the opposing view. Jones cited Kant's doctrine of "critical reason" (expressing determinism) and "practical reason" (expressing voluntarism) as an example of a philosophical attempt to integrate the apparently antithetical positions. Jones then proceeded to provide a psychological explanation for the various beliefs from extreme determinism (fatalism) to extreme voluntarism. His own view was that psychoanalysis provides an essential part of the understanding which enables one to see "much better than he [Kant] had an opportunity of doing, a chance of reconciliation between the two in place of regarding them as an insoluble antinomy" (p. 187). However, Jones also thought that free will, from the point of view of scientific objectivity, was an illusion, even though a necessary one. This type of compatibility between causality and the freedom of the will is not acceptable to some philosophers.

in historical inevitability has had no social impact (Popper, 1963). But what is relevant for us is that the inadequacy of an explanation in terms of overt and conscious interests alone is used as an opening for implying unconscious motivation: "All this is very odd . . . we cannot detect any difference it makes to his life or conduct according as he adheres to one answer or to its very opposite. Surely this remarkable fact calls for much consideration" (Jones, 1924, p. 181). If and insofar as we have sufficient independent reason for saying that unconscious as well as conscious motives are engaged in these particular matters, well and fine. But if the alleged disparity between the degree of concern actually shown and the objects of that concern is to be interpreted as a reason for saying that, alternatively or additionally, the interest must have an unconscious origin, then we must first make sure that complete justice has been done to the possible overt sources.

4. Actual Philosophical Problems of Free Will

Let us now attempt to state briefly and with a minimum of assumptions what the philosophical problems of free will are. We can then reconsider the possible contribution of psychoanalysis to the two sorts of discussion distinguished in section 2. Briefly, the philosophical problems of free will and determinism consist of questions posed by the logical analysis of two ranges of concepts and expressions, focusing on the issue of whether the presuppositions and implications of the application of members of the one set are or are not compatible with those of the application of members of the other. The one range may be characterized as those used in the ascription of responsibility—e.g., "he acted of his own free will," "he had a choice," "he could have done otherwise." The other range comprises the key notions of classical scientific explanation—e.g., "the behavior was predictable," "it was causally determined," "it can be subsumed under universal laws of nature."

Typically, problems arise from an apparent conflict between the assumptions and implications of two sets of ideas both of which we have strong justifying reasons for applying. What we take to be our everyday knowledge of ourselves and others seems to show that it is often truly said that someone could have done differently. Yet according to the presuppositions and achievements of deterministic science, apparently nothing really ever could have been other than it was, is, or will be, and everything that occurs happens as the inevitable outcome of sufficient antecendent causes. One sort of answer to these philosophical questions urges that the apparent conflicts are indeed irreconcilable (the incompatibility thesis). Anyone who defends this position becomes thereby committed to discovering and stating what, of that which had appeared to be true, has to be rejected as false.

The opposite sort of answer, represented by Hume's "reconciling project," insists that the conflicts are only apparent (the compatibility thesis), and hence that it is possible to be with a clear logical conscience what Jones would call ambivalent (Hume, 1748).

One extremely important special case is that in which the second set of ideas takes a theological form and the presuppositions are those of theism. The supposed antinomy is then between free will and predestination rather than between free will and determinism. It is important even here to note that someone may reasonably maintain the compatibility thesis in general, but insist—as again Hume did—that this nevertheless leaves the theologians in intolerable difficulties (Hume, 1748). It is one thing, and that sufficiently disputatious, to urge that sometimes I could have done other than I did, notwithstanding that what I did was predictable by scientific methods. It is quite another thing to argue that we are the absolutely dependent creatures of an omnipotent God, who can justifiably call us to account—even subject us to eternal penalties—for actions which, as creator, he ensures that we perform (Flew, 1955). One has to realize that creation, in the theological sense, is a matter of constant ontological underpropping and not, as in the lay sense, a matter of making something and then possibly leaving it more or less to its own devices.

5. Conscious Concern and Unconscious Motivation

Once the nature of the philosophical problems of free will has been delineated, it is easy to see that these provide plenty of purchase for familiar and conscious interests and motives. Indeed, there seems to be no pressing need to look to the unconscious for psychological explanation, either of interest and concern or the lack of them. This is not to say no unconscious interests or motives are engaged or that, with particular persons, there is no need for some explanation in these terms. To say the former would be reckless, since we know that in human psychology overdetermination, even at the level of consciousness, is common and that people have desires, interests, and motives which, being overridden by others, are not implemented in action.

There is no pressing need to seek unconscious motivation because the interests engaged on both sides of the apparent antinomy are as powerful as they are obvious. As for the ambivalence which Jones points up, this is precisely what we should expect when dealing with a conflict both sides of which possess more or less compelling attractions. Finally, the alleged practical irrelevance of the issues at stake in philosophical debate is not sufficient reason for insisting that consciously manifested desires and interests cannot adequately explain the intensity of philosophical concerns, unless, with arbitrary philistinism, we take it as self-evident that no one could really care about such purely theoretical issues. Psychoanalysis may throw light on why philosophers and others have certain desires and interests. But such genetic discoveries cannot show that the phenomena thus explained do not really occur, or that they are really the same as their origins. On the contrary, the one relevant peculiarity of analysis is that a derivative interest may disappear if the patient comes to recognize its origin, e.g., he may cease to be interested in philosophy as a result of his analysis. However, that is scarcely sufficient for analysis to claim that he was never interested in the first place.

So much for the philosophical problems of free will and determinism in general. The special case of theology is slightly more complicated. It may be argued that the "incontrovertible lack of authentication" of religious ideas requires explanation in light of the fact that they "have exercised the strongest possible influence on mankind" (Freud, 1927, p. 29). But, this still does not justify the need for psychoanalytic explanation. It shows only that such explanation is required for the holding of theist ideas in general, but not that there is a special need to explain the interests and ambivalences of the theist theologian with regard to the problems of free will and predestination.

6. Some Common Mistakes about Free Will and Choice

Let us consider again Jones's (1920) conclusion that "A knowledge of unconscious motivation is indispensable, even for philosophical discussion of determinism." He was arguing that "the intense feeling of conviction that we have a perfectly free choice in the performance of many acts . . . only means that the person is not aware of any conscious motive." The relevance of psychoanalysis is that it is supposed to show that, "What is left free from the one side receives its motive from the other—from the unconscious—and so the psychical determinism is flawlessly carried through" (pp. 77-78). This passage is representative of so many in the classics of psychoanalysis that it is well worth examining more closely.

The first point to be made is that in the everyday, nontechnical sense to act of one's own free will is neither to act without desires nor to act unpredictably; it is to act without constraint. Certainly, it is often very difficult to decide what forms of pressure short of physical coercion ought to count as constraint, and to what degree. But if without any coercion and under no pressure I do exactly what I want it would be simply ludicrous to suggest that the fact that I wanted to do what I did was in and of itself sufficient to show that I was not acting freely. Nor would it be any less inept to urge that my predictable determination to vote for the most hopeful anti-Labor candidate, based upon my convinced hostility to socialism, shows lack of freedom. On the contrary, what surely would show lack of freedom would be if, whether predictably or not, I responded to some coercion or constraint by acting against my own wishes and convictions.

Free will in this sense needs to be distinguished from free will in the technical sense. In the latter case, free will presupposes the capacity to act in a way which is in principle unpredictable. Exercises of freedom in this special, philosophical, libertarian sense must be as such "uncaused causes"—causes with posterity but without ancestors. It is because he construes free will in this second way that Jones (1924) claims that psychoanalysis tends to show that no one ever acts of his own free will: "it is in a position to reveal the apparently unknown causes of our wishes" (p. 183).

At this point someone might very naturally object that, since Jones is writing about an aspect of the relations between philosophy and psychoanalysis, it is only to be expected that he will use a term like free will in the technical, philosophical rather than in the ordinary lay sense, and hence that to refer here to its everyday meaning is a piece of diversionary trifling. Yet, in truth, questions of culpability are decided on the basis of whether a person has acted "of his own free will," in the lay sense, or under some form of coercion or constraint. It is also in the lay sense of the term that we know that, from time to time, we act entirely of our own free will. It may be argued that no one can properly be called to account for anything which he did not do of his own free will, in the philosophical sense, but it is not permissible to take this highly controversial conclusion for granted simply on the basis of what everyone is prepared to concede about the relevance of free will, in the ordinary sense, to questions of inculpation and exculpation. Similarly, we must not assume that the reasons for saying that we know that people act of their own free will, in the lay sense, are decisive for the conclusion that they possess free will in the philosopher's sense. Since the expression, "of his own free will," interpreted in the lay sense, seems to carry no necessary implication of either predictability or unpredictability it appears that the second of the last two conclusions, if it is true at all, must be established in different ways.

Construing free will in the philosophical, libertarian sense—albeit without recognizing how greatly it differs from its everyday meaning—Jones (1953-1957) observes:

> . . . man's belief in free will seems to be stronger in proportion to the unimportance of the decision. Everyone is convinced that he is free to choose whether to stand or to sit at a given moment, to cross his right leg over his left or vice versa 'as he wishes.' With vital decisions, on the other hand, it is characteristic that he feels irresistibly impelled towards one and one only, and that he really has no choice in the matter nor desires to have any. Luther's famous 'Hier stehe ich. Ich kann nicht anders' . . . is a classical example [2: pp. 181-182].

It is indeed an excellent example, and nonetheless valuable for being—it seems—easily misunderstood. Certainly Luther's words were as truly spoken as they are magnificent. But they must not be taken to imply he was somehow paralyzed, literally unable to do other than he did. It is not as the victim of a paralysis that anyone admires Luther, but rather as the dedicated incarnation of the protestant conscience. The point is not that he could not have done otherwise had he so chosen, but that he discounted all available alternative options as totally unacceptable. Jones made the mistake of taking Luther at his word, quite literally.

Typically, when someone claims that he had no choice this is to be interpreted as meaning only that he had no tolerable alternative option, not that he had no other option at all. Even when we act under compulsion—in the ordinary, not the psychoanalytic sense of the term—we do have another choice: the very choice whose unacceptability we are claiming when we plead compulsion in the first place. Thus, taking Aristotle's (III [i]) illustration, I can just tell the bandit to fire away, but—and who will blame me or refuse to accept my excuse?—I prefer to open the safe meekly as directed. The point is underlined if we change the illustration and—modernizing Aristotle's example—suppose that the alternative is not just opening a safe for a bank-robber but assisting in the work of an Auschwitz. It then becomes far from clear that my death ought to be for me an intolerable option or that my plea of overwhelming compulsion deserves to be accepted.

Again, with choice as with free will, it is wrong to think that in the ordinary meaning of the word as opposed to some special sense, the presence of strong motivation, or predictability negates its existence. Jones (1924) writes: "With vital decisions, . . . it is characteristic that he feels irresistibly impelled towards one and one only, and that he really has no choice in the matter nor desires to have any" (p. 182). But that a particular choice is so easy to make that there is no attendant anguish of decision does not preclude the existence of alternative choices. Nor does the fact that everyone knew which choice I would make negate the fact that I made it.

A main reason why these rather pedestrian points do not seem obvious to Jones is that he confuses questions about the origins of our desires with questions about the existence of choice. The argument seems to be that if we have some strong desire which we did not choose to have, then this desire impels us, and we have no choice in what we do. Yet, although our desires may not be a matter of choice, this is no reason for suggesting that they must be considered as impulsions driving us to act.

Again, the fact that we want something, even that we want it very much indeed, does not show that we have no choice but to express our desire in action. Thus it may very well be that a man may find himself hard-put to explain why he fell in love with a particular woman. However, his inability to account for his infatuation does not make him any the less infatuated. Nor does it make the subject of the infatuation any the less himself, or the infatuation any the less his. If brought to task for his unfortunate selection of a love object, he might reply as Jones suggests: "I couldn't help it. I just had to." (However, if he said this in response to the exasperated question why he, an atheist, had to go and fall for a devout Roman Catholic he could, surely, very reasonably be told that under the circumstances it was asking for trouble to frequent Aquinas Society socials!)[4] Yet none of this affects the real crux that to have a desire does not necessarily guarantee its implementation. He may or may not, directly or indirectly, wholly or in part, have chosen to fall in love with her. However, his desire for her no more entails that he will take steps to win her than these steps, if taken, guarantee the success of his suit. What is being suggested is diametrically opposed to the truth, for, in fact, to say that he desires the woman is not to say that he has no choice but to pursue her, but rather to suggest that it is open to him to decide whether or not he will do anything about it at all.

7. Three Wider Morals

What has been said in the previous section is likely to distress both the psychologists and the philosophers, the former because it will seem too pat, and the latter because it will seem too crude and too peremptory. The answer to both sorts of objection is that the points being made are fundamental, and that only insofar as they are insisted on, however crudely, can we hope to form

[4] *Editors' note:* This might be compared with the case of a former alcoholic who knows that if he takes even one drink he will slip back into alcoholism. Prior to taking the drink he is "free" either to take it or not to take it; after the drink, he is no longer free not to go on. A person can choose a course of action which will deprive him of the power to choose.

a correct view of the philosophical implications of psychoanalysis. Thus Jones rightly insists upon the psychic determinism which is presupposed, and which also tends to be confirmed, by psychoanalysis. He assumes that it precludes any choice whatsoever. Yet we are now in a position to appreciate that, here again, we have what might seem to be an obvious assumption which is nevertheless the exact reverse of the truth.

As pointed up in section 1, to believe in psychic determinism is to believe that behavior is an expression of the motives, desires, wishes, purposes, intentions, and plans of the agent. But to say that an agent's action is so determined is not at all to imply that he could not help himself, that even if he had wanted to do something else he would have been unable to do it. On the contrary, it is to say, and to say only, that what he does is done because he wants this and intends that.

This is not only compatible with, but actually presupposes the possibility of his having done something else had he so chosen. For unless there were other things which he could have done had he so wished—unless he could at least have abstained from doing it—it would be redundant to state that his desires caused the action. What happened did not happen because he wanted or intended it to happen, but for some quite different reason. His desires and his plans had nothing crucial to do with it. If there were not in fact any such alternatives open to him, then the very most one could properly say would be that he acted.

But even this may be erroneous, for the practice of ascribing actions to people—indeed the very idea of agency—presupposes that for every action, there is an alternative action. Thus it would be wrong to say even that someone was the agent of an action if he had no other alternative, i.e., not just no tolerable alternative, but literally none. If it really is the case (incompatibility thesis) that universal causal determinism leaves no room for any such alternatives, then it would seem that psychoanalysis, far from being a natural ally of such determinism, must itself be threatened by it. On this assumption, psychic determinism and universal causal determinism stand not as species to genus but as mutual incompatibles.

In sum, the logical situation as regards psychic determinism seems to be this: (a) The whole enterprise of psychoanalysis presupposes psychic determinism. It is precisely and only insofar as this sort of determinism obtains that there can be room for psychoanalytic work, while the successes of that work constitute verifications of that presupposition. (b) Psychic determinism, far from being incompatible with teleological notions, is itself defined in terms of just such concepts. (c) These notions, particularly that of conscious desire,[5] are applicable only to agents who have a choice, who could do other than they do. (d) If this notion of having a choice involves the philosophical, libertarian concept of free will, then the psychic determinism presupposed by psychoanalysis must be logically incompatible with universal causal determinism. This must be so because universal causal determinism precludes any uncaused causes or any occurrences which are unpredictable, not just in practice but in principle, whereas the philosophical, libertarian notion of free will conceives of choice as an uncaused cause, a cause with descendents but without ancestors. (e) The conclusion on which the incompatibility thesis is based can be persuasively contested. The thesis has been rejected by a great many of the philosophers and philosophical theologians who have addressed themselves to the issues. If, as I myself believe, they have been right to reject it and to defend the opposite conclusion, the compatibility thesis, then it becomes possible consistently to hold—with Freud and Jones—both psychic determinism and universal causal determinism.

However, since Jones took the incompatibility thesis for granted, and since he was, as a psychoanalyst, also committed to psychic determinism, it would have been consistent for him to have regarded those who have tried to interpret developments in

[5] It is important to note that whatever may obtain with conscious desires, purposes, and so on is not applicable to their unconscious analogues.

particle physics indeterministically as allies against the common enemy of universal causal determinism. Instead—and, I think, fortunately—when it comes to dealing with the suggestions of Sir Arthur Eddington and Sir James Jeans, he remembers his philosophical materialism, his commitment to universal causal determinism, and his consequent rejection of any philosophical, libertarian notion of free will. Thus Jones (1924) notes how:

> . . . recently some arguments derived from atomic physics have given a fresh turn to this ancient controversy and have illustrated once again how in the endeavor to sustain belief in the objectivity of free will support is sought in every possible direction. Starting from Planck's quantum theory and Heisenberg's uncertainty principle some physicists, notably Sir Arthur Eddington and in more ambiguous ways Sir James Jeans, hold that determinism is absent on the atomic plane and apparently present on the macrocosmic one only because of the effect of statistical averages [pp. 187-188].

Jones (1924) quotes, with disapproval, Eddington's statement: "A complete determinism of the material universe cannot be divorced from determinism of the mind. . . . Conversely if we wish (*sic*) to emancipate mind we must to some extent emancipate the material world also" (p. 188).

Jones brings up two main points against this curiosity of our recent intellectual history. The first is that our present inability to discover determinants is not sufficient reason for postulating a universal objective indeterminism. In this he ranges himself with Einstein and other critics of the Copenhagen School, who refuse to concede that what no doubt is characteristic of one stage in the development of physics must be a permanent feature of the universe itself. The second, which alone is relevant here, is borrowed from Cassirer:

> To mistake the "choice" *(Auswahl)* which an electron has between different quantum orbits with a "choice" *(Wahl)* in the ethical sense of this word would signify becoming the victim of a purely linguistic equivocality. To speak of an ethical "choice" there must be not

> only different possibilities but also a conscious distinction between them and furthermore a conscious decision about them. To attribute such acts to an electron would be to relapse into a gross type of anthropomorphism [Jones, 1924, pp. 188-189].

What Cassirer says is, of course, correct, but it does not dispose of Eddington and Jeans so completely as Jones believes. If, like Eddington, Jeans, and Jones himself, you are thinking in terms of a philosophical, libertarian notion of free will, and if, like Eddington but unlike Jones you wish "to emancipate mind" by showing that there is such a thing as free will in this sense, then you presumably hope that the corollary of the existence of libertarian free will, which is the falsehood of universal causal determinism, also obtains. It therefore becomes entirely reasonable for you to seek, and happily to seize when found, whatever looks like evidence against universal causal determinism.

The evidence of particle physics, if Copenhagen is correct, would be sufficient to refute that sort of determinism as a general proposition: one negative instance defeats any universal generalization. What it would not do would be to show that anyone possesses free will in the philosophical, libertarian sense, much less that—type-fallaciously—electrons are endowed with such an essentially personal characteristic. Eddington and Jeans probably felt no need to draw these conclusions as illegitimate corollaries. They would have had no wish to maintain the second because their religion committed them to assert, rather than to deny, a categorical distinction between things and persons. And they would probably not have wanted to try to derive the first conclusion in this particular way, because they no doubt thought to reach it more surely and more immediately by another route. Since they had good reasons for believing that we are all continually making choices, and doing one thing when we could have done another, they were no doubt as inclined as most men are to construe these reasons—in my view wrongly—as a proof that we have free will in the philosophical, libertarian sense. Eddington and Jeans may have made, and no doubt did make, several fundamental mistakes here. But they were not wrong in believing that the defender of libertarian free will has an interest in trying to show that universal causal determinism is false. For to show this would be part, although of course not the whole, of showing that this sort of free will is a real phenomenon.

As I have argued elsewhere (Flew, 1956), the extension of meaning required to permit us to speak of unconscious as well as conscious desires permits us to speak of behavior not presently under our conscious control as being nevertheless the expression of our (unconscious) motives.[6] Correspondingly, we may also speak by extension of obsessive actions—notwithstanding that these may be genuinely compulsive, in the sense that we cannot help performing them however much we may wish to, and hence notwithstanding that they are not in the strictest sense actions—i.e., things which we do.[7]

The emancipating moral can, and at this stage must, be put in an equally stylized and dogmatic way. Consider Freud's account (1915-1917) of the nature of a classical analytic cure: "for every symptom of every neurotic illness . . . analysis regularly shows that these symptoms are derivatives of unconscious processes but can, subject to a variety of favourable circumstance, be made conscious." He goes on to say: "Symptoms are never constructed from conscious processes; as soon as the unconscious processes concerned have become conscious, the symptom must disappear" (pp. 278-279). The crux for us is that as soon as the unconscious psychic determination becomes conscious, the symptomatic behavior which it determined comes under the patient's control. It is precisely for this reason—and because the patient presumably does not, now that he has become able to stop himself, want to go on performing as ordinary, non-

[6] See footnote 5.

[7] They are, in so far as they really are uncontrollable, no more things which we do than the uncontrollable degeneration of our tissues is something which we do.

compulsive, true actions what formerly were symptomatic, "compulsive actions"—that the symptoms vanish. For, presumably, no one would want to claim that, for instance, Freud's (1915-1917) patient, who used to suffer from uncontrollable urges to spill ink on the tablecloth and then to summon the servants to see (p. 262), became as the result of successful psychotherapy simply *unable* to repeat the performance.

What has been said here about psychic determinism must be limited to cases where the determinants are conscious. But, insofar as all unconscious desires are potentially conscious, insofar as all conscious psychic determination presupposes alternative actions and inasmuch as analysis is a process of bringing the unconscious into consciousness, we may conclude that the development of psychoanalytic therapy is essentially, distinctively, and characteristically emancipatory. The true philosophical implication is not, as Jones thought, that we can now be shown that, even where we had previously believed we had a choice or that we acted of our own free will, we really did not. Rather it is that, in at least some cases, where we were certainly right in thinking that our behavior was not under our control, that behavior may, in the future, be subdued to our wills by analytic therapy. This paper, by disentangling some of the confusions behind the misconception that any advance by psychoanalysis must necessarily involve a contraction of the area of possible choice, provides a further gloss to that great dark slogan of enlightenment: "Where Id was, Ego shall be!"

REFERENCES

Aristotle, *Nichomachean Ethics.*

Berg, C. (1946), *Deep Analysis.* London: Allen and Unwin.

Edwards, J. (1754), *The Freedom of the Will,* ed. P. Ramsey. New Haven: Yale University Press, 1957.

Flew, A. G. N. (1954), Crime or Disease. *Brit. J. Sociol.,* 5:49-62.

——— (1955), Divine Omnipotence and Human Freedom. In: *New Essays in Philosophical Theology,* ed. A. Flew and A. C. MacIntyre. London: S.C.M. Press, pp. 144-169.

——— (1956) Motives and the Unconscious. *Minnesota Studies in the Philosophy of Science,* 1, ed. H. Feigl and M. Scriven. Minneapolis: Minnesota University Press, pp. 155-173.

——— (1959), Determinism and Rational Behaviour. *Mind,* 68:377-382.

——— (1964), *Body, Mind and Death.* New York: Collier-MacMillan.

——— (1965), A Rational Animal. *Brain and Mind,* ed. J. R. Smythies. London: Routledge and Kegan Paul, pp. 111-131.

——— (1966), *God and Philosophy.* London: Hutchinson.

Flugel, J. C. (1934), *Men and Their Motives.* New York: International Universities Press, 1947.

Freud, S. (1915-1917), *Introductory Lectures on Psycho-Analysis. Standard Edition,* 15 & 16. London: Hogarth Press, 1963.

——— (1927), The Future of an Illusion. *Standard Edition,* 21:5-56. London: Hogarth Press, 1961.

Hume, D. (1748), *An Inquiry Concerning Human Understanding,* ed. E. W. Hendel. New York: Liberal Arts Press, 1955.

Jones, E. (1920), *Papers on Psychoanalysis.* London: Bailliere, Tindall and Cox, 1950.

——— (1924), Free Will and Determinism. *Essays in Applied Psychoanalysis,* 2:178-189. New York: International Universities Press, 1951.

——— (1953-1957), *The Life and Work of Sigmund Freud,* 3 vols. New York: Basic Books.

——— (1956), B.B.C. Broadcast. *The Listener,* p. 589.

——— (1959), *Free Associations.* London: Hogarth Press.

MacIntyre, A. C. (1957), Determinism. *Mind,* 66:28-41.

Miles, T. R. (1966), *Eliminating the Unconscious.* London: Pergamon.

Popper, K. R. (1945), *The Open Society and its Enemies.* London: Routledge and Kegan Paul.

——— (1963), The Nature of Philosophical Problems and their Roots in Science. *Conjectures and Refutations.* London: Routledge and Kegan Paul, pp. 66-96.

Ryle, G. (1949), *The Concept of Mind.* London: Hutchinson.

ON BEING AND DREAMING

CHARLES HANLY, PH.D.

Locke's "historical, plain method" for investigating the human understanding, which was an early and important step toward the formation of empiricism, can now be supplemented and improved in a significant respect. Locke's method took into account only physical disturbances of the exact representation of things in perceptions, images, and thoughts. Locke appears to have assumed that the human mind *per se* instinctively credits only those ideas that can be observationally confirmed. But this assumption does not account for the credence given to metaphysical systems which contain ideas that cannot be observationally corroborated and which are valued precisely because they do not replicate natural entities in any way. Despite these epistemological defects, metaphysical ideas have been claimed to provide answers for the ultimate questions about the origins and nature of man and the universe. Empiricism, when limited to Locke's point of view, cannot provide an understanding of philosophy itself, since it

Dr. Hanly has taught at University of Toronto since 1959. He is Associate Professor in the Department of Philosophy. He was President of the International Forum Foundation (1965-1967), and is currently President of the Canadian Peace Research and Education Association. Dr. Hanly is a member of the Academic Advisory Board of the Toronto Psychoanalytic Forum of the Humanities.

cannot account for the kind of claims on which much of philosophy is based. Neither can it account for the actual history of ideas through which civilization has evolved to the epoch when empiricism could arise.

The source of these limitations in empiricism was its failure to take the work of unconscious psychological factors into account. Locke, of course, was logically debarred from doing so because of his assumption that consciousness is a defining property of mental elements and activities. However, this assumption is not essential to empiricism. It was introduced by Locke as an *ad hoc* assumption in order to construct a further argument against innate ideas. When it is corrected in this respect, Locke's "historical, plain method" provides an indispensable orientation in philosophy. It simultaneously focuses our attention on the physical as well as the psychological origins of ideas. Empiricism, when modified in this way, becomes a co-operative investigation into the human understanding in which psychoanalysis and philosophical analysis have complementary tasks.

Recently, the verification theory of meaning has been put forward as the cornerstone of empiricism. However, in its original formulation and use, it contained an error similar to Locke's.[1] It was held that statements which are in principle verifiable are meaningful, whereas statements which do not have this logical property are nonsensical. However much one might welcome the verification theory of meaning as a weapon against such metaphysical statements as Hegel's *"Sein ist Nichtsein; Nichtsein ist Sein* [to be is not to be; not to be is to be]," it does not provide an adequate analysis of meaning for at least two reasons.

There are statements that are meaningful without being verifiable in principle. An example is Berkeley's hypothesis that physical bodies are really collections of sense impressions and are, therefore, mental entities. Berkeley set up his hypothesis in such a way that any observation must confirm it. Consequently,

[1] Ambrose (1966) has presented a detailed analysis of this error.

no observation can disconfirm it, which means that it is unverifiable. Nevertheless, Berkeley's hypothesis purports to describe a basic and unexpected fact about every *apparently* physical body in the universe, and anyone with a little imagination can form an accurate impression of what Berkeley is affirming and what he is denying. Even deliberate "nonsense" statements such as Lewis Carroll's " 'Twas brillig and the slithy toves/Did gyre and gimble in the wabe" are meaningful in that they guide us to sketch out in our imagination a surrealistic twilight-, watery world populated by slippery quasi-reptiles somewhat resembling seals. Vague and elusive meanings are still meanings. They are worthless as components of scientific statements. But from the fact that they are not scientifically significant, it does not follow that they are not meaningful in any respect. Neither does it follow that they cannot be made the object of an investigation which can result in an elucidation of the meaning of the vagueness—which elucidation need not be itself in the least vague. After all, we often say of a person that he is vague about something. What is sometimes meant in such contexts is that the vagueness is part of a strategy of avoidance by which the person keeps himself protectively in the dark about something.[2] However, cognitive avoidance does not occur *ex nihilo*. It has a motive. Connected with the motive, there is a constellation of associations which, when uncovered, will reveal its significance. Similarly, vague ideas which have elusive meanings—the stock-in-trade of metaphysics —may also take their origins from experiences and thoughts that are motivated to be vague and elusive. The error inherent in the typical use of the verification principle as a weapon against metaphysics is that it causes philosophers to fall short of understanding philosophy itself, insofar as philosophy is metaphysical.[3]

[2] In other situations, we may mean that vagueness represents simply the absence of perceptions and information concerning the subject at hand or of a well-formed plan of action. The alternatives are not exclusive of each other.

[3] This point was first made and elaborated upon by Lazerowitz (1955, pp. 49-51).

The verification principle assumes that meaning is uniquely a property of language. Prior to the word there is no meaning. But this assumption overlooks the prelinguistic meanings that invest the individual's field of experience and which, as we shall see, determine, in a general way, the significance of language itself. Before the human infant develops the physical capacity to use language, he is able to participate in a situation that is invested with meaning. Reference, which is an essential function of language, is intrinsic to significance. And reference occurs prelinguistically in the infant's symbolic use of parts of his own body or external objects to bring the gratification of his sucking instinct within his own reach. So long as there is a modicum of unity in the infant's experience, this substitutive activity will refer beyond itself to the greater satisfaction of the breast. These elementary symbolic experiences may well prepare the way for the incorporation of sounds as substitutes for things and the acquisition of the use of words to refer beyond themselves to things.

However, the artificial nature of linguistic entities is not a self-evident fact to human consciousness; it is a gradual discovery. As Piaget (1929) has shown, the childish attitude to words preserves the elementary symbolic situation of the infant (pp. 81-84). Children inhabit a world in which words repeat in themselves the nature of the objects to which they refer. A small girl can be threatened and enraged by an adult who, pretending not to know her name, teases her by calling her boys' names. The reason for this is that to the small child her name is not only descriptive of her feminine nature, but it contains, as vocalized by her parents and other adults, the magical substance of her nature. Her name is the ground of her being. To apply a wrong name to a child is to communicate to her that she is not what she believes herself to be. Hence, there is a prelinguistic significance that establishes the significance language itself will have. It is only later that the world comes to acquire its intrinsic physical and mechanical aspect within the field of experience and words are "cleansed" of their magical efficacy.

Psychoanalysis has shown that this transformation of the field of experience, with its reduction of the world and language to reality, is made possible psychologically by the repression of the childhood conflicts which sustain the "animated world." However, the repression preserves intact the experiences and beliefs of childhood as memories, thoughts, and impulses that cannot be integrated by association or logical connection with ongoing perceptions either consciously or preconsciously. Nevertheless, and for this very reason, the "world" and "language" of childhood remain as latent, unconscious presences marking the origins of the mentality of the adult. The degree of influence that these early memories have on adult emotions, attitudes, moods, perceptions, imaginings, thoughts, and actions varies according to individual and circumstance. At the very least, there is always dormantly present in our mentality the primitive belief in the sacred power of words. Thus the domain of the meaningful is wider than language. The error inherent in Locke's "historical, plain method" has been repeated by the positivistic use of the verification principle. The verification principle is a good criterion for scientifically significant statements, but it is not an adequate theory of meaning. Metaphysics needs to be understood rather than legislated out of the domain of the meaningful by arbitrary *fiat*.

Would it then be appropriate to classify metaphysics with poetry? Does metaphysics adumbrate a more fundamental universe transcending the natural world, while differing from it, just as Carroll's "nonsense" verse sketches out for us a world of imagination that refers back to the world we perceive, but also acquires a structure and furniture of its own by taking nature as a point of departure for a new creation? The comparison cannot be pressed. Metaphysics claims scientific truth. Poetry, however, is, for the most part, explicitly narrative, lyrical, fanciful, expressive, or mythological. Its express domain is the intuitive, the emotional, and the imaginative: the psychologically significant. By contrast, metaphysics is logical, suppositional, discursive, and descriptive. It claims to provide true statements about a nonphysical reality that lies hidden beyond the range of normal awareness in the way in which atoms and the curvature of space are imperceptible to normal observation. Metaphysics is supposed to reveal the hidden nature of being. If the verification principle has done nothing else, it has rendered such claims on behalf of metaphysics permanently suspect by clarifying the logical difference between metaphysical speculation about being and scientific descriptions of space and atoms. Perhaps metaphysical theories are formed of hybrid propositions combining the logical syntax of scientific statements (without their verifiability) and the anthropomorphic meanings of poetry. This, in any case, is the point of view of this paper.

But one further provision must be introduced. Even though metaphysical theories cannot be *experimentally* verified, metaphysicians have claimed *experiential* verification for their ideas. The idea that the metaphysician enjoys some kind of special experience that has been given to him while remaining unavailable to others, except when they fall under the influence of his words and arguments,[4] is as old as Plato's *Symposium*. By implication the experience in question is supposed to be epistemologically unique in that it can, by itself, justify a sweeping critique of the evidence of the senses. Intrinsic to it is an intuition of a "hidden" dimension of reality that eludes scientific experimentation and understanding. This intuition is psychologically embedded in an attitude of reverential certainty. The metaphysician works out the intellectual residue of the experience into a philosophical theory about what exists, its nature and structure.

In the *Symposium* Plato described a mental process leading to metaphysical intuition. It began with the transference of homosexual desire for the persons of young men to their souls, to

[4] These notions are also contained in the *Phaedrus* and *Epistle VII*, 341, C.

civil law (the source of beauty in human souls), culminating finally in the detachment of the affect from any specific natural object. This detachment of "eros" from nature, it was claimed, would generate an oceanic experience of Beauty. The intellectual residue of the experience is the metaphysical axiom: there exists an eternal form of Beauty that far surpasses in perfection the natural beauty of physical objects which derive their inferior quality of beauty from the eternal archetype.[5] Thus Plato's philosophical theory of forms and the theory of knowledge he built around it were germinally present in the experience itself. The mind of the metaphysician is converted to a new way of thought by the experience. The metaphysician becomes intellectually certain about what is unapparent, and uncertain about what is evident to natural observation. It is of importance to philosophy to be able to understand and evaluate the nature and quality of the "metaphysical experience"—something that empiricism and positivism have failed for the most part to do.

An interesting test case for our hypothesis in the philosophical literature is Parmenides' philosophical poem. It contains one of the first abstract, deductive arguments in Greek philosophy as well as a poetic fantasy in its proem. Parmenides' poem is divided into three parts. The Proem is a fanciful account of a chariot trip taken by the philosopher as a youth. The chariot is drawn by sapient mares and is guided by sun maidens up to the seat of a goddess who reveals to him his true identity, vindicates his life mission, and gives him the name of Reality, "Being." The Way of Truth is an abstract argument to demonstrate the existence and nature of Being. The Way of Opinion is an account of the world as a system of illusory appearances which generate inconsistent beliefs concerning its nature and dynamics in the minds of a deceived mankind.

It is a remarkable fact that, despite the centuries of study of this work, its cognitive origins remain almost as much a mystery

[5] The continuing influence of this experience on Plato's perceptions is evidenced in the *Phaedo,* 75, B.

as they must have been to Parmenides himself. The reason for this state of affairs derives from the tendency to base interpretive studies of Parmenides' thought exclusively on Lockean (or Cartesian) premises concerning the functioning of human reason. Consequently, the metaphysical theory of being and the argument by means of which it is analytically constructed are abstracted from the life and times of the philosopher who created them. From a textual point of view, the Proem has been segregated off from the Way of Truth as something extrinsic to its comprehension (Owens, 1959, pp. 58-59). Those who have taken it more seriously, such as Jaeger (1947), Kirk and Raven (1962), view it as a religious experience symbolically expressed. But we are not told what the origin and nature of the religious experience was. Kirk and Raven reduce its purpose to a rhetorical device against potential Pythagorean critics. Cornford (1912), who has attempted a further explanation, refers the Proem to the Orphic version of a collective religious experience (p. 214). But Parmenides was an original metaphysical genius who set Greek philosophy off along a new path. Therefore, a correct explanation must take his individuality into account. Furthermore, religious meanings arise first within the individual's experience and only later interact with the cultural residue of ancestral experience imbedded in custom and tradition. It is unlikely that Parmenides was *simply* the passive recipient of the religious ideas of others.

We are alerted to a significant relationship between the Proem and the Way of Truth by Parmenides himself, since the deductive argument of the Way of Truth is put into the mouth of the goddess who appears in the Proem. What we need first of all to consider, then, is the nature of the experience in the life of the philosopher from which the Proem derived. The hypothesis to be considered is that the Proem originated in an oracular dream.

The evidence of the occurrence of dreams that have a manifest content which is spontaneously interpreted by the dreamer after waking as having a philosophical significance is presumably not great. Dreams that are interpreted as revealing the fate of the individual are perhaps more common. For example, a young woman who dreamed that she saw herself as a middle-aged woman lying dead in a coffin spontaneously formed the belief upon awaking that the dream revealed the time of her death. Subsequently, she developed severe hysterical symptoms. Essential to her intellectual understanding of her dream was the substitution of ontology for psychology. Her interpretation, having bypassed the associations from which the dream actually derived, referred the dream to the work of a divine power that, for some unknown reason, had sealed her fate. Her interpretation may be considered as part of the dream itself, since it is defensive secondary elaboration. Consequently, the dream in this extended sense, which includes its secondary elaboration, comes to acquire an ontological significance and contributes to the definition of the individual's "world" and "destiny."

Another example is yet more pertinent. A mathematics teacher once recounted a dream from his boyhood (latency period). He dreamed that he was walking through a beautiful pastoral world. A radiance suffused everything as though from a vast sphere like a sun. The thought occurred to him that his life and the world were the dream of a divine dreamer. The manner in which the dream was reported indicated some temptation to believe that it disclosed something about the hidden nature, structure, and dynamics of reality despite the dreamer's waking, adult, rational recognition of the validity of a common sense which had been reinforced by his scientific training and work. Indeed, his dream did contain a "vision" of the nature of being. The metaphysical premises suggested by the manifest dream are these: "to be is to be dreamed" and "to be is to dream." An obvious substitution of "perceived" for "dreamed" and "perceive" for "dream" yields Berkeley's metaphysical equation for being. The premise shared alike by the dream and the metaphysics is that substance is uniquely a mental activity while natural bodies are the mental entities that are conjured up by its activity. They differ only in that the latter substitutes perceiving for dreaming (waking for sleeping) as the essence of the activity in question. Thus, in modern times, dreams occur whose manifest content suggests a religious or philosophical idea to waking thoughts. Therefore, the hypothesis is not *prima facie* absurd.[6]

However, this dream did not convert the dreamer to philosophy out of the conviction that he had been vouchsafed a unique insight into the nature of things. Despite the absence of the interpretation of the dream through the recovery of the unconscious associations, the dream represented little more than a mild intellectual temptation to philosophize. The thoughts generated out of the conscious manifest dream had been tested against reality either via perception or learning and rejected as unjustified speculation. But had the following four conditions obtained for the person in question, it is probable that the dream would have been differently incorporated into waking thought. These conditions are (1) the overestimation of the epistemic worth of visionary and, in particular, dream experiences in the culture; (2) the absence of scientific knowledge and education in the culture; (3) a diminution of the efficacy of the senses in reality testing; (4) an increase in the amount of affect bound to the unconscious associations at the roots of the dream. Of these conditions, the first pair are social and the second are individual. Parmenides differed from our modern dreamer in that, in his case, all four conditions obtained as the following considerations will show.

There existed in Parmenides' day a vigorous belief in the occurrence of veridical dreams. Dodds (1951) has pointed out that this belief was sufficiently widespread that it could take the form of a cultural pattern (pp. 102-134). The pattern was made possible by the occurrence of dreams which had a similar manifest content in many individuals. This fact has not been ex-

[6] Jung, of course, took this fact at its face value and erected on it his theory of dreams. Jung (1938) was right in saying that "often dreams, visions, even hallucinations, were mixed with the great philosophic opus" (p. 69), but he repeated the error of the philosophers in question in his own theory.

plained, but for the fact itself there is ample evidence. The ancient Greeks had made a differentiation between significant and nonsignificant dreams. Significant dreams[7] were further classified into the visionary or preenactment dream (replicated in the experience of the modern-day mathematics teacher, cited above) and the oracular dream "when in sleep the dreamer's parent, or some other respected or impressive personage, perhaps a priest or even a god, reveals without symbolism what will or will not happen, or should or should not be done" (Dodds, 1951, p. 109). The suggestion that Parmenides' Proem originated in an oracular dream is based on the striking similarity between the content of the Proem and the description of the crucial element in this type of dream. Certainly, if Parmenides had experienced such a dream, its epistemic authenticity and importance would have been vouchsafed by the organized beliefs of his own culture. Far from being motivated to treat it with skepticism by his scientific environment, he would have been encouraged to accept its manifest content as a veridical intuition.

This assumption is made yet more plausible by the fact that Socrates, who has come to epitomize the rational, critical capacities of the Greek mind and who was found guilty of impiety by an Athenian tribunal, nevertheless claimed that his critical investigation of his contemporaries' pretensions to knowledge had been motivated by a religious oracle.[8] Furthermore, Plato reports that Socrates received the indications of his mission in life through a repeated dream experience of the oracular type under discussion. In the *Phaedo,* Plato reports Socrates as having made the following statement:

> Often in the course of my life the same dream-figure has visited me, differing in its visible form but always saying the same words, "Socrates be diligent and make music." In the past I had supposed that

[7] This classification was known to Freud and discussed by him in *The Interpretation of Dreams* (Freud, 1900).

[8] An account of this episode in the life of Socrates is given by Plato in the *Apology,* 190, 22E.

> it was urging and encouraging me to go on with what I was doing . . . the highest music was philosophy. But now that my trial was over . . . it occurred to me that possibly the injunction of the dream might be to compose music in the commonly accepted sense . . . it was safer, I felt, not to depart until I had fulfilled my sacred obligation by composing what the dream enjoined [*Phaedo,* 60E].

It is plausible to suppose that Socrates' confidence in the religious oracle and his obedience to the dream oracle are interpersonal and intrapersonal expressions of one and the same unconscious process issuing in the conscious admonition to "hearken to the fateful voice." Parmenides was not a skeptic.

Yet another converging consideration should not be overlooked. Although the ancient study of dreams reveals the Greek genius for classification, the classification itself was premised upon the assumption that the manifest contents of dreams contain their meaning. Thematically disordered dreams (the nonsignificant dreams of the classification) were treated in a manner consistent with this basic error. They were referred to organic causes. Thematically coherent dreams (the significant dreams of the classification) were prized as being sources of prophesy and wisdom. Psychoanalysis has shown that dreams with a thematically coherent manifest content have been subjected to greater amounts of distortion in their formation than their incoherent counterparts. Their superficial meaningfulness provides protection against the discovery of their unconscious meaning (Freud, 1900, 1915-1917). The Greek genius for classification went awry given the absence of any perceptions of the psychodynamics of dream formation.[9] The error inherent in the classification made possible the synthesis of the dream theory with a demonic ontology through which Greek mentality could retain a cognitively distorted relationship to its own unconscious origins.[10]

[9] This fact reinforces Brenner's observation in his contribution to this volume concerning Freud's discovery of a new method for observing mental processes.

[10] A repetition of this intellectual orientation and formation is to be found in the case of the young woman cited above.

It might be argued against this thesis, which assigns a decisive influence to irrational factors that the Pythagoreans, with whose work Parmenides must have been familiar, had made major advances in mathematics, geometry, and harmonics and that, furthermore, Parmenides himself contributed to the development of logic and analysis. But mathematics and logic are not by themselves sufficient conditions for an adequate grasp of reality, as is demonstrated by the fact that the Pythagoreans confused numbers with substances. The Greek mind had a philosophically fatal tendency to treat new categorical and conceptual inventions as though they were themselves conatural with and even superior to the entities they were designed to comprehend. Plato, for example, having discovered the classifiability of human types, actions, natural objects, common properties, and artifacts, treated the generic names of classes as though they had an existence more substantial than the natural entities they classified.[11] In general, traditional philosophical scholarship has exaggerated the scientific nature of pre-Socratic thought either by projecting much later scientific ideas back into their works in complete disregard of their ancient idiom, or by legitimately finding similarities with nineteenth-century German idealism, the scientific and philosophical worth of which they already have over-estimated.[12] The former error derives directly from the naïve adoption of Locke's epistemology. An example of this tendency is the interpretation of Empedocles' fragments on animal creation which finds in them the elementary insights of the theory of evolution, although, as Simpson (1949) has shown, they are of a type with primitive creation myths (p. 124). Despite some starts along the road toward scientific thinking, there was among the Greeks little well-established scientific knowledge to nourish and stabilize a

[11] Even Aristotle, who was aware of the tendency and criticized his predecessors for succumbing to it, repeated the mistake in his own system in his identification of class concepts with the physical organizing principles of natural species.

[12] Cornford (1912) and Dodds (1951) are notable exceptions. See also Woodbury (1958).

rational picture of reality that could help to secure the mind against intellectual submission to irrationally favoured beliefs.

However, the individual can always mobilize aggression against the traditions of his culture and go in search of something better than it offers. Furthermore, Greek culture was not monolithic. There already existed a skeptical reaction to the institutions of superstition and mysticism. Therefore, it is necessary to consider Parmenides himself in terms of the last two conditions enumerated above which pertain to the individual rather than his culture. The first item of biographical information appears to be disastrous to our thesis. Xenophanes[13] was a major contributor to the skeptical reaction; tradition has it that he was also Parmenides' teacher (Kirk and Raven, 1962, p. 268). However, Parmenides, according to Diogenes Laertius, "did not follow him [Xenophanes]." He adopted instead, as his philosophical mentor, an obscure Pythagorean, Ameinias, to whom Parmenides built a shrine when he died.[14] As Dodds (1951) has shown, Pythagoras and his school were much occupied with the occult. It is reasonable to suppose, therefore, that Parmenides was motivated to absent himself from the influence of Xenophanes and be "converted to the contemplative life" by a Pythagorean precisely in order to acquire external confirmation for his own inner conviction of his chosenness for "the philosophical life." Better for this purpose the obscure Pythagorean who would sanction the sources of his inspiration without demanding doctrinal acquiescence than the imposing, skeptical intelligence of Xenophanes—especially if a goddess in a dream has told him that he is not one of the monstrous "two-headed" mortals and has vouchsafed to him the *word* that is the truth and the way of truth: the contemplative philosopher's talisman.

There is also crucial internal evidence for the third condition in Parmenides' philosophy. An essential element in Parmenides'

[13] For an account of Xenophanes' role, see Dodds (1951, p. 118).

[14] "It was by Ameinias rather than Xenophanes that he was converted to the contemplative life . . ." (Kirk and Raven, 1963, p. 264).

philosophy is the notion that anything that is real is motionless. This idea entails that nature, which is always changing, is an illusion. The senses, therefore, deceive mankind into taking an illusion for a reality. There is, of course, an element of truth in Parmenides' evaluation of the functioning of the senses during that epoch. Levy-Bruhl (1910) and Freud (1901) have pointed to the overwhelming role of projection in ancient man's experience of nature. It is obvious that projection impairs the individual's sense of reality and his ability to carry out reality testing. But it was not the dawning awareness of this fact that caused Parmenides to claim that the senses are cognitively disfunctional; it was, instead, the inability of the senses to deliver up to the mind the vision of a unitary, motionless, uniform, bounded and identical being that moved him to reject their communications as deceptions. Therefore, Parmenides' conception of the function of the senses was only accidentally insightful; the operative force of his philosophy was to provide a rationalization for not cultivating the senses—a rationalization that Plato eventually elaborated into a theory of knowledge. Parmenides' attitude to the senses must be construed as a derogation of reality testing in the interests of a subjectively generated vision.

The fourth condition must have been present as well because it is dynamically related to the third condition. Although projection was often a major determinant of ancient man's perceptions,[15] it is probable that the principal defense at work in the formation of Parmenides' disparaging attitude toward the senses was denial. Everything in nature seemed to have reminded Parmenides of something that he profoundly feared expressed in nature's differentiation, indefinite extension, and motion. In any case, as Brenner (1957) has pointed out, denial and projection are equally incompatible with effective reality testing. The abandonment of reality testing is necessarily an abandonment to the

[15] An important psychic difference seems to be reflected in the epistemologies of Plato and Locke. In their respective analyses of perception, Plato attributed agency to the subject, whereas Locke attributed agency to the object.

influence of intuitions, visions and dreams. It places the intellect and its logical capacities in the service of the unconscious which means, among other things, a commitment to the identification of wanting with being, words with their objects, and a conviction of timelessness.

The hypothesis that Parmenides' metaphysics of being had its origin in an oracular dream coheres well with a new understanding of Parmenides' philosophy advanced by Woodbury. According to Woodbury (1958) "Parmenides' holy mystery is the reality of a name" (p. 157). In essence, what the goddess told Parmenides was that the name of the world is being. Although trivial to us because of our more realistic grasp of the nature of language, such a "discovery" was by no means trivial to a prescientific Greek.[16] Given the magical identification of the name and the named, to have the name of the Real is to be placed in the position of being able to enter into an ontological, moral, and cognitive identification with the Real; just as for the child to be properly named is to be himself, to be properly himself, and to know that he is himself. The goddess enjoined Parmenides to think and say of Reality only that "it is" and never that "it is and is not." Reality is sheer static positivity and identity. To think or speak of Reality otherwise is to fall into intellectual and moral error—the direct result of misnaming. Philosophically, the consequence of not having the true name of Reality is the construction of a cosmology based on antithetical or contrary words which Parmenides came to think was the basic error of Pythagoreanism.

Woodbury bases his argument, apart from his textual thesis, on the historical fact that words did not present themselves to the ancient mind simply as artifacts to be used in thinking and speaking to stand for things, but rather as idols infused with the force, nature, and destiny of the objects they symbolized. How-

[16] Cf. the biblical Jews' attitude to the word "Jahweh" or the contemporary fundamentalist Christian's refusal to allow his children to call him by the word "father" because it is the name of God.

ever, the picture is complicated by the fact that the belief in true naming must be accompanied by the capacity to recognize occurences of false naming. In the latter cases, a name would have *only* a referential function. It would have no truth in it. Its use would, in fact, tend to undergo a reduction to reality. Hence, intrinsic to the animistic experience of the significance of language is a potentiality for a development beyond it. Some Greeks must have already begun to treat the reduced and real significance of nouns (their referential function) as their only genuine cognitive function.[17] However, the primitive identification of words with things is unconsciously retained in the repressed memories and fantasies out of which dreams are formed. Therefore, even if Parmenides was familiar with the idea that nouns have only a referential and not a descriptive function, the dream origin of Parmenides' metaphysical doctrine would account for his philosophical retention of the traditional, sacred view of names. The hypothesis that the Proem originated with an oracular dream experience corroborates the Woodbury thesis and conversely.

The climactic event of the Proem is the speech by the goddess in which she welcomes Parmenides to her dwelling, assures him that it is justice and not "ill chance" that has guided him to her, and admonishes him to "hearken and carry her word away." The Way of Truth, in which Parmenides sets out his deductions of the properties of being, is represented as part of the goddess's address. Parmenides integrated the core of the original dream experience with the subsequent philosophical meditations arising out of it. In this way Parmenides correctly expressed the causal link between dream experience and philosophical argument and authentically directed our attention to the importance of the goddess.

The goddess is one of the more charming examples of the fallacy known as *argumentum ad verecundiam*. Her logical role

[17] In the *Cratylus,* Plato verbalized the distinction between the descriptive and denotative use of language and correctly rejected the notion that names could have a real descriptive function.

is to lend moral authority to Parmenides' premise: the real name of Reality is Being. Kirk's and Raven's (1962) statement that the Proem is merely a rhetorical device against Parmenides' Pythagorean opponents leaves entirely unexplained how the Proem acquired its moral authority. Parmenides must himself have credited the authority of his goddess. If our assumption is correct, the cultural pattern centered on the oracular dream would guarantee its influence with others. The fact that Parmenides thought that his deductive argument required the support of such authority speaks for itself.

The awesome presence of the goddess in the Proem has the nonverbal, implicit significance of the imperative, "all should speak and think as Parmenides." This moral function of the goddess can be linked, by means of one of Isakower's findings, to the verbal nature of her revelation. According to Isakower (1954), "speech elements in dreams are a direct contribution from the superego to the manifest content of the dream" (p. 3). His observations suggest further that "speech phenomena in dreams not infrequently have a portentous, awe-inspiring character and tone, particularly reminiscent of oracles or quotations, and thus suggesting a common origin" (p. 6). The portentous nature of the dream would be further enhanced by the incorporation into it of the speaker (in this case, a distorted maternal image) with the speech. This additional determination from the superego could be explained by a dangerous strengthening of id impulses against which special repressive measures have to be taken. In this respect oracular dreams must have been the extreme polar opposite of the dreams reported by Plato (*Republic,* 571), which were naïve wish fulfillments of oedipal strivings. Thus the derivation of the central image of the Proem from an oracular dream explains its peculiar ability to function as a privileged vision of Reality. The oracular dream could guarantee its own credibility. It was a key to the locked door of the future: the warrior's guide to heroism, the poet's inspiration, or the philosopher's way of truth.

It is not possible to establish this interpretation with more than some degree of plausibility. An obvious alternative is the idea that the Proem is *simply* a waking poetic fantasy. But once the word "simply" is removed, the alternative interpretation amounts to the same thing. The psychological processes whereby waking poetic fantasies and dreams are formed are not fundamentally different. The one factor that might otherwise differentiate them —the greater role of the ego in the formation of daydreams—is of no importance in this instance because of the peculiar contribution made by the superego to dreams of the oracular type. Hence, the interpretations of the Proem as a poetic elaboration of an oracular dream or as a powerful waking fantasy of oracular significance are psychologically equivalent. Therefore, given the fact that some uncertainty as to which specific interpretation is correct is irremedial, the hypothesis that the Proem represents an oracular dream has been preferred in this paper not only because of its plausibility, but also in the hope that it may act as a heuristic argument against the trivializing use of the word "simply" that too often qualifies the alternative classification.

Let us now turn from the oracular dream to the oracle herself. The representation of cunning in the guise of a woman was a common enough phenomenon in ancient Greek culture. Three examples follow. First, there is the image of Gaia (drawn by Hesiod in his *Theogony*) who contrived to have Kronos castrate his father Uranos. Homer attributed to Achilles a hallucinatory experience in which Athena appeared to counsel him against a physical attack on Agamemnon and to hold out to him as an inducement to abate his rage something better later on—an immortality of fame as a hero.[18] Plato claimed (*Symposium,* 201d-202c) that Socrates received his understanding of the nature of love from Diotima, a priestess. In each case, the plan and, scarcely less obviously, the motive for a fateful life decision were located in the mother or her substitute. From a moral point

[18] The passage is to be found in Bk. 1 of the *Iliad.*

of view, the life plan underwent some improvement. Gaia's exhortation to Kronos amounted to this: "Unless you want to live in obscurity forever, come to my aid, castrate your father and take his place." Athena counseled Achilles differently, "Despite your wish, do not kill the king, only attack his reputation with words. Forebearance will be compensated with fame." Diotima's formula for the birth of the philosopher was: "If you want to be remembered by your descendants only, then gratify the sexual instinct physically and beget children. If you want to be remembered by the descendants of your people, gratify the instinct mentally and create works of art. But if you want to re-establish the soul's affinity with the eternal, procreate ideas of the forms in the minds of noble, intelligent young men." What remains a constant in this changing pattern is the dominance of the incorporated maternal image. Parmenides and his goddess were by no means unique in ancient Greek civilization.[19] If we range the maternal images with respect to primitiveness and civility, it would appear reasonable to place Gaia at the primitive end of the spectrum followed by Hera with Parmenides' goddess as the antecedent to Diotima.[20] Plato's *Symposium,* therefore, provides a basis for a retrospective interpretation of Parmenides' Proem just as Parmenides' Proem refers back to the themes bound to

[19] Devereux (1963) has examined the conflict between matrilinear and patrilinear succession to political power in the evolution of ancient Greek political institutions. The patrilinear inheritance was a late development and at first involved a compromise solution in which, although "his abstract claim is based on the principle of patriliny; his method of seeking to gain his inheritance is, however, related to the ancient principle of kingship acquired with the help of, and in a manner agreeable to a goddess" (p. 209). Devereux also points out the mythological expression of the conflict in the quarrelling of Hera and Zeus as Hera (to render the psychological fact in its inversed projective form) refused to give over to Zeus the hegemony which "according to the ancient local pattern, mother-goddesses exercised over their boy-son lovers, who were designated by the term *paredros*" (p. 207). The Proem appears to establish Parmenides as a late manifestation of the matrilinear tradition. The fact that he was said "to have legislated for the citizens of Elea" is congruent with this assumption.

[20] It is obvious that Diotima does not yet represent the ideal mother who is able to guide her son toward the achievement of a personality that combines sexual maturity (heterosexuality) with work in science or the arts.

the more primitive maternal images that abounded in Greek culture of which two examples have been selected.

If the Proem shows the predominant influence of an idealized maternal figure in the formation of Parmenides' philosophical aspirations, what can be reconstructed concerning Parmenides' attitudes to the fathers of his world? The extant biographical data suggests that Xenophanes was Parmenides' first teacher but that he was converted to the "contemplative life" by an obscure Pythagorean, Ameinias. Kirk and Raven (1962) claim that "there seems to be no good ground for rejecting the scanty evidence we possess about the life of Parmenides" (p. 265). The reason for treating the evidence with skepticism is the tendency of the Hellenistic scholars, from whose writings the data are derived, to fabricate biographical and social counterparts for philosophical filiations. However, this argument would not tell against taking the biographical fragments seriously even if the historical tutelary relationship between Parmenides and Xenophanes were fabricated, for the fabrication might nevertheless point to an important psychological fact, that is, Parmenides' emotional adoption of Xenophanes as a philosophical mentor. That such an adoption as an emotional and relational underpinning for the submission to an effective intellectual influence is a reasonable assumption for the Hellenistic scholars to have made is verified by the importance of just such relationships in Platonic dialectic, as well as other ancient philosophical schools such as the Pythagoreans. Furthermore, such a basis for philosophic filiation is practically inevitable when logic, methods of demonstration, and experimentation are at a primitive stage of development. That this type of self-adoption occurs even with the acquisition of precise and impersonal methods of observation and reasoning is demonstrated by Harvey who, according to his biography, claimed to have found his discovery of the circulation of the blood in the works of Galen. Therefore, it is a safe assumption that the biographical fragments do record significant truths about Parmenides' intellectual development, if there is internal evidence in

Parmenides' philosophy of the influence of Xenophanes' thought. In fact, there are two premises, one ontological and one epistemological, that Parmenides must surely have derived from Xenophanes: that the Real is unitary; and that mankind is deceived by appearances. To be sure, Parmenides developed from these ideas further notions that are entirely his own, but the internal evidence, nevertheless, supports Kirk and Raven's estimation of the biographical evidence.

Parmenides then undertook a tutelage to Ameinias with whom he appears to have formed a highly ambivalent bond. The amount of veneration and fear that he felt toward Ameinias is measured by the shrine he built to him after his death. His contempt for Ameinias is expressed in the fact that he had his goddess classify Ameinias' Pythagoreanism in philosophy as "that way on which mortals wander, knowing nothing, two-headed" (Kirk and Raven, 1962, p. 271).[21] Furthermore, a highly competitive motive appears behind his instruction in Pythagorean "nescience." Parmenides' goddess informed him that "the whole ordering of these I tell thee as it seems likely, that so no thought of mortal men shall ever outstrip thee" (p. 279). So much the darling of his goddess was Parmenides that he had to be the master even of the Pythagorean dialectic of error: Parmenides could acquire Pythagorean philosophy if it could be used for the purpose of dialectically surpassing the "mortal men" who were its advocates.

The elementary pattern of development appears to have been, first, the adoption of two cardinal ideas from Xenophanes, followed by the reworking of these ideas, and culminating logically in the deductive analysis of the properties of being and, psychologically, in the masking of their real origin through their fusion with the goddess fantasy. This coincided with Parmenides' turning to Ameinias for confirmation of the dominance and authority of the goddess's oracle only to be followed by Parmenides' "lov-

[21] "Two-headedness" denotes Pythagorean use of antithetical categories to explain phenomena such as generation and death, motion in space.

ing destruction" of his consciously acknowledged masculine mentor Ameinias. A constant in the pattern is conflict with father surrogates and the reference of ideas assimilated from males to a central feminine superego image which then comes to be identified as their source.[22] Parmenides was enthroned in his metaphysical realm as was Oedipus in Thebes.

An examination of the theme of conflict in Greek culture and in Parmenides' philosophy substantiates this interpretation of the biographical fragments. Conflict had three types of significance for the Greek mind which can be conveniently classified as human, cosmological, and logical. The prototypical meaning of conflict as Cornford (1912) has shown was sexual.[23] An extreme form of patriarchal family structure in which the son remained a minor in every essential respect with duties to his father but no rights persisted down to the sixth century. This structure was a social symptom of conflicts between fathers and sons so powerful as to make their peaceful coexistence in a shared adult world inconceivable to them. Cosmologically, Greek thought explained the formation of the natural world out of elementary substances (the four elements, earth, air, fire and water) which were caused to interact by strife. Cornford (1912) has described the original representation from which the cosmologies made their departures as follows:

> The world began as an undifferentiated mass, without internal boundaries or limits. This mass separated into two parts, which were opposed or "contrary"—male and female. Finally, the male and female were united by Eros, the countraries were combined, and gave birth to individual existence—to Gods, or to things [p. 68].

[22] It has been pointed out that Descartes' philosophy underwent a similar evolution toward the misidentification of ideas he had acquired from others with ideas he believed to be innate to his own mind. It is also reported, as mentioned above, by Singer (1925) that Harvey, by a reverse process, attributed his own discovery of the circularity of the system of veins and arteries to Galen.

[23] Plato's *Republic,* especially the recommendations it contains for the censorship of literature and the regulation of society, provides a striking confirmation of Cornford's point of view.

These sexual identifications of the elements were made explicit by Empedocles.[24] In the more highly rationalized systems of Plato and Aristotle the same sexual connotation remains fixed to the cosmic contraries, Form and Matter. The logical connotation of conflict as a relation of contrarity between propositions (contrary propositions cannot both be true, but may both be false) was a relatively late development. As we have already seen from an examination of the biographical fragments, Parmenides' critique of Pythagoreanism had the psychological significance of an attack on the father. There is no evidence, however, from the fragments themselves that Parmenides' critique of Pythagoreanism was also based on the logical point that they adopted contrary postulates in their philosophical system. Had he done so, Parmenides would surely have been wrong, since the Pythagoreans did not assert the axioms "everything is male" and "everything is female." On the contrary, the Pythagoreans postulated that pairs of opposite principles (among which are male-female, light-dark) are elements of things. Such a dualistic system is not logically invalid *per se*. It is Parmenides' system that encounters difficulties with logical contrariety, since the Way of Truth and the Way of Seeming, when taken together, include the contrary statements "everything is a unified, single totality" and "everything is differentiated into discrete individuals." Parmenides' contributions to logic fell short of the discovery and use of the logical concept of contrariety.

There is evidence that Parmenides found the Pythagorean cosmology to be abhorrent because of the sexual connotation of its basic principles, ". . . in the midst of them is the goddess who steers all; for she it is that begins all the works of hateful birth and begetting, sending female to mix with male and male in turn with female (Parmenides, fragment 358). And Parmenides was not making the philosophically important objection that the

[24] "Here first the four roots of all things: shining Zeus, life-bringing Hera, Aidoneus and Nestis who with her tears fills the springs of mortal men with water" (Empedocles, fragment 417).

Pythagoreans had failed to differentiate biological from chemical categories. Parmenides did not deny the sexual and conflictual nature of cosmic dynamics. He claimed only that its status was that of an illusion in comparison with the absolute, fixed unity of Being. He was objecting to the work of the sexual instinct as such and its differentiation into male and female. Thus his rejection of Pythagorean animism was, like his critique of the cognitive value of the senses, only accidentally insightful. Parmenides had not yet grasped the physical nature of the universe —a cognitive flaw that can be found in every ancient cosmology with the sole exception of the Democritean-Epicurean system.

The question then arises as to the sexual nature of Being in Parmenides' thought. The world of illusion in which day is succeeded by night and in which summer must give way to winter is also the world in which males and females periodically unite to bring into existence beings that undergo growth, maturity, and death. The conflict between light and dark (that works the daily and seasonal alterations of light and dark) functions, according to the doctrine of the Way of Seeming, in co-operation with a sexual force differentiated into male and female to produce the phenomena of generation and death. Is Being, which stands to nature as reality to appearance, an asexual entity or is it an entity that has a special sexual nature in sharp contrast with the physical manifestations of sexuality in nature?

Parmenides left the idea of Being vague. He derived a series of ontological properties for it among which were unity, sameness, individuality, and stasis. It is uncreated and uncreating. He also conceived of it as finite and spherical. These last two properties were deduced from the special assumption that Being is bounded equally on all sides by necessity. This assumption merits some attention. Since Being is everything that is real, necessity must be internal to it. Parmenides goes on to explain that this "Strong Necessity" which causes Being to be finite results from the fact that Being lacks nothing (Parmenides, fragments 350, 351).

The predicates taken together fall short of establishing what Being is. Scholars have been left in something of a quandary. Burnet (1892) claimed that "there can be no real doubt that this [Being] is what we call body" and that Parmenides is asserting that "the universe is a *plenum*" (pp. 178-179). However, Kirk and Raven (1962) stated that "had he been asked whether his 'Being' was solid [or 'body'] his answer would have been a hesitant negative" (p. 270). Jaeger and Cornford have emphasized the religious nature of Parmenides' idea. Cornford (1912) took Parmenides' ultimate premises to be "God alone is" and "he is One. It is from the divinity of *physis* that his system is deduced" (p. 216).

Cornford is surely right in thus emphasizing the spiritual nature of Being. Any tangible body is so manifestly either in motion or movable, discrete, divisible, and multifaceted that it is most unlikely that Parmenides would also have said of the sum total of physical reality that it is immobile, uniformly fused, indivisible, and undifferentiated.[25] Furthermore, nature—the system of tangible bodies—was declared by Parmenides' goddess to be an illusion. This declaration implies that natural objects lack the ontological properties of Being which is inconsistent with Burnet's interpretation. Parmenides' own body must have been a constant reminder to him of his individuality, separateness, and difference from other things. Finally, other philosophers in the tradition—Plato, by implication, and Aristotle, explicitly—assigned to matter the ontological role of differentiating universal species (forms) into discrete collections of spatiotemporal, changing, individual entities. It is, therefore, unlikely that Parmenides would have found the Unitary Thing to be the sum total of matter in the universe. However, it is likely that he conceived of it as a mysterious spiritual entity which uniformly pervades the whole of nature and which coincided with his own

[25] Descartes, who did conceive of the universe as an extended plenum, also attributed divisibility, numerability, infinity, and motion to it.

inner identity. Waking experiences of fusion with a mysterious, unifying unity in nature have been described by romantic poets and writers. Being is nature in the guise of such a spiritual entity given in an ecstatic experience in which the normal differentiation between knowing subject and known object has been effaced. Once Being is understood in this way, the appropriateness of Parmenides' claim that the expression "it is" renders the significance of Being becomes obvious: Being obliterates the nature of the world and the self in a static, yet vital, neutralizing fusion of existence. The return from this "spiritual" union to the reality of the physical world would be experienced as a declension into perceptual and physical relationships with isolated and differentiated objects that make up an inferior, illusory, and derivative domain; hence, Parmenides' derogation of the senses. Plato's *Symposium* presents another example of a mystical experience, generated by the sublimation of the sexual instinct, providing the experiential ground for the formation of a metaphysical theory. Thus Cornford's error lies not in his theological interpretation of Being, but in his view that Being is masculine.

The two major hypotheses of this paper (1) that the Proem originated in an oracular dream and (2) that the doctrine of Being was a verbal and logical articulation of a mystical, pantheistic experience can be united in the proposition that the dream and mystical experiences must have been logically interdependent complementary elements in a total life pattern. Perhaps, then, a further specification of the nature of Being can be inferred from the symbolism of the Proem.

Three features of the Proem are particularly striking.[26] Every living thing included in it, the horses, sun maidens, Justice, and goddess, apart from its hero—the philosopher himself—are female. Certain motions are highlighted with vivid detailed descriptions. They are worth repeating. First, there is the description

[26] I am indebted to P. G. Thomson, M.D., with whom I discussed the symbolism of the Proem.

of the axle and wheels of the chariot. "And *the axle blazing in the socket—for it was urged round by well-turned wheels at each end*—was making the holes in the naves sing, while the daughters of the Sun, hasting to convey me into the light, threw back the veils from off their faces and left the abode of night." Second, there is the description of the action of the hinges of the great doors that lead beyond "the ways of Night and Day" to the goddess. "Then, *when the doors were thrown back,* they disclosed a wide opening, *when their brazen posts fitted with rivets and nails swung in turn on their hinges*" (italics added). Finally, in a more general way, the Proem describes a journey through space in defiance of the force of gravity ending with the hero's audience with goddess.[27]

What is needed is an interpretation that will make sense of three connected elements in Parmenides' Proem: first, the theme and imagery of the Proem; second, the notion of Being in the Way of Truth; and third, the repudiation of sexual differentiation as an illusion in the Way of Seeming.[28] Corelated with the dominance of female objects in the imagery of the Proem is the dominance of feminine properties in the definition of Being. Being is spherical and passive. At the same time Being possesses a quite peculiar power: it is perfect self-sufficiency; it lacks nothing; it needs no relationship; it need not reach outside itself either through perception or act; it is both finite and *causa sui.* The world of illusion, on the other hand, which is not created by Being but simply exists indefinitely as its illusory counterpart, is worked by a sexuality that is differentiated into male and female thus causing the existence of need and insufficiency and the necessity of events of union and separation.

An interpretation that integrates these elements is the follow-

[27] One is reminded of the symbolic organization of space and flying bodies in certain of the paintings of Chagal.

[28] It is of interest that Plato advanced the last thesis explicitly rather than symbolically in the *Republic* (V, 453-457). Plato was unable to grasp the fact of feminine and masculine psychic differentiation and identity.

ing: Being is a bisexual entity; the psychic original of the metaphysical idea is the repressed fantasy of the bisexual mother.[29] This hypothesis has a number of advantages. One obvious advantage is that it explains the highly eroticized quality of Parmenides' philosophical curiosity as expressed in the Proem. But there are others. It provides an additional clue to our understanding of Parmenides' dissatisfaction with Xenophanes and his preference for Ameinias. Xenophanes' deity was male. In contrast, the Pythagorean One, which was thought to be the ultimate source of the dualistic cosmic principles such as light-dark and male-female, provided a conception of ultimate reality that would have been congruent with such an unconscious fantasy. As Cornford observed (1912) "the Even and the Uneven they held to be, respectively, female and male; while the undivided monad, the One, was bisexed" (p. 70). In order to construct an intellectual cosmic representation of his fantasy, all that Parmenides had to do was deny a generative function to the Pythagorean One and reclassify its cosmological theory based on the table of opposite categories as a system of "empty" names with reference only to an illusory world.

There can be no doubt that the ancient Greeks correctly recognized the fateful nature of the sexual instinct. The philosophical way, as the *Symposium* amply demonstrates, dealt essentially with the problem of coping with it. Furthermore, Parmenides, like Empedocles, Plato, and Aristotle identified Being with knowing: "like knows like." Thus the bisexed woman has perfect knowledge of this fateful instinct and, consequently, of human destiny. Her conscious replica—the goddess or the priestess—becomes the oracle that communicates the secrets of life and the way of wisdom: the path that a creature who has

29 A mirror image of the fantasy of the self-sufficiency of the female is the belief in the self-sufficiency of the male as expressed by Plato in the *Symposium* and *Phaedrus* in his idea of philosophical dialogue between males as a procreative activity involving insemination, pregnancy, birth, and loving care of the progeny-philosophical ideas.

been separated off from Being should follow in order to be re-united to Being. Thus the cause of Parmenides' preference for Ameinias over Xenophanes, of the oracular dream and the mystical experiences that informed his notion of Being, and of his fearful hatred of the sexually differentiated, conflictual, natural world, was the unconscious fantasy of the bisexed mother from whom he wished never to separate. A later philosopher, Kierkegaard, wrote a book to which he gave the title *Purity of Heart is to Will One Thing*. Parmenides had purity of heart.

Finally, a paradoxical mood of aggressive self-protectiveness pervades Parmenides' fragments. Natural sexuality with its, to him, grotesque processes of begetting, bearing, and bringing forth is something hateful and to be avoided as unreal. Indeed, any change in nature, its colours, and its multifaceted objects is to be avoided. These are things that benumb and confuse the mind. Similarly, persons who are intrigued enough by them to seek to understand and explain them are "hordes devoid of judgement." There is a mood of aggressive exaltation involved in such a wholesale repudiation of the world and its investigators. At the same time there is an intense self-protective fearfulness in the refusal to yield the self to nature and its processes. Lazerowitz (1964) has pointed to this element in Parmenides' philosophizing in connection with Parmenides' denial of motion—a denial that is logically bound to his denial of empty space, "the fear of empty space when intellectualized in the form of a theory and displaced onto the phrase 'empty space' (or its equivalents) can be coped with more easily and with less pain than it can in its original form" (p. 180). Now, "empty space" or "void" had a quite special meaning for the ancient Greeks. It was "void" that separated the original union of Gaia and Uranos. And the cosmological notion of "void" was itself a disguised, intellectual representation of castration as Kirk and Raven (1962) have pointed out. Parmenides' Being is *emphatically,* and at any cost to logic or fact, the entity that cannot undergo the awful drama described in Hesiod's cosmogony.[30] The philosophical denial of empty space within Parmenides' system of ideas appears to be the intellectual correlate of a rigid psychological denial of the reality of guilt. In substance, Parmenides' metaphysics is no improvement on Hesiod's *Theogony*. Parmenides' constructive genius was logical. It was by giving his ideas the form of a deductive derivation which exhibited the logical interdependence of the properties he attributed to Being that Parmenides made his contribution to the advancement of philosophy.

So far we have been begging the question of the relationship between the psychological explanation of an idea and its truth value. Freud (1913) adopted the position that the question as to whether or not a religious idea serves as a wish fulfillment psychologically is logically distinct from and irrelevant to the question of its truth (p. 179). That they are logically distinct questions is obvious, but that they are always independent is not so obvious. It depends on the nature of the relationship of the conscious, intellectual representation to the unconscious fantasy with which it is psychologically associated. If the association is only *contingent,* then the fact of a causal relation between an unconscious fantasy and a conscious thought process would not affect our estimation of its truth value. This situation would obtain in the case of the latent metaphysical idealist-physicist who is influenced by unconscious fantasies to believe that every discovery of a new fact or law in physics is a progressive unfolding of the mental nature of the universe. The content of his conscious thoughts about physical systems would not, however, be influenced by the secondary personal significance they would have for him. If, on the other hand, the relationship is *constitutive* and the unconscious fantasy determines the content and use of the conscious ideas, the psychological explanation will disqualify

[30] Thus it was not simply logic but rather a logic dominated by fear of what might happen if mother nature were to become productive that caused Parmenides to repudiate Pythagoreanism and fail to see what Aristotle found to be obvious—that it is logically absurd to doubt the existence of nature.

truth claims on their behalf.[31] Evidence for a constitutive relation is the systematic repudiation of an empirical verification for the ideas in question.

The effect of the psychological explanation is to disqualify the substitute claim of a privileged experiential verification which is introduced as the special ground for the objectivity of the metaphysical idea in the absence of observational or experimental evidence. Thus a psychological explanation and interpretation is indicated for ideas that are both vague and protected from falsification by an epistemology that repudiates observational verification. Parmenides' notion of Being qualifies as an idea in the formation and use of which a nexus of unconscious fantasies, hopes, and fears have played a constitutive role.

Metaphysical significance and poetic significance are very similar. The difference is one of the mental faculty at work (imagination or intellect) and the syntax adopted for verbalization. The transition from the Proem to the Way of Truth is not one of substance, but one of form only. Metaphysics is visionary poetry in the logical syntax of mathematics and natural science.

REFERENCES

Ambrose, A. (1966), Metamorphoses of the Principle of Verifiability. In: *Current Philosophical Issues,* ed. F. C. Dommeyer. Springfield, Mass.: Charles C Thomas, pp. 54-79.

Brenner, C. (1957), *An Elementary Textbook of Psychoanalysis.* New York: International Universities Press.

Burnet, J. (1892), *Early Greek Philosophy.* New York: World Publishing Co., 1961.

Cornford, F. M. (1912), *From Religion to Philosophy.* New York: Harper, 1957.

Devereux, G. (1963), Sociopolitical Functions of the Oedipus Myth. *Psychoanal. Quart.* 32:205-214.

[31]The distinction between contingent and constitutive unconscious associations can be clarified by comparing the idea of the curvature of space in contemporary geometry and physics with the idea of the sphericity of Being in Parmenides' metaphysics.

Dodds, E. R. (1951), *The Greeks and the Irrational.* Berkeley: University of California Press.

Freud, S. (1900), The Interpretation of Dreams. *Standard Edition,* 4 & 5. London: Hogarth Press, 1953.

——— (1901), The Psychopathology of Everyday Life. *Standard Edition,* 6. London: Hogarth Press, 1960.

——— (1913), The Claims of Psycho-analysis to Scientific Interest. *Standard Edition,* 13:165-190. London: Hogarth Press, 1955.

——— (1915-1917), Introductory Lectures on Psycho-Analysis. *Standard Edition,* 15 & 16. London: Hogarth Press, 1963.

Isakower, O. (1954), Spoken Words in Dreams. *Psychoanal. Quart.,* 23:1-6.

Jaeger, W. (1947), *Theology of the Early Greek Philosophers.* Oxford: Oxford University Press.

Jung, C. G. (1938), *Psychology and Religion.* New Haven: Yale University Press.

Kirk, G. S. & Raven, J. E. (1962), *The Pre-Socratic Philosophers.* Cambridge: Cambridge University Press.

Lazerowitz, M. (1955), *The Structure of Metaphysics.* London: Routledge & Kegan Paul.

——— (1964), *Studies in Metaphilosophy.* London: Routledge & Kegan Paul.

Levy-Bruhl, L. (1910), *Primitive Mentality.* London: Allen & Unwin, 1923.

Owens, J. (1959), *A History of Ancient Western Philosophy.* New York: Appleton Century Crofts.

Piaget, J. (1929), *The Child's Conception of the World.* London: Routledge & Kegan Paul.

Simpson, G. G. (1949), *The Meaning of Evolution.* New Haven: Yale University Press.

Singer, C. (1925), *A Short History of Anatomy and Physiology from the Greeks to Harvey.* London: Paul, Trench & Truebner.

Woodbury, L. (1958), Parmenides on Names. *Harvard Stud. Classical Philol.* 63:145-160.

ON SOLIPSISM

William E. Kennick, Ph.D.

"The real reason why so few philosophical questions have received a definite answer in all the centuries they have been pondered on," Ernest Jones (1959) remarked in his autobiography, "and why there is such an astonishing contrast between the diversity of philosophical opinions and the widespread agreement in scientific work, is that the questions have more important subjective origins than has hitherto been discernible" (pp. 60-61). That philosophical problems and theories have unconscious determinants, and therefore areas of significance hidden from the philosophers themselves, is no longer subject to serious doubt. But Jones's "real reason" goes only part of the way in explaining the astonishing absence of assured, or even reasonably assured, results in philosophy. Philosophers clearly *appear* to be engaged in a kind of scientific work, one in which hypotheses are framed to explain phenomena of various kinds and in which evidence is adduced to support the hypotheses. And scientific work too may have "important subjective origins." An important part of the explanation of the contrast between philosophy and science,

Dr. Kennick is presently Professor of Philosophy at Amherst College. He has taught at Boston University and at Oberlin College, and has written articles for a variety of philosophical publications.

therefore, is to be arrived at only through the question of whether philosophy is indeed a kind of science and whether in reality, and not only in appearance, it is about the phenomena it purports to investigate. The following analysis of solipsism is a case study aimed at answering this question in part, and at showing how that answer, at least in this case, may connect with Jones's hypothesis of "subjective origins."

I

"Whoever wishes to become a philosopher," Russell (1912) said, "must learn not to be frightened by absurdities" (p. 20).[1] Among the apparent absurdities of philosophy, one of the most striking and interesting, and yet least studied, is solipsism. Derived from the Latin words *solus* and *ipse,* meaning "I myself alone," the name applies to several discriminable philosophical views. Price (1931) has recognized three distinct types of solipsism, and they may be identified with the following assertions: (1) "Nothing exists but myself and my present mental states"—sometimes referred to as solipsism of the present moment; (2) "nothing exists but myself and my mental states past and present"; (3) "nothing exists but myself, my mental states, and the material world, i.e., there are no minds other than my own." In addition to these, there is at least one other form of solipsism, what might be called the skeptical as opposed to the negative existential form, namely: (4) "I cannot know that anything exists other than (4a) myself and my present mental states, or (4b) myself and my mental states past and present, or (4c) myself, my mental states, and the material world."[2] Actually, as I

[1] Russell (1918) has also said, "The point of philosophy is to start with something so simple as not to seem worth stating, and to end with something so paradoxical that no one will believe it" (p. 193).

[2] Cf. Price (1931), "It was formerly supposed by almost all philosophers that a given human mind has strictly speaking no knowledge of other minds at all, but only beliefs about them" (p. 53) which, if true, would mean that formerly almost all philosophers were solipsists, whether they knew it or not.

shall try to show, the skeptical form of solipsism reduces to or entails one of the negative existential forms, which is why most, if not all, arguments for solipsism are epistemological in character; they establish the skeptical conclusion and move from that to one of the negative existential claims.

For the purposes of this paper I shall ignore the distinctions between Price's three types of solipsism and the special arguments that might be adduced for one of them as against the others. I shall restrict my discussion to the following two general claims: (a) "I cannot know that there are minds other than my own," and (b) "There are no minds other than my own." And these I shall take to imply, if not to be equivalent to, (a) "I cannot know that there are persons other than myself," and (b) "There are no persons other than myself."

II

One of the first curious but noteworthy features of solipsism is that it has been openly avowed by so few philosophers. This cannot be because it is more outrageous on the face of it than many things philosophers have not scrupled to avow. Philosophers have not hesitated to argue for the unreality of matter, of plurality, of motion, of space and time, and so on; but very few have admitted to being solipsists, and this despite the fact that solipsism can be shown to be a consequence of widely held philosophical views, particularly those of an idealistic or phenomenalistic bent. Foulquié (1962) describes solipsism as a "doctrine sans partisans, mais logiquement impliquée dans toute théorie idéaliste de la connaissance et de la réalité."[3] But if every idealistic theory of knowledge and of reality *logically implies* solipsism, then, since there have been many philosophical idealists, solipsism is not really "sans partisans" at all; it has many adherents. (They might be called cryptosolipsists to distinguish them

[3] Trans.: "A doctrine without partisans, but logically implied in every idealistic theory of knowledge and of reality."

from those few philosophers who have openly avowed the position.)

Broad (1925) observes:

> Many philosophers have *wanted* to deny the reality of material objects, and have felt that it was a feather in their caps when they succeeded in doing so to the satisfaction of themselves and their followers. But, seemingly, no one *wants* to be a solipsist; and scarcely anyone has admitted himself to be one. It has been left to rival philosophers to tell him that, on his principles, he ought to be one; and this has generally been regarded as a charge to be repelled and not as a compliment to be thankfully acknowledged [p. 317].

Broad goes on to say that he does not think that "this difference can be ascribed to the fact that the evidence for the existence of other minds is more cogent than the evidence for the existence of matter, or to the fact that we have a stronger instinctive belief in the former than in the latter." The "real explanation" lies, he thinks, in the fact that "certain strong emotions are bound up with the belief in other minds, and that no very strong emotions are bound up with the belief in matter." This may be so; but *what* strong emotions? All that Broad offers us is loneliness—the loneliness that comes from believing that I am the only person in the world. I shall suggest below (VI) why this will not do.

III

In the second of his *Meditations on First Philosophy* Descartes claimed that the propositions "I exist" and "I am a thinking or conscious being (*res cogitans*)" are and must be true every time I assert them either to myself or to someone else; in short, they are somehow necessary or *a priori* assertions. If I assert that I do not exist, what I assert *must* be false; and if I assert that I am not a thinking or conscious being (a mind, self, or person), that too *must* be false, for a thinking being simply is, among other things, one that asserts or denies. Whatever necessity may characterize such statements as "I exist" and "I am a thinking being," however, that same necessity does not characterize the claim that there are or exist *other* thinking beings. As Russell (1912) has put it, "No logical absurdity results from the hypothesis that the world consists of myself and my thoughts and feelings and sensations, and that everything else is mere fancy. . . . There is no logical impossibility in the supposition that the whole of life is a dream, in which we ourselves create all the objects that come before us" (p. 22). Russell rejects this "hypothesis" on the sole ground that it is "less simple" as a way of accounting for the facts of our life than the "common-sense hypothesis" that there really are objects and people independent of us; although that solipsism *is* "less simple" than the "common-sense hypothesis" is not obvious—one might have supposed just the opposite!—and Russell fails to make clear *how* it is, or even what "simplicity" has to do with the matter. In any case, not being an *a priori* true assertion, the assertion that there are other people in the world is either contingently true, contingently false, or necessarily false. Russell, at least at the time he wrote *The Problems of Philosophy,* apparently took it to be contingently true. But, as I shall try to show, *as the solipsist understands it,* the claim that there are other persons in the world is *necessarily false.*

Now the solipsist's claim—either "I cannot know that there are other persons in the world" or "There are no other persons in the world"—appears on the face of it to be blatantly false. After all, one is inclined to say, "can't he *see* that there are other people in the world?" The answer to this, I think, is: "Yes, of course he can, but he regards what he sees, or can see, as irrelevant to the issue; all that counts, or can count, is his argument. And this—that only argument counts, that observation is irrelevant—must affect the way in which we understand the solipsist's claim."

IV

Arguments for solipsism are numerous, at least as numerous as the well-known arguments for (subjective) idealism and for phenomenalism. Bradley (1893) gives us an epitome of the idealist argument for solipsism: "The argument in favor of solipsism, put most simply, is as follows: I cannot transcend experience, and experience must be *my* experience. From this it follows that nothing beyond my self exists; for what is experience is its [my self's] states" (p. 218). Hence, as Schopenhauer (1818) expressed it, "The world is my idea [*Vorstellung*]."[4] Solipsism is not integrally tied to idealism or phenomenalism, however, and to show this I offer the following argument based on neither position.

An Argument for Solipsism

That persons other than myself exist is not a necessary or an *a priori* truth; it appears to be a contingent truth. But if it is a contingent truth, then it must, in principle, be possible for me to obtain evidence relevant to its truth or probable truth. Yet what evidence can I have for the existence of persons other than myself—not just other bodies similar to my own, but other minds or selves, beings that have, or can have, thoughts, feelings, desires, hopes, fears, and so on? Either I must be able directly to apprehend another's thoughts, feelings, and so on, or I must be able reliably to infer from the behavior of another body that it is the body of another person, i.e., the body of one who has thoughts, feelings, and so on. The only way of directly apprehending a thought or feeling is to have it, and it is logically impossible for me to have another's thoughts or feelings. On the other hand—

[4] This is the famous first sentence of *The World as Will and Idea.* But Schopenhauer continues, "this is a truth valid with reference to every living and knowing being, although man alone can bring it into reflective, abstract consciousness"—as if "The world is *my* idea" did not entail that there is only one living and knowing being, namely, myself!

to take the second member of the disjunction— there can, in principle, be no reliable way in which I can infer from the behavior of another body that it is the body of a person, i.e., the body of one who has thoughts or feelings. In the first place, no description of the behavior of a body entails a proposition referring to a mental act, state, or attribute. Hence, if I am reliably to infer another's thoughts or feelings from the behavior of a body, I cannot do so by way of logical inferences from statements about behavior. The only other mode of reliable inference open to me requires that if I am reliably to infer *x* from *y* (the thought or feeling from the behavior) I must know that whenever *x* occurs *y* also occurs, or does so with a certain probability. To know this, however, it must be possible for me to know that *x* has occurred, and to do so in some way *other* than by the method of inference in question. Thus it must be possible, somewhere along the line, to know directly, i.e., noninferentially, that *x* has occurred. But this, as we have seen, is logically impossible. Therefore, it is in principle impossible for me to know that there are persons other than myself.

But if it is logically impossible for me to know that there are other persons, then there are no other persons. In general, if *p*, then it must be possible to know that *p;* conversely, if it is not possible to know that *p,* then not-*p*.[5] As we have already shown, however, it is impossible for me to know that other persons exist. Therefore, there are no other persons, which is to say that I am the only person in the world—Q.E.D.[6]

[5] This, I take it, is the principle of Berkeley's rejection of Locke's material substratum and of Hegel's rejection of Kant's thing-in-itself.

[6] I do not offer this argument as the strongest possible argument for solipsism, or as one that I myself "accept." The following passage contains the main elements of the argument and shows how close even a scientific psychologist such as Hebb (1955) comes to solipsism: "Speech, and introspective description, is not a sort of pipeline direct to the consciousness of another, giving us first-hand knowledge. It is behavior, from which we may infer, correctly or incorrectly, the nature of the underlying processes that determined what the subject has said. All that we can know about the conscious processes of another, or about what the psychiatrist calls the unconscious, is *an inference from behavior,* verbal or nonverbal" (p. 4).

V

In his Introduction to *The Philosophy of Mind* Chappell (1962), after giving an argument for solipsism similar to, though more elaborate than, the one I have just given, makes the following interesting remark:

> As I have stated it, the argument is, I think, plausible. It begins from obvious truths and contains no obvious mistakes of fact or logic. But its conclusion is, nonetheless, quite unacceptable. Solipsism is at least false; it may be necessarily false or even unintelligible. In any case, it follows that something in the argument is illegitimate. Something has been stated or assumed as a premise that is false, or a step has been taken that is logically fallacious, or both (p. 6).[7]

This is a natural and, some would say, a healthy response. But if we look at what Chappell goes on to say about his own argument, we note something curious. After canvassing a number of very sophisticated and cogent attacks on the argument—not all of them directed at the same "error" by any means—he finds not one of these attacks decisive or convincing. One would suppose that he is therefore left with the unpalatable conclusion that solipsism is true. But this, he affirms, is not the case: solipsism is simply false; therefore there *must* be something wrong with the argument, even if we, or he, cannot say just *what* is wrong with it.[8]

Stebbing's response is much like Chappell's: In her British Academy lecture of 1933 she said: You will notice how frequently in the course of this lecture I have tacitly denied solipsism. For instance, I just now said that (under certain conditions)

[7] Note the amazing discrepancy between the second and the last sentences of this quotation!

[8] One can always "play it either way" in philosophy: one can, like Hume (see *A Treatise of Human Nature,* Book I, Part IV, Section VII), accept the argument and thereby accept its valid conclusion, however unpalatable it may be; or one can reject the conclusion and thereby reject *every* argument from which it validly follows.

'*we* are forced to solipsism.' This was not a slip; it was intentional. I have the best grounds for denying solipsism, namely, that I know it to be false. You who are listening to me, and enable me to speak in the plural, *also* know it to be false" (p. 77).[9]

Philosophical jokes are not plentiful, but one of the best of them concerns a letter written to Bertrand Russell by a distinguished psychologist and logician, a woman who, braver than most men, openly admitted that she was a solipsist. As Russell (1948) tells the story: "I once received a letter from an eminent logician, Mrs. Christine Ladd Franklin, saying that she was a solipsist, and was surprised that there were no others." "Coming from a logician," he adds, "this surprise surprised me" (p. 196).[10] But why was Russell surprised? Did he suppose that Mrs. Ladd Franklin's philosophical position committed her to believing that he, Bertrand Russell, did not exist, in the way that some classical scholars have supposed that there never was a poet named Homer? And did her writing to Russell "show" that she was not really a solipsist?

More recently, Anscombe (1959) has expressed surprise at Russell's surprise at Mrs. Ladd Franklin's surprise and has observed that maybe the joke was on Russell:

> The necessity of solipsism is very arguable; why should a solipsist not argue it with everyone capable of arguing? Nothing would follow, even if two solipsists exchanged views with mutual congratulation, about any cession by either to the other of the unique position he conceives for himself. If two people discuss Descartes' "Cogito," they can agree that "This is an argument I can administer to myself alone," and each can hold the other would be incorrect

[9] Alluding to Wittgenstein's *Tractatus,* she says, "Any philosophical view which leads to the conclusion that what solipsism *means,* or *intends,* to say is quite correct is, in my opinion, obviously false" (p. 74).

[10] In an earlier book Russell (1927) told the story this way: "I once received a letter from a philosopher who professed to be a solipsist, but was surprised that there were no others! Yet this philosopher was by way of believing that no one else existed. This shows that solipsism is not really believed even by those who think they are convinced of its truth" (p. 291).

to have disputed that; if snow fell in appropriate sentences, one could dispute, agree and disagree with, those sentences [p. 168].

It is Anscombe's view that Mrs. Ladd Franklin did nothing surprising at all in writing to Russell as she did, and that by doing so she by no means showed that she was not really a solipsist.

This brings us to the heart of the matter. Is solipsism "at least false"? Do we "know it to be false"? And does the solipsist's speaking to and about other people, as he most obviously does, "show that solipsism is not really believed even by those who think they are convinced of its truth"?

VI

Moore was fascinated by the kind of philosophical claim of which solipsism is typical. He could never quite understand how intelligent men can say such absurd things as that time and space are unreal, that there are no material objects, and so on. To refute such claims, to show that they are false, Moore (1922) employed a technique he referred to as "translating a proposition into the concrete." To employ this technique, you take a philosophical claim, *p*, and ask what it implies. If you note that it implies a number of propositions, *q*1, *q*2, *q*3 . . . *q*n, any or all of which you know to be false, then clearly *p* must be false. For example, if "Time is unreal" is true, then nothing ever happens before or after anything else; but some things do happen before or after other things—e.g., I got out of bed this morning before I ate my breakfast—therefore, "Time is unreal" is false. Let us apply this technique to solipsism. If "There are no persons other than myself" is true, then there is no one other than myself in the United States; but there are persons other than myself in the United States; therefore, solipsism is false.

Apparently Stebbing, Chappell, and Russell (at least at the time at which he wrote about Mrs. Ladd Franklin's letter) would accept this sort of refutation as a genuine refutation of solipsism;

and most people, I think, would reject solipsism on the same or similar grounds. But logically, note, the Moorean refutation of solipsism rests on the assumption that "There are no persons other than myself" *implies* such propositions as, "There is no one other than myself in the United States"—taking the latter sentence as it would normally be used. But does the solipsist's claim have such implications? I think not.

Just as the same proposition can be expressed by different sentences (e.g., sentences in different languages), so different propositions can be expressed by the same sentence, or tokens of the same sentence type (e.g., "I am six feet tall," as spoken by each of several men only some of whom are six feet tall). It is important to notice that the argument for solipsism given—and I think this is true of all arguments for solipsism—is entirely *a priori*. Seen as the validly derived conclusion of an *a priori* argument, the solipsist's thesis, either "There are no persons other than myself" or "I cannot know that there are persons other than myself," is a necessary or *a priori* proposition.[11] And yet the propositions that are held, in the manner of Moore, to be implied by it are contingent or empirical. But an *a priori* proposition by itself *cannot* imply a contingent or empirical one in the way required by the putative refutation. In other words, you cannot deduce a factual proposition from a necessary one alone. Hence, the truth of the *contingent* proposition, "There are persons other than myself in the United States," is totally irrelevant to the truth-value of "There are no persons other than myself," *as the solipsist uses that sentence*. Hence, the plain man's "There are other people in the world" and the solipsist's "There are no other people in the world" are logically compatible and might be uttered jointly by a solipsist, provided that he utters them in different logical tones of voice, i.e., as expressing logically different types of propositions. Hence, there need be nothing surprising in

[11] Cf. Malcolm (1963): "in order to find out what kind of thesis a philosopher is maintaining, we have to consider the kind of support he offers for it" (p. 181).

Mrs. Ladd Franklin's joint assertion of the contingent proposition "Bertrand Russell is a person and Bertrand Russell exists" and the *a priori* proposition "There are no persons other than myself."

To see this more clearly, consider what might be called "The Case of the Lone Survivor." I know what it would be like for everyone in the world other than myself to die or to vanish, what it would be like to be the lone survivor of the human race. I therefore know what it would be like for the contingent proposition expressed by the sentence "There are no persons other than myself (left) in the world" to be true. So does the solipsist. And just as I know that this proposition is now false, so does the solipsist. Note that the Lone Survivor would not necessarily be a solipsist even though, *ex hypothesi,* it would be true, and he might know it to be true, that he was the only person in the world. Hence, Broad (1925) must be wrong when he speaks of the solipsist's fear of loneliness. We have no reason to suppose that solipsists fear loneliness any more than do the rest of us. Or, as Wittgenstein (1948) put a similar point, "Does a realist pity me more than an idealist or a solipsist?" (p. 48).[12]

Even if the solipsist is an idealist or a phenomenalist, one who holds that contingent statements about all objects other than himself, including other persons, are equivalent to logical functions of statements about his own experiences, "ideas," sense data, or how things appear to him, still he knows quite well that the relevant experiences, sense data, and so on, just do not occur. Hence even a solipsist of this stripe knows that the *contingent* proposition expressed by the sentence, "There are no persons

[12] See also (p. 59): "Now the man whom we call a solipsist and who says that only his own experiences are real, does not thereby disagree with us about any practical question of fact, he does not say that we are simulating when we complain of pains, he pities us as much as anyone else, and at the same time he wishes to restrict the use of the epithet 'real' to what we should call his experiences; and perhaps he doesn't want to call our experiences 'experiences' at all (again without disagreeing with us about any question of fact)," e.g., without disagreeing with us about the number of persons that there are in the world.

other than myself" is false. And this has, and logically need have, no effect whatever on his solipsism.

VII

As a putatively true *necessary* proposition, however, the solipsist's claim leads to some curious results. According to a widely held view, sentences expressing necessary or *a priori* propositions reflect verbal usage in roughly the following way. Consider the three sentences:

S_1: An even number is an integer divisible by two without remainder.
S_2: The expression "even number" means an integer divisible by two without remainder.
S_3: The expression "even number" means the same as the expression "integer divisible by two without remainder."

S_1 is typical of sentences that would be said to express necessary or *a priori* true propositions. S_2 and S_3, however, clearly express propositions about how certain English expressions are used and hence express contingent propositions. The proposition expressed by S_1, therefore, is not logically equivalent to that expressed by S_2 or S_3. The proposition expressed by S_1, however, is often said to be true by definition or true *ex vi terminorum*. This means that if I know that S_2 or S_3 expresses a true contingent proposition about the meaning of the expressions in question, then I know, *eo ipso*, that S_1 expresses an *a priori* true proposition; conversely, if I know that S_1 expresses an *a priori* true proposition, I know that S_2 or S_3 expresses a true contingent proposition. The same holds, *mutatis mutandis*, for sentences expressing necessarily false propositions.

On this interpretation of sentences expressing necessary propositions, the solipsist's claim, either "There are no minds other than my own" or "I cannot know that there are persons other than myself," is in effect the claim that phrases such as "other mind" and "other person," like the phrases "four-sided triangle" and "colorless red object," express absurdities and have no possible application to anything. But *if* this is what the solipsist is in effect asserting, then certain curious things happen to solipsism itself (see section VIII), and this might be taken as a reason for saying that solipsism is obviously false (see section IX).

VIII

If what the solipsist says is necessarily true, then not only would all phrases and sentences containing such expressions as "other person," as well as all phrases and sentences containing personal and possessive pronouns in the second and third persons, have no application to any possible state of affairs, but, by the same token, all phrases and sentences containing personal and possessive pronouns in the *first* person would be pleonastic or otiose. For example, if what the solipsist says is necessarily true, then "The world is my idea" reduces to "The world is someone's idea," for in "The world is my idea," "my" *can* contrast with nothing. Similarly, "I have a headache," "I alone exist," and "I think (*cogito*)" reduce respectively to "Someone has a headache," "Someone exists," and "Someone has a thought."[13] In short, if the solipsist's argument proves what it appears to prove, viz., that it is necessarily the case that I am the only person in the world, then language is in principle incapable of expressing the fact about the world that the solipsist appears to want to

[13] See Ludwig Wittgenstein in *The Yellow Book* (notes taken by Margaret Masterman and Alice Ambrose in the intervals of dictation of *The Blue Book;* supplied to me by Alice Ambrose): "If it is logically impossible for me to say that another person has toothache, it is equally so for me to say I have. To the person who says 'Only I have real toothache,' the reply should be, 'If only you can have real toothache there is no sense in saying 'Only I have real toothache.' Either you don't need 'I' or you don't need 'real'. . . . 'I' is no longer opposed to anything. You had much better say, 'There is toothache.' " See also Geach (1956) and Shoemaker (1963) who have made similar points. But Bradley (1893) put the point in this way: "You cannot . . . construct a self which will swallow up and own every element from which it is distinguished."

assert, viz., "I am the only person in the world." Clearly, "I have a headache" and "Someone has a headache" do not mean the same thing. Although the proposition normally expressed by the first sentence entails that normally expressed by the second, the converse does not hold. This brings us to the possible refutatory use that might be made of this point.

IX

Malcolm (1963) has given a different interpretation of Moore's method of refutation from that suggested by my presentation (section VI).[14] Referring to an argument by Prichard to show that we cannot see a body (which is obviously analogous to the solipsist's "I cannot know that other persons exist"), Malcolm notes that, in the light of Prichard's argument, Prichard's claim is *a priori:*

> When Prichard's view is drawn out in the only direction in which it can go, it turns out to be the claim that it is an *a priori* truth that we cannot see bodies. He is holding that the very notion of *seeing a body* is absurd. . . . Prichard is holding that there is a conceptual absurdity in saying such a thing as "I see a racoon in your corn patch," or in making *any* affirmative statement expressed by a sentence whose main verb is some form of the verb "see," used in a visual sense and taking for its object the name of a body. . . . When he [Moore] said, against the skeptics, such a thing as "I now see that door," it did not matter whether he was actually looking at a *door*. He did not have to produce an example of a *true* perceptual statement. In order to refute the claim that there is an absurdity in the concept of seeing a body, Moore did not have to present a *paradigm* of seeing a body. . . . He only had to remind his listeners and readers that the sentence "I see a door over there" has a correct use and, therefore, *can* express a true statement. . . . The philosophical positions that Moore opposes can, therefore, be seen to be false *in advance* of an examination of the arguments adduced to support them. We can know that there is something

[14] In an early paper (1942) Malcolm presented yet another interpretation of Moore's method. I consider only the later one here.

wrong with Prichard's reasoning before we study it [pp. 178-179, 181].

Applying this to the case of the solipsist, we can say: To refute the solipsist, it does not matter whether there are in fact other people in the world or whether we know that there are other people in the next room. In order to refute the claim that there is an absurdity in the very concept of another's mind or in that of knowing that there are other persons, we need only to remind ourselves (it "is necessary and sufficient . . . to point out") that the sentence, "There are other people in the world" or the sentence, "I know that there is a person in the next room" has a correct statement-making use and therefore *can* express a true proposition. Hence, solipsism can be seen to be false in advance of an examination of the arguments used to support it.

But this, I think, will not do. The solipsist's reasoning, as Malcolm sees it, has blinded him to the obvious contingent linguistic fact that sentences such as, "There is a person other than myself in this room" or, "I know what's on his mind" have a correct statement-making use and therefore can express true propositions. Unfortunately, however, we have no reason to suppose that the solipsist is blind to this at all. Mrs. Ladd Franklin knew English as well as Russell; and Hume, who seems to have been a solipsist, knew it as well as Moore. The solipsist knows quite well that the English sentences at issue have a correct use—as do the corresponding sentences in other languages—and his extraphilosophical behavior, e.g., writing letters to or playing backgammon with his friends, shows that he does. We cannot, therefore, refute his position, show that it is *false,* by adducing contingent propositions about the uses of phrases and sentences—propositions which he does not deny—any more than we can refute his position by adducing true contingent propositions about other people. The solipsist's claim is no more a denial of the obvious linguistic fact that expressions such as "other person" have a possible application than it is the denial of such attested facts as that there are more than 150,000,000 people living in the United States. The *only* apparent evidence that the solipsist supposes either that there are no people other than himself in the world or that expressions such as "other person" have no possible application is *what he says as a philosopher;* everything else, including what he says in daily life, e.g., about and to his friends and family, stands solidly against either interpretation of his philosophical claim. He does not, to use Berkeley's well known words, think with the learned and speak with the vulgar. Or rather, when he is doing philosophy, he both thinks and speaks with the learned, and when he is not doing philosophy, he both thinks and speaks with the vulgar; and he apparently senses no logical disparity between the two.

X

What, then, does solipsism come to? What can the solipsist be doing when he says, "There are no persons other than myself" if he is *not* denying the obvious fact that there are persons other than himself and if he is *not,* via the expression of an *a priori* proposition, denying the obvious linguistic fact that certain words and sentences have a correct referential or statement-making use? The answer I am inclined to give to this question is one that has been suggested to me by the work of Lazerowitz (1959, 1964).

The solipsist's statement *appears* to express a contingent proposition analogous to the one that might be expressed by the Lone Survivor. As we have seen, however, it does not. In the light of the solipsist's argument, the only kind of proposition he can reasonably be taken to be asserting is an *a priori* one. However, on the interpretation of sentences expressing *a priori* propositions given, the solipsist *appears* to be asserting, in effect, that certain words and sentences express absurdities. This, however, he is also not doing. Still, if sentences expressing necessary propositions do reflect linguistic rules or practices in the way suggested, the solipsist's claim must be appropriately construed. Since it does not, and since, as his behavior shows, he knows that it does not express a false proposition about English or any other generally employed language, the solipsist's statement may (must?) be taken to reflect a rule of a language that he, the solipsist, has devised, through the appropriate revisions of English (or whatever other language he speaks), not for general use but for some private purpose. This is the only plausible explanation for his use of the solipsistic idiom or notation *only* when he is doing philosophy.

Now if we ask *why* the solipsist makes the linguistic "moves" that he does, it will hardly do simply to refer to his argument. As is well known, the argument that persuades one philosopher often fails to persuade another (consider the vexed history of the ontological argument for the existence of God); and what, in a way, we are asking is why the solipsist is persuaded by his own argument when the vast majority of men, including the vast majority of other philosophers, are, as he knows, left unmoved by it —and this in spite of the fact that they may be unable, like Chappell, to find anything wrong with it. The solipsist does not see his own conclusion to be false *in advance* of an examination of his argument for it, although he ought to, if he is saying what he is said to be saying. To put the point another way: if the conclusion of the solipsist's argument reflects a rule of a revised version—what might be called a private or soliloquistic version— of the language he normally speaks, then, assuming that his argument is formally correct, since sentences such as "There are no persons other than myself in the world" *do not* express necessary statements in English, as does the sentence "There are no colorless red objects in the world," one or more of the premises of the solipsist's argument must also represent a linguistic revision —a revision that many philosophers may feel the temptation to make, although they resist accepting the conclusion that logically follows from making it. In short, since we can find no empirical evidence, about language or about anything else, on the basis of which the solipsist could support his claim and since, nevertheless, in the face of this fact he persists, or can persist, in holding his philosophical view, we have no alternative but to suppose that he has another motive for saying what he says than the desire to say what he knows or believes to be the case. Moreover, in the case of solipsism, unlike analogous cases in, say, ethics, aesthetics, or political philosophy, we can imagine no moral objective, aesthetic ideal, or political cause in the interest of which we might conceive him to be working. We are thus forced to the conclusion that what the solipsist does, he does from some, perhaps fleeting and evanescent, psychological motive.

XI

Having reached this point, I am able only to speculate, in the most unprofessional manner, on what that motive might be. But to take a shot in the dark, I offer the following observations for whatever they may be worth.

I am impressed by what might be called a thematic affinity between solipsism and what psychologists refer to as narcissism. Following Freud, psychoanalysts recognize a stage in human growth that Freud referred to as "primary narcissism," a stage in which the infant does not distinguish, or distinguishes only imperfectly, between himself and the outside world, i.e., things other than himself. In his paper "On Narcissism" Freud (1914) says that he was driven to an investigation of this phenomenon and to a recognition of its importance by the inaccessibility of schizophrenics (or, as he called them, paraphrenics) to analytic treatment. Paraphrenics, he says, "display two fundamental characteristics: megalomania and diversion of their interest from the external world—from people and things" (p. 74). He speaks of our developed interests in things and persons other than ourselves as like the pseudopodia that a protoplasmic animalcule puts forth: our interests in objects too "can be put forth and drawn back again." It is his view that in paraphrenia patients have withdrawn their interest in objects and in other people and have thereby "regressed" to the narcissistic stage. Speaking of these same patients, Fenichel (1945) writes:

> Such individuals react to any narcissistic hurt in later life [any hurt to their self-esteem] in the same way that they attempted to react to their first narcissistic hurt, namely, to the realization that they are not omnipotent; they deny the hurt and increase their self-esteem in overcompensation. For such persons a regression to narcissism is also a regression to the primal narcissistic omnipotence which makes its reappearance in the form of megalomania [p. 420].

In narcissistic daydreams people often imagine themselves to be kings, conquerors, great movie stars, and even God; and when these daydreams cease to be daydreams and become delusions, a psychosis is the result. Fenichel (1945) claims this to be characteristic of all schizophrenia:

> The differentiation of the ego coincides with the discovery of objects. An ego exists in so far as it is differentiated from objects that are not ego. Therefore, the following formulae mean one and the same thing, only varying in point of view: the schizophrenic has regressed to narcissism; the schizophrenic has lost his objects; the schizophrenic has parted with reality; the schizophrenic's ego has broken down [p. 415].

I do not say, nor do I wish even to suggest, that solipsists are psychotic. On the contrary: the characteristic mark of a psychotic is that he is unable to distinguish between fantasy and reality, but, as I have insisted, this distinction is precisely one that the solipsist can and does make. Yet there may be—and surely no harm can come from exploring the possibility—a connection between solipsism as a philosophical position and the evanescent narcissistic daydreams by which quite normal people deny psychic hurt and increase their self-esteem. The words of the solipsist's claim, as we have seen, do not say what they seem to say; rather, they express a necessary truth in a revised notation. But in spite of the fact that his words are being used in a novel way, their apparent content is not lost, as can be seen from the way in which critics of solipsism uniformly take them. His words, then, create what might be called a philosophical illusion: they must say one thing, and yet they appear to say another. That what they appear to say the solipsist himself knows to be false, and thereby must have some awareness of the fact that his words do create an illusion, is made manifest by his behavior. But what is consciously dismissed may be unconsciously accepted; and from the content of the illusion we can perhaps gather the nature of the unconscious thought his words express, namely, a wish to return to a very early stage of development the psychic content of which is aptly captured by the apparent sense of the solipsist's words.

Ayer (1957) says that if we take the logical step from "I am seeing x" (where 'x' stands for something publicly observable) to "it seems to me that I am seeing x" and then take the further step from "it seems to me that I am seeing x" to "I am seeing a seeming x," then "here by a stroke of the pen we create a whole new realm of private objects and, what is more, imprison ourselves inside it" (p. 219). If one can so easily create a world of private objects and imprison himself inside it, why can one not by a similar stroke of the pen, i.e., by means of a semantically rationalized re-editing of language, effect the equation "I = the world" and so "create" a world in which one alone exists?

REFERENCES

Anscombe, G. E. M. (1959), *An Introduction to Wittgenstein's Tractatus.* London: Hutchinson University Library.

Ayer, A. J. (1957), Perception. In: *British Philosophy in the Mid-Century,* ed. C. A. Mace. London: Allen & Unwin, pp. 213-236.

Bradley, F. H. (1893), *Appearance and Reality.* Oxford: Clarendon Press, 1930.

Broad, C. D. (1925), *The Mind and Its Place in Nature.* London: Routledge & Kegan Paul.

Chappell, V. C. (1962), *The Philosophy of Mind.* Englewood Cliffs, N.J.: Prentice-Hall.

Foulquié, P. (1962), *Dictionnaire de la Langue Philosophique*. Paris: Presses Universitaires de France.

Freud, S. (1914), On Narcissism: An Introduction. *Standard Edition*, 14:73-102. London: Hogarth Press, 1951.

Fenichel, O. (1945), *The Psychoanalytic Theory of Neurosis*. New York: Norton.

Geach, P. (1956), *Mental Acts*. London: Routledge & Kegan Paul.

Hebb, D. O. (1955), *A Textbook of Psychology*. London: Saunders.

Jones, E. (1959), *Free Associations: Memories of a Psycho-Analyst*. New York: Basic Books.

Lazerowitz, M. (1959), *The Structure of Metaphysics*. London: Routledge & Kegan Paul.

——— (1964), *Studies in Metaphilosophy*. London: Routledge & Kegan Paul.

Malcolm, N. (1942), Moore and Ordinary Language. In: *The Philosophy of G. E. Moore*, ed. P. A. Schilpp. Evanston: Northwestern University Press, pp. 345-368.

——— (1963), *Knowledge and Certainty*. Englewood Cliffs, N.J.: Prentice-Hall.

Moore, G. E. (1922), *Philosophical Studies*. London: Routledge & Kegan Paul.

Price, H. H. (1931), Our Knowledge of Other Minds. *Proceedings of the Aristotelian Society*, 32:53-78.

Russell, B. (1912), *The Problems of Philosophy*. London: Oxford University Press.

——— (1918), Logical Atomism. In: *Logic and Knowledge: Essays 1901-1950*, ed. R. C. Marsh. London: Allen & Unwin, 1956.

——— (1927), *Philosophy*. New York: Norton.

——— (1948), *Human Knowledge, Its Scope and Limits*. London: Allen & Unwin.

Schopenhauer, A. (1818), *The World as Will and Idea*. New York: Humanities Press.

Shoemaker, S. (1963), *Self-Knowledge and Self-Identity*. Ithaca: Cornell University Press.

Stebbing, L. S. (1933), Logical Positivism and Analysis. *Proceedings of the British Academy*. London: Oxford University Press, pp. 53-87.

Wittgenstein, (1948), *The Blue and Brown Books*. Oxford: Blackwell.

THE PROBLEM OF JUSTIFYING INDUCTION

MORRIS LAZEROWITZ, PH.D.

Philosophy of science is *als ob* science in the service of the unconscious.

Ernest Jones has described his encounters with philosophy in words which cannot fail to strike a responsive chord in the minds of many people. He wrote (1959):

> Time and again I have emerged from a course of reading in philosophy with the conviction that the authors were really avoiding specific problems by converting them into tenuous sophistries that had little real meaning. Then after a while I would feel that this was an unfair judgment on what were obviously great minds, and that it was more likely to be due to my limited powers of intellectual apprehension, which have always been obviously deficient in abstract fields [p. 60].

The impression these words make on one is that philosophy caused a division in Jones' mind, between the idea that philosophers are great thinkers and the conviction that their intellectual labor has produced nothing better than tenuous sophistries. It

Morris Lazerowitz is Sophia and Austin Smith Professor of Philosophy at Smith College. He has written extensively in philosophy and metaphilosophy. (For an explanation of the coined word "metaphilosophy," see Lazerowitz, 1964, Vol. 1, No. 1, p. 91.)

seems that his way of healing the breach was to dismiss the conviction. The judgment he finally came to was that philosophers are "people who have been impelled to deal with various personal problems in their unconscious by making serious efforts to think consciously; they have intellectualized the emotional conflicts" (p. 60). He went on to remark that in saying this he was paying philosophers a "high compliment," because so little real thinking is done in this world. It is not difficult to discern the original conviction behind the compliment.

It is difficult to conceive of the goal of philosophy as different from the goal of science and to consider that its arguments and pieces of analysis are not attempts to establish or confute propositions about various phenomena; but a difference between the two to which Jones refers tends to produce uneasiness about the kind of science philosophy is. It demands an answer which can only be reached by a re-examination of the subject: the explanation of the difference has to be found *within* philosophy itself. Jones (1959) has referred to the "astonishing contrast between the diversity of philosophical opinions and the widespread agreement in scientific work" (p. 61). This is a contrast for which philosophers have ready explanations, but other people will be deeply perplexed. Jones' explanation is that in philosophy "the questions have more important subjective origins than had hitherto been discernible" (p. 61), and this no doubt is part of the explanation. John Wisdom (1966) has said that some people have "exaggerated the degree to which philosophy is an expression of unconscious inclinations, nevertheless it now appears how very powerful unconscious causes are in philosophy."[1] He has also pointed out (1955) that "the more a question is finally settled by observation and, or, calculation on well established lines, the less scope have unconscious causes" (p. xii). It may well be that philosophical questions are not the kind of questions that are settled either by observation or calculation. This, if true, would

[1] In a letter to me, February 21, 1966.

help us understand the strange difference between philosophy and the sciences. And it may be that the unconscious is able to play in philosophy the role suggested by Jones because of the malleability of its theories and arguments, something in its nature which makes possible permanently irresolvable disputation and which accounts for the odd lack of concern by philosophers over the complete absence of stable results in their subject. What needs to be looked into are the properties of philosophical statements which will enable us to understand the contrast between science and philosophy. The purpose of this study is to examine a long-standing philosophical problem which looks to be scientific, the problem of justifying inductive inference.

In the practice of science, as well as in ordinary life, the possibility of making predictions with varying degrees of assurance and success is taken for granted, and it enters no one's head to think that inductive inference in general stands in need of justification. Statements about the future which are based on inductive evidence are ordinarily considered to be of two kinds. Some of them are made with complete certainty, which is to say that inductive evidence is taken to have established conclusively propositions about the future. Thus, for example, everyone would think it silly to say, in an ordinary, everyday circumstance, "It is not certain that tomorrow salt will dissolve in water" or, "Probably water will freeze at 32° Fahrenheit." It is, of course, easy to imagine salt no longer dissolving in water and water not solidifying at the lowest temperatures. Nevertheless, though we may not be able to identify the mistake, we would think that a person who stated that salt *probably* will dissolve in water tomorrow was laboring under some sort of misapprehension about either fact or language. To put the matter differently, some statements about the future do not count as *predictions:* there is an impropriety in the words, "I predict that the next teaspoon of salt will dissolve in water." Other statements about the future that are backed by inductive evidence are of course put forward more or less tentatively, as predictions to which some degree of probability attaches. To be sure, we may challenge particular inductive inferences as assigning a probability to a prediction in excess of the evidence, but the legitimacy of inductive procedure itself is not, either in the scientific laboratory, in the factory, or in the kitchen, thought to be something which might be brought in question.

In philosophy the matter is otherwise. As is well known, one of the main problems in philosophy concerns the justification of induction. What does not arise as a question in the actual practice of science or in the conduct of everyday life occurs in philosophy as a serious problem which is represented as being of more than just theoretical interest. It is represented by many philosophers as a problem on the solution of which hang matters of the utmost gravity. Thus, Russell (1912) has written:

> The question we really have to ask is: "When two things have been found to be often associated, and no instance is known of the one occurring without the other, does the occurrence of one of the two, in a fresh instance, give any good ground for expecting the other?" On our answer to this question must depend the validity of the whole of our expectations as to the future, the whole of the results obtained by induction, and in fact practically all the beliefs on which our daily life is based [p. 101].
>
> The general principles of science, such as the belief in the reign of law, and the belief that every event must have a cause, are as completely dependent upon the inductive principle as are the beliefs of daily life. All such general principles are believed because mankind found innumerable instances of their truth and no instances of their falsehood. But this affords no evidence for their truth in the future, unless the inductive principle is assumed [p. 107].

The picture these passages give us of the scientist is that of a person who, for all he knows, is living in a fool's paradise which may some day dissipate before his eyes. Many philosophers give the impression of thinking that the scientist is in the situation of a gambler who is experiencing a run of luck, and that science rests on nothing more solid than an assumption that philosophy alone is capable of investigating but which it has not been able to change into a proposition with a known truth-value. It is hard to think that scientists, even those who become enmeshed in the philosophical problem of justifying induction, will accept this idea of the insecurity of science, or, if any accept it, will *feel* that science is insecure. And some philosophers who have thought about the problem also reject this idea. Thus, for example, Ayer (1936) has urged philosophers to ". . . abandon the superstition that natural science cannot be regarded as logically respectable until philosophers have solved the problem of induction" (p. 49). It may be observed that philosophers who harbor the "superstition" about the insubstantial foundations of natural science do not, as will be obvious to anyone who troubles to look, give any sign of feeling or thinking that science is not logically respectable or that its structure of results may crumble at any moment. We cannot fail to notice the curious bifurcation that exists between their portentous philosophical talk and the rest of their talk and behavior; and this bifurcation suggests the possibility that the *philosophical* uncertainty about the security of science is not the familiar kind of uncertainty we experience in everyday life. More than this, if we stop to think on the matter we may soon find ourselves wondering whether the problem of justifying induction is the sort of problem it appears to be.

About philosophers who persist in looking for "power or agency" in conjunctions of events Hume said that ". . . they seem to be in a very lamentable condition, and such as the poets have given us but a faint notion of in their descriptions of the punishment of *Sisyphus* and *Tantalus*. For what can be imagin'd more tormenting than to seek with eagerness, what forever flies us; and seek for it in a place, where 'tis impossible it can ever exist?" (1739, Book I, Part IV, Section III). It may be that these words also describe the plight of philosophers who seek the solution to the problem of justifying induction. It may be that the answer they pursue is a will-o'-the-wisp, not because it is beyond the grasp of mortal minds but because philosophers have, at the conscious level of their thinking, misconstrued the nature of their problem. Wittgenstein epitomized the intellectual condition of the philosopher in the phrase, "the fly in the fly-bottle," and the bottle, we may begin to think, is of a special design. It is an existentialist bottle, one with no real exit. If this should hold in general for technical philosophical problems, it would help us understand the philosophers' protracted imprisonment in their problems, an imprisonment the duration of which has become sufficiently embarrassing to philosophers such as Harrod (1963) to make them fall back on the transparent rationalization of "the appalling difficulty of philosophical problems" (p. 241).

In this essay, I shall examine the question concerning the justification of induction, not with the object of discovering the answer, but with the object of arriving at a clear understanding of the nature of the question. Wittgenstein sometimes spoke of philosophical problems as having a *dissolution* rather than a solution; and it may be that dispersing the mists surrounding the problem and arriving at a clear understanding of it is equivalent to solving it. It may be that insight into what the question asks will have the effect of dispelling the problem-appearance which surrounds the question, and thus will remove the compulsion to look for a truth-value answer to a question which has none. Before taking up the problem of justifying induction, however, it will be useful to consider briefly a related problem.

The claim has sometimes been advanced that inductive inference is really deductive inference. Thus, Ewing (1951) has written: "Inductive arguments are, after all, inferences, and for an inference to be valid the conclusion must follow from the premises. But for this to be so the premises must entail the conclusion. . . . It is difficult to escape this argument" (p. 168). Other philosophers apparently have experienced little or no difficulty escaping this argument and have put forward the view that inductive inference is not really inference. One view professes to tell us what inductive inference really is; the other professes to tell us that there is no such thing as inductive inference, that what goes by the name of inductive inference is not inference. These views appear to make incompatible claims about inductive inference, but scrutiny shows that looked on as *factual* claims they vanish into each other. A philosopher who declares that inductive inference is really deductive inference is saying that all inference is deductive. He tells us there is nothing that counts as an inference which is not deductive. The point of his claim may be clarified by stating that there is no inference, actual or conceivable, which is not a deductive inference. What a philosopher who declares that inductive inference is not really inference wishes to place before us is the proposition that all inference is noninductive inference. This view comes down to the claim that no conceivable inductive inference is an inference, or that all possible inferences are noninductive.

Regardless of whether his claim is correct or not, a philosopher who states it is making no sort of statement about the *nature* of inference. This can be seen by noticing that according to his implicit claim that all possible inferences are noninductive, the term "noninductive" (or its equivalent) used in the expression of his claim does not mark a difference between kinds of inferences, e.g., it does not function in the way in which the term "formal" functions in the sentence, "All inferences occurring in *Principia Mathematica* are formal inferences." So far as its descriptive content is concerned, it says no more about inference than does the sentence, "All inferences are inferences." It is as barren of information about inference as the tautology, "If it is raining, then it is raining" is barren of information about the weather. The same consideration applies to the view expressed by the words, "All inferences, including inductive inferences, are deductive." The term "deductive," is not used in the philosophical sentence to set off a special class of inferences, and so does not characterize inferences. The sentence conveys no information (or misinformation) about the nature of inference. Like the words, "All inference is noninductive," the words, "All inference is deductive" are no more a characterization of the nature of inference than are the words, "All inference is inference." Strange as it may seem, the two antithetical philosophical theories coincide in respect to their informative content.

The more specific claim expressed by the sentence, "Inductive inference is deductive," or to put it in a way which lends an air of discovery to the claim, "Inductive inference is really deductive," can be seen also to have the characterizing force of a tautology. As the argument in support of the claim shows, what is being maintained is that all conceivable inductive inferences are deductive. Construed as making a claim about inference, the underlying implication is that "inductive" is not used in the expression of the claim to distinguish among inferences, nor to refer to a class of inferences some or all of which look to be nondeductive. Contrary to the impression it undoubtedly fosters, the statement does not distinguish between inductive inferences which do not look to be deductive but are, and inductive inferences, actual or possible, which neither are nor look to be deductive. In respect to characterizing inferences, it is as contentless as "All inductive inference is inference," or as "All inference is inference."

It is puzzling to realize that the views, which create such a vivid impression of being about the nature of inference, are equally devoid of information about inference, deductive or inductive. Like tautologies, which according to Wittgenstein (1922) ". . . say nothing" (4.461), they are all mute with regard to the subject on which they appear to be deliverances. Realizing this has the effect of dispersing some of the fog which prevents us from getting a clear view of the nature of the philosophical theories and of the questions they are designed to answer, and it enables us to move on to a different appearance they sometimes present. Like the Eve of the three personalities, philosophical theories are capable of presenting different faces to different people; and when their ontological mask, i.e., their appearance of being about things or processes, is removed, it is often replaced by a verbal mask. Nowadays philosophers have developed a tendency to adopt without much ado the position that philosophical theories are verbal in character, that they are reports about the uses of expressions in a language. These philosophers bypass the notion that philosophical questions are requests for factual information about things, and that philosophical theories are truth-value propositions about the existence or properties of things, and proceed directly to the notion that the questions are requests for factual information about accepted usage and that the theories report, or misreport, usage. One trouble with this overquick procedure is that the ontological appearance is not dissolved but is, instead, submerged. It is subjected to intellectual repression but continues to lead a vigorous life behind the philosophical investigation of language, where it is all the more difficult to get at. It gives rise to the curious idea, which is difficult to cope with because it is for the most part hidden, that knowledge of important things about the world is to be gained from the study of language. Behind the analysis of linguistic usage traditional metaphysical philosophy flourishes, and is, in fact, the life of linguistic analysis.

The view that inductive inference is actually deductive, when construed as amounting to a verbal claim about the accepted use of terminology entering into inference expressions, comes to saying that "deductive" applies to every inference to which "inductive" applies. According to the present interpretation, the philosophical view brings to our attention, in the nonverbal mode of speech, the linguistic information (or misinformation) that the term "inductive inference" denotes a form of deductive inference. Similarly, the views that all inference is deductive and that all inference is noninductive are to be construed as conveying, respectively, the claims that "nondeductive inference" has no use, or that the use of "deductive" dictates its application to whatever the word "inference" correctly applies to, and that "inductive inference" has no use, or that "inductive" applies to nothing to which "inference" correctly applies. Looked on as being about the nature of inference, the views turn out to be empty imitations of theories. They are verbal counterfeits which say nothing whatever about inference. But if taken to be about the correct use of inference terminology, they are just false. It is not the case that "inductive" is used in the English language to refer to a form of deductive inference. Neither is it the case that "deductive" applies, in point of usage, to whatever "inference" applies to, or that "inductive inference" is a literally meaningless expression. It hardly needs remarking that a philosopher who expresses his view by the words "Inductive inference is a form of deductive inference" knows perfectly well that "inductive inference" does not refer to a kind of deductive inference. It is the same with regard to the other views. A philosopher who says, "It is impossible for any inference not to be deductive," knows that "nondeductive inference" has a use in the language; he knows perfectly well that, in point of usage, the application of "deductive inference" is not coextensive with the application of "inference." A philosopher who says, "All inference is noninductive," is not ignorant of usage; he knows that "inductive inference" has a use and what that use is. He experiences no difficulty in using the phrase to identify inferences.

If we place on the views the constructions which they naturally lend themselves to, i.e., constructions which represent them as being oblique deliverances about the correct use of terminology, we come to a deadlock, with no prospect of understanding what the protracted disagreements are about. It would be reasonable to think that the interpretation was correct if bringing the philosophers back to actual language had the effect of resolving their disagreements. But this does not happen: Britain's Chancellor of the Exchequer, Maudling, was reported as quoting his tutor at Oxford to the effect that, "Philosophy progresses not by finding the answers but by progressively clarifying the questions." This is a clever rationalization behind which philosophers can cover their chagrin at never coming to undisputed answers to philosophical questions. Interestingly enough, in the rationalization itself is to be found the recognition that philosophical questions can have no incontestable answers: reaching incontestable answers is not part of the progress of philosophy. Without elaborating the paradoxical consequences[2] which emerge from construing the theories to be lexicographical reports, it is plain that recourse to known facts of usage will not resolve the disagreement among philosophers who hold the theories. This is why the philosopher's pursuit of a stable, generally accepted answer stirs up the image of a Tantalus who thirsts for knowledge which forever eludes him. When put to it to explain the glaring difference between the condition of philosophy and the steady and secure advances in the sciences, natural and mathematical, he understandably falls back on such rationalizations as that philosophical problems are prodigiously difficult, or that philosophical theories cast a spell over people's minds which blinds them to their mistakes, or that philosophical questions stand in never-ending need of clarification, or that answers are not to be expected since the important task of philosophy is to sharpen the concepts used in other disciplines. It can no longer be doubted that the philosopher labors under a misapprehension of the nature of his question and the theories put forward in answer to it, and that he can only liberate himself by getting clear about their nature. Wittgenstein is said to have remarked that the philosopher "tries the window but it is too high. He tries the chimney but it is too narrow. And if he would only *turn around,* he would see that the door had been open all the time!" (Malcolm, 1958, p. 51). What the philosopher needs to do is to resist the conventional notions of what a philosophical question asks and to explore the idea that it is the kind of question that does not have true or false answers.

If, to use Wittgenstein's expression, we turn around to the open door, we can understand the philosophical theories about inference. We can see that, underneath their surface appearance, they are introductions of alterations in the use of terminology. The sentence, "All inference is deductive inference" expresses

[2] For detailed discussion of these see Lazerowitz (1955), especially chapters 9 and 10, and Lazerowitz (1964), the first parts of chapters 2 and 3.

neither a theory about the nature of inference nor a verbal theory about the actual use of "deductive inference"; it introduces a stretched meaning of the word "deductive," a use that is academically superimposed on ordinary language. The sentence is not to be taken as a declaration that the accepted criteria for the use of "deductive" dictate its application to whatever "inference" applies to. It is, instead, to be understood as presenting an innovation in the use of "deductive," i.e., a stretched use which represents the nonworkaday decision to apply "deductive" to whatever "inference" applies to. Similarly, the philosophical sentence, "No inference is inductive," brings before us the academic, verbal decision to contract to the vanishing point the use of "inductive," i.e., to deprive it of its textbook application to inferences. It is, so to speak, made to suffer banishment by linguistic fiat. By way of a brief excursion, it is interesting to note what Austin (1962) has said about the use of the term "direct" in connection with the philosophical theory of perception: "We have here, in fact, a typical case of a word, which already has a very special use, being gradually stretched, without caution or definition or any limit, until it becomes, first perhaps obscurely metaphorical, but ultimately meaningless. One can't abuse ordinary language without paying for it" (p. 15). Clearly, this philosopher has permitted himself a glimpse into the linguistic workings of philosophy but has come away with the opinion that at least some philosophical retailorings of terminology are abuses of ordinary language. The implication is that they are mistakes, to be corrected by an analysis which explicates actual usage. But this is one of the familiar views about the nature of philosophical statements. It has advanced the understanding of philosophy not one whit nor has it brought philosophers any nearer to resolving their differences. It is fair to conclude that a philosopher who characterizes a view as constituted by a stretched (or contracted) use of a word but unites his characterization with the notion that the new use is mistaken has, to use Wittgenstein's metaphor, turned around, and then around again. The reshaping of usage by philosophers, their stretching, contracting, or eliminating the use of words, does not result from mistaken ideas about established usage. They are the free creations of philosophers, whose error lies in their interpretation of the nature of their creations, not in their grasp of usage.

It is not difficult to see that construing the statement, "All inference is deductive," as introducing a creatively[3] stretched use of "deductive" and the statement, "No inference is inductive," as introducing a purposely narrowed application of "inductive" frees the views from paradoxical consequences. These constructions also dissipate the problem-appearance of the questions, which are not now to be interpreted as requests for information about inference or inference terminology. They also remove or weaken the temptation in philosophers to refute each other's views and replace this temptation by the wish to understand them.

The view that inductive inference is really deductive, which strikes many philosophers as being manifestly false, is open to a like interpretation. What has happened in this case is that the actual application of "inductive" has been retained unaltered but the use of "deductive" has, in a purely idle way, been stretched beyond its textbook use so as to apply to inferences to which "inductive" applies. The way in which the philosopher presents his artificial redrawing of the boundaries of inference terminology makes it look as if he fancies himself to have made a discovery about the true nature of inductive inference, whereas all he has done is add a sham use to the term "deductive." The philosophical, illusion-creating language alterations embodied in the argument for the view that inductive inference is really a form of deductive inference are readily discernible in the following passage, quoted earlier: "Inductive arguments are, after all, inferences, and for an inference to be valid the conclusion must follow from the premises . . . the premises must entail the conclusion." In the interest of notational uniformity, "valid" (and

[3] Creative in the interests of unconscious fantasy.

with it, "follow" and "entail") is stretched so that it applies not only to correct deductive inferences but also to correct inductive inferences. That is, it is made to apply to all correct inferences, so that in this new way of speaking, "valid inductive inference" has a use as well as "valid deductive inference." As a next step, the term "valid inference" is made to apply to whatever "correct deductive inference" applies to, resulting in the view that inductive inferences belong to the category of deductive inferences.

To come now to the problem of justifying inductive inference, the fact that philosophers have taken a remarkable variety of positions with regard to it suggests that, like the problem about the nature of inference, it too has only a dissolution. It suggests that the problem has kept philosophers imprisoned through their misapprehension of its nature and that, as in the preceding case, finding the way out is equivalent to breaking the spell of a verbally contrived mirage. In this connection, one thing that needs to be noted is how utterly different the philosophical problem is from the practical or technical problem of justifying particular inductive conclusions. For example, when a sociologist states that the repeated experience of the consequences suffered from transgressing a certain rule of ownership teaches us that "the sense of interest has become common to all our fellows, and gives us confidence of the future regularity of their conduct," his proposition may, conceivably, be challenged on the ground that the evidence has not been gathered by trained observers using accredited formulas for random sampling, or on the ground that the evidence is insufficient to support it. But circumstances could be described in which people who are practiced in this kind of scientific procedure would withdraw their objections and accept the proposition as well-founded and reliable. The philosophical problem regarding the justification of induction is in an altogether different case, for it remains after all scientific experts have been satisfied that the accepted conditions for gathering and evaluating evidence have been fulfilled and that the evidence does justify the conclusion. This is so not because philosophers are less easily satisfied than scientists are. Their question is not the kind of question to which any sort of examination of the evidence or of strengthening the evidence or recasting criteria for what is to count as evidence is at all relevant. Rather, it asks whether what counts in science as evidence for a proposition about the continuation of an observed regularity can, in principle, count as evidence at all.

The problem has usually been formulated in the following way: When two things have in a number of cases and without exception been found to be associated, does a new occurrence of one of the two give any ground whatever for expecting the other? Common sense and science take the principle expressed in this question for granted, namely, that past concomitances, no exception having been observed, are grounds for further expectations —the greater the number of observed concomitances the better the grounds. Common sense has been described as having "natural confidence" in this principle. As is well known, Hume came to the conclusion that this natural confidence was unfounded and that the inductive principle had to be given up. In the words of Kneale (1949), "The source of Hume's despair was his discovery that reflection destroys our natural confidence in induction, and his only remedy was social intercourse, which distracted his attention from the question of justification and so enabled him to believe and act again" (p. 226). Hume's investigation of the problem led him to the conclusion that the past can provide us no rules for the future, that there is no rational justification for any expectation based on past experience: "Even after the observation of the frequent or constant conjunction of objects, we have no reason to draw any inference concerning any object beyond those of which we have had experience" (*Treatise,* Book I, Part III, Section 12). In other words, Hume was of the opinion that the problem of justifying induction had been solved. Inductive inference cannot be justified; no number of observed cases apparently exemplifying a law gives grounds for or lends any probability to the proposition that such cases will continue in the future.

Russell (1912) has gone on to develop a number of further positions. At times he implies that induction cannot be justified (or, sometimes, that it has not yet been justified) but that we cannot, for practical reasons, give it up. Like solipsism, which he thinks is theoretically irrefutable but cannot be accepted, the inductive principle cannot be established or justified but must be assumed. Sometimes he says that the inductive principle is to be accepted on the ground of its "intrinsic evidence" (p. 106). He has also expressed the opinion (1945) that the principle of induction is a logical axiom: ". . . induction is an independent logical principle, incapable of being inferred either from experience or from other logical principles. . ." (p. 674).

To these views about the problem Ayer (1936) has added still a further position. Against such a solution as that offered by Russell and others, that induction is a logical principle he maintains that it is an error to suppose that a logical principle (or a tautology) could be about the world or could make a claim as to matter of fact. Accordingly, the principle that past experience is a trustworthy guide to the future cannot be an *a priori* proposition nor can it be deduced from one. Neither can it be rendered probable, as he thinks Hume has correctly argued, by inductive procedures. Ayer's conclusion, which is different from any of the views put forward by Hume or Russell, is ". . . that there is no possible way of solving the problem of induction, as it is ordinarily conceived. And this means that it is a fictitious problem, since all genuine problems are at least theoretically capable of being solved: and the credit of natural science is not impaired by the fact that some philosophers continue to be puzzled by it" (p. 50). In Hume's and in Russell's view the problem is certainly genuine; in Ayer's view it is fictitious. Hume's solution is that the principle of induction is unsound. One of Russell's views is that it is a logical axiom. Ayer's positive view is that the principle has passed the test of success in practice, which is the only test a self-consistent principle requires for its justification, and that there is no real problem regarding its soundness.

A curious lapse should, perhaps, be noticed in connection with the considerations which led Ayer to reject as spurious the philosophical question regarding the justification of induction. His argument, for one thing, comes to maintaining that the inductive principle is not analytic, which is to say that the sentence, "When two things, *x* and *y*, have frequently and without exception been observed together there is some probability that a fresh *x* will be accompanied by a *y*," does not express an analytic proposition. For another thing, his argument comes to maintaining that the inductive principle is not open to verification in sense-experience, by a series of observations. And this is to say that the sentence does not express an empirical proposition either. The question, thus, cannot be answered by recourse to logic or to empirical procedures and is, according to his well-known criteria for literal intelligibility, a pseudo question. The curious thing is that he did not, in conformity with the criteria he laid the greatest stress on, draw the conclusion that the sentence expressing the putative inductive proposition in fact expressed no proposition and was literally senseless. Instead, he concluded that the proposition is all right but that the question is all wrong.

It is worthwhile mentioning one variant of Ayer's stand, that it is senseless to ask whether induction can be justified as a scientific procedure. This variant represents the question as not having been given sense, the implication being that the rules of usage of the language in which the question is framed do not prevent its having sense, although they do not provide it with a sense. The explanation of why it has been thought to have sense is that the inductive proposition has been confounded with propositions for which it is appropriate to ask for justification. That is, the philosophical question—"Is the belief in the soundness of induction justified?"—which has not been assigned a sense, is thought to have sense because of its outward grammatical similarity to such questions as, "Is the belief in the wish-fulfillment theory of dreams justified?" Thus, with regard to the philosophical question, Strawson (1952) has written:

> No sense has been given to it, though it is easy to see why it seems to have sense. For it is generally proper to inquire *of a particular belief,* whether its adoption is justified; and in asking this, we are asking whether there is good, bad, or any, evidence for it. In applying or withholding the epithets 'justified,' 'well founded,' etc., in the case of specific beliefs, we are appealing to, and applying, inductive standards. But to what standards are we appealing when we ask whether the application of inductive standards is justified or well grounded? If we cannot answer, then no sense has been given to the question [p. 257].

The explanation of what it is that makes philosophers dupe to their own senseless question undoubtedly carries with it a certain amount of appeal. But it does not bear close scrutiny. A philosopher like Russell, who has expanded on the point that to ask for the inductive grounds of induction is to involve oneself in a *petitio,* knows the difference between the philosophical question and a similarly phrased factual question. In fact, his own considerations make perspicuous the difference between them. The implication of Strawson's words is that a philosopher can cling to his mistaken notion about the intelligibility of a question despite his having been aware of distinctions which should prevent, and certainly remove, the mistaken notion. This recalls Moore's (1925) paradox,[4] which, in the present context, provokes the observation that it is easier to think that philosophers can remain lost in familiar territory than that their questions are vastly different from what they appear to be. That is why unrealistic explanations are given and why they are so easily accepted.

If we disengage ourselves from the continuing controversy and look at it from a distance, we shall become increasingly perplexed. The failure of philosophers, after so much labor, to dis-

[4] "The strange thing is that philosophers should have been able to hold sincerely, as part of their philosophical creed, propositions inconsistent with what they themselves *knew* to be true . . ." (p. 203).

cover an answer on which they could agree, together with their constant restatement and re-evaluation of the arguments clustering around the problem, will naturally suggest the Oxford tutor's notion as to where progress in the investigation of the problem lies. Moore's well-known dictum that before we can hope to answer a question we must first try to get clear about precisely what the question is, may at first seem to provide an explanation of what has been taking place behind the debates of philosophers. This is that the problem is still in process of clarification and that we should curb our impatience for a definitive answer. But this is an idea from which we shall soon be disenchanted, if we attend to the kinds of turnings the debate has taken and to the attitudes of the debaters. Some practiced philosophical thinkers are convinced that there is a problem of justifying induction, that the words "Can past experience ever provide good grounds for future expectations?" do actually express a question. Other practiced thinkers are equally certain that there is no problem. And some of these think it makes no literal sense to ask for a justification of induction, while others, like Ramsey (1931), think it is *unreasonable* to ask for this, that to do so is to "cry for the moon" (p. 197). Still other philosophers are undecided about whether there is a problem. An oddity immediately forces itself on our attention, for what would enable a philosopher to decide that there is a problem, or that there is none, cannot be anything he is unaware of.

To continue with the catalogue of positions with regard to the problem, among those who take it to be genuine, some think it has not yet been solved. Others are persuaded that it has been solved, but they are divided on what the solution is. This is certainly a bewildering variety of positions both with regard to the question and with regard to its correct answer, a variety which hardly suggests the presence of a disciplined effort to clarify a question. Indeed, to imagine that the dispute is constituted by an attempt to clarify the question is to let fantasy take over. If anything, looking from a distance at the philosophical battlefield must soon create the impression of a battle that is waged in a thickening fog. The only hopeful idea which suggests itself is that the present problem is akin to the earlier problem about whether inductive inference is really deductive.

The mystery surrounding the problem deepens when we go on to consider the standard arguments, well known since Hume, that are brought to bear on it. We find that there are striking and inexplicable differences of opinion among philosophers over what the arguments show, how they are to be understood. Like the question itself, the argumentation appears to have a plastic character; it seems capable of presenting itself in different guises to different thinkers, and in different guises to the same thinker on different occasions. Ayer (1936) has described the problem of induction as one of finding a way to prove that certain empirical generalizations which are derived from past experience will hold good also in the future. Following Hume, he states that there are only two approaches to the problem which could possibly lead to its solution. He writes:

> One may attempt to deduce the proposition which one is required to prove either from a purely formal principle or from an empirical principle. In the former case one commits the error of supposing that from a tautology it is possible to deduce a proposition about a matter of fact; in the latter case one simply assumes what one is setting out to prove [p. 49].

The conclusion he draws from this is that the problem is bogus. According to his assessment of the force of Hume's considerations, what they show is something about the nature of the problem. They are not the kind of considerations which isolate one of several putative answers and establish its truth.

Russell, as has already been noted, thinks that the arguments bear a different interpretation, that they show one of the traditional answers to be the true answer. In his judgment, Hume's arguments prove that induction is an "independent logical principle." To Ramsey (1931) the outcome of Hume's reasoning appears to be that induction cannot be a logical principle:

> Since the time of Hume a great deal has been written about the justification for inductive inference. Hume showed that it could not be reduced to deductive inference or justified by formal logic. So far as it goes his demonstration seems to me to be final . . . [pp. 196-197].

As is well known, Hume's own assessment of his reasoning is that it shows the principle of induction to have no justification whatever, neither empirical nor *a priori*. But although he supposed himself to have shown induction to be entirely without foundation, there is no indication that he imagined his reasoning to show that the question is senseless. It is quite safe to say, instead, that, as against Ayer, he thought the question, "Can induction be justified?" made perfectly good sense and that the reasoning, far from showing the question to lack intelligibility, gave the correct answer to the question: "Induction cannot be justified." To sum up the different points of view with respect to Hume's reasoning: according to one assessment, it shows that there is no question; according to another, it shows the principle of induction to be *a priori;* according to still another, it shows that the principle is not *a priori;* and according to Hume's appraisal, it shows that the principle is without foundation and that no inductive inference can be justified.

What makes it possible for Hume's lines of reasoning to look so very different to different philosophers is a riddle which is not answered by saying that some philosophers have read them wrongly and that others have read them aright. The argumentation is remarkable for its clarity and simplicity; and to suppose that philosophers divide, and remain divided, over what it shows is on a footing with supposing that mathematicians might divide over which one of a number of elementary theorems is implied by a certain demonstration. How rightly to understand the philosophical divisions of opinion remains a puzzle. On the surface they appear to be disagreements over what a line of reasoning shows, but the reality cannot be this. What the disagreements are about becomes even more puzzling if we re-examine Hume's own words:

> What is possible can never be demonstrated to be false; and 'tis possible the course of nature may change, since we can conceive such a change. Nay, I will go farther, and assert, that [one] could not so much as prove by any *probable* arguments, that the future must be conformable to the past. All probable arguments are built on the supposition, that there is this conformity betwixt the future and the past, and therefore can never prove it. This conformity is a *matter of fact,* and if it must be proved, will admit of no proof but from experience. But our experience in the past can be a proof of nothing for the future, but upon a supposition, that there is a resemblance betwixt them. This therefore is a point, which can admit of no proof at all, and which we take for granted without any proof [*Abstract,* p. 15].

Hume's words make it evident that he wished to bring out in a perspicuous way a difference between entailment, or deducibility, and causation, i.e., a difference between the "if, then" of logic and the "if, then" which occurs in causal statements. When he states in the *Enquiry* that "it implies no contradiction that the course of nature may change, and that an object, seemingly like those which we have experienced, may be attended with different or contrary effects" (Section IV, Part II), what he is doing is calling attention to the great difference between causal propositions, such as "Friction generates heat" and "A body submerged in a liquid is buoyed up by a force equal to the weight of the displaced liquid," and an entailment proposition such as, "Being a tree entails being a plant." The proposition that heat is generated by friction does not imply that it is logically impossible for things to be in friction without heating; and the proposition that if a body is submerged in a liquid it will be buoyed up by a force equal to the weight of the displaced liquid does not entail the logical impossibility of a contrary state of affairs occurring. But the proposition that a thing's being a plant is logically necessitated by its being a tree entails the logical impossibility of anything being a tree and not a plant. In effect, what he remarks on and wishes to call to our special attention is a linguistic point, viz., that causal terms do not fall into the category of entailment words and that in certain important respects they do not function in the language in the same way. He achieves his aim by pointing out in the nonverbal mode of speech that the conjunction of the entailing concept with the denial of the entailed concept yields an "impossibility of thought" i.e., a logical impossibility whereas the conjunction of the cause concept with the denial of the effect concept does not yield a logical impossibility. It is something that is "distinctly conceivable." What Hume has done amounts to remarking the difference in use, in the language in which he makes his point, between causal descriptions and entailment expressions. The expression formed by the conjunction of the antecedent term with the negation of the consequent term in the one case has no descriptive function in the language, while in the other case it does function descriptively. In English, "tree but not a plant" does not describe what does not exist; it has no descriptive sense. The phrases, "in friction but not heating" and "submerged but not buoyed up by a force equal to the weight of the displaced liquid," have descriptive sense, although they describe what does not in fact happen.

The point that comes through quite plainly is that to distinguish between the way in which entailment expressions function and the way in which causation expressions function is to make perspicuous features of the use of "logical implies," or "entails," and the use of "causes." The sentence, "Being in friction entails heating up," uses the word "entails" improperly; for "in friction but does not heat up" has descriptive use. The sentences, "Being a tree causes a thing to be a plant" and "Being a mother is the cause of her having a child," use the word "cause" improperly; the expressions "childless mother" and "tree but not a plant" lack descriptive use. Hume's consideration simply makes us aware of criteria for the use of "causes" and "logically implies" which we naturally employ. Parenthetically, it may be noted that philosophers who hold an entailment view of causation do not have an imperfect grasp of these criteria, which they themselves employ in everyday speech. The fact that they do not give up their view, despite what Hume and others have so often said, cannot, to use D. E. Moore's expression, be accounted a "mere mistake." Their view has to be understood as presenting in a veiled form of speech an academically stretched use of "logically implies" and of "entails," a use which is semantically empty, but which apparently gives some sort of satisfaction.

The first thing that Hume was concerned to show, to put the matter in Russell's way (1912), is that "the fact that two things have been found often together and never apart does not, by itself, suffice to *prove* demonstratively that they will be found together in the next case we examine" (pp. 101-102): the past is not a "logical guarantee" for the future. The second thing which he sought to show is that such a fact could not even suffice to make it probable that they will be found together in a fresh case.[5] His main argument for this thesis rests on what appears to be an empirical investigation of attested causal occurrences, an investigation in which looking is represented as playing a decisive role. His famous report of the investigation he made was that observation discovers no tie between objects, nothing which transpires between them that could be identified as that feature in the action of the one which brings about the expected change in the other. We do not, in addition to seeing the action of the one and the change in the other, see the action producing the change. The

[5] Thus he says, "All probable reasoning is nothing but a species of sensation" (*Treatise,* Book I, Part III, Section 8). According to Russell (1945), part of Hume's view is that "However many instances we may have observed of the conjunction of A and B, that gives no *reason* for expecting them to be conjoined on a future occasion . . ." (p. 667). Hume's way of putting it is that from the repetition of a conjunction "we can draw no inference . . . nor make it a subject of our demonstrative or probable reasonings . . ." (*Op. Cit.,* Section 14).

outcome of his search for the tie of causation, or for what might be called productive causation as against mere joint occurrence, is that "objects have no discoverable connexion together." He wrote: ". . . there appears not throughout all nature, any single connexion which is conceivable by us. All events seem entirely loose and separate. One event follows another; but we never observe any tie in them. They seem conjoined but never connected" (*Enquiry,* Section VII, Part II). The conclusion to be drawn from this, and it would seem so straightforward and unambiguous as to rule out the possibility of its being misunderstood, is that past experience, no matter how comprehensive, can furnish no ground for any inference with regard to future occurrences: "Even after the observation of the frequent or constant conjunction of objects, we have no reason to draw any inference concerning any object beyond those of which we have had experience" (*Treatise,* Book I, Part III, Section 12).

According to Hume's description of his investigation, the careful scrutiny of conjunctions of occurrences which would normally be taken by everyone to be instances of a change brought about by one thing acting on another, e.g., the change brought about in water by the action of heat on it, brings to light the fact that the occurrences are conjoined but not connected. This is to say that what is revealed by observation is that they are independent of each other, the one occurrence having nothing to do with the existence of the other. Water is not made to boil by the flame but boils on its own concurrently with the fire burning. They are, so to speak, cases of parallel action. Occurrences which happen together, no matter how much they may appear to be bound up with each other, turn out to be merely chance conjunctions of independent events. As no series of known chance conjunctions of *y*'s with *x*'s can be counted as evidence for the proposition that a new *x* will be accompanied or succeeded by a *y*, just as no pure run of luck in a game of chance counts as evidence that the next bet will also win, the inductive principle is groundless. It is clear that the use of "probable" makes it an impropriety of language to say, "The frequent but wholly *accidental* conjunction of *y* with *x*, no exceptions having been observed, makes it probable that the next observed *x* will be accompanied by a *y*." The statement, "No number of occurrences of a known chance conjunction of *y* with *x* counts as making probable the occurrence of *y*, given *x*," in an oblique way, tells us something about the use in the language of the word "probable."

Hume's investigation of causation has the air of an empirical investigation; and the language in which he couches his conclusion, "So on the whole there appears not, throughout all nature, any single instance of connexion which is conceivable by us," makes it look like a generalization that is founded on an examination of instances. A number of things, however, one being the fact that philosophers have been able to divide on what Hume's arguments show, suggest that the idea created by Hume's language may not correspond to what he was actually doing. Only two of these need be touched on here, one relating to an enigma of nature he alludes to, the other relating to the talk with which he surrounds his investigation and conclusion. The enigma to which he alludes concerns the regularities we observe around us daily, regularities which made Galileo declare, "Nature is governed by immutable laws which she never transgresses." Hume was impressed by the regularities in nature, but was satisfied (superficially at least) simply to dismiss them as inexplicable. In his own words, "We cannot penetrate into the reason of the conjunction."[6] He should, in conformity with his claimed findings and expressed view, have said, instead, that there is no reason to be discovered, that the conjunctions are and remain mere chance happenings, and that that is all there is to it. It just is a fact that we are everywhere surrounded in nature by prodigious improbabilities. But if this is what Hume really wished to hold he could not have failed to

[6] And also: ". . . that in the most usual conjunctions of cause and effect we are as ignorant of the ultimate principle, which binds them together, as in the most unusual and extraordinary" (*Treatise,* Book I, Part IV, Conclusion).

realize how vast was the probability that what he had looked for actually existed, despite his failure to find it. According to Russell's (1945) account,

> Hume's 'real' argument is that, while we sometimes perceive relations of time and place, we never perceive causal relations. . . . The controversy is thus reduced to one of empirical fact: Do we, or do we not, sometimes perceive a relation which can be called causal? Hume says no, his adversaries say yes, and it is not easy to see how evidence could be produced by either side [p. 669].

If the controversy were as represented by Russell, i.e., about a matter of empirical fact, it is easy to see how evidence could be produced for one side and against the other. The evidence which no one could fail to have noticed would be the astronomical improbability of the regular concomitances we encounter everywhere in nature being pure coincidences. The words of an adventuress in a recent play sum up the point: "I know that luck can only run a certain distance." The probability of the claim that, in addition to the conjunction of the occurrences, there is the production of one occurrence by the other would be so great as to make everyone, including Hume, laugh the counterclaim out of court. This throws the weight of evidence in favor of those who claim to perceive a causal tie, and against those who might claim that there is none to be perceived—providing, of course, that the dispute is empirical, about whether something is being perceived in occurrences or is only imagined to be there.

The second thing which goes against the idea that Hume's investigation and conclusion are empirical is the talk with which he links them. If we become attentive to this, a different picture from the one he himself apparently entertained begins to emerge. A phrase like "seem conjoined but never connected" creates the impression that "connected" is used to denote something in addition to what is denoted by "conjoined": the phrase "connected as well as conjoined" appears to mean something more than what is meant by "conjoined." Hume's claimed discovery would seem to be that experience has shown that there are no instances denoted by the term "connected," just as experience has taught us that there are no instances of the concept *unicorn*. But surrounding remarks he makes soon change this impression. Such observations as, "there appears not throughout all nature, any single connexion which is *conceivable* by us" and "we have no other *notion* of cause and effect, but certain objects which have been always conjoined together"[7] compel us to think that Hume, whether he was aware of it or not, supposed himself to have discovered an important fact about the concept of cause, namely, that it is identical with the concept of constant conjunction, and that "connected as well as conjoined" does not express anything "conceivable," i.e., does not denote a concept. The idea which these observations bring into focus is that some sort of *a priori* investigation is being conducted behind the false façade of an empirical investigation of an empirical position. Elsewhere I have tried to show (1964, pp. 202-211) that on Hume's own account his search for the tie of causation was a piece of unconscious humbug. It has to be said immediately, of course, that his search was bogus not in the sense that he pretended to look for something he did not find, but in the sense that the words he used to describe what he was doing in fact described no search but only imitated language which does describe one.

Hume gave expression to at least four different theories about causation: one of these, which if he did not state in so many words, he implied, is that nature works by hidden causes; another is that causation is nothing more than constant conjunction or unvarying sequence; another still is that there are no causes in nature, but only co-happenings; and finally, that "cause," "power," "necessary connexion" are terms which have no literal sense. These views are, in fact, bound up with each other and, strange as it may seem, in the end come to the same thing. Only the last two views will be considered here.

Take first the view, expressed by "Nothing is ever the cause of

[7] Italics my own.

anything; all conjunctions of occurrences are chance conjunctions; they are all loose and separate." It is quite clear that anyone who asserts these words will not be made to give them up by any state of affairs to which we might call his attention. Cases of water coming to a boil on the gas flame, stationary billiard balls being activated by collision, or billiard balls having their direction changed by impact with other bodies, etc., which are of course already known to him, would be dismissed as not really being cases of something causing something else. They would be characterized, instead, as consisting of chance conjunctions of occurrences. No single conjunction of occurrences or any number of repetitions of the conjunction we might get him to examine would move him to give up his skeptical view, or tend to make him less assured of its truth. He does not accept the ordinary variety of occurrence which we take to be causal as in any way contradictory to his view.[8] And this is not because he somehow overlooks what we see in such occurrences. He sees what we see, behaves pretty much as we behave, and in his nonphilosophical moments talks like the rest of us who are not at all in doubt about the existence and operation of causes. He does not see less in the causal picture than we see, any more than a person who declares da Vinci's *Last Supper* is not an arresting painting sees (or need see) less in it than others. This is mystifying, but there can be no denying that what counts with us as a case of causation (and also with him when he is not in one of his metaphysical moods) does not count as such in his philosophy. The view once expressed by Wittgenstein that "Belief in the causal nexus is a superstition" (5.1361) not only remains impervious to theoretical falsification by any of the occurrences we refer to, but is also impervious to falsification by any hypothetical occurrences we may describe. If we ask the skeptic himself to

[8] Philosophers who are led by metaphysical reasoning to deny the existence of a well-attested phenomenon normally allow the existence of the corresponding appearance. Interestingly enough, Blanshard (1966) thinks that some metaphysicians would deny the existence of the appearances if consistency with a line of reasoning demanded this sacrifice (p. 348).

supply us with a description of an occurrence which if it existed he would accept as upsetting his claim, we find that he is in like case with us. He no more than we can describe any occurrence or set of occurrences, over and above those we encounter in science and in daily life, which, if they existed, would be taken to falsify the claim. This can only mean that as he is using the words, "All conjunctions of events are loose and separate, there is no causal nexus," they do not express a proposition which has a theoretical falsification.

It would thus seem either that he thinks these words, in their actual use, express an *a priori* proposition or else that as he, in some unfamiliar way, is using them they express one. These two ideas about the sentence, "No conjoined events are causally connected; all co-occurrences happen by chance or accident," are not the same, but both are in accord with the fact that nothing, actual or describable, would be accepted by the philosopher as falsifying what it states. The first idea comes more naturally than the second, and it seems to square better with remarks like those already noted, e.g., that there is in nature no conceivable instance of connection, which implies that causal connection is in principle inconceivable. If we adopt the first hypothesis, the sentence, "No conjoined occurrences are causally connected; all conjunctions of occurrences are accidental," will be understood as stating that it is logically impossible for events to be related as produced effect to producing cause and that being a conjunction of occurrences entails being a chance conjunction or, what is the same thing, that it is logically impossible for there to be a non-chance conjunction of occurrences.

The question regarding the nature of logical necessity and logical impossibility is an important question to get clear on, but here no more can be said than that a sentence which denotes an *a priori* true proposition serves as a medium for placing before us a fact about the use of terminology in a given language.[9] It is

[9] See Lazerowitz (1955), pp. 254-276.

a sentence which does not explicitly mention terminology but nevertheless has only verbal import; but this is not to say that the proposition it expresses is verbal. The sentence shares its outer form, i.e., the form of speech in which it occurs, with sentences which state nonverbal propositions; but it shares its content with sentences that express verbal propositions about usage. Without attempting an accurate description of the form and function of the sentence, we may say that it exhibits what the corresponding verbal sentence mentions: e.g., the sentence "An uncle is someone's brother" exhibits the fact of usage about which the sentence "Part of the meaning of the word 'uncle' is being someone's brother" makes an explicit declaration. Like the Delphic oracle, a sentence denoting an *a priori* truth neither mentions nor conceals what it communicates. In the present connection the important thing to notice is that to a sentence which denotes a necessarily true proposition, *p,* there corresponds a sentence which expreses a true verbal proposition, such that anyone who knows that the first sentence denotes *p* knows that what the verbal sentence states is true.

On the hypothesis that the position of the skeptic with regard to causation comes to his advancing an *a priori* rather than a factual claim, there will correspond to the sentence, "There is no such thing as causal connection; events, by necessity, are loose and separate," the following verbal sentence: " 'Causal connection' has no descriptive function in the language; the rules for the use of 'loose and separate' dictate its application to whatever 'conjoined occurrences' correctly applies to." To say that the first sentence states a logical truth is equivalent to saying that the proposition about usage expressed by the second sentence is as a matter of fact true. The first sentence might be said to exhibit the verbal usage to which the second sentence refers. On the assumption that the skeptic thinks the first sentence functions in the language to express a necessary proposition, it follows that he believes that the corresponding sentence makes a true declaration with regard to usage. We should have to think he has the idea that in the English language the term "causal nexus" (and terms like "produced" and "made") have no more use than does "unrelated siblings," and also that "loose and separate" and such terms as "chance conjunction" and "accidental combination" apply, as a matter of usage, to all pairs of occurrences. But this is a notion which, apart from his philosophical view, is not to be taken seriously. So far as his grasp of everyday language is concerned, there is no doubt that he knows as well as anyone that "caused occurrence," etc. has a perfectly good use and that usage does not dictate the application of "chance conjunction" to everything denoted by "conjunction of occurrences." It is to take refuge in fantasy to say that he forgets usage or that he misdescribes usage while under the spell of philosophy. It would be unrealistic to think he is under a spell which weds him to a mistaken view about usage. And even while philosophizing he does not fail to use causal terminology in the correct, accepted way. The conclusion which forces itself on us is not that his mind is bewitched into adopting mistaken notions about usage but rather that he unconsciously changes terminology, stretches or contracts usage, or banishes words from the language, for whatever gratification such unconscious play with words brings him.

This, the second of the two hypotheses, although perhaps less natural and certainly less appealing than the first, is nevertheless the more plausible. This becomes clear if we consider with care the hypothesis that the philosopher autocratically uses words to express a necessary proposition. The verbal counterpart of his philosophical utterance, e.g., the sentence, "The expressions 'causally connected' and 'nonchance conjunction of occurrences' have no descriptive use," would then be understood, not as making a flagrantly false claim about conventions operating in ordinary language, but as describing conventions in a privately reconstructed language having a special, and one may guess, subjective purpose. This hypothesis makes understandable various mystifying features that are not explained by the first hypothesis. We can understand, for instance, how anyone who takes a sceptical position regarding causation can, without having to develop a bizarre kind of amnesia, resist correction of any sort, either by an appeal to ordinary language, which he of course continues to use correctly, or by an appeal to occurrences in the world. No state of affairs serves to correct him, and neither does a fact of verbal usage. The reason for this, provided by the second hypothesis, is that his view is neither about the world nor about actual language. The skeptic is not, to use Wittgenstein's (1958) description, "a man out of his senses, a man who doesn't see what everybody sees" (p. 59). He is a man who introduces nonworkaday changes in language, or it would be better to say, superimposes the changes on it. He does this in such a way as to create a convincing illusion, an illusion realistic enough to make some people think that he sees more deeply into things or into language than the common man does.

The two hypotheses about the nature of the philosophical rejection of causation,[10] one representing the philosopher as describing actual usage, the other as in some way changing usage, have now to be brought into connection with the problem of justifying the principle of induction. It will be remembered that, on the natural assumption that the rejection of causal agency was founded on observation, any number of observed conjunctions, however great, has the status of a gambler's run of luck and cannot be used for calculating future chances. By way of a brief excursion, it is worth noting a puzzling argument which is sometimes brought against what may be called the pragmatic justification of induction, i.e., an objection to the contention that the use of the principle of induction is justified by its passing the test of "success in practice" (Ayer, 1936, p. 50). Russell (1912) expressed the objection in the following words:

[10] This sometimes takes the form of a redefinition of the word "causation." See Hume (1739, Book I, Part III, Section 14), especially the last part.

> It has been argued that we have reason to know that the future will resemble the past, because what was the future has constantly become the past, and has always been found to resemble the past, so that we really have experience of the future, namely of times which were formerly future, which we may call past futures. But such an argument really begs the very question at issue. We have experience of past futures, but not of future futures, and the question is: Will future futures resemble past futures? This question is not to be answered by an argument which starts from past futures alone [p. 100].

One plain implication of this argument is that past successful forecasts are not rational grounds for expecting equally successful predictions in the future, any more than a gambler's run of luck is rational ground for believing that his future bets will win. As Russell graphically epitomizes the situation, "The man who has fed the chicken every day throughout its life at last wrings its neck instead" (p. 98).

There is a temptation to import into the argument metaphysical considerations about time, such as that the future is hidden from us because, being future, it does not yet exist and is not available for our inspection. These are considerations which are comparable to those created by the sign above the Checkerboard Inn in Yorkshire, "Beer served free tomorrow"; and they only succeed in enshrouding the argument in unnecessary philosophical mystification. At one level of interpretation, the argument can be seen to be only another way of saying that we cannot look into the future, not because tomorrow is not today, but because all occurrences are independent, i.e., because those which are paired are paired by mere chance and so provide no data for an inductive reckoning of the future. In a world in which everything happens by chance the future is veiled, but not for the tautologous reason that what has not happened yet is not happening now.

As has been seen, the idea that the words, "All conjunctions of events are loose and separate; there is no causation or law in nature," state a proposition about the world turns out to be wrong. But taking them at face value, the words imply that the world is so constituted that the inductive principle does not apply to it. To put the point more concretely, the combination of statements, "All conjunctions are accidental" and "*x*'s and *y*'s have frequently been observed together, the one never without the other," does not imply that given an *x* it is probable that a *y* will occur. But the skeptic with regard to causation does not, despite his language, actually take the stand that it is an empirical fact, grounded in observation, that all conjunctions of occurrences are fortuitous. The way in which he expresses himself gives rise to the false picture that this is what he is doing and that with the help of observation he is demonstrating the inapplicability of induction to our world. Behind the façade of his form of speech he takes a different view. What this is, often makes its appearance in the guise of an *a priori* proposition, to the effect that it is logically impossible, impossible in conception, for a conjunction of occurrences to be nonfortuitous, or for one occurrence to bring about another occurrence. Construed in this way, the view implies that the inductive principle is logically inapplicable to the world. More specifically, it implies the logical impossibility of one event being causally dependent on another, or of a change being produced rather than just happening. This in turn implies that, regardless of how often *x*'s and *y*'s have been associated, it is logically impossible for it to be probable that *x* and *y* are not independent. Restated so as to bring into plainer view the verbal point involved, the philosophical claim implies that it makes no literal sense to speak of nonaccidental conjunctions of occurrences. The conclusion is that, with regard to occurrences which have been constantly associated, it makes no literal sense to say that probably their association is not mere chance. It is hardly necessary to remark that in the English language it is perfectly intelligible to speak of the probability of conjunctions of occurrences not being accidental, and that everyone knows this.

The last hypothesis, like the one about the nature of the claim that inductive inference is really deductive, construes the Humean position regarding causation and chance as presenting in a veiled form retailored terminology: a vacuously stretched use of "chance" and "accidental," which dictates their application to all conjunctions of occurrences, and a contracted use of "cause of" which prohibits its application to any occurrence or thing. On this construction of what has been done with language, according to which the philosopher does not use terminology to describe fact or to exhibit a linguistic rule but to gerrymander with words, the problem of justifying induction has a dissolution rather than a solution. Correspondingly, the sceptic's position with respect to the problem has an explanation rather than a truth-value. Along with his contracted use of "cause" and "connexion," i.e., along with his academic deletion of these words, as well as with his stretched use of "chance," he introduces a contracted use of the word "probable" (and related terms). This word is academically shorn of at least part of the use it normally has in such phrases as "*x* is the probable cause of *y*" and "probably *y*'s following *x* is not mere chance." This is what Hume's solution of the question, "Can induction be justified?" comes to. His negative answer, i.e., his rejection of the inductive principle, sometimes expressed in the words, "The past can provide no standard for the future," is a statement which presents, in the fact-stating idiom, the pretended banishment of an important use of the word "probable." The question—"Can the inductive principle be justified?"—is not a request for factual information about the applicability or workability of a principle, but is a request, made in the spirit of a language game, for a redecision regarding one of the uses of "probable." The arguments which Hume adduced to back his verbal decision are themselves moves with terminology. The sceptical position and its supporting arguments constitute, under cover of the ontological form of speech in which the philosopher expresses himself, a complex verbal game that produces a dramatic effect. In part, this is achieved by the mode of speech in which the game with words is played. When the altered use of cause, chance, and probability terminology is paraded against the backdrop of the language which remains in everyday use, the result is the intriguing picture of the sceptic looking behind the appearance of a world governed by immutable law and finding that it works only by accident and chance. Like the Platonic metaphysician who returns to the Cave from the realm of true reality to tell us that we, scientists and common folk, mistake shadows for things, the Humean investigator of reality steps out in front of the curtain of illusion to tell us that the world we live in does not justify the use of induction.

The game Hume plays with the words "chance," "cause," and "probable" appeals to many people. And when a philosopher accepts the arguments and declares their outcome inescapable, it means that he has made the game his own, for whatever satisfactions living under its spell may give him. Some philosophers, however, reject the game wholly or in part, or introduce modifications of their own. Ramsey (1931), for example, has stated that what Hume showed was that inductive inference "could not be reduced to deductive inference or justified by formal logic" (pp. 196-197), but this interpretation of Hume did not lead him to reject the inductive principle. Thus, he said:

> We are all convinced by inductive arguments, and our conviction is reasonable because the world is so constituted that inductive arguments lead on the whole to true opinions. . . . It is true that if any one has not the habit of induction, we cannot prove to him that he is wrong; but there is nothing peculiar in that. If a man doubts his memory or his perception we cannot prove to him that they are trustworthy; to ask for such a thing to be proved is to cry for the moon, and the same is true of induction . . . no one regards it as a scandal to philosophy that there is no proof that the world did not begin two minutes ago and that all our memories are not illusory [p. 197].

A number of shifts in terminology can be discerned in this passage, and some of these become visible in the comparison of the absence of a proof that the world was not created two minutes ago or that sense perception is trustworthy with the absence of a proof that induction is reliable. The linguistic alterations which enter into the philosophical view that it is impossible for anyone to know that his senses do not deceive him are a contracted use of the word "know," which confines its application to statements about an immediate experience, and the assimilation of statements denoting logical possibilities to the class of statements denoting physical possibilities. It is, of course, *logically* possible for a person to be constantly deceived by his senses, which is only a nonverbal way of saying that it makes *literal sense* to speak of his being constantly deceived. In the philosophically refashioned way of speaking, we can say we do not really know that we are not the dupes of our senses or that we are not being hallucinated by a Cartesian demon. In the same way, the assimilation of statements about the logical possibility of a break in the series of observed associations to the class of statements about physical possibilities, when conjoined with a suitably modified use of the word "proof," gives rise to the philosophical complaint that we cannot prove the reliability of induction. The next step is to point out that no finite number of observed associations can prove, or logically guarantee, that the association has not been accidental, and that nothing short of an infinite number of observed associations with no known exceptions would establish this. All this delusively creates the picture of a goal that remains forever beyond our reach. In this atmosphere, it seems a fitting rebuke to say that to ask for a logical guarantee is as unreasonable as to ask for the moon. But the theory, complaint, and rebuke are only such in appearance. A philosopher who adopts Ramsey's language game may later reject it, or he may accept it with part of his mind while rejecting it with another part of his mind. Something like the latter seems to have happened in the case of Ramsey. His remarking that it is not a scandal that there is no demonstration of the reliability of induction suggests that he plays the Humean game with one part of his mind; but he does not take it seriously with another part of his mind.

However, what comes through more distinctly than this in Ramsey's words is his unwillingness to play part of Hume's language game. In the light of our understanding of the nature of Hume's theory, Ramsey's statement that "the world is so constituted" that induction can on the whole be relied on is not to be taken as making a claim either about the constitution of nature or about the correctness or adequacy of a part of the language used to describe nature. Instead it is to be understood as an oblique expression of the decisions not to give up the word "cause" and not to stretch "accidental" so that it applies to whatever "conjunction of occurrences" applies to. It is reasonable to assume that he rejects a part of Hume's terminological maneuvering, that part which eliminates one important word and stretches the use of other important words. It is much as if he were saying that on the whole he prefers not to engage in a philosophical game with the terminology of science. By accepting one of Hume's arguments, which he takes to show that inductive inference "could not be reduced to deductive inference or justified by formal logic," he resists playing one game some philosophers play with induction terminology, viz., stretching "entailment" to cover causal statements. And by rejecting another of Hume's arguments, he resists still another game philosophers play with terminology, viz., stretching "chance association" to cover cases of causation, on which hangs the philosophical denial of the validity of the inductive principle.

Ayer's position with regard to the problem of justifying induction is similar to Ramsey's. It is not implausible to suppose that a philosopher who dismisses metaphysics on the ground that it is nonsense, who wishes to save philosophy from its excesses and restore its good name,[11] would like to see Hume's arguments given a different direction from the one Hume himself gave them. He would wish to see them directed against the philosophical question itself, rather than against the principle of induction. Thus we find Ayer (1936) thinking that Hume has been misinterpreted, that he has been charged with denying causation whereas he only sought to define it.[12]

[11] Ayer's words, even out of context, make this plain: ". . . if the philosopher is to uphold his claim to make a special contribution to the stock of our knowledge . . ." (p. 51).

[12] "He has been accused of denying causation, whereas in fact he was concerned only with defining it" (p. 54).

It is an interesting and curious fact that philosophical arguments often have remarkable adaptability, and that it is sometimes the case that the same considerations will lead equally to antithetical views. To illustrate, the consideration which leads to the view that there are no things, but only processes, leads as well to the view that things are processes. Hume's considerations can be seen to lead to the view which denies the existence of causal connections among happenings and also to the view which professes to explain the nature of causation, i.e., the view that a causal statement analyzes into one which asserts an invariable conjunction of occurrences. Ayer elects the second path in order, it would seem, to make room for induction and at the same time to discredit the philosophical notion that induction stands in need of justification. In his opinion Hume's answer to the question concerning what is meant by saying that one event is a cause and another its effect shows:

> first that the relation of cause and effect was not logical in character, since any proposition asserting a causal connection could be denied without contradiction, secondly that causal laws were not analytically derived from experience, since they were not deducible from any finite number of experiential propositions, and, thirdly, that it was a mistake to analyse propositions asserting causal connections in terms of a relation of necessitation which held between particular events, since it was impossible to conceive of any observation which would have the slightest tendency to establish the existence of such a relation [pp. 54-55].

One thing that can be clearly seen in Ayer's words is that instead of using the first and third observations as reasons for banishing the word "cause" he uses them as justifications for *redefining* the word. The redefinition brings out a point of similarity as well as a point of difference between the use of "conjoined events" and the use of "causally connected events," or "events related by a law": the similarity lies in the fact that the relations they refer to differ in kind from entailment, and their dissimilarity lies in the fact that between the relations they refer to there is a difference of degree. Russell's (1912) formulation of the inductive principle brings out the latter feature in the redefinition of "cause." He wrote that inductive evidence can "make it nearly certain that A is always associated with B, and will make this general law approach certainty without limit" (p. 105).

It can be expected that the philosophical redefinition of "cause" will be linked with a curtailed use of "know," a use such that "knows with certainty that ø is a law of nature" expresses what is logically impossible. Just as according to one view knowing with certainty that a physical object exists is impossible because an infinite number of sense tests would have had to be completed, so knowing that *x* and *y* are related by a law is impossible because an infinite number of conjunctions would have had to be observed. In this way of speaking, "knows with certainty that ø is a law" has no application in any theoretical circumstance, which is to say that the phrase has no literal sense. In the usual way of speaking, it makes perfectly good sense to say "S knows that *x* is cause of *y*" and "S knows that ø is a law of nature." In non-philosophical speech it is correct English to say, "The inductive principle helped us to discover causes and laws the existence of which has now been a long-established fact." But this is not the idiom of some philosophers. A philosopher who points out that causal laws are not analytically derived from experience, since they are "not deducible from any finite number of experiential propositions," is informing us that he is redefining "cause" and "know."

Without going into the complicated linguistic maneuvering, it may be pointed out that the inductive principle is so restated as to make it appear that the principle used in science had been given a more careful formulation, viz., a statement of a causal law is and remains a hypothesis which is made probable by observed instances of the law, and that its probability can be made to approach certainty "without limit." This is not the way the inductive principle is understood in the practice of science. No practicing scientist would say that further observations would continue to make, for example, "Friction generates heat," even more probable. Only a philosopher of science indulges in this sort of talk. However, the philosophically reformulated principle outwardly resembles the principle the scientist uses in his practice and, moreover, is presented as a corrected version of the principle. We can see now, in the new verbal setting, how Hume's arguments could be construed as showing that the philosophical problem is fictitious, and that the security of science, which uses the principle, does not hang on its solution.

It will be remembered that Ayer had the idea that the inductive principle is "a proposition about a matter of fact," i.e., an empirical proposition roughly expressible by the words, "the past is a reliable guide to the future." What Ayer's idea suggests is that there is a philosophical problem of classifying the principle. Its denial does not imply a formal contradiction, but it is not subject to disproof by appeal to experience. Thus, while certain features of the inductive principle incline Ayer to categorize it as empirical, other of its features incline some philosophers to categorize it as logical. In a way that is typical in philosophy, each classification is achieved by artificially stretching words, in the present case, the words "empirical" and "logical." Ayer's classification of the inductive principle, together with his idea of what Hume's arguments reveal about the nature of causation, opens the way to the position that Hume's considerations *really* show the problem of justifying induction to be fictitious. The view that causation is nothing more than constant conjunction, unlike the view that no such thing as causation or agency exists, does not require the excision of "nonchance conjunction" and the stretching of "accidental conjunction." It only requires readjustments in their definitions. Hence Hume's arguments are no longer to be construed as showing that induction is groundless; instead they are to be taken to show that the inductive principle is a unique empirical proposition, one which has no verification. It becomes, so to speak, a higher-order empirical proposition, one which is about empirical propositions asserting the existence of a law of nature and cannot have the kind of evidence they have. The inductive principle thus becomes a kind of empirical proposition that is incapable of confirmation by induction but is presupposed by particular inductive propositions: it is represented as a proposition which stands by itself among empirical propositions, one for which it is nonsense to demand justification or evidence. The manipulation of terminology that gives rise to this view can be seen to be extremely complex, involving the words "empirical," "chance," "law," "infinite," etc., and here little more than a glimpse into its linguistic structure has been achieved.

Russell, whose position coincides with Ayer's at a number of points, disagrees both about the nature of the inductive principle and about what Hume's arguments establish. In one place Russell (1912) remarks that the principle recommends itself on the ground of its "intrinsic evidence" (p. 106), and in another place he characterizes it outright as not empirical but as being a logical principle. He also disagrees with Ayer's type of position regarding what Hume's arguments show the character of the inductive principle to be. According to Russell (1945) they prove that it is ". . . an independent logical principle, incapable of being inferred either from experience or from other logical principles . . ." (p. 674). These words have to be read in relation to the notions that, (1) Hume's arguments are to be reckoned as analytically laying bare the nature of causation, rather than as disproving its existence; (2) propositions declaring the existence of a law cannot be conclusively established; (3) because it can neither be rendered probable nor disproved by experience, the principle of induction is not empirical. It then is possible to see in Hume's arguments an attempt to show that the inductive principle is an *a priori* axiom, or an independent logical principle. In the linguistic setting furnished by (1), (2), and (3), the arguments are to be understood as demonstrating that the inductive principle is not an empirical proposition and, inasmuch as its negation does not yield a formal contradiction, that it is not a tautology.

The remaining construction to be placed on the arguments is that they show it to be an *a priori* but not an analytic principle, one which is to be accepted on its intrinsic evidence. Lewy (1939) has said something which helps us see what leads a philosopher to describe the principle of induction as an independent logical principle and to look on Hume's arguments as supporting this idea:

> . . . it seems to me that the following proposition "Whenever I have heard barking in the past there was always a dog somewhere near, I'm hearing barking now, but I have no reason whatever to believe there is a dog in the neighbourhood" is *self-contradictory*. I cannot prove that this is so, but I should ask you to reflect on how we *use* expressions like "I have good reason to believe," "It's probable," "It's very likely" etc. If you reflect on how these expressions are actually used, I'm sure you will see that the proposition I've just stated is self-contradictory in the very same way in which it is self-contradictory to say "All men are mortal, Smith is a man but Smith is not mortal" [pp. 89-90].

It will be remembered that according to Russell the "real" question we have to ask with regard to induction is: Do *any* number of cases of a law fulfilled in the past afford evidence that it will be fulfilled in the future? Lewy maintains that the affirmative answer to this question is guaranteed by its negation being a formal self-contradiction. His inability to prove that there is a contradiction in the statement, "No number of cases of a law ϕ being fulfilled in the past affords evidence for or makes probable the proposition that ϕ will be fulfilled in the future," fits in with Russell's claim that the inductive principle is a logical axiom, the truth of which cannot be demonstrated but which is self-evident. Lewy's direction for getting to see for ourselves the contradiction he sees is to pay heed to the use *in the language* of such terms as "probable," "likely," "good reason for believing." Indeed, if we become sensitive to the criteria for their use we see what might be called "nonspecific definitions." That is, what we become aware of by following Lewy's direction are such linguistic facts as that an *unspecified* number of observed unbroken associations of x with y is *called* "a good reason for believing that a fresh x will be accompanied by a *y*," "ground for its being probable that . . . ," "makes likely that . . . ," etc. The sentence, "No number of correlations of *y* with *x* affords evidence for or makes probable that the correlation will continue," has verbal import which goes against the use of "is evidence" and "makes probable"; it violates what we *mean* by these terms. But since no specific number is included in their definition, the sentence is not formally self-contradictory.[13] It nevertheless states a logical impossibility. The words, "*Some* number of constant associations of *y* with *x* makes it probable that *x* is a cause of *y*," express an *a priori* proposition but not a tautology. For since "some" refers to no specific number, no statement of the form "*n* associations have been observed, with no exceptions noted, but it is not probable that . . ." implies a formal contradiction.[14] What these considerations bring to our attention is that the sentence expressing the principle of induction is a *definition* of the word "probable": it gives one meaning of the word in the language. Its being formulated in the nonverbal mode of speech in part explains its appearance of being an axiom of some sort. Its outer dress also makes it possible for other philosophers to view the definition as being about how the world works, and is part of the verbal material that is required for weaving various theories around the principle.

The philosophical problem of justifying induction is not a problem of determining the validity of a basic scientific procedure. The various positions put forward as solutions of it present, in an unrecognized form, academic maneuverings with the language of induction and have nothing to do with induction itself. We may justifiably wonder what it is about the philosophical tinkering with language that has continued to hold the attention of people for so many years. Psychologically speaking, it would be unrealistic to imagine that what absorbs them is just the game played with inference vocabulary. To be sure, the verbal game

[13] For a detailed discussion of this point see Ambrose (1966, pp. 200-202).

[14] It is this sort of fact which has led some philosophers to characterize the inductive principle as synthetic *a priori*.

brings to life the appealing illusion of the philosopher as a super-scientist who investigates the presuppositions of science—an illusion which caters to the unconscious wish for omnipotence of thought. But there is more to it than this. It is reasonable to think that the profound spell is cast over his mind by something he perceives behind the verbal content of the game, a cluster of ideas he unconsciously associates with it. What invests the problem with the importance it has for the philosopher, what gives it its charge, are its "subjective origins." Unconscious ideas which he reads into the problem keep him thrall to it, and the special linguistic character of the problem makes it adaptable to the expression of subterranean mental contents. In sum, behind the appearance of attempts to solve a scientific problem is the artificial redistricting of the applications of induction-expressions, which produces the appearance; and below that, deep in the mind, are emotional problems which are given expression by the rearranged pieces of language.

We may permit ourselves a guess at one of the subjective determinants of the philosophical problem. It does not require much reflection to see the possibility of a link between the concern with the philosophical problem and a need to cope with a tendency to obsessional doubt. In connection with the problem of free will and determinism, which is an ingredient in the problem of justifying induction, Jones (1964) has written:

> . . . there must be few serious thinkers who have not in some period of their life been perplexed by the antinomy that seems to inhere in every solution. The perplexity may even reach the intensity of the *folie de doute* of those afflicted with an obsessional neurosis, who endlessly oscillate between two opposite conclusions or decisions [pp. 178-179].

A character in a Restoration play illustrates this tendency beautifully: he cries to his friend that while he is with his mistress he feels no uncertainty about her exclusive love for him, but the moment he is away from her doubt and suspicion set in.

To take up briefly one solution of the problem of justifying induction, Hume's position that the past provides no rule for the future can be seen to lend itself to the interpretation that it gives hidden expression to a disposition to doubt. Hume's view about what the past cannot teach us is not a theory about how nature works; rather, it reveals a tendency in him to fall prey to doubt.[15] Proving his claim that the past is no guide for the future, which is a way of convincing himself that the tendency is "natural," would then function psychologically as a reassurance formula: instead of suffering from a private affliction he satisfies himself that he participates in one that is common to all. He unconsciously consoles himself with the thought: I am not out of the ordinary, underneath we are all the same; it is the lot of everyone to fall prey to obsessive doubt. The well-known example which Russell used to show why we can never be certain that the next instance will be like its predecessors is that of the chicken that is fed every day but eventually has its neck wrung. The meaning of this is not overly concealed, and it tells us one of the ideas that is linked with anxiety and doubt.

REFERENCES

Ambrose, A. (1966), *Essays in Analysis.* London: Allen & Unwin.

Austin, J. L. (1962), *Sense and Sensibilia.* Oxford: Clarendon Press.

Ayer, A. J. (1936), Language, Truth and Logic. London: Victor Gollancz (Second ed., 1948).

[15] The following passage from the *Treatise* (Book I, Part IV, Conclusion) gives a clear indication of a tendency to what he called "philosophical melancholy": "The *intense* view of these manifold contradictions and imperfections in human reason has so wrought upon me, and heated my brain, that I am ready to reject all belief and reasoning, and can look upon no opinion even as more probable or likely than another. Where am I, or what? From what causes do I derive my existence, and to what condition shall I return? Whose favour shall I court, and whose anger must I dread? What beings surround me? and on whom have I any influence, or who have any influence on me? I am confounded with all these questions, and begin to fancy myself in the most deplorable condition imaginable, environed with the deepest darkness, and utterly deprived of the use of every member and faculty."

Blanshard, B. (1966), In Defense of Metaphysics. In: *Metaphysics: Readings and Reappraisals,* ed. W. E. Kennick and M. Lazerowitz. Englewood Cliffs, N. J.: Prentice-Hall, pp. 331-355.

Ewing, A. C. (1951), *The Fundamentals of Philosophy.* London: Routledge & Kegan Paul.

Harrod, R. (1963), "Sense and Sensibilia." *Philosophy,* 38:227-241. London: Macmillan.

Hume, D. (1739), *A Treatise of Human Nature,* ed., L. A. Selby-Bigge. Oxford: Clarendon Press. 1941.

——— (1740), *An Abstract of a Treatise of Human Nature,* ed. J. M. Keynes & P. Sraffa. Cambridge: Cambridge University Press, 1938.

——— (1748), *Enquiries Concerning the Human Understanding and Concerning the Principles of Morals,* ed., L. A. Selby-Bigge. Oxford: Clarendon Press, 1902.

Jones, E. (1959), *Free Associations: Memoirs of a Psychoanalyst.* New York: Basic Books.

——— (1964), Free Will and Determinism. In: *Essays in Applied Psychoanalysis,* 2:178-189. New York: International Universities Press.

Kneale, W. C. (1949), *Probability and Induction.* Oxford: Clarendon Press.

Lazerowitz, M. (1955), *The Structure of Metaphysics.* London: Routledge & Kegan Paul.

——— (1964), *Studies in Metaphilosophy.* London: Routledge & Kegan Paul.

Lewy, C. (1939), On the "Justification" of Induction. *Analysis,* 6(5 & 6): 87-90. Oxford: Blackwell.

Malcolm, N. (1958), *Ludwig Wittgenstein: A Memoir.* New York: Oxford University Press.

Moore, G. E. (1925), A Defense of Common Sense. In: *Philosophical Papers.* London: Allen & Unwin, 1959, pp. 32-59.

Ramsey, F. P. (1931), *The Foundations of Mathematics,* ed. R. B. Braithwaite. New York: Harcourt, Brace.

Russell, B. (1912), *The Problems of Philosophy.* London: Oxford University Press, 1943.

———(1945), *A History of Western Philosophy.* New York: Simon & Schuster.

Strawson, P. F. (1952), *Introduction to Logical Theory.* London: Methuen.

Wittgenstein, L. (1922), *Tractatus Logico-Philosophicus.* London: Routledge & Kegan Paul. Translated by D. Pears, B. F. McGuinness, 1961.

THE NEED TO PHILOSOPHIZE

Ben-Ami Scharfstein and
Mortimer Ostow, M.D.

No one who knows them will doubt that philosophers need to philosophize. They are too rational to suffer anything that is not altogether clear. They spend many of their waking hours thinking deeply. And yet, philosophers, as they say of other philosophers, are not entirely rational, and perhaps not even entirely reasonable. This evidence that they remain human is worth stressing only because it is contrary to their ambition. Philosophers, as one sees, are not simply, but passionately rational, or at least passionately convinced of their rationality. It should therefore be part of their ambition to understand how the passionate and rational are related, especially in such men as themselves. They need not be afraid of self-disclosure. Not enough is or will ever be known to explain all philosophy away,

---

Ben-Ami Scharfstein has taught at Brooklyn College, Hunter College, The University of Utah and Tel-Aviv University where he is chairman of the Department of Philosophy.

Mortimer Ostow, M.D. has served on the visiting staffs and taught at Beth Israel and Montefiore Hospitals, and currently at Mount Sinai Hospital and Medical School in New York City. He occupies the Edward T. Sandrow Chair of Pastoral Psychiatry at the Jewish Theological Seminary. He directs the research groups on Sexual Perversion and Drug Therapy of the Psychoanalytic Research and Development Fund.

and an understanding of the need to philosophize can be to their profit and pleasure.

To reach the understanding, we must be careful to avoid some of the traditional problems of philosophy itself, even though the philosopher must regard them as inescapable. The notion of "reality" that will appear in these pages is unanalyzed and undefended. It is whatever psychiatrists and other unphilosophical persons mean by it. The problem of self-reference, that is, of the reference of our analysis to our own need to analyze, will likewise be ignored.

If we may anticipate objections, the philosopher who reads our psychiatric remarks is likely to claim that the evidence we present is inadequate. He will be right. This is no more than a general essay, which indicates the kind of evidence that might, if worked out rigorously, make our position plausible. For this reason, we appeal to the reader to draw on his own experience to supplement the examples that we give here.

The philosopher is also likely to claim that our evidence is irrelevant to philosophy as such. This objection is right in a sense. As a philosopher, he must concern himself above all with the correctness of his logic and adequacy of his evidence. It is beyond question that one's motives, of whatever sort, cannot establish the correctness or incorrectness of one's views; and psychiatric analyses, which have their own motives, must also be defended in reasonable ways. Reasoning cannot be totally analyzed into nonrational factors or totally judged in their terms.

Yet we cannot leave the objection of irrelevance without qualifying it. If motives are formally irrelevant to the correctness of the philosopher's statements, this irrelevancy is itself irrelevant to the desire to understand motives. Not only do they have an obvious practical importance in our lives, but the irrelevancy is the crux of a notable problem, of the man who is able to transform his subjective difficulties into objective truths, mathematical ones, for instance. And then, if we discover the motives that animate, shall we say, mathematicians, we may be able to educate them more effectively and preserve them from their own impulses that threaten their lives or abilities. Keeping mathematicians alive and mathematical is of some use to mathematics, though not formally.

It must also be noted that formal relevance does not explain everything in formal arguments. These are constructed of symbols and rules for their use, which in philosophy become assumptions about the nature of things and rules for correct or efficient reasoning. But formal reasoning is unable to explain why these assumptions and rules were chosen. The usual explanation, as we know from experience, is that the chooser has anticipated what they will lead to. If so, motives explain just that in formal reasoning which formal reasoning is unable to.

The understanding of motives has an additional explanatory value. In any given person, including a philosopher, there is a structural likeness between his unconscious processes and his explicit reasoning. The likeness is not predictable in detail, and its discovery is largely retrospective. But it often illuminates not only the choice of conscious assumptions and rules, but also the lapses, obscurities, and contortions in the reasoning. The philosophical interpreter's normal impulse is to fill in or smooth these away by additional reasoning, which makes it all, as he says, consistent; but in making it so, he may be concealing the evidence for another, more realistic interpretation.

Since we are considering the philosopher's need to philosophize, we may begin by asking who this philosopher may be. There is of course no one such being, and there are general differences among Greek, medieval, modern, and contemporary philosophers. Rather than choose our examples from all of these, we shall draw them mostly from two groups. The first is made up of the classic philosophers of the seventeenth and eighteenth centuries, who seem, at this distance, to be at the core of the modern history of philosophy. The second group is of approximate contemporaries, both Anglo-Saxon and Continental, around whom the present-day philosophical battles are fought. Restriction to these two groups makes it easier to refer to the philosopher, without sociological or other commentaries.

Apart from restricting the choice of examples, we may try, very briefly, to distinguish the philosopher from the artist and scientist. Psychologically speaking, the artist is unhappy with the world's appearance. He tries to change and re-create it to please his eyes better. The scientist, on the other hand, tries to catch sight of the unknown, in order to change the world by understanding and controlling natural mechanisms. Like the artist or philosopher, he often begins with an intuition, but he must either close the logical gap between intuition and conclusions based on it, or give empirical evidence that the intuition holds true. The closing of the gap or provision of the evidence allows the sciences to have a fairly linear, progressive history that unites all scientists in an ideal fellowship.

The philosopher, however, neither handles appearances to remake them, nor learns to control natural forces. He creates trains of ideas, often organized into a system, which are meant to reveal and perhaps to be the structure of reality. He differs from the scientist in that he has no technique by which he can convince his professional fellows. He logicizes, but the logical gaps remain; they can be closed only by the unconscious mechanisms he ignores. The empirical evidence he relies on is never enough, except to the rare souls who share his preconceptions or psychic needs. He demonstrates, in the sense of proving to himself and a few disciples, and the latter find it exorbitantly hard to convince him that they really grasp what he has been proving. There is more agreement in religious fraternities, such as that of the Thomists, but their members, too, soon diverge among themselves and, in any case, have no proofs acceptable to other philosophers.

Philosophers have therefore come to be in a strange position. They consider their views of great importance, they expend much effort in trying to prove that they are right, and they remain frustrated in their attempt. The fact is that they have accidentally or deliberately chosen a profession that lacks the publicly recognized methods of proof which we have come to identify with those of science. Their use of formal logic does not change this absence of proof, because they subject the logic to interpretations that do not convince their colleagues.

If, as their language suggests, the ambition of philosophers is to prove their case, why have they chosen a profession which will frustrate them? Are they somehow choosing to deceive themselves, choosing to fail, or choosing to deal with insoluble problems because endless dealing with them is exactly what they want? The answer to the last question is a qualified "Yes." It depends on the nature of the curiosity which is essential to philosophers and scientists, and so we begin by repeating what the psychiatrist has learned about the need to know.

Curiosity has primitive roots. We can see its analogue in the exploratory behavior of animals. Monkeys can be induced to work by the reward of an interesting sight. The senses, as we have learned from recent experiments, require stimulation. To be deprived of it is painful and incapacitating. Curiosity, exploration, and change, are needed to maintain good health. Curiosity and exploration are also needed to resolve perceptional, emotional and ideational conflicts. If too many of the conflicts are left unresolved, we are unable to orient ourselves and act effectively.

Clinical evidence teaches us, however, that in human beings there is a peculiar heightening of curiosity as the result of unfulfilled desires for sexual knowledge and for power. Young children, we discover, do not understand the functioning of the sexual organs or see their parents' sexual organs as much as they want to; they cannot solve the mystery of birth to their satisfaction. No matter how many facts they accumulate as they grow older, they continue to feel that a secret of great importance has been withheld from them. It is this residue of frustrated infantile sexual curiosity that is at the basis of the search for knowledge.

The heightening of curiosity that results from the desire for power is due to the equation we make between power and knowledge. The equation is true even in the primitive sense that when an individual sees what he biologically needs, e.g., food or a sexual partner, the very sight excites, releasing his instinctual energies. More generally, when he sees what he is looking for, he feels motivated and powerful. It is true, of course, that the more one knows, the more likely one is to have control over the environment, human or other. Thus it is no wonder that knowledge gets to feel like power. The fruit of the tree of knowledge, we recall, was believed to have made Adam and Eve godlike, from God's standpoint, dangerously so.

Can these generalizations be related in detail to the philosophers we are familiar with? The idea that knowing the truth will protect the philosopher and grant him a tranquil or ecstatic eternity is one of the oldest and most persistent in all of philosophy. Back in the seventeenth century, Descartes hoped that science based on metaphysics would give mankind a new power. It is a measure of the same hope that he urged an ill friend to hold on until he, Descartes, had speculated his way to the cure. Spinoza, more nearly a mystic, assumed that the clear-thinking philosopher would love God, that is, Nature, intellectually, and would enter into the impersonal and yet mysteriously personal bliss of eternity that he had earned.

If we turn now to the twentieth century, to Edmund Husserl, considered by many Europeans as a paradigmatic, pure philosopher, we again find the theme of knowing or seeing clearly as the very power of life. It was Husserl's belief that science was unable to grasp ultimate truth. He was able to grasp it, he thought, by making every mental process the object of a pure seeing and understanding, stripped of anything practical or adventitious. Yet he was emotional about pure seeing. At a time when he felt depressed, he told a story about himself as a child. He had received a pocketknife, but was not satisfied with its condition. "Considering that the blade was not sharp enough he ground it again and again until it became smaller and smaller and finally disappeared" (Spiegelberg, 1965, p. 76).

This story is a version of a common childhood fantasy. It expresses the fear that potency is destroyed by excessive masturbation. Potency, in Husserl's version, is equated with the sharpness of the knife. Knowing his lifelong concern with fundamental clarity and his alternating extreme feelings of success and failure at achieving it, we must also equate the sharpness of the knife with sharpness of vision and clear-cut analysis. When he was depressed, he felt he had lost both potency and vision.

Husserl's feeling that clarity was the whole value of life was most emphasized in his diary, where he wrote, in an entry of 1906: "I have been through torments from lack of clarity and from doubt that wavers back and forth. . . . Only one need absorbs me: I must win clarity, else I cannot live; I cannot bear life unless I can believe that I shall achieve it" (Spiegelberg, 1965, p. 76).[1]

The examples we have given can be no more than suggestive. But our contention that curiosity has a sexual basis is supported by the sexual fearfulness of a remarkable proportion of the major seventeenth- and eighteenth-century philosophers. We hold that philosophical curiosity is sexual curiosity, sublimated, of course, and is also hope for the power that seeing is felt to confer. It may seem that a man should be able to gratify his sexual curiosity directly, through natural, physical, intimate love. The fact is, however, that the philosophers to whom we refer were unable to sustain a normal intimate love relationship with a woman.

Neither Descartes, Leibniz, Locke, Hume, nor Kant married. Except for Descartes, who had a child as the result of a brief liaison, and possibly Hume, it seems that none of these men ever

[1] We wish to thank Professor Rulon Wells, of Yale University, and Dr. Haim Ginott for having commented on this essay while it was in tentative form. Because documentation would have been disproportionate to the essay's length and technicality, we have decided against it. But we have based our characterizations of the philosophers mentioned on a study of reliable sources.

have had intercourse with a woman, although their psycho-sexual histories were not identical. Descartes had a nurse as his substitute mother. As a man of the world, he courted one Mme. de Rosay and disarmed a rival who attacked him; but as a philosopher he did not neglect to tell her that no beauty compared with that of Truth. He resisted not only marriage, but other social conventions, and human intimacy in general. In later life he formed some Platonic friendships with women, especially Princess Elisabeth of Palatine. As for Spinoza, his mother died while he was young; his relations with his family were bad; he was the subject of one brief romantic story; he spoke of romantic jealousy as if he had experienced it; and looked down on women. Leibniz seems to have been bolder; he even proposed to a woman. She asked for time to reflect. This gave him, he said, the same opportunity, which he used to regret and retract his unphilosophical offer. Kant's inner debate on marriage was so prolonged that the lady who provoked it had moved to another city before it ended. Locke, not yet the confirmed bachelor, exchanged love letters with women, one of whom, Lady Masham, took him in as a permanent guest when he found London unbearable. She remained more or less in love with him and described him, after his death, as "a second father." Hume, a keyhole-witness tells us, was seen on his knees, courting a young noblewoman, unsuccessfully. The good, brave Hume slowly gathered courage for matrimony, but by the time he was sixty and ready, his fatal illness had begun.

Whatever the personal qualities or the rationalism or empiricism of these philosophers, they all shared the fear of sex. We find the same fear, no less accentuated, in more recent philosophers, Kierkegaard, C. D. Broad, and Wittgenstein, for example. Modern counterexamples could, no doubt, be cited. Russell, with his many affairs and several marriages, might be one, though this very restlessness is psychiatrically suspect. Whitehead, with his equable monogamy, might be another. But the proportion of philosophers both professionally influential and sexually fearful is nevertheless high. So fundamental a fear must be related both to their need to speculate and to the character of their speculations.

Clinical evidence indicates that a man's fear of marrying is most often the result of his love for his mother. Afraid of expressing this love, he becomes afraid to express any tender or even untender love for a woman. The philosophers mentioned are frightened lovers of their mothers. They keep approaching their fantasy equivalents of mothers, but the closer they get, the more frightened they become. Finally, when the secret threatens to become bared, they go blind. The secret is too like a void, or a vortex, or a mother's sexual organs. So it, the secret or void, and she, the mother, are veiled in philosophic decencies or ultimates—infinity, ideal clarity, perfected humanity, God, and so on.

Philosophers are naturally attracted to ultimates, but they either see them with a purifying eye like a mystic's, or, like Kant, they make them necessary and impossible. Kant remains a powerful philosopher because, as a believing skeptic, he expresses the necessity and impossibility of the philosopher's objective. He argues that perception and reason cannot lead to faith, but that faith is necessary. He thinks that we see and reason only about the world of phenomena, which is formed by ourselves out of we know not what. But this unknown substance, the thing-in-itself, though veiled from us, is still somehow present in our moral and esthetic sensitivities.

By the contention we have previously made, Kant's thing-in-itself is, at the most primitive level, his dangerously beloved mother. The truth is that his mother was the one person for whom he revealed deep love. Jachmann (1804) states that tears came into his eyes when he mentioned her. "She often took me outside the city," he said, "directed my attention to the works of God, expressed herself with pious rapture over His omnipotence, wisdom, and goodness, and impressed on my heart a deep reverence for the Creator of all things" (pp. 170-171).

This sentence recalls another, in which Kant said that two things filled his mind with ever-new and increasing awe and admiration—the starred heaven above him and the moral law within him. The conjunction of the sky and the moral law was just that which had been made by his mother. This helps us to understand why Kant linked them with his awareness of his existence. It was she who linked him with all he valued, and she, the only person he could love, who sustained him intimately and gave him the confidence that behind appearances there was the unknown *x*, reality.

What might be regarded as hypothetical in Kant's case is stated openly by the English philosopher, Broad (1959). He tells of the exclusiveness of his mother's love for him, his difficulty in expressing love for her or for anyone, and of his resulting sense of guilt:

> I was her only child, and as the years went by she gradually lost all objects of personal interest and affection except myself. . . . I could not even *feel* an emotion towards her commensurate in intensity and concentration with that which she felt towards me. Still less could I *express* such emotions as I did feel in ways that would satisfy her. For one thing, as I have said, I find it most distasteful to utter the language and make the gestures of strong personal affection. For another, I knew that any attempt to do so would lead my mother to clutch at straws and overestimate the strength of the emotion which I felt and to respond with a still more embarrassing warmth . . . [p. 27]. My mother lived until I was in my fifty-second year, and in the course of the 21 years by which she survived my father I had more and more to do with her. The ambivalence of my feeling toward her, and the second-order reflexive emotions of self-reproach which this engendered in me have been a very disturbing factor in my life [p. 52].

Not surprisingly, Broad refused to catch his foot "in the man-trap of matrimony." But he drew a surprising picture of the price he had paid, in weakness and childishness, for his dependence upon his mother:

> The really fundamental defects have been cowardice, physical and moral, and lack of drive and resolution . . . to take the physical side first. Let the reader consider the following list of quite ordinary accomplishments which I have never managed to acquire. I cannot dance, or skate, or ski, or swim properly, or play tennis or cricket or golf, or ride a horse, or sail a boat, or drive a car. . . . I cannot, fortunately, give equally palpable instances of lack of moral courage and of its ill-effects on me. I have lived an exceptionally sheltered life, not unlike that of a monk in a monastery, only without the duties of asceticism [p. 67].

If he were to survive, what could this man do but try to recover, in a creative medium, the reality he could not have, and the other realities, the experiences of other, ordinary men, he had sacrificed for her sake?

The theme of the ultimate which is very near but difficult or impossible to see or touch is characteristic of the whole of existentialist philosophy. Heidegger believes that Western metaphysics has been no more than a forgetting of being. This forgetting, he says, creates anxiety in the true thinker, who must try to recover being in its truth, which is openness, unconcealedness. When this unconcealedness comes to an end, the philosophical Logos, the revealer and concealer, loses its moorings in being and drifts about aimlessly. The West must return to its hidden, forgotten, primordial source—being.

Such Heideggerian conceptions are illuminated with a grotesque simplicity when one substitutes the words "mother" and "child" for "being" and "Logos." If the philosopher, unknown to himself, is the fearful lover of his mother, who is also, in fantasy, a void or vortex, we understand why Heidegger (1929) says, "We are familiar with things in being—but being itself? Are we not always attacked by dizziness when we are to define or only to grasp such matters?" (p. 204). We understand, too, why Heidegger (1961) describes being in a series of contradictory superlatives, as "the emptiest and the richest, the most general and the most unique, the most intelligible and the most refractory to conceptualization, the most in use and still arriving, the most reliable and the most treacherous, the most mentioned and the most passed over in silence" (pp. 250-53). Almost every mother's son will agree with Heidegger's statement that man needs being, and being needs man. Both, as he says, belong together.

The relationship of the French existentialist, Merleau-Ponty, to his mother is stressed by his close friend, Sartre (1947-1949), in a tribute written after Merleau-Ponty's death. Sartre also explains how this relationship was translated into the themes of his friend's philosophy:

> One day in 1947, Merleau told me that he had never recovered from an incomparable childhood. . . . Seeking his golden age, and with that as his point of departure, he forged his myths and what he has since called his "style of life." . . . This naivete, by starting from *what has happened,* also discovered the meaning of *what is happening,* and finally, it made a prophecy based on this inventory and its evaluation. This is what he felt as a young man, without as yet being able to express it. Through these detours, he had finally arrived at philosophy. He wondered—nothing more. Everything is played out from the beginning, and we continue in spite of this. Why? Why do we lead a life which is disqualified by its absences? And what does it mean to live?
>
> He suffered in his relations with others. Everything had been too wonderful, too soon. The form of Nature which first enveloped him was the Mother Goddess, his own mother, whose eyes made him see what he saw. She was the *alter ego.* By her and through her, he lived the "intersubjectivity of immanence" which he has often described, and which causes us to discover our "spontaneity" through another. With childhood dead, love remained, equally strong, but bereft. Certain it was that he would never again find this destroyed intimacy, he was only capable of demanding [pp. 162, 210].

Merleau-Ponty's mother died. Her death renewed death for him, including that which had been his first separation from her in birth. It renewed the tension between appearance and disappearance, the "primordial historicity" he speaks of. He wanted her death to be her rebirth in him. "For this reason, he found more powers in absence than in presence. . . . When his mother died, and childhood was abolished with her, absence and presence, Being and Non-Being, glowed into one another. Through phenomenology, and without ever departing from it, Merleau hoped to rejoin the imperatives of ontology. That which is no more, is not yet, and never will be" [p. 216].

Merleau-Ponty's philosophy, to rephrase what Sartre tells us, perpetuates his symbiosis with his mother and also expresses the impossibility of doing so. Sartre himself, whose closeness to his mother and reluctance to marry are well known, is harsher in tone. He uses psychoanalytic ideas, interpreted mostly in the light of Adler and Stekel. But the themes of absence, frustration, and the void are obsessive for him, and he speaks of his own feelings when he describes the fascination and frightfulness of women. Women are, according to Sartre (1943), a gaping obscenity:

> In herself woman appeals to a strange flesh which is to transform her into a fulness of being by penetration and dissolution. Conversely woman senses her condition because she is "in the form of a hole. . . ." Beyond any doubt her sex is a mouth and a voracious mouth which devours the penis—a fact which can easily lead to the idea of castration. The amorous act is the castration of the man; but this is above all because sex is a hole [p. 350].

Sartre believes that the threat of "the hole" is presexual. But if we pay attention not to this abstract idea but to the tone of the passage, we must find it both cruel and pained, as his writing often is. Sartre (1963) says of his books, "I've often written them against myself, which means against everybody, with an intentness of mind that has ended by becoming high blood pressure" (p. 102).

Sartre's philosophy is constructed on sadomasochistic lines. The chief participants in *Being and Nothingness* are, as the name indicates, Being, which is full, imperturbable, and godlike, and

Nothing, or human consciousness, which cannot exist without Being, yet which must prey on it. Consciousness is Nothing because it is a constant grasping, a yearning and a failure to become Being. In Sartre's world, man is free, but only in the consciousness of his lack, and therefore in anguish. Love, too, therefore, is sadomasochistic and doomed. One tries to enslave the Other's freedom, but succeeds only in appropriating the Other's body. Love is necessary and yet futile. Because this is the world as Sartre sees it, he is telling us, in effect, that nothing and no one can sustain him with love. Being is full of itself, human Others are inaccessible, and so one lives in an environment empty of any gesture that can strengthen humanity with humanity. A human self is a nothing-self. It is true that Sartre means to say that consciousness is Nothing because it is only a grasping of that which is different from itself; but his notion of consciousness is strongly affective. He, as consciousness, is loveless, disappointed, depressed. He is, so to speak, a constantly-pricked balloon.

The sadomasochism we find in Sartre is usual, if rarely as open, in other philosophers. This is what we should expect. The philosopher, we have said, is likely to love but be afraid to love his mother. The ultimate object, the ideal, in his philosophy is a substitute for her; but he must keep his distance from it, because she is unattainable. He therefore uses his abstract ideas to create an ambivalent, sadomasochistic distance from the object. And because he often cannot allow himself any sensual love play, he substitutes the pleasure of sadomasochistic reasoning for it. In the process, he may well choose to hurt others; he surely hurts and pleases himself. He prefers to continue to enjoy the pleasure than to end it by "solving" the problems.

If this is true, we can deepen our understanding of philosophers by discovering their sadomasochistic mechanisms. Kant is an interesting example. He was closer to the masochistic pole. Afraid of emotion, he kept his distance from it by repelling it constantly. That is, he was distressed by anything that threatened to become uncontrolled—by metaphysics, the "lack of character" of artists and musicians, the death he heard in music, the wildness or madness he felt in unrhymed poetry, the shapelessness of untrimmed trees, the fantasies in novels. By his own admission, he was also hypochondriacal. He thought he had a narrow chest; but a narrow chest, he also thought, resulted from the leading-strings by which parents enslaved children.

Kant's closeness to and distance from his thing-in-itself can now be understood as his sadomasochistic repulsion of the dangerous object. But his cruel streak comes out most clearly in his ethics. It is well known that he upheld the absolute sanctity of human life. It is less well known that he thought that a criminal could lose his humanity and ought then to be punished inhumanly, as the crime demanded, for the absolute sanctity of human life no longer applied to him. Everyone, he said, would laugh in the face of a murderer who claimed that it was unjust to condemn him to death. He believed that sexual crimes put their perpetrators beyond the pale of humanity. For rape and pederasty, he recommended castration, for sodomy, perpetual banishment from human society.

Kant, it seems, was so on guard against his own impulses that he could not think unvindictively about crime. He suffered the inner consequences. He balanced himself on life, he said, as on a tightrope. He grew so tired of life that only the criminality of suicide kept him from it. According to Wasiansky (1804), in his old age, his dreams grew murderous, and he was their repeated victim:

> His frightful dreams became more and more horrible. Out of individual scenes of the dreams his imagination composed entire frightful tragedies which made so strong an impression that their influence persisted long after he awoke. Almost every night he thought himself surrounded by thieves and murderers. This nightly disturbance by dreams developed in such a frightful progression that in the first few moments of awakening he would take his servant, who was hurrying to come help him, for a murderer [pp. 278-279, authors' translation].

To return from Kant to contemporary philosophers, we find sadomasochistic traits in two of the most influential, Husserl and Wittgenstein. Husserl would grow elated and then paralyzingly discouraged. His sadomasochism, that is, his characteristic love, attack on the beloved person, and resulting attack on himself, is expressed in a letter to his teacher, Brentano (Spiegelberg, 1965):

> Probably no other urge in my constitution is more developed than that to revere, to follow those whom I love reverently, and to take their side with eagerness. But as my nature unfortunately has two sides, there is also in me an indomitable critical sense which, unconcerned about my emotional inclination, analyzes coolly and rejects ruthlessly what appears to it untenable. Thus bound by sentiment, free by intellect, I pursue my course with scant happiness [p. 89].

Husserl's "ruthless rejection," which, we must assume, was not purely rational, was exorcized against himself no less than others.

Wittgenstein made a harsh Kantian point in his *Tractatus*. Like Kant, he argued that we can know only that which does not finally matter or does not have an independent existence. Judging by the successive remarks in his notebooks, he equated his painful search for the meaning of life with that for logical primitives. Sadomasochism permeated his personality and teachings. He often felt suicidal, and his later project for philosophy was suicidal by implication, for he wanted, essentially, to do away with philosophy by means of the clear understanding of ordinary language. Furthermore, he believed that one could think well only by hurting oneself.

Broad (1959) judged others by his own nature, and therefore cruelly:

> If I may judge others by myself, I would say that a *façade* of good sense and sweet reasonableness often conceals a boiling pit of half crazy suspicions and emotions:—*turris super cloacam,* to borrow and adapt a medieval monk's description of the female human body [p. 16].

Broad's sadomasochism became frightening *reductio ad absurdum* when he spoke of Hitler as dear to him and, in the same breath, as fiendishly cruel:

> I share most of the likes and dislikes of our late dear *Führer,* though I hope and honestly believe that, "if all earthly power were given," I should not put them into practice with the insensate folly and fiendish cruelty of that lunatic [p. 38].

The attractively dangerous, sadomasochistic pursuit of philosophy generates obsessions and compulsions (such as we have seen in Kant and Husserl), and unions of docility and protest (as we have seen especially in Broad and Husserl). The typical offensive-defensive weapon of the philosopher is his logic, i.e., his system of concatenating ideas. It allows him to express his impulses in a limited way, but serves even better to protect him against them. It is not impossible that a philosopher who puts great emphasis on formal reasoning should be explosive, intolerant, and emotionally immature.

We need not make so severe a comment on Descartes to see how he draws up rules to keep himself and other men at a peaceable distance, and how he elaborates his step-by-step method to keep him going straight in the world—not, as he dreamed, blown irresistibly aside; not, as he feared, curious beyond reason; and not, as he repented on his deathbed, condemned by God.

Spinoza, whose philosophical method was inspired by Descartes, but who was more thorough in his use of it, was a passionate, withdrawn man, hostile toward people in general and afraid of his own emotions. He allowed himself to be delighted by the wars of bees, the jealousy of doves, and the like, but his logic was designed to make human actions and appetites into the thought-equivalents of planes, lines, or geometrical bodies.

Though we shall not attempt the demonstration, it could be shown how the favorite logical mechanisms of the philosopher are used by him to build just the world he needs to live in. That is, philosophers have certain characteristic contradictions, alternations, conjunctions, or logical conditions, and these are projected into their choice of logic. Their lives and philosophies are on the models of yes-no, either-or, and-and, or if-then. Likewise, inductive logicians are what they have become because they have personal problems they solve in imagination by the painstaking accumulation of evidence. They are always hoping to learn how to tip the scales in their favor.

The preoccupation with logic can become utterly irrational. We see it at its psychotic extreme in the memoirs of Schreber, whose illness provides a magnified illustration of the way in which suffering can be countered by words with unknown magical values.[2] Philosophers also counter their suffering by creating new, safe worlds for themselves. The medium of creation is the concept rather than the isolated, magically valued word of the schizophrenic. Yet philosophers may fall in love with the words that state their beloved concepts.

Kierkegaard provides a paradoxical example of the philosophical lover of words. Philosophers of positivistic or analytic leanings may disown him, yet, he is, ironically, an acknowledged father of the existentialists. He attacked abstraction, formal logic, and verbalism. The example is therefore apposite and ironic.

[2] Landis's (1964) quotations from Schreber's *Memoirs of My Nervous Illness* provide a vivid portrait of his confusion. Schreber, painstakingly exact and proud of his accomplishments, says:

> For years I have heard daily in hundredfold repetition incoherent words spoken into my nerves without any context, such as "Why not?" "Why if," "Why, because I," "Be it," "With respect to him" . . . (together with) certain fragments of sentences which were earlier on expressed completely; as for instance 1) "No I shall," 2) "You were to," 3) "I shall," 4) "It will be." . . . Throwing into my nerves unconnected conjunctions expressing causal or other relations ("Why only," "Why because," "Why because I" . . . etc.) forces me to ponder many things. . . . It is often not at all easy, particularly in the case of sensations and feelings, to account for reasons ("But why") satisfactorily. . . . Nevertheless this question is stimulated in me by the voices and moves me to think; but as I said before continual thinking is too wearying. . . . An extremely simple observation ["This is Mr. Schneider. But why?"] under the pressure of compulsive thinking becomes the starting point of a very considerable mental task, usually not without bearing fruit [p. 132].

When Kierkegaard was a child, it seemed to him that his father could make the world come into existence by talk alone. In imitation of this god, the boy would shut himself in his room and say loudly, "I will it," demanding that what he had imagined should come true. After he had grown up, he remained a willful dreamer, avid for every experience he could not have. The theater fascinated him. Theatrically, he spent a whole week thinking, feeling, and living like a miser. He had the desire to commit a real theft so that he might live in fear of exposure. He was friendly with members of the criminal police and entertained the ideal of a master thief. He would also describe, as if he saw them before his eyes, the pleasures of the ancient Greeks and the sufferings of the ascetic. He imagined himself dying, though only if there were no one at the scene to argue with.

The power of words and the effect of their order fascinated Kierkegaard most of all, for words were characters he could manipulate in an endless drama of his own making. He fell in love with Latin and Greek grammar. When he learned the rules for the indicative and conjunctive, an extraordinary change took place in his consciousness. For the first time he sensed that everything depended upon how a thing is thought. Grammatical form was the invisible soul by which a thought was given life and reality form. He talked to his thoughts, and when he wrote them down he lived in their birth and discovery of form. His words were not, he said, merely literary ones, a mere game. He was playing for higher stakes, reduplicating his words in his life and his life in his words, each taking on substance, sincerity, and reality from the other. He was in love with the sound of words, and he felt the pregnancy of thoughts they echoed. It occurred to him to imagine that if a man could bear children, the birth would be very difficult, for a man does not allow himself to scream.

Words, his love, could be painfully real to Kierkegaard, but also painfully unreal. At times he saw himself not as a natural being, but as the horrible, mouthing compendium of a man, an epitome of feelings and concepts. He imagined himself writing a novel in which one of the characters went mad, and imagined himself going mad while writing it and finishing it in the first person. Words, he said, are both the medium for truth and existence and for untruth and nonexistence. Language is no less dangerous to man than the carnal appetites. There should be a special police to strip rhetoricians, teachers, and professors down to their linguistic skins, to tear off their linguistic disguises, and to say to them, "Hold your tongue and see what your speechless life can say for you!" Language is the gift by which we are judged or judge ourselves. In language, man constitutes himself as an original text of his individual and human existence. This was Kierkegaard's attempt to use words to conceal what was painful and to gain what was missing in his life. He tried to make words carry the whole burden of existence, and when they failed, he grew angry with them, but remained no less dependent on them. He attacked abstractions for being what they are, abstractions, but had the impossible ambition of turning them into nonverbal existences. It must have given him great pleasure to create his world of words, concepts, and dreams; he lapsed into unhappiness all the same.

Kierkegaard's introspections on the nature and value of his writing and his fantasies of pregnancy raise the question of the philosopher's attitude toward his own work. Philosophy, like other creative endeavors, exhibits its creator's potency. The exhibition is sometimes explicitly sexual as with Kierkegaard with his continual talk of seduction, and with Sartre. Heidegger's overwhelming desire to reveal being, no doubt, had its unconscious sexual aim. Slightly concealed sexual metaphors are frequent in philosophy. For instance, to choose a random example, Bergson (1911, p. 247) describes the creation of the world as beginning in an enormous jet of energy which falls back on itself and congeals into material things. His metaphor is reminiscent of Neo-Platonism; but then the whole of Neo-Platonism is based on the potency metaphor of an absolute reality giving perpetual birth to all that exists, which is only its own self relaxed into apparent otherness.

The philosopher, like the artist, interposes his work between himself and everything else. It functions for him rather like a child's favorite toy or blanket which has an objective presence of its own, but is so imbued with his handlings, stains, odors, and fantasies, that it mediates for him between the realm of pure wishful thinking and the realm of crude, painful reality. But the analogy with birth may be more revealing. Philosophies are parthogenetically created children, born of partnerless marriages and pleasures. The fathers who bear them are, like other fathers, proud and fiercely defensive. They show them off and try to get others to proclaim their charms. The world which a philosophy is designed to become can be ratified by consensus which the philosopher is naturally happy to obtain. While it lasts, his distortions of reality, if they are distortions, are harder to make out. If his philosophy becomes embedded in lasting social attitudes, an acquired intuition begins to confirm its truth.

But philosophy is not always successful, even for its creator. It must in part be an effort to escape reality and real object relations. If the philosopher is predisposed to mental illness, if he is weakened for any reason, or if the defensive power of his philosophy is exceeded by the pressures against which it defends, he may grow psychically ill, or he may make the ultimate rejection of reality by committing suicide. But although Hume once tried to commit suicide, and Kant and Wittgenstein were concerned with it, we do not know how frequent the impulse is among philosophers.

Perhaps the philosopher's creative impulse, in its relation to both health and disease, is best described in terms of the pattern of destruction and rebirth. This pattern is the basis of schizophrenic pathology, for the schizophrenic, unable to bear the real world, abandons it psychically. He destroys it in his mind and builds a new world of fantasies. But this tendency to destroy and rebuild is universal, in the healthy no less than the psychotic.

The applied scientist tries to change the world, the artist to change its appearance, and the revolutionary to destroy and rebuild it politically. The destruction-rebirth pattern is a fantasy of omnipotence. The philosopher unconsciously imagines himself omnipotent because he changes the world, he feels, by manipulating his ideas. The mystic tries to achieve omnipotence by creating the right state of mind. But only the paranoid schizophrenic actually sees himself as an omnipotent being.

This concludes our description of the philosopher's need to philosophize. Philosophy only begins in this need. Its superstructures are quite different from the psychic foundations we have been tracing. But if what we have said fits the facts even approximately, they ought not to be evaded.

REFERENCES

Bergson, H. (1911), *Creative Evolution*. New York: Holt.

Broad, C. D. (1959), Autobiography. In: *The Philosophy of C. D. Broad*, ed. P. A. Schilpp. New York: Tudor.

Heidegger, M. (1929), *Kant und das Problem der Metaphysik*. Frankfurt/M.: Klostermann, 1951.

——— (1961), *Nietzsche*, 2. Pfullingen: Neske.

Jachmann, R. B. (1804), *Immanuel Kant geshildert in Briefen* an einen Freund. Königsberg: Nicolovius.

Landis, C. (1964), *Varieties of Psychopathological Experience*. New York: Holt, Rinehart & Winston.

Sartre, J. P. (1943), *Being and Nothingness*. New York: Philosophical Library, 1953.

——— (1947-1949), *Situations*. New York: Fawcett, 1966.

——— (1963), *The Words*. New York: Fawcett, 1964.

Spiegelberg, H. (1965), *The Phenomenological Movement: A Historical Introduction*. The Hague: Martinius Nijhoff.

Wasiansky, A. C. (1804), *Immanuel Kant in seinen letzten Lebensjahren*. Königsberg: Nicolovius.

OBSERVATION, HISTORICAL RECONSTRUCTION AND EXPERIMENT: AN EPISTEMOLOGICAL STUDY

ROBERT WAELDER, PH.D.

Clinical and historical disciplines and disciplines engaged in field studies have often been confronted with the request to validate their claims by experiments or by statistically fortified mass studies, and they have been criticized for failing to do so. Compliance with such requests has sometimes been seen as indispensable before the claims of these disciplines can be taken seriously. At times it has even been seen as prerequisite for their continued toleration.[1]

Requests and criticisms of this kind have come from both

Published posthumously. Dr. Waelder was an eminent psychoanalyst and teacher, and for many years a prolific contributor to the literature of the social sciences as well as psychoanalysis.

[1] For example, the philosopher, Michael Scriven (1959) said, with reference to psychoanalysis: "As a set of hypotheses [psychoanalysis] was a great achievement fifty years ago; as no more than a set of hypotheses it is a great disgrace today. The logical reason is that experimental design in this area is difficult. It is far from being impossible, however, and we have the resources, the need, and the absolute moral obligation to execute such experiments before encouraging or *condoning* the future practice of psychoanalysis" (p. 226).

outside and inside these disciplines. The criticism may at times be justified, but often the critics seem to have given insufficient weight to the following considerations:

1. That the application of laboratory methods is limited by the nature both of the questions asked and of the subject studied.

2. That attempts at applying laboratory methods to areas in which the conditions for their proper applications are lacking may lead to erroneous results.

3. That for certain types of questions there are other approaches available which, if carefully executed, can in many cases lead to answers which are secure, if not beyond all possible doubt, at least beyond what lawyers call reasonable doubt; and that no rational life would be possible, and with it no laboratory science, if this kind of reasoning were denied all validity.

An attempt will be made in the following to distinguish between different types of questions that we may ask of reality, and to formulate the ways of validation appropriate for each.

Problems Related to Types of Questions Asked

Men may ask different questions about the world accessible to our senses. There are, accordingly, different ways of proceeding in trying to answer them, of testing the validity of answers, and of demonstrating them to others so that one man's knowledge may become part of a common body of knowledge.

First of all there are questions regarding *contemporary* phenomena. Among these are such questions as—What is the shape of the surface of the earth? How high are its mountains, how deep its seas? How are minerals distributed in the shell of the earth? What is the condition of the coronary arteries of a particular person? How much arithmetic does he know? Does this man love his wife?

Answers to such questions are found by observation. They are demonstrated to others by pointing at the respective objects and encouraging others to observe them, too. It may be observation of *spontaneous* phenomena (unaltered except for whatever change may be effected by our looking at them), or it may be observation of the response of the system to *probing stimuli* (measurement, testing).

Then there are questions about the *past,* involving reconstruction and explanation of past events. We here have to do with questions such as: When did our planet come into being? When did life first appear on earth? What was the condition of the earth (or the solar system) at that particular time? When did *homo sapiens* appear on earth? Did he appear in one place or in several places independently? If the latter, did it happen at different times and in different forms? What was the average life-span of man at a particular time and place? From what diseases did he suffer? What is the core of historical truth in the Gospel story of the ministry and execution of Jesus? Who killed John F. Kennedy?

Again, there are questions such as: How did life come into being? How the human mind? What were the causes for the Decline and Fall of the Roman Empire? Through what conditions did modern civilization, characterized by a self-perpetuating science and its regular application to medicine, technology and industry, come into being? Why did it happen in Europe at a particular time and not, for instance, in Hellenistic antiquity or in China? Why did the American Civil War or the First World War break out? Why does a person acquire a particular psychoneurosis, or by what circumstances or forces has his character been shaped? What motivated a particular person to commit suicide? How did a traffic accident come about? What started the fight in the nursery?

At stake in all these instances is a *reconstruction of the past.* In the first group of examples, emphasis is on the various *elements* in a time sequence, while in the second group, emphasis is on the *connection* between these elements, i.e., in the way things follow from their antecedents.

Reconstructions are based on *memories* of human beings, including those that have been entrusted to records (written, pictorial, or other), and on *circumstantial evidence,* evaluating clues in the light of our knowledge of, or opinion about, regularities and probabilities in events of nature or human affairs. This, in essence, is the *historical method.* It follows, by and large, what lawyers call the *rules of evidence.*

Finally, there are questions regarding *repetitive patterns:* Such patterns may be purely *empirical regularities,* like the movements of the sun, the moon, and the planets; the life cycle of plants and animals; or the typical stages of maturation and decay in the ages of man. Or they may be what are thought to be *universal laws,* manifestations of a necessity inherent in the nature of things, like the law of gravitation, the law of the preservation of energy, or Gresham's law of bad money driving good money out of circulation.

Regularities and laws are tested and demonstrated by prolonged *observation* and, in particular, by the *possibility of predictions.* Sometimes it can only be the prediction of phenomena that will occur spontaneously in the natural course of events, as the prediction of an eclipse of the sun; or the prediction, on the basis of Newton's law of gravitation, of the appearance of an as yet unknown planet at a particular time and place. But sometimes the situation is sufficiently subject to our control so that we can not only check on the prediction of events under ordinary conditions, but can vary the conditions at will and so check on predictions for a whole spectrum of conditions. This is the case of the *experiment.* Obviously, testing and demonstrating in the latter way, corroborating a whole spectrum of predictions, carries greater conviction than corroborating one, or a few, predictions in the natural course of events. Hence, testing of general propositions by experiment is clearly preferable, *provided* experiments are possible, i.e., provided that all factors of the situation are actually under control and can be varied independently.

Problems Related to Observational Science

The reality testing of images is a constant occupation of the mind, and the demonstration to others of observations accepted as real is a constant part of social interaction. It works well enough in a myriad of ways in daily life.

But there are two pitfalls in observation and hence in science built upon it. One has to do with inadequacy of perception and errors of observation; the other, with the impact which observation, and, in particular, probing, has upon the facts observed.

There are, first, the inadequacies of the sense organs. Some people are totally blind; many more have visual impediments such as myopia, or a greater or lesser degree of color blindness. There are illusions to which all men are prone, such as the fata morgana of the desert or hallucinations under toxic influence; there are also the hallucinations of the psychotic. We can easily deal with sense deceptions of the fata morgana type or of the toxic type by showing that they depend on certain conditions—atmospheric, in the first case; physiological, in the second—and that they do not fit in with an otherwise coherent body of perceptions. In the case of inadequacies of sensual perception and in the case of psychotic hallucinations, we accept a coherent world picture of a majority as standard against a number of dissident individual perceptions which are mutually irreconcilable.

But in practice, things are not always as smooth as the theoretical formulation suggests, and it often comes down to this: those perceptions are held to be correct which are so considered by the *scientific community* in a particular field (and, often enough, by something less than unanimous consent, at that). Because the scientific community is, for all practical purposes, a self-perpetuating body, we come uncomfortably close to accepting *power* as the criterion of truth.

But these difficulties are still not overwhelming so long as we confine ourselves to physical data. They become very serious once we deal with the data of an *inner life*—such as love, fear, anguish, hope, desire; or, more particularly, when we deal with an inner life not subject to selfobservation, i.e., with *unconscious* psychic phenomena.

The data of psychic life have often been called subjective, or private, data, accessible only to the subject himself, to distinguish them from physical data, which are public and, "in principle," accessible to all. Psychic data, in this viewpoint, are therefore not demonstrable to others and so cannot be part of a common body of knowledge.

This raises the question: how do we come by our knowledge of the psychic life of others? For no matter how subjective or private psychic life may be, there is no doubt that it does exist and that it greatly influences physical behavior. The husband reacts to what he senses about his wife's feelings; the diplomat or labor negotiator, to what he feels to be his opponent's intentions; even the infant reacts—and, it seems, reacts strongly—to his mother's moods.

With the exception of those of us who believe in extrasensory perception, we are all agreed that the psychic life becomes known to others through physical manifestations. But how this comes about is another question.

There are theories according to which man *infers* the inner state of another person, on the basis of the physical manifestations, by processes of association, intuition or reasoning. Scheler (1954) was perhaps first to suggest that we do not infer the existence of another mind and its contents but *perceive* them immediately, i.e., that we actually *see* that someone is elated, enraged, suspicious, or afraid.

We may stand on the speaker's platform and see a man in the audience yawning. Can we say that we see he is bored, or have we merely concluded it on the basis of experience with ourselves or others, experience which has taught us that whenever we have made this facial grimace, we have been bored, or whenever we have seen it in others, we have had independent reason for believing them to be bored? Or can we say that we see they are bored? This is a relatively simple case, inasmuch as most people will probably agree that yawning indicates boredom; thus, the question is, in this case, practically not very relevant. But there may be another man who does not yawn, and we may feel we "see" that he, too, is bored. More than that, we may perhaps be sure, not only that he is bored, but also that he tries hard to hide his boredom and to give the impression of concentration.

The development of concepts pertaining to our understanding of psychic activity in others parallels the development of views dealing with perceptual theory in the visual field. Here, too, there is an older theory according to which a raw material of sense impressions is organized and integrated into perceptions by mental operations; and a more recent school of thought which considers this distinction artificial, holding that "gestalt" is part and parcel of the process of perception from the very beginning. Do we see a field of colored dots and *conclude* that here is a chair, a desk, a davenport? Or do we actually *see* a furnished room with a chair, a desk, a davenport?

Modern theory of perception (Gibson, 1950) has gone in the direction of the second possibility, a position strongly supported by observation of patients suffering from severe visual impediments due to cerebral lesions (Goldstein, 1942). Some of these patients have a syndrome called *agnosia,* viz., the failure to see gestalts. A patient suffering from this condition may actually see only a field of color dots. With time he will probably learn to adjust to living with his defect and even make up for it, to some degree, through the development of substitute activities which are carried out without conscious awareness. The eye will perhaps trace with very rapid movements the contours of objects, and the patient will then *conclude* that here is a chair, a desk, a davenport. Thus, what older concepts had supposed to be the *normal* process of perception turned out to be a *substitute performance* in *pathological* cases in which the ability of normal perception had been impaired. Psychological research militates, therefore, in favor of the proposition that gestalt perception is an integral part of the process of perception itself and not a mental process superimposed upon it.

The ethologist, Konrad Lorenz, pleaded recently (1959) for the admission of gestalt perception as a source of scientific knowledge. His thesis is summed up in these words:

> . . . among the functions participating in the total performance of the human organism, none, not even that of quantification, possesses a primateship over some other, with regard to being the source of scientific cognition; and . . . in the sum total of all cognitive performances, the perception of complex gestalt plays a part which is not only scientifically legitimate but completely indispensable.

But there are *epistemological* difficulties which stand in the way of this proposition.

People vary enormously in their gestalt perceptions (and in what they "perceive" of the inner life of others). Many people are more or less "gestalt blind" (or "psychologically blind") just as many people are in some degree color blind. Hence, gestalt perception and the perception of the inner life of others are not directly *intrasubjektiv verifizierbar* (objectively verifiable).

This is a source of difficulty when one wants to demonstrate one's observations to others in order to make them into a part of a common heritage of knowledge. The difficulty looms particularly great in matters involving the *perception of the inner life of others.*

Thus, if we admit, as a source of knowledge, gestalt perception and, in particular, perception of the inner life of others, we must accept that people who are equal before the Law are not equal before the doors of knowledge, i.e., *admission of gestalt perception implies an aristocratic rather than a democratic theory of knowledge.*

It was readily accepted in the past that people differ vastly in their abilities and that some can see more of the truth than others. The German poet, Stefan George (1868-1933), formulated it defiantly. "Ein Wissen gleich für alle ist Betrug" (A knowledge equal for all is a fraud). Constitutional endowment, learning, and inspiration or genius, define for him the steps of knowledge which "only the deluded fancy can be leaped over."

Such a theory is distasteful and unacceptable to moderns, not, it would seem, because it has been proved to be incorrect, but rather because it is inconvenient, and because it goes against the grain of our moral sentiments. It is inconvenient to base a theory of knowledge on authority, and it seems immoral that knowledge should be accessible to some and inaccessible to others. Democratic ideology demands that all good things are equally accessible to all. In the confusion of the moral with the factual, of the "ought" and the "is," which is common to all ideological thinking, it appears that what is not moral cannot be true; i.e., what is not accessible to all cannot be knowledge.

However, we are not quite consistent in this. From the fact that some people are blind or deaf and that most people are to some degree color-blind, we do not conclude that colors do not exist; rather, we think that they exist to the full score of the color discrimination of the perfect eye of a tiny minority and that the rest of us must accept the fact that our vision is in some degree defective.

It is also not literally true that the results of the exact science can be demonstrated to all. One cannot really demonstrate the validity of, say, the theory of relativity or the quantum theory, to all people; the great majority is not sufficiently adept in abstract thinking to be able to really understand these doctrines. The universal consent boils down, in practice, to the consent of the academic community in the respective discipline—in other words, to the consent of a self-perpetuating group; hence, the ultimate court of appeal is authority, power. Moreover, the agreement of the academic community is not always total; there are, in even the most exact disciplines—i.e., in the measuring disciplines—some heretics who hold views which are considered false by the bulk of their colleagues. *Universal* consensus is almost always a fiction.

It is nevertheless true that there is a *higher degree* of agreement about elementary sensations than there is about gestalts. More people can agree that somewhere red exists than can agree that anxiety or hatred exist. *The democratic philosophy demands the reduction of data to those over which there is least controversy;* hence, the elimination of gestalt perception.

This trend appears first in the 17th Century, when the sense of touch was given preference over the perception of the eye. As the historian, Wolfram von den Steinen, (1949), put it:

> The pioneering scientists of the 17th Century and the enlightened thinkers of the 18th, fully conscious of what they were doing, gave preference, in accordance with Condillac, to the sense of touch over the eye. The divine, sun-like, sense was subordinated to the one that man has in common with the jelly fish [p. 49].

The modern attempt, in science, to exclude "subjective impressions" and replace them entirely with objective dial readings is actually a move in this direction. *For dial readings, in the last analysis, do not need the eye at all.* Apparatus could easily be so constructed that all "readings" can be done by the *touch of the fingers.* Elimination of gestalt perception thus amounts to reducing perceptions to the sense of touch which, in von den Steinen's words, "man shares with the jelly fish."

The roots of this approach are largely *ideological:* the postulate of equality of all men, which is a moral aspiration rather than an established fact of nature.

A *second difficulty* in admitting gestalt perception as a legitimate source of knowledge lies in the fact that gestalt perception may be faulty, i.e., that people may see gestalts which are not there. That is typically the case with the paranoiac; he *sees* clearly the hand of a conspiracy behind the daily events—events which, for the most part, seem trivial to others—and he cannot understand how others can be so "blind" as not to see it. Adolf Hitler "saw" clearly the hand of "World Jewry" behind Capitalism, Labor Unions, the Peacemakers of Versailles and Bolshevism. Yet his vision was faulty. The percentage of Jews among capitalist enterpreneurs, labor leaders, and revolutionaries was relatively high, but so has the share of Jews been, for centuries, in all innovations, and in the emancipation from tradition, and the rationalization of life. But neither in capitalist development nor in the socialist movement was their participation decisive, as later events showed. Above all, the participation of Jews in various heterogeneous movements, such as capitalism and socialism, was a spontaneous expression of individual inclinations, a centrifugal phenomenon, and not a concerted, centrally directed activity. An integrated, homogeneous "World Jewry" never existed, except perhaps in moments of grave common danger.

I once suggested the term *hypergnosia* to signify the trend of seeing more gestalt in reality than there is justification for; the word was constructed in analogy with "agnosia," the established term for the inability to see gestalt in the visual world (Waelder, 1926).

The demand for universal demonstrability has led to a concentration on subjects that do not require gestalt perceptions but can be easily reduced to dial readings, with other questions being neglected. Karl Mannheim (1929) charged that social scientists

> instead of attempting to discover what is the most significant, with the highest degree of precision possible under the existing circumstances . . . [tend] to attribute importance to what is measurable merely because it is measurable [p. 46].

For a long time psychology remained limited to questions which permitted reduction to dial readings or their equivalent, as, for instance, questions concerning perception or memory. Questions regarding character formation, life conduct, and psychopathology remained outside, presumably to be approached later, when, hopefully, one would have learned to reduce them too, to dial readings. When Freud appeared and attacked just these questions by way of prolonged observation in depth in an appropriate set-up, his efforts were widely rejected as unscientific. Today, clinical psychology, which to a great extent developed in response to the impulses provided by Freud, has grown immensely in the number of practitioners, and so in voting power. But there is still (or again) a wide gap between experimental and clinical psychology, a gap which even threatens to split the psychologists' professional organization.

Together with the trend of limiting study to subjects reducible to dial readings, there has also been a trend toward quantifying phenomena which do not easily lend themselves to quantification. Out of this trend have come public opinion polls, taxonomic studies, such as the Kinsey report on sexual practices, or sociological studies, such as Middletown and Yankee City. Some of the results may well be examples of what one critic (Tresolini, 1961) called "the bogus quantification of the obvious."

More recently, there have also been voices from within the natural sciences, expressing regret that their disciplines insisted on the requirements of reduction to dial readings, and demanding that entrance requirements into the sacred precincts of Science be changed so as to make allowance for observation of psychic content and for gestalt perception. Among them is the voice of Konrad Lorenz, whose views were mentioned earlier. The microbiologist René Dubos (1965) put forth a similar argument:

> It is a moral obligation for the scientific establishment to devote itself in earnest to the study of ecosystems, both those of nature and those of men. But ecosystems cannot be studied by the use of over-simplified models which constitutes the stock-in-trade of orthodox experimental science. . . . The study of natural and man-made ecosystems, as well as of man's response to environmental forces, has as much intellectual dignity and deserves as much academic support as the study of isolated particles and elementary reactions [p. 241].

But these voices have been few, and their influence on the Powers in Being has been small.

Problems Related to the Nature of the Observer

Different people find different kinds of evidence convincing; some trust their eyes, others trust only the dials.

Two examples may illustrate the situation:

Example I. Jones (1965), an experimental psychologist, studies conformity as a tactic in ingratiation. His theses amount to approximately this: It is common for people to try to ingratiate themselves with others by playing up to them and agreeing with them. Professor Jones considers this fairly general, but he also notes that "in this particular area" he has "learned through research experience that people are extremely likely to deceive themselves," and that therefore "only by comparing appropriate experimental and control treatments can we begin to specify the variables essential to construction of a theory concerning it" (p. 145).

There exists what the author calls "the dilemma of the ingratiator": The more dependent a person is upon another's goodwill, the more interested he is in using this kind of tactic—but the more will the other be on his guard. And if the ingratiator makes himself too obvious, the whole thing may boomerang. Experiments were devised which showed that people find a way out of this dilemma through a more sophisticated form of ingratiating behavior—mixing agreement with disagreement, i.e., hiding the substance of the former under a pretense of the latter.

The conclusion will seem obvious to many. Instances of it abound in the world's literature, are narrated in novels, enacted in plays, commented on in works of worldly wisdom and satire, and described in treatises on diplomacy and salesmanship; they are even reflected in idioms of the language: "laying it on too thick."

The behavior in question is very much like flattery. Many a

young man knows that flattery, skillfully dosed so as to be credible, is a way of "making" a girl. Some young men even conduct a preliminary study of where the weak spots of their prospective prey lie—girls who have heard time and again that they are beautiful may be hungry for reassurance about their intelligence, others who have been assured on the latter score, may be grateful for appreciation of their bodies. All this is so obvious, it could well be used in a psychological test. Beyond a certain age, those who do not know these things are either not very bright or emotionally blocked.

But for Professor Jones and for many people with him, all this is apparently not "scientific"—i.e., it is not trustworthy and needs to be shown in the laboratory before it can be accepted as true.[2]

Example II. The historian, Jacques Freymond (1960), published a study on the Saar conflict during the first decade after the second World War. He proceeded in the way common to historians (or criminologists), assessing motives and consequences of human actions according to experience and common sense psychology. He supplemented this traditional historical approach with quantifying methods more recently developed in the systematic social sciences, such as observation of the frequency with which an issue turns up in parliamentary debates or in the

[2] It may be worth noting that the author of the above-mentioned paper does, in fact, make some judgments that do not stem from laboratory experiments but from observations with the unarmed eye. These judgments manifest a credulity such as would hardly be found in those who openly accept natural observations as a valid source of insight and are accustomed to subject their impressions to critical scrutiny. Professor Jones assumes that the ingratiator has to be circumspect about the way he goes about his business, not only because his purpose may become too transparent and so incur sales resistance, but also because of a "natural reluctance to see himself as deceitful or manipulative."

That seems to me an unwarranted generalization. Many people have no compunction whatever about "manipulating" others; in fact, they enjoy it. Boys sometimes boast about the "line" they hand the girls. (Guilt feelings may come later, but then, as a rule, not simply because of manipulation as such.) Perhaps, if the mind is absorbed by laboratory studies, it is less open to experience of daily life.

press. But Freymond treated these data with a certain amount of caution and used them only as supplementary evidence: "These few quantitative analyses have no value as proof, but the information they supply reinforces what we already obtained from a careful survey of the newspapers" (p. 277). "These polls are unfortunately so few as to make all generalisations open to question and, moreover, they provide only vague indications as to motives . . ." (p. 280).

Thus, one side takes it as rather obvious that in an age of nationalism the destiny of the Saar would be important to Germans and that the persecution of national leaders would, under ordinary circumstances at any rate, enhance their prestige among their followers. It takes these propositions for granted on the basis of historical experience and psychological plausibility. At the same time, it is cautious about drawing conclusions from, say, the frequency with which an item appears in the newspapers, because these appearances are only counted, not weighed, and because their appearance or nonappearance may be due to a variety of motives, not all of which are historically significant.

The other side, however, considers assumptions about human reactions like those made by Freymond as extravagant, wild conclusions based on a view of the statistical elaboration of data without evaluative judgment of their significance.[3]

[3] The following is an extreme example of the latter from my personal experience.

I recently received a circular letter from a research group in one of the country's most prestigious institutions; it contained a long list of statements, and recipients were invited to indicate with regard to each statement whether they approved or disapproved, strongly, moderately or mildly.

I replied that however much I wished to cooperate, I could not fill out the questionnaire because my opinion could not usually be compressed into a simple 'yes' or 'no'; I would have to add qualifying comments. I demonstrated this in connection with one of the statements and showed that, without amplifying comments, my answer was bound to be misconstrued.

I thereupon received a letter from the head of the research unit, admitting that "it is certainly difficult to respond with a 'yes' or 'no' answer to complex statements," but adding that "nevertheless, for the purpose of research, such a task must be imposed and your discomfort in it can be readily understood."

Thus, the research leader apparently believed that I had been complaining

As has been suggested earlier, neither side seems to me to be entirely right. Both hold fragmented views, reflecting the fact that some people are stronger in synthetic intuition than in critical analysis, while others are stronger in analysis than in intuition.

The situation appears to be this: *If we do not admit gestalt perceptions and limit ourselves to dial readings,* we are in danger of losing a great part of reality; *we have purchased demonstrability at a price*—sometimes an enormous price—*in terms of content and depth. If we admit gestalt perception, we are defenseless against hypergnosia* and may fall prey to paranoid systems. In order to avoid the latter, we would have to establish an *authority* to decide whose gestalt perceptions are trustworthy and whose are not; and that creates a problem which cannot be decided by immanent criteria. It would, once again, make truth a question of power.

We must try to minimize both dangers. While *admitting gestalt* perceptions, we must constantly *check* them against *elementary* experience, i.e., experience reducible to dial readings.

There is no foolproof road to Truth, and the belief that such a road exists in something called "The Scientific Method" is an illusion, a modern analogy to ancient fantasies like the philosopher's stone or the fountain of youth. But the best approach in matters of mind and society still seems to be to try (in the words of Justice Oliver Wendell Holmes to a 50th Reunion of the Harvard Class of 1861) "to see as far as one may," i.e. to have the results of prolonged observation by those most perceptive checked wherever possible by dial readings.

Problems Related to the Influence of the Observer

Another set of problems arises if observation is not limited to the passive reception of sensual impressions, but if the observer

---

about personal discomfort and did not see, or pretended not to see, the point, that the data he was about to collect "for the purpose of research" were meaningless.

is *probing* nature in order to elicit responses. We must then ask whether the probing is sufficiently thorough so that the responses can be taken as characteristic; and if it is, to what degree it has itself changed, or even produced, the phenomena it was meant to test.

The first question must be considered whenever the probing is applied to a relatively small sample of reality: How representative of the whole subject was the sample selected for study? Was, for instance, the piece of liver sucked up in a liver biopsy characteristic of the composition of the entire organ? Are the people interviewed by the Kinsey group representative of the American population as a whole as far as sex practices are concerned?

The second question presents itself whenever the forces involved in the probing are of an order of magnitude comparable to that of the phenomena themselves. In such cases, our study teaches us only about the *response of nature to the probing stimuli*. The question remains of how to infer from these data the behavior of nature not so irritated.

This question of the influence of the measuring device has been particularly important in the physics of the very small. One might think that the influence of measuring devices can itself be investigated by means of finer instruments and so gradually corrected. But it was found in this century that, in the range of the very small, the atomistic structure of the universe makes such asymptotic elimination of errors impossible and sets insurmountable finite limits to the accuracy of measurement. This realisation, while setting limits to man's aspirations, has itself been the source of a deepened understanding of the phenomenal world.

In the field of psychology and behavior, animal or human, the attempt to consider and to diminish or, if possible, to eliminate the error due to the fact of probing, has led to various devices. The anthropologist may live for a considerable time in the midst of the people whose culture he studies, hoping to be accepted as part of the landscape; or he may camouflage his research interests by other pursuits so that the people, he hopes, are not aware of being observed. The psychoanalyst makes the analytic situation itself an object of observation and probing, trying to understand it himself and then making his analysand aware of it and its implications, with a view to thus weakening or eliminating it.

PROBLEMS RELATED TO HISTORICAL RECONSTRUCTION AND EXPLANATION

The following are typical examples of reconstructions of the past:

Example I. Objects found at the site of a crime may show fingerprints which are then traced to a particular person. The conclusion is then drawn that the person has had his hand on the object in question. This reconstruction of the past is based on the wide experience that the pattern of the fingerprints is not duplicated but is a unique personal characteristic.

General biological experience has taught us that the ratio between radioactive and non-radioactive isotopes of carbon can determine the time when a once living organism died. The age of a particular level in excavations is thus determined by a reasoning based on certain regularities known from accumulated experience.

Example II. An elderly lady is found shot dead in her home; the location of the wound and the absence of any weapon seem to rule out suicide. Suspicion turns to her impecunious nephew, a spendthrift continually in need of funds. Suspicion is intensified through evidence that the nephew was actually in a financial squeeze, that he had appealed to his aunt for help and had been turned down. It gets a further boost when a man appears who testifies to having seen the nephew in the vicinity of the old lady's home in what appeared to him an excited condition. When evidence is supplied that the fatal bullet fits a gun that was in the nephew's possession, the case for the State is sufficiently strong for prosecution. At the time when the matching of bullets to weapons was exclusively a matter for the judgment of experts, with the possibility of disagreements, the efforts of the lawyer for the defense may have been concentrated on forcing the expert witness to qualify his statements and to admit the possibility of error, or to undermine his authority before the jury. Today, this approach would probably not be tried, and the attorney for the defense may concentrate on suggesting a missing link in the chain of causality. Perhaps the gun has been purloined by unknown hands for the purpose of framing the nephew.

There is a point at which circumstantial evidence seems so conclusive that the attorney for the defense does not challenge it at all but prefers to enter a plea of "not guilty by reason of insanity" or pleads for mercy on account of mitigating circumstances.

The reconstruction of the crime, or explanation of observed facts (an old lady shot dead) is based on the consideration of all possibilities, both as they appear in the beginning and as they suggest themselves in the course of the progressing investigation, ruling out those which, in the light of all circumstances, are impossible or highly improbable. If the range of alternatives under consideration is complete (in terms of our knowledge of nature and human events), if one reconstruction is possible and psychologically plausible and covers all data, and if all others are ruled out as impossible or extremely improbable, the case of the reconstruction and explanation is well established. It is, as lawyers say, proved *beyond reasonable doubt.*

Example III. One of the most famous Corinthian vases, the so-called François vase, was reassembled from some two thousand potsherds found over a wide area, presumably scattered by tomb robbers. A few fragments are still missing. As described by Pfuhl (1955), the vase is richly decorated with paintings which illustrate mythological stories, ". . . the details of incredible finish, even to the almost microscopic friezes in the decorated bands of certain garments . . ." (p. 25). It is universally accepted among archaeologists that the object assembled from these shards and now exhibited in Florence is, but for minor imperfections due to the ravages of time, identical with an object manufactured in the 6th century B. C. by human hands and meant to be a vase. This is a statement about events of the past.

It is thinkable that the shards actually did not belong together but came from many different vases, fitting together only by accident, as it were; thinkable, but so unlikely as to be hardly worth considering. There are cases in which reconstructions seem dubious, but when things fit together completely, down to "the almost microscopic friezes," archaeologists do not doubt the substantial correctness of the reconstruction. It is similar with jigsaw and crossword puzzles; perhaps there is a solution completely different from the one we have worked out, but we discount this possibility.

The reconstruction of the past is accepted in such cases on the strength of the consideration that *any other explanation is extremely improbable.*

Example IV. Several cases of typhoid fever have turned up in a major city, and the Health Department searches for the origin of the epidemic. The Department holds a list of persons known as carriers. All persons who have fallen ill are interviewed with a view to reconstructing all their movements and contacts at the time they contracted the disease. It turns out that all patients but one have been customers in a produce store located in a building complex in which one known carrier has his apartment. A follow-up on this clue reveals that the sewage pipe from the carrier's apartment leads over the ceiling of the produce store, and that the pipe is defective at that point, with moisture accumulating in the ceiling.

This seems to explain all cases but one: A patient who lives in an entirely different section of town and who has claimed never to have been in the district in which the produce store is located. This patient is interviewed again and encouraged to retrace all his movements during the critical time. He suddenly remembers that he once drove through this part of town on his way to a suburb and, suffering from the heat, stopped at a fruit store and bought a bunch of grapes. It turns out that this was the store in question.

The ring is now closed. All produce found in the store is destroyed, the defective pipe is repaired, and no new cases are reported. Afterwards, we feel justified in assuming that the events have been adequately reconstructed and the outbreak of the epidemic adequately explained.

Example V. The deciphering of hieroglyphs is another example of reconstruction of the past. The Rosetta stone carried three inscriptions: one in Greek, one in hieroglyphs, and a third one in still different characters. Deciphering started with the hypothesis that all told the same story, i.e., that it was a trilingual announcement—a plausible enough hypothesis, yet one that could not be taken for granted. Then came another hypothesis to the effect that a number of hieroglyphs framed by a cartouche were the Egyptian equivalent of the name of the king found in the Greek version. In proceeding further, hypothesis was piled upon hypothesis. All of them found their justification in the fact that they eventually permitted the reading of the text; and that they permitted the deciphering of numerous other inscriptions as well. Today, ancient Egyptian, like ancient Greek or Sanskrit, can be learned from textbooks, and, but for possible occasional errors and inaccuracies, no scholar doubts that the reconstruction is not just a concatenation of speculations and delusions, but is substantially correct.

All reconstructions of the past contain an *implicit prediction:* If the past has been correctly reconstructed, one can predict that no evidence will turn up in the future that will invalidate the reconstruction. That means, in the case of Example I, that no evidence will ever turn up to suggest that the person to whom the fingerprints have been traced could not have touched the object in question, perhaps because he was dead before it had been manufactured. It means, in the second example, that no evidence will turn up to show that the nephew could not possibly have killed the old lady. It means, in the case of the third example, that no evidence will ever turn up to indicate that the François vase did not exist in antiquity in the form of, and with the decorations shown by, the object exhibited in Florence.

These predictions are purely negative, and because they have been borne out over a considerable period of time adds little to the persuasiveness of the reconstruction.

But not so in the last two examples. We can predict, in the fourth example, that no new cases of typhoid will appear, once what we believe to be the source of the infection has been dried up. We can predict, in the case of the fifth example, that other Egyptian inscriptions, including those not yet excavated, will be understandable on the basis of the reconstructed script, requiring, at most, minor additions or modifications.

That these predictions have been borne out by subsequent events adds substantially to the persuasiveness of the reconstruction; in the case of the deciphering of the hieroglyphs, it virtually makes any other explanation seem absurd.

The reason for this difference between the implicit predictions in the first three and in the latter two cases seems to lie in the fact that the reconstruction, in the earlier cases, refers to purely *individual* events (a person touched an object, a person killed another one, a potter made a vase), while in the later examples reconstruction refers to *typical* events—situations likely to be repeated in other instances (people getting sick in an epidemic, people using language and script). From the fact that John has touched a piece of furniture, or that a young man has shot his aunt, nothing follows for the behavior of others. But if there is a source of infection in a populated city, it is reasonable to expect that others will come down with the disease, and that that no longer happens, once some measures have been taken, supports the hypothesis on which these measures had been based. So too, script and language are collective rather than individual phenomena, and if one person has used a semantic system, others also must have done so.

At the time of the deciphering of cuneiform script, the Royal Asiatic Society sent a newly discovered Assyrian inscription to four scholars then working in the field, asking them to decipher it, independently of each other. The translations made by these four scholars were remarkably similar, encouraging the scientific community to accept the claims of the assyriologists. The fact that a number of scholars understand a text in the same way does not in itself prove that their translations are correct; they may all be guilty of a common error. But it is unlikely that a delusional system could be applied to a *text as yet unknown*.

The deciphering appears to be fully proved as more and more texts are read with results which are consistent with each other and with data from other sources. The more such interconnected results accumulate, the less likely is it that it could all be the play of coincidence; eventually, the chances of coincidence become infinitesimal.

The situation in intelligence work is similar. If counterintelligence "breaks" the enemy code, his coded messages yield a meaning that makes sense. If further intercepted messages can be read according to the same system, and if the conclusions drawn from these translations are borne out by facts, the decoding will be considered correct.

In all these instances, a course of events has been reconstructed from available clues which can completely explain what happened, while possible alternative explanations are highly improbable.

The great historian of science, Charles Singer (1941) once said about the theory of evolution:

> Evolution is perhaps unique among major scientific theories in that the appeal for its acceptance is not that there is any evidence for it but that any other proposed interpretation of the data is wholly incredible [p. 487].

But in this lies the appeal for the acceptance of *all historical*[4] *interpretations;* (Waelder 1962, p. 624) and the theory of evolution *is* a historical interpretation. Professor Singer's astonishment was probably due to the fact that he had not often to deal with historical reconstructions and explanations.

It should be added, however, that historical interpretations can rarely, if ever, be proved *beyond all possible doubt*. The gun of the old lady's nephew and heir could have been taken from the drawer by an unknown intruder and returned to it without leaving discoverable traces. The corroboration, by fact, of the predictions implicit in historical interpretations adds weight to the interpretation, particularly in those cases in which the interpretation refers to typical rather than to unique events. The theory of evolution, for instance, finds support in the daily experience of micromutations of organisms in response to the introduction of antibiotics and pesticides. But even then, reconstruction is rarely beyond possible doubt; the epidemic of our example may have had a different, undetected source, and its termination could have been a matter of coincidence. Even the deciphering of hieroglyphs and cuneiform may yet be shot through with fundamental errors, although, in this case, it seems absurd to maintain that the deciphering is entirely invalid—a mere delusional system.

Thus, a reconstruction can be highly probable, sometimes overwhelmingly probable. But very improbable things do occur occasionally. The Law takes account of these limits of certainty and requires only that a case be proved *beyond reasonable doubt,* thus making allowance for a residual uncertainty in all things human.

On this area of uncertainty rests the view that historical and clinical disciplines are inexact and therefore not scientific at all

[4] The term "historical" is used here, and in what follows, in the broad philosophical sense of a reconstruction of the past by any means, not in the specific sense of the academic discipline "History," which is limited to the reconstruction of the past of literate peoples from written records.

or are, at best, "proto-sciences," i.e., collections of experiences and more or less clever guesses out of which a science may some day be developed. But, as we have seen, historical reconstruction can often be proved beyond reasonable doubt, with a very high degree of probability. The reconstruction of ancient Egyptian language and script is perhaps, on the whole, more convincing than some experimental verifications of theories even in the natural sciences.

The high degree of probability that can often be achieved in historical studies is quite sufficient for human purposes; and in any case, whether sufficient or not, it is all that *can* be had in some circumstances. No rational life would be possible if we considered all these conclusions untrustworthy.

It should be added, however, that there are some historical problems for which an answer is close to impossible. One may, for instance, inquire into the motives of Abraham Lincoln's policies prior to the Civil War. Was Lincoln motivated (a) by a distaste for the institution of slavery; or (b) by a determination to preserve the Union; or (c) by the interest of the bourgeois class in industrialisation; or (d) by personal characteristics due, perhaps, in varying proportions, to genetic endowment, early childhood experiences, or later indoctrination, religious or otherwise? Or was he moved by several, or by all of these factors, and if so, to what degree did each contribute to the final result?

These questions are unanswerable, and the historian's fantasy and bias have free sway.

Situations of this kind and the fact that the same events are continuously interpreted differently by different writers, with agreement never in sight, has probably contributed to the widespread belief that history—whether the history of nations, groups, institutions, or cultures which we commonly have in mind when we speak of "history" or the reconstruction of the history of an individual, as in psychoanalysis—is not a science but an "art." But it should not be forgotten that while some historical questions —both of the group and the individual—are fairly unanswerable, there are many others which can be answered beyond reasonable doubt. To discard the latter because of the intractability of the former would be pouring the baby out with the bath water.

On the other hand, because it is often possible to demonstrate facts of the past and explanations of unique events beyond reasonable doubt, it does not follow that all historians—those studying the history of groups and those studying the history of individuals—have always been proceeding painstakingly, with proper regard for pitfalls. There are also what Carl Becker called historians *sans peur et sans recherche*—without fear and without research—who present historical explanations as fiat, so to speak, without adequate attention to the rules of evidence.

There is yet another pitfall in historical studies both of groups and of individuals: the inclination to project later events back into the past, to see the past in the light of events that crystallized later. The Austrian poet, Grillparzer (1791-1872) once said: "It is difficult to know the future, but it is impossible to know the past because we can never emancipate ourselves from the knowledge of what came out of it in the meantime."

Thus, it is extremely difficult to realize what Rousseau, Marx, or Nietzsche actually meant. When Rousseau speaks of the General Will and the need to "bring all particular wills in conformity with (it)," we cannot help thinking of Robespierre and the *Terreur;* when reading in Marx about the dictatorship of the proletariat, we see Lenin and Stalin; when reading in Nietzsche about *Herren-Moral* and *Sklaven-Moral* and the coming of the superman, we see Auschwitz. Yet, Rousseau, Marx, and Nietzsche almost certainly meant nothing of the kind, and it had probably never occurred to them that their words, uttered against the background of a fairly stable culture in which much could be taken for granted, might be so translated into practice by their followers.

To sum up: historical investigations, guided by the rules of evidence, will often lead to results that are secure beyond reasonable doubt; but they will do so only *if* they are actually guided by these rules.

It is unfortunately true that the most absurd propositions have been advanced by some historians. Thus, A. J. P. Taylor, the prominent Oxford historian, argues that the Austrian crisis of March 1938, which led to the *Anschluss,* was brought about not by Hitler but by—Schuschnigg. David Hogan, an American historian, argues that the Second World War was not brought about by Hitler's aggressiveness but was "forced upon" mankind by, of all people, Lord Halifax.

The existence of this kind of literature, written by professionals, goes a long way toward discrediting the historical method in the eyes of the public. Yet, this conclusion is not justified. These absurd results are reached by leaving relevant facts out of consideration, and neglecting chronology. If a laboratory technician were to do similar things with his samples, he could produce equally absurd "results," but this would be no argument against the reliability of chemical analysis, properly conducted.

Problems Relating to the Role of the Experiment in Historical Investigations

We cannot find the causes of a past event by experiment, for we cannot put the clock back and have things played over again with conditions varied at will. If we want to experiment with unique situations, past or present, we can do it only by *constructing a model* which we think is like the real system in question or approximates it sufficiently, and experimenting with this model. But that involves the question of how similar the model actually is to reality. Sometimes the similarity is sufficiently established beyond reasonable doubt, as, for instance, when an illness is attributed to some hitherto unknown or unsuspected agent—say, a chemical used as food preserver—and experiments are made to determine whether this agent actually produces these consequences. If this turns out to be the case, we will probably be satisfied that the previously observed cases had the same etiology, i.e., we assume that the model closely parallels reality.

But conditions cannot always be so simply reproduced in the laboratory, and the correspondence between reality and the model may be more tenuous. This is particularly the case in the social sciences. Once it had become known that Chinese intellectuals and Western prisoners had been subjected to "coercive persuasion" (Schein, 1961)—more vulgarly called "brainwashing"—Western scientists experimented by studying the suggestibility of individuals under various artificially produced stresses.

Such studies are valuable for what they tell, but claims that they throw light on the process of coercive persuasion in Chinese prison camps are based on the assumption of a fundamental similarity between the real situation and the laboratory situation, i.e., between the predicament of the person subjected to the real procedure and the predicament of those who participated in the experiments. This assumption is highly questionable because the terror of an individual who finds himself helpless in the hands of ruthless fanatics, without any material or moral support from his own people, is different by many orders of magnitude from any stresses that can be artificially produced in an American laboratory.

The question of whether or not, or to what degree, the model constructed for an experiment is analogous to the reality under study, cannot in itself be decided by experiment. It rests on operations of reasoning, commonly called judgment; and judgment, in its more explicit activities, involves the very kind of reasoning we have discussed as criteria of historical interpretations.

If, then, the experiment was brought in so as not to have to rely on judgment believed to be subjective and inexact, it must be noted that, however clear the outcome of the experiment, the undertaking has not been entirely successful. For judgment, that unreliable, subjective agent that was to be ousted in favor of an exact procedure, actually still remained indispensable in the original choice of the model with which experiment was to be made. This fact was clearly understood by Kant (1790-1796):

> It is obvious that there needs to be an intermediary link between theory and practice regardless of how comprehensive the theory may be; for the theoretical intelligence [*Verstand*] which has conceived a rule must be supplemented by a judgment, so that the practitioner can decide whether or not a certain thing falls under sway of this rule. It is not possible to formulate any rules according to which that could be judged, as this could go on *ad infinitum*. Hence, there may be theorists who can never become practical because they lack judgment, e. g., physicians or lawyers who have done well in school and don't know what to do when called in for consultation [p. 127].

This is true with but one qualification. Sometimes it may be possible to check experimentally on the accuracy or the probable accuracy of a model by so constructing it that it can *make predictions about facts which are already known but which had not been built into the model itself*. A case of this kind was described by Dennis Gabor (1962). The model, in that case, was not constructed with a view to explaining events that had already taken place but with a view to predicting the future; nevertheless, the principle is the same.

A large silt bar about seven miles wide had accumulated across the entrance of Rangoon River in Burma. By 1931 the depth had decreased to about 12 feet and was still decreasing. The authorities, concerned about the situation, called in a civil engineer, Sir Alexander Gibbs, as consultant. Gibbs constructed a model of the harbor in the proportion of 1:200. The tides of the sea were mechanically reproduced, alternating at great speed, so that 15 hours in the model were equivalent to one year in nature, or about one week in the model equivalent to 11 years in nature. The model was constructed so as to reproduce the conditions of the harbor, not at the time of its construction (1932), but rather the conditions that had existed 57 years earlier, in 1875. The model was then put into operation. The first five weeks should have brought things up to 1932. That was actually the case; after five weeks the silt bar in the model had reached the size corresponding to nature in 1932. This was taken as indication that the model did actually reproduce reality correctly. It was then operated for one more month to bring things up to 1982. It turned out that the silt bar would grow until 1937 and then shrink, a conclusion that was borne out by later events.

There are also occasions in which experiments are made as an auxiliary of a historical investigation. In the investigation of an airplane accident, it may seem that the plane disintegrated in the air. Suspicion is voiced that the building material may have disintegrated under stress, and experiments are made by subjecting the same kind of material to similar stresses. An affirmative outcome of these experiments does not necessarily prove that this is what actually happened in the accident. The plane, even though earmarked for destruction by structural weaknesses of the material, may yet have come to ruin by, for example, a bomb explosion, before it reached its destined doom. But the experiment proves that structural weakness could have been responsible and was, in fact, bound to cause the plane to disintegrate some time, and, in the absence of any clues pointing to other sources of destruction, we will accept it as actual cause.

This is only a special case of the general condition that all historical reconstructions are made *on the basis of known regularities or laws*. When the police identify a particular person from fingerprints, they do so on the basis of the general experience that fingerprints are a personal characteristic, not duplicated in others. When the archaeologist determines the age of an object through carbon dating, he applies his knowledge of the speed of radioactive carbon decay. The only difference between these cases and the case of the plane which disintegrated in the air is that, in the former cases the respective regularities of nature had already been known prior to the study of the individual case, while in the latter case the existence of the respective regularities had only been suggested in the course of the investigation of the particular case and ascertained thereafter. Hence, what we have before us in the latter type of case is not really an application of experiments to historical investigations, but rather an *experimental study of regularities of nature which are relevant for the historical case under study.*

When experiments were most effectively applied to psychoanalytic problems, it was in the same way in which experiments appear in historical investigations in general, viz, as an *auxiliary*, demonstrating the possibility rather than the reality of a reconstruction. The classic examples are the experiments regarding sexual symbols. Schroetter (1911) and Roffenstein (1923) showed their existence by producing them artificially through posthypnotic suggestion; Betlheim and Hartmann (1924) by provoking them in a patient suffering from Korsakoff's psychosis, a condition characterized by loss of memory and confabulations. These experiments proved that sexual symbols exist; they did not prove that a particular image which might be a sexual symbol was in fact one in a specific case.

Problems Relating to Regularities in Nature and in General Laws

We can make two types of statements regarding repetitive phenomenological patterns. First are the purely empirical statements with respect to repetitive events: Kepler's planetary laws, for example, or the life cycle of animals. The second type are general laws establishing such repetitiveness as the consequence of the inherent nature of things: Newton's derivation of the planetary movements from his law of gravitation, for example, or the laws of thermodynamics, electrodynamics, of relativity, and quantum mechanics.

Since, in the statement of regularities of the first type, no claim is made with regard to their causes, and thus no implied claim that those causes are inherent in the objects, the discovery of discordant facts does not invalidate the statement; it merely restricts its range. But a discordant fact disproves a presumed *law*.

There are children whose development does not quite conform to the maturational scheme, or who do not reach this or that stage of development at all, or reach it much before or much after the typical time. Such findings restrict and qualify the schemes of typical development described in medicine and psychology but do not make them useless. The schemes are still valid for the majority of individuals. Rational large scale planning can still be based on them.

Essential hypertension was discovered around the turn of the century, and its clinical manifestations and possible development were described. It was later found that essential hypertension has a more sinister prognosis among American Negroes than among Caucasians. This discovery did not invalidate the clinical researches that had been done with Caucasians; it merely defined their limits and added new knowledge to the old. New knowledge can easily be assimilated in the tolerant, "pluralistic," atmosphere of purely empirical patterns.

But things are different once the existence of a law has been proclaimed. A law is a jealous authority that does not tolerate rival authorities. A single refractory fact that cannot somehow be subsumed under it, destroys its validity.

Prolonged observation discovers regularities. Laws are never definitely proved, because their claims, implying inner necessity, go beyond what can ever be observed. But if *predictions* made on the assumption of these laws are borne out by observation, the laws become widely, or generally, accepted.

In some instances we cannot manipulate reality at will and have to wait until nature offers the occasion to observe the predicted phenomenon, as in the case of eclipses of the sun or the moon, or in the case of the bending of light passing close to the gravitation field of the sun. In such cases, the persuasive power of an observation bearing out a prediction largely depends on the *precision* of the prediction which has been so borne out. The fact that Leverrier could locate the planet Neptunus precisely on the spot predicted was decisive for the general acceptance of

Newton's law of gravitation. But the fact that "capitalism"—in itself an imprecise concept—has disappeared over vast parts of the world has not proved the validity of Marx's theory of history, except in the eyes of those already unalterably convinced, and it will not be proved if market economies should disappear in the remainder of the world, too; for the prediction that would have been borne out was not very specific. Every past political or economic system has been superseded by others, and every present one will probably be superseded at some future time.

In other cases, phenomena are so completely under our control that we can corroborate, not only a few predictions of isolated events, but a whole continuum; i.e., we can predict what will happen under any combination of parameters. Such is the case of the experiment, which makes the experiment the incomparable tool in the search for general laws, the *via regia* toward the discovery of what is inherent in nature. But the experiment, all but indispensable for the formulation of general laws, is not universally applicable. It does require a subject matter which in all relevant aspects, i.e., in all aspects known to have an influence on the phenomena under study, can be manipulated at will. It must be possible to vary individual parameters independent of each other. As the mathematician Warren Weaver (1955) put it, the parameters must be "loosely coupled" (p. 1256). When this is not the case, when the change of one parameter is bound to be accompanied by changes in a number of others, experiment, in the strict sense of the word, is not possible. The more intimate the coupling, the more will the efforts at *disentangling* the various factors *depend on reasoning of a different kind*. And there is no basis for an *a priori* assumption that under such conditions the data of the so-called experiment will always permit more exact inferences than could be drawn by historical reconstruction. In fact, it seems to me that outside the realm of its proper applicability, i.e., outside the area in which parameters are loosely coupled and can be varied independently, the evaluation of "experimental" data requires the apparatus of the historical method and may be altogether misleading without it.

The Ideological Roots of Scientism

Modern Western civilization, which may be said to have had its earliest infancy in the age of Humanism, which grew and gained momentum with the so-called Scientific Revolution in the 17th century, and gathered momentum with the Industrial and political Revolutions in the 18th century, and which is now encompassing the entire globe, storming ahead in the rapidly expanding movements of science and technology, and political and social reform, seems to be propelled by two powerful impulses: the one an impulse toward mastery, by man, of his habitat, viz., a *manipulative* impulse; the other a *moral* impulse toward social justice, usually seen in terms of equality.

There is little doubt that these movements have bestowed immense benefits on the great majority of men. The first of these impulses has, in the most advanced countries, added many years of life, and of productive and enjoyable life to boot, to the human life span, and it has all but emancipated man from the ancient curse of a constant struggle against hunger and of back-breaking toil. The second impulse has meant that the anonymous masses of mankind, who all through history had to serve the purposes of their masters and could pursue their own only after their masters' had been satisfied, had come into their own.

But while it would be ridiculous to underestimate the magnitude of the achievement, it would be equally erroneous to overlook the fact that achievements are bought at a price. Whatever does not serve either the manipulative or the egalitarian drive has been neglected and has withered.

In the field of human knowledge with which we are here concerned, the *first* of the two modern orientations has meant that all attention has been focused on what can be manipulated. Subjects which cannot be manipulated but can be approached only in a receptive attitude—contemplation, philosophy—either have shrivelled into insignificance, or vain attempts have been made to emulate the triumphant manipulative disciplines in these matters, too. Hence, the nearly exclusive interest in the formulation of general laws that would permit the manipulation of things and that require for their proof the experiment which requires that its subject can be manipulated at will. Hence, the loss of interest in historical fact. "The depreciation of historical fact," said the historian of science, Thomas S. Kuhn (1962) "is deeply, and probably functionally, ingrained in the ideology of the scientific profession, the same profession that places the highest of all values upon factual details of other sorts" (p. 137).

The *second* orientation has meant that knowledge has to be justified in egalitarian terms, and that knowledge which is not accessible to all—or cannot be made to appear accessible to all, with the benefit of some maneuvering— is not knowledge at all.

No branch of human life can avoid being touched by the prevailing attitudes of men, by what F. M. Cornford (1950) called their "unwritten philosophy." Disciplines which approach the world in a nonmanipulative fashion and which make allowance for the possibility of a knowledge not equal to all, are pressed against the wall. The best they can hope for is to somehow survive until a day when the present imbalance of outlook will be corrected and the pendulum of alternating human extremisms will swing back again. One may hope, without too much confidence, that it will not be toward another extremism, for human beings, as Sir Richard Livingstone (1959) said, "rarely walk in the center of the road; they reel drunkenly from the ditch on one side to the ditch on the other" (p. 43).

THE EPISTEMOLOGY OF PSYCHOANALYSIS

The empirical basis of psychoanalytic claims is exclusively the prolonged observation of individuals. These individuals are studied both dynamically and historically (Hartmann, Kris,

1945). An attempt is made to find: (a) what "makes a person tick," that is, in what way his inner life and his behavior grow out of varying and, as a rule, conflicting motivations both conscious and unconscious, i.e., both accessible or inaccessible to self-observation; and (b) how, out of the raw material of constitutional endowment and environmental influences, he has become the kind of person that he is (pp. 11-30).

For the purpose of this investigation, the individual under study is instructed to follow the so-called analytic rule, i.e., during the sessions of study, to permit every idea to enter his mind, regardless of whether or not it seems relevant to the purposes pursued at the moment, and to communicate to the observer the total content of the mind rather than only a selection made from one point of view or another. This setting permits the observer to acquire a more complete knowledge of a person's mental life than could be had otherwise. It also opens to view aspects of life and feeling which are ordinarily withheld from one's own and, even more, from anybody else's attention. These communications form the raw material in which the observer searches for a dynamic and historic understanding of his object.

He sets himself three tasks: (a) To discover the way the mind of his analysand works; (b) To find in it gestalts, such as repetitive patterns; (c) To reconstruct their development in the past.

In the *first* of these activities, he proceeds largely by trying to see what is going on. Anybody who denies the possibility of perceiving mental content in others and believes that perception is limited to physical data only, while everything else is a matter of inference, will look upon psychoanalysis as a matter of speculation.

What has been said before in general terms about different people putting their trust in different kinds of evidence, can be applied here. For some, the evidence of what they feel they "see" is immediately convincing. Little is added to their conviction by corroborative "objective" data—i.e., data which in the last resort could be reduced to dial readings. In fact, there are some who approach corroborative objective data with distrust, wondering whether the result was not brought about by some hidden *petitio principii* or by faulty reasoning. Others, on the other hand, look upon the perceptions of the former group as subjective impressions and accept the indirect proof by objective reasoning as convincing.

The different approaches, which have previously been described in relation to investigations involving psychic life or gestalt perception, should now be brought to bear on psychoanalytic propositions in particular. There is, for instance, the psychoanalytic doctrine of the relations between paranoia and (unconscious) homosexuality: in the delusion of persecution the paranoid person is seen as desperately denying and disclaiming a sexual attachment to the persecutor who is (or stands for) a person of the same sex. In some cases at least, direct observation puts this contention beyond reasonable doubt for some people (including the present writer).

On the other hand, psychologists have tried to check this thesis by objective methods: by investigating the frequency of overt homosexual behavior or of obvious homosexual symbolism in paranoids or by their rating on a masculinity-femininity test scale. The results showed a significant correlation between paranoia and homosexuality (Gardner, 1931; Strahosch, 1934; Page and Warkentin, 1938).

Some people who are unimpressed by gestalt perception will accept such studies as a convincing proof of a relationship. Others will be unconvinced, feeling that the correlation may be due to unknown causes.

The same is the case with the psychoanalytic interpretation of what Freud called the psychopathology of everyday life. For instance, Freud (1916-1917) reports the following story:

> I was once the guest of a young married couple and heard the young woman laughingly describe her latest experience. The day after her return from the honeymoon she had called for her un-

> married sister to go shopping with her as she used to do, while her husband went to his business. Suddenly she noticed a gentleman on the other side of the street, and nudging her sister had cried: "Look, there goes Herr L." She had forgotten that this gentleman had been her husband for some weeks. I shuddered as I heard the story, but I did not dare to draw the inference. The little incident only occurred to my mind some years later when the marriage had come to a most unhappy end [p. 57].

For some people, forgetting the fact that one is married to a person and reacting to him as a stranger will be a rather convincing indication of a less than complete acceptance of the relationship, or of an estrangement; but how could this be proved by objective data? One might follow up a number of such cases with a view to establishing whether their divorce rate is significantly different from that prevailing at their time and place. But since the slip can only indicate alienation at the particular moment, i.e., may be only temporary, while divorce, presumably, is the consequence of a more lasting alienation, one would need a sizeable number of cases before conclusions would have any significance. And it may be difficult to find a sufficient number of comparable, well-documented incidents of this kind. Yet, even if these were found, and if the investigation showed no statistically significant difference in the subsequent divorce rate of these cases, there would still be some who would continue to believe that the slip did indicate a lack of involvement, and that the fact that it did not show up in the divorce rate was probably due to undetected minor causes.[5]

There are many instances of this kind. In practical life situations many people respond to slips as though they understood the

[5] Considerations of this kind are not limited to psychological matters. In the physical sciences too, a theory can seem so well established that the scientific community disregards incongruous data, satisfied that they are due to secondary, if undetected, causes. Half a century ago physicists disregarded F. Ehrenhaft's reports of having measured electric charges smaller than the elementary quantum of electricity. They did so, even though Ehrenhaft's observations had never been satisfactorily explained.

meaning which Freud attributed to them, even though they may not be willing to endorse the Freudian view in its abstract formulation. If a young man does not turn up for a date, his girl will hardly accept it as a valid excuse that he has "just" forgotten about it; rather, she will probably feel that this explanation adds insult to injury.

During the Italian campaign of the second world war, 23 villagers of Caiazzo in Southern Italy were machine-gunned at the order of a German officer. He had asked the villagers in which direction "the enemy" had gone and they, inadvertently, did not point in the direction of Allied troup movements but in that of the Germans. The barbarism of a mass execution of people for an inadvertent show of sympathy needs no emphasis; but who will question that the slip of the villagers did, in fact, betray where their sympathies lay?

However, it must be emphasized that in a properly conducted psychoanalysis, the psychoanalyst should not rely exclusively on his impressions, no matter how strong. While believing that the psychic life of others is accessible to observation, he must be aware of the fact that this kind of observation is subject to many errors and illusions. Even in the story of the newlywed quoted above, Freud (1916-1917) emphasized that

> our interpretation is . . . no more than a suspicion to which we ourselves do not attach too much importance. Later, however, something happens which shows us how well-justified our interpretation has been [p. 57].

This later event, in the case of the story, is the unhappy ending of the marriage. Freud, as we see, operated by *combining psychic insight with objective corroborations.*

In a similar way, the psychoanalyst checks his "perceptions" by means of external data which do not require the same "looking into" the mind (Waelder, 1966). He is therefore constantly *oscillating between gestalt perceptions and checking by way of nongestalt operations.*

The *second* part of the psychoanalytic procedure, the search for repetitive patterns, is a matter of (logical) reasoning.

The *third,* or historical, part of the psychoanalyst's job is pure reconstruction of the kind that is practised by historians, archaeologists, criminal investigators, accident investigators, supervisors who conduct surveys, and many others. It is subject to the same criteria that these activities are, i.e., the fact that a reconstruction is plausible does not prove it to be correct. We may have a plausible explanation of a person's character in terms of the family constellation in his childhood—father, mother, siblings, their characteristics and interrelations—but that does not mean it is necessarily the correct one. In order to accept it as such, it must also be shown that it can account for all phenomena, that all its implications can be found in reality, and that all alternative explanations can be ruled out.

In some instances, a psychoanalytic reconstruction can also acquire the same predictive and manipulative aspect that we have noticed in some historical reconstructions (as, for instance, in the case of the typhoid epidemic). If a psychoanalyst has succeeded in "solving" a neurotic symptom, i.e., in understanding it as a manifestation of an inner conflict, the reappearance of the symptom in a given constellation of circumstances becomes predictable. So does its disappearance, once its emergence under the circumstances has been understood and the underlying conflict, of which it appears to be a manifestation, has found a different solution. There are cases (Waelder, 1962) in which a person who has satisfactorily understood his neurosis can, on the basis of this understanding, virtually make and unmake his symptoms at will.

Thus, psychoanalytic interpretations properly arrived at can, in my opinion, reach a very high degree of probability—beyond all reasonable doubt. This does not mean, however, that such near-certainty can be claimed for all explanations suggested by psychoanalysts, any more than all interpretations of the past advanced by historians, or all measurements made in a laboratory, are necessarily correct. There is little doubt that the quantitative measurement required in some fields serves as a useful restraint on the flight of the imagination in those whose restraints are otherwise not too strong. But that, in turn, does not mean that the responsible application of a subtle procedure should be discredited because some people fall short of its stringent requirements.

But psychoanalysis is not only a collection of individual case histories; it has a doctrine, and that doctrine serves in the study of individual cases by suggesting directions for the search.

The doctrine consists of *generalizations from individual case studies* and formulates regularities rather than universal laws. Among these are developmental and maturational patterns: the phases of psychosexual development, for example, including concepts such as latency, or the stages of ego and superego development. They describe typical patterns and are tolerant to qualifications and exceptions. The anal-sadistic phase of infantile development may be all pervasive in some cases and barely hinted at in others. Latency may be all but lacking, with infantile sexuality continuing virtually uninterrupted into puberty. "Post-ambivalent" genital attitudes may never be reached at all, etc. The conditions, biological or environmental, for this spectrum of variations is a subject for study.

A particularly interesting case of this kind is the theory of the Oedipus complex which, according to Freud, is the culmination of infantile sexuality. It represents a kind of anticipation of adolescence, and, because of the child's physiological immaturity, is doomed to failure. Under conditions of family life, the Oedipus complex ordinarily assumes the form of a desire reaching out toward the parent of the opposite sex and competition with the parent of the same sex. There are, however, variations according to circumstances, and the Oedipus complex of the institutionalized orphan, whose parents live only in fantasy, or of the child of a prostitute who receives different men every night, necessarily shows deviations from the typical form. There is also the "inverted Oedipus complex" (Freud, 1923) wherein the child takes the parent of the same sex as object, in competition with the parent of the opposite sex.

In recent decades, anthropologists have described societies which are not assemblages of monogamous families, but in which children live with the maternal clan, and the mother's brother is the dominant male figure in their early life. Clearly, a variation of the pattern typical in partrilinear structures must be expected under these circumstances; but there is no reason why this should invalidate the basic assumption of a premature flowering of genital sexuality, with adults as important objects.

Once the data about these societies had become known, many anthropologists proclaimed that the psychoanalytic theory of the Oedipus complex had been exploded; they acted on the assumption that psychoanalysis had claimed that the Oedipus complex is a manifestation of a universal law of nature rather than a regular maturational stage, and that the form which the Oedipus complex tends to take in children growing up in "normal," monogamous, families is its only possible form. Neither of these claims had in fact been made; and even if they had been made, the new material would require only qualification, not abandonment, of the theory.

We have an outside observer's report of Freud's reaction to Malinowski's description of societies in which children are brought up by their mothers and their maternal uncles. From the anthropological writings referred to, one should expect Freud to have felt that a decisive shot had been fired at one of his doctrines. But that had apparently not occurred to him at all. Victor von Weizsaecker (1954) reports a conversation with Freud in 1926:

> When the extent of the application of psychoanalysis came up, Freud implied that psychoanalysis would have interesting material for about another fifty years. He mentioned, for example, the psychology of the African matrilinear tribes where the Oedipus com-

plex is directed, not against the father, but against the brother of the mother, since he represented the authority of the family [p. 66].

Thus Freud saw in these anthropological findings material for a refinement of psychoanalytic knowledge; it had not occurred to him that others might look upon them as evidence against fundamental propositions of psychoanalysis.

Perhaps the most important piece of psychoanalytic doctrine is the theory of neurosis. According to Freud, psychoneurosis is due to an unresolved inner conflict which involves libidinal strivings. The conflict has been evaded by repression which has succeeded only in making the strivings unconscious but not in incapacitating them. The neurotic manifestations represent a return of the repressed, distorted so as not to be recognizable.

This concept, too, must be considered an empirical finding rather than a universal law. Perhaps the *return of the repressed* may turn out to be the essential factor in neurosis, if we define neurosis as a condition in which men are forced to behave against their better judgment, to think what they do not want to think, to do what they do not want to do. But the fact that a *sexual* impulse is involved is purely *empirical.* In fact, Freud himself (1936) once ascribed a feeling of unreality, a phenomenon akin to neurosis, to a guilt feeling that had not been recognized as such and that had forced its way into consciousness in this distorted form ("it is not true" instead of "it should not be true"). There seem to be other such cases (Waelder, 1960) in the realm of psychoneurosis proper. But such findings are refinements of, rather than contradictions to, the original theory. They will be important if and when the ultimate principles or laws are some day distilled from the wealth of experience. But that day is not yet. We are not yet at the point where we can safely proceed to the highest level of abstraction and formulate all-embracing laws.

Which leads to the final point. Psychoanalysis consists of individual case studies and generalizations drawn from them. But what about universal laws in psychoanalysis?

Laws that define the *necessary and sufficient conditions* of phenomena do not, in my knowledge, exist. There are many rules that formulate *necessary though not sufficient* conditions of an event; and many more that formulate probable ones. These rules are a matter of experience, and intrinsic necessity can hardly be claimed for them. They are more like Kepler's laws than like Newton's. Their verification must therefore be sought through observation rather than through experiment. The role which the genuine *experiment,* the *via regia to the validation of general laws,* can play in the verification and falsification of psychoanalytic propositions is correspondingly small.

The day may come—will come, I hope—when a few grains of intrinsic necessity can be extracted from a ton of known and well-studied patterns of phenomena, so that the latter can be derived from the former. If and when this day dawns, experiments will be called for to prove or disprove these propositions.

Summary and Conclusion

There seem to me to be three basic approaches to the study of the empirical world: the observation of contemporary events; the reconstruction of the past; and experimentation to establish universally valid cause-effect relations.

Observational science struggles with the question of the admissibility of gestalt perceptions and the question of observer bias. In the first of these questions we have to do with genuine differences in the ways men perceive and think, and universal agreement cannot be expected.

The rationale of *reconstruction* of the past is fundamentally the same, whether an astrophysicist studies the origin of the solar system, an archaeologist reconstructs the living conditions of a prehistoric people, a historian evaluates the reliability of written records, or a psychoanalyst tries to uncover the formation of a neurotic symptom. It is always a reconstruction of the past on the basis of clues available at present, in the light of assumed regularities, whether physical, biological or psychological.

Reconstruction has to steer its course between a naive confidence in the plausible, and a radical skepticism which, if taken seriously, would make all life, and with it also all laboratory science, impossible.

Experimentation is the royal road toward the formulation and demonstration of universal laws. Its applicability is limited to conditions that can be manipulated in relevant aspects. Outside of this area, the ambiguities of experimental research multiply rapidly. Application of laboratory results to life situations requires, in any case, an act of *judgment* which in itself can only rarely be tested experimentally.

The various doctrines advanced by philosophers of science or of history, from positivism to historicism, contain (greater or lesser) elements of truth and have therefore their areas of applicability. But their claims have often been extended beyond this area of legitimate application; this is partly because generalizations from experience, natural to the intellect, are likely to go beyond what is justified—experience is almost always more contingent than we appreciate at the time—and partly because of a "will to believe." In particular, the currently prevailing scientistic and positivistic assumptions appear to be largely ideological, i.e., rooted in attitudes and aspirations rather than in facts.

REFERENCES

Betlheim, S. & Hartmann, H. (1924), On Parapraxes in the Korsakoff Psychosis. In: *Essays in Ego Psychology,* ed. H. Hartmann. New York: International Universities Press, 1964, pp. 353-368.

Cornford, F. M. (1950), *The Unwritten Philosophy.* Cambridge: Cambridge University Press.

Dubas, R. (1965), Science and Man's Nature. *Daedalus,* 94:223-244.

Freud, S. (1916-17), Introductory Lectures on Psycho-Analysis. *Standard Edition,* 15:15-239. London: Hogarth Press, 1963.

——— (1923), The Ego and the Id. *Standard Edition,* 19:13-66. London: Hogarth Press, 1961.

——— (1936), A Disturbance of Memory on the Acropolis. *Standard Edition,* 22:239-248. London: Hogarth Press, 1964.

Freymond, J. (1960), *The Saar Conflict 1945-1955.* New York: Praeger.

Gabor, D. (1962), Predicting Machines. *Scientia,* 47:113-117.

Gardner, G. E. (1931), Evidences of Homosexuality in 120 Unanalyzed Cases with Paranoid Content. *Psychoanal. Rev.,* 18:57-62.

Gibson, J. J. (1950), *The Perception of the Visual World.* Boston: Houghton Mifflin.

Goldstein, K. (1942), *After Effects of Brain Injuries in War.* New York: Grune & Stratton.

Hartmann, H. & Kris, E. (1945), The Genetic Approach in Psychoanalysis. *The Psychoanalytic Study of the Child,* 1:11-30. New York: International Universities Press.

Jones, E. (1965), Conformity as a Tactic of Integration. *Science,* 149:144-150.

Kant, I. (1790-1796), Über den Gemeinspruch: Das mag in der Theorie richtig sein, taugt aber nicht für die Praxis. *Werke in sechs Bänden.* Darmstadt: Wissenschaftliche Buchgesellschaft.

Kuhn, T. S. (1962), *The Structure of Scientific Revolutions.* Chicago: University of Chicago Press.

Livingstone, R. W. (1959), *The Rainbow Bridge.* London: Pall Mall Press.

Lorenz, K. Z. (1959), Gestaltwahrnehmung als Quelle wissenschaftlicher Erkenntnis. *Zeitschr. exper. angewandte Psychol.,* 6:118-165.

Mannheim, K. (1929), *Ideology and Utopia.* London: Routledge & Kegan Paul, 1936.

Page, J. & Warkentin, J. (1938), Masculinity and Paranoia. *J. Abnorm. Soc. Psychol.,* 33:527-531.

Pfuhl, E. (1955), *Masterpieces of Greek Drawing and Painting.* New York: Macmillan.

Roffenstein, G. (1923), Experiments on Symbolization in Dreams. In: *Organization and Pathology of Thought,* ed. D. Rapaport. New York: Columbia University Press, 1951, pp. 249-256.

Schein, E. H., Schneier, I., & Backer, C. H. (1961), *Coercive Persuasion: A Social-Psychological Analysis of the "Brainwashing" of American Civilian Prisoners by the Chinese Communists.* New York: Norton.

Scheler, Max (1954), *The Nature of Sympathy.* New Haven: Yale University Press.

Schroetter, K. (1911), Experimentelle Träume. Experimental Dreams. In: *Organization and Pathology of Thought,* ed. D. Rapaport. New York: Columbia University Press, 1951, pp. 234-248.

Singer, C. (1941), *A Short History of Science in the Nineteenth Century.* Oxford: Clarendon Press.

Steinen, W. von den (1949), *Das Zeitalter Goethes.* Bern: Verlag.

Strahosch, F. M. (1934), *Factors in the Sex Life of Seven Hundred Psychopathic Women.* Utica: New York State Hospital Press.

Tresolini, R. J. (1961), Letter to the Editor. *Amer. Political Sci. Rev.,* 55:885.

Waelder, R. (1926), Schizophrenic and Creative Thinking. *Internat. J. Psycho-Anal.,* 7:366-376.

——— (1960), *Basic Theory of Psychoanalysis.* New York: International Universities Press.

——— (1962), Psychoanalysis, Scientific Method and Philosophy. *J. Amer. Psychoanal. Assn.,* 10:617-637.

——— (1966), *Basic Theory of Psychoanalysis.* New York: International Universities Press.

Weaver, W. (1955), Science and People. *Science,* 122:1256.

Weizsaecker, V. von (1954), Reminiscences of Freud and Jung. In: *Freud and the 20th Century,* ed. B. Nelson. New York: Meridian Books, 1957, pp. 59-75.

FREUD AND MELANIE KLEIN: PSYCHOLOGY, ONTOLOGY, AND *WELTANSCHAUUNG*

J. O. Wisdom, Ph.D.

Empirical Content vs. Ontology of a Theory

Classical and postclassical psychoanalysis are largely, even though not completely, to be equated with the work of Freud on the one hand and of Melanie Klein on the other. Between the two lies a large area of overlap and a small area of divergence, but the small divergence is large in significance. So far as the relation between Freud's and Melanie Klein's theories has been discussed, attention to date has been confined to content. My concern here is to investigate an area that has remained virtually unexplored, the general outlook that goes with the content.

In order to make the contrast clear, it is necessary to outline the anatomy of the content. The body of psychoanalytic theory would generally be regarded as consisting of clinical hypotheses and of so-called metapsychology. Elsewhere I (Wisdom, 1956)

Professor Wisdom, a former President of the Society for Psychosomatic Research, for many years edited *The British Journal for the Philosophy of Science*. He has written extensively on philosophy, psychoanalysis and psychosomatic medicine.

have distinguished the two by specifying examples. Thus, the hypotheses of the castration-complex and the Oedipus complex, of condensation and displacement, of introjection and projection, etc., are clinical. This means that they have direct application to clinical material, may be used in giving interpretations, are either true or false, and presumably are testable by clinical means.[1] For example, part of the Oedipus theory is that a son hates his father unconsciously, and when certain free associations are produced by a male patient his analyst may give him this interpretation. In contrast, there are nonclinical theories, such as those of the id, libido, wish-fulfilment, discharge of tension, etc., which Freud called "metapsychology." These were introduced to try to make sense of clinical discoveries, to explain them; i.e., metapsychology forms a body of explanatory theories.[2]

However, in addition to these two groups (clinical hypotheses and conceivably explanatory metapsychology), there is a new area I wish to open up: that is, a class of theories *embedded* in many clinical hypotheses. To explain briefly:

Consider the statement "All physiological changes are produced by physical causes." This is not empirically testable because failure to find a physical cause in a given case is not a refutation; it may only mean we have not yet run the physical cause to earth. But the idea has proved a fine policy directive (even if the scope of its usefulness now seems to be restricted) in yielding dividends in physiology. It is paralleled by Freud's wish-fulfilment theory of dreams, which is untestable in that whenever we fail to locate a wish that a dream fulfils this does not refute the theory because it may only mean that we have not obtained

[1] There is a widespread belief among philosophers that psychoanalysis is totally untestable. Whether or not some of its theories are untestable, I have put forward a method by which its clinical hypotheses could in fact be tested (Wisdom, 1966).

[2] At least ostensibly. Whether these nonclinical theories succeed in being explanatory depends on whether they are testable. No one has yet shown any of them to be testable; hence judgment has to be suspended whether or not they really are *empirical* theories, i.e., explanatory theories with empirical content. But this problem lies outside the scope of the present paper.

enough free associations to enable us to unearth the wish. Again, the idea has proved a magnificent policy directive (which has by no means outlived its usefulness) in yielding dividends in dream interpretation and therapy.

Or consider Newton's inverse-square law of gravitation. The content is empirical and is testable. Now bracket with it the theory that space is absolute. This is not testable by any known observation. One cannot lay down that it is untestable by observation at all, for some test might be devised, but it is difficult to conceive what sort of observation might test it. Yet this theory is part of classical mechanics, is part of the warp and weft of it, and constitutes what I call the "embedded ontology" of the theory. *Empirical theories carry an ontological commitment,* which is one of the specific forms that metaphysics assumes. (Likewise the theory of relativity contains the embedded ontology that space-time is absolute in a certain respect, namely invariance of metric and law; and quantum mechanics, the embedded ontology, for instance, of a limited indeterminism and of an absolute discreteness, e.g., of energy-values.)

Now although the embedded ontology is not refutable by observation, it is not necessarily unscientific on this score, for, as I have been at pains to show elsewhere (Wisdom, 1963a), science normally contains untestable components alongside theories with empirically testable content. Embedded ontology may become refutable in another way—by means of a *new theory*. The embedded ontology of absolute space is incompatible, not with relativity observation, but with relativity theory. When you have a theory, such as relativity, that is testable, tested, and corroborated, you are commited to its consequences and therefore committed to the rejection of what is incompatible with those consequences. Thus *absolute space, which is not observation-refutable, is theory-refutable.*

The question then arises whether any of Freud's untested explanatory theories might become theory-refutable. To this we can give only a conditional answer: if, for example, the theory of early object relations should be testable, tested, and corroborated, then as a consequence Freud's libido theory would be falsified.

We are now in a position to say that the broad theory put forward by Freud consists of clinical hypotheses that are testable by observation, of possibly explanatory theories, and of an embedded ontology pervading testable clinical theories (the possibly explanatory theories, if they proved untestable, might be of this last type). We are now in a position to consider Freud's and Melanie Klein's similarities and divergencies. I (Wisdom, 1956) have outlined them before, but a slight expansion is desirable.

Empirical Difference between Freud and Melanie Klein

Melanie Klein accepted Freud's theory of dreams, his ideas on wish-fulfilment, masochism, condensation, displacement, etc., the castration complex, Oedipus complex, superego, forms of defense, the ideas of the early phases, and forms of instinct—the great body of his work. Wherein did she diverge? And why?

I would hazard that Melanie Klein's problem arose when she attempted to treat very young children with psychological disturbances, because she found object relationships dominant and found psychoanalysis of toddlers feasible. How was she to understand these two phenomena, seeing that according to classical theory they were impossible? Confronted with such a problem, she diverged from Freud in the following ways.

(i) One broad difference is that, in her view, the infant, instead of basking for the first months of life in a warm bath of primary narcissism, is involved intimately with persons or parts of persons from the beginning of life. Whereas Freud conceived of a psychical aim of expenditure of energy purely in the service of the pleasure-principle without regard to any object that might be required to satisfy it, she held that all psychical life is object-relational. This difference alone has wide implications. For example, it leads to the extension of the theory of the Oedipus complex backwards in time and also backwards from the genital level to the oral phase. And it entails a modification of Freud's libido theory, a theory central to his whole approach.

(ii) Freud, in his scheme of explanation, gave overriding importance to sex as opposed to aggression, to which he attached some, though relatively minor, importance. Melanie Klein on the other hand gave to aggression comparable, indeed in certain ways superior, weight. This leads to a significant change of slant throughout.

(iii) Melanie Klein developed the idea of the superego into an idea of internal objects in general (thus bringing in part objects as well as whole objects). Freud's explanatory scheme took account of this process but in only a rudimentary form and fairly late. Melanie Klein incorporated it completely so that it played a significant part in all her thinking. This development can also be described as an emphasis on fantasy.

(iv) She produced a wholly new view of the nature of guilt. Freud's idea was that the sense of guilt was due to an internalized fear of punishment; Melanie Klein's, that it stemmed from aggression toward a loved object. Melanie Klein's concept could be called "depressive guilt" and Freud's, "persecutory guilt."

(v) She laid enormous stress on three mechanisms, which, though present in Freud's work, play an inconspicuous part: introjection, splitting, and projective identification.

(vi) Though seemingly a difference over a detail, considerable significance may emerge from their different interpretations of the castration complex in the female.

She also linked (ii) and (iii) by means of a fresh view of the death instinct, which operated, in her theory, somewhat differently from Freud's conception of it.

These differences are all to be found as ingredients in Melanie Klein's two new theories, with which she filled the temporal gap of the first three years of life up to the development of the Oedipus complex (genital level). Freud had a few ideas but no worked-out view for this period. Her new theories are: the theory of the paranoid-schizoid position and the theory of the depressive position.

I have elsewhere elaborated in considerable detail the theory of the depressive position (Wisdom, 1962) and the theory of the paranoid-schizoid position (Wisdom, 1963b). Prior to this there was an admirable, though brief, account of the former (Scott, 1949). However, the lack of a full account of the whole body of Melanie Klein's theories has now been compensated for by an outstanding elementary treatment written by Hanna Segal, the most distinguished of her pupils to work within her framework (Segal, 1964).[3] It will therefore suffice to sketch the main features of the theories.

The depressive position has to do first with the growth of whole objects through the mastery of ambivalence, the integration, that is to say, of a good object and a bad object kept apart to avoid the distress of ambivalence. Secondly, when the depressive position is tolerated, i.e., the ambivalence is tolerated, this comes about through a process that compensates for the damage done to good objects by ambivalence, known as reparation.[4] (Thus reparation is not only a defense against ambivalence but also an "acceptance-mechanism.")

Concern for another, in Freud's view, is a by-product of libidinal desire; for Melanie Klein, it arises out of the need to repair damage done to valued objects.

[3] The special merits of the book are the straightforward style of writing and the host of excellent examples. Despite its elementary nature, the book occupies a curious position in that it is really for specialists. The author openly says she assumes a thorough knowledge of Freud. She does not, however, explain Melanie Klein's problem; nor does she discuss the overall difference of approach, the *Weltanschauung* to which most of the present paper is devoted. This paper might indeed be regarded as a supplement to Segal's book. The author, incidentally, published the first case history in the literature of the psychoanalysis of a schizophrenic (Segal, 1950).

[4] Freud explained man's rising above the animal as a result of sublimation and reaction-formation, respectively a displacement from, and a reversal of, the object of desire. Melanie Klein's principle of reparation concerns compensation for aggressive damage; it is, therefore, an additional "civilization-mechanism."

This position is most pronounced between four and nine months. It is a highly organized position and stems from something more primitive, which is easily touched off when something goes wrong in the depressive position.

The theory of the paranoid-schizoid position is this: Prior to the unification of good and bad objects (i.e., the depressive position), these are in a state of isolation; the good object is uncontaminated, i.e., idealized; the bad object is wholly intolerable or persecutory. The isolation of the two characterizes the position as schizoid; the idealization-persecutory structure characterizes it as paranoid. Idealization easily passes into persecution, and the infant in this position, the first four months of life, cannot escape from what I have described as a malignant cycle. The way out, i.e., into the depressive position, occurs through the growth of the capacity for reparation, which makes the persecutory less dangerous and diminishes the need for maintaining an idealization.

Parallel with this is the theory of oral envy, according to which the infant projects part of itself into the breast and defiles it. This would seem to be a specific form of the cycle of the paranoid-schizoid position.

Anterior to this theory is another—the death instinct, which plays a role quite different from that in Freud. For Melanie Klein, the death instinct creates certain fantasies, namely bad internal objects, and is at the root of envy.

The theory of the depressive position has been rejected by many other psychoanalysts, but it is hard to see why. It is essentially a theory of emotional integration centering around ambivalence, and all analysts hold that there is emotional integration and that there is ambivalence; further, it is not at all easy to provide an alternative theory to Melanie Klein's. In any case her opponents have produced no alternative, and there are indications that they are arriving at a similar view, though in a somewhat weakened form. So one is led to suppose that the theory of the depressive position has been rejected, not so much for its content, but because in some way it reflects one or another of these differences of overall views or the general image people form of the infant mind. I think it is possible that Freud himself in the end would have been willing to accept this theory. However, if we go on to the theory of the paranoid-schizoid position, I think Freud would not have acquiesced. The relevant features here concern the split nature of the infant's mind in the first four months of life, according to which it lives at some moments in an idealized world of perfect objects and at other moments in an absolute hell of persecuting objects. What Freud would have been unable to accept was not the idea of idealization or of persecution, but the view that these worlds were object-relational. For him they would have been worlds of primary narcissism, and, since the theory of primary narcissism was at the very heart of his theory and his overall view of man, it is most unlikely that he would have accepted the object-relational theory of the paranoid-schizoid position. He probably would have also objected to the Kleinian modification of his death instinct theory and of oral envy to fit an object-relational mold.

Melanie Klein's theories, forming a new basis for the explanation of neurosis, involve aggression toward split-off valued internal objects together with a projective defense, and unification by reparation.[5] And the superstructure of most of classical analysis, such as the Oedipus complex, is built up on these theories as a foundation.

To summarize, the ingredients that are different in Melanie Klein, or at least so much more emphasized as virtually to constitute something new, are: (i) early object relations as opposed

[5] This is not the place to elaborate the difference for technique that ensues. But it has to do with constant interpretation of transference, both positive and negative, interpretation of internal objects, interpretation of introjection, splitting, and projective identification—these in addition to the classical interpretations. The new interpretations enabled Melaine Klein to analyze infants and psychotics for the first time, i.e., in the classical sense of analysis by interpretation alone, without the use of reassurance, etc. The first analysis of a psychotic (a manic-depressive) I know of to be reported in the literature—carried out strictly in this way—was done by Scott (1947) in the late 1930's.

to primary narcissism; (ii) aggression given cabinet rank along with sex; (iii) internal objects, part and whole, good and bad, or structure and function of fantasy; (iv) depressive guilt as opposed to persecutory guilt; (v) mechanisms of introjection, splitting, and projective identification; (vi) the role of the castration complex in the female. And the new theories are: (1) the theory of the death instinct as applied to fantasy; (2) the theory of oral envy; (3) the theory of the paranoid-schizoid position; (4) the theory of the depressive position; (5) the theory of the Oedipus complex at oral level, this complex being a component of the depressive position.

Freud's and Melanie Klein's Ontologies

If we now have a picture of Melanie Klein's problem, and of her solution, i.e., the respects in which she went beyond or in a different direction from Freud, we are in a position to entertain another question, namely what was their difference in ontology. I do not think this has been discussed at all, even by Guntrip (1961), although he did discuss Freud's own ontology.

Horizontal or Vertical Cleavage of the Unconscious

The basic mental processes on which Melanie Klein relies are introjection, splitting, and projection. Consider splitting of the personality, for instance, occurring in the early weeks of life and continued in normal development as well as in schizophrenia throughout life. Here we have a theory of the nature of the unconscious different from that held by Freud, although he acknowledged the existence of splitting. For in Melanie Klein's view, a person avoids distress by keeping two aspects of the personality split off into different compartments, both of which may be accessible to consciousness. But if this is so, the relationship between the two is not conscious. This division of the unconscious is, as it were, a vertical cleavage, whereas Freud's division, based on the idea of repression, is a horizontal one, in which an unconscious section of the superego represses an unconscious section of the id or ego. Not that Melanie Klein denies the existence of repression; for her, however, it would be a derivative mechanism resulting from underlying processes of introjection, splitting, and projection. Further, the cleavage of the unconscious vertically by splitting is accompanied for her by a further division between inner and outer, for one of the split-off aspects of the personality is usually projected. Again, Freud was perfectly familiar with this, but he regarded it as exceptional, as in paranoia, rather than a universal characteristic of infancy, as did Melanie Klein.

There is nothing here that should provide a fundamental divergence of opinion between Freud and Melanie Klein, at any rate so far as empirical theory goes. But Freud's strong emphasis on repression shows that it amounted to a model in terms of which he saw the entire mental structure, and explained many other features of man's world. Correspondingly, Melanie Klein's model of splitting and projection is basic to her outlook and explanation of many aspects of man's world. So to some extent the difference approaches one of overall outlook.

Etiology: Sexuality vs. Aggression

Now consider Freud's ideas on etiology, which are common to those of ordinary medicine. He has widely been regarded as supposing that sexual disturbance was the cause of all the neuroses. In fact, what he held was a perfectly sensible framework of etiology, namely that an untoward episode in the environment acts upon the dispositional factor or subsoil, which he held was sex, aggravated by contributory causes, against a background of heredity. Now Freud certainly held that sexuality was a predisposing cause of all neuroses, and here a larger difference begins to open up. It was true that Melanie Klein, while regarding sex as playing a fundamental role in pathology, nonetheless thought that aggressive factors were more significant in giving rise to neurosis.

According to Freud, the problem arises over sexuality imperfectly directed toward the sexual object, whereas in Melanie Klein it concerns aggressiveness ambivalently directed toward the sexual object. This difference does not here concern us very much; in both cases the psychological consequences are somewhat similar, namely, with Freud this sets up anxiety and the possibility of punishment, whereas with Melanie Klein aggression toward the sexual object arouses a sense of guilt. For both, the subsequent fate of the individual, whether to become neurotic or not, depended upon the way that individual sought to defend himself against the anxiety or guilt.

Etiology: Biological vs. Psychological

However, a difference at this point does emerge: for Melanie Klein a neurotic consequence is of a purely psychological kind, that is to say, it is the result of attempting to defend one's self against anxiety or a sense of guilt, but inadequately, in such a way as to provoke a chain of further disabilities from which one never breaks loose. Now with Freud, while this was also true, there was a further consideration. Being imprisoned in a neurosis from which there is no escape has its distressing effects not simply because of the frustrations involved but because of one very special frustration. In Freud's view, neurotic consequences will ensue if the sexual aim cannot be fulfilled, and for Freud it is the frustration of the sexual aim that is at the root of neurosis. Here the explanation becomes not completely psychological but quasi-biological, because his view was that if sexuality was inhibited, say physically, then the very inability to obtain the sexual discharge itself constituted a neurosis. That this was Freud's view is, I think, fairly clear from the passages in which he wrote about discharge of tension. But there is one specific piece of evidence which comes from his treatment of what he called the *actual* neuroses, which he contrasted with the *psycho*neuroses. Typically, an actual neurosis was a syndrome of debility, listlessness, and the like, on the one hand, or irritability, over-sensitiveness, and the like, on the other, by no means florid conditions but still definite: in such conditions he held that there was no sexual inhibition, but that the disturbance arose simply and solely from faulty sexual discharge. He gives as an example the practice of *coitus interruptus* and he held that when the tantalizing situation was put right then the disorder would clear up, which would not be the case with a psychoneurosis. It is clear here that dislocation of discharge of sexuality was, in his view, fundamental in causing the neuroses.

Here we have a difference between a basic view that in the last resort attributes explanation of the neuroses and human activity in part to a theory of biological or bodily tensions, and an alternative theory that gives explanations entirely in psychological terms. In the absence of a test, the view that one adopts may well depend upon temperament or upon whether one takes naturally to the view that biological factors actually help to determine the form of the outcome, or alternatively to the view that biological factors simply provide the motor force but not the direction of the outcome.

Scope of Object Relations

We come now to another broad difference. The pleasure principle which has been mentioned was a principle of a rather impersonal kind, according to which an infant sought pleasure, irrespective of who it was from, how obtained, or where. In contrast, Melanie Klein held that an infant sought to establish contact with an object, that is, a person or part of one, from the very beginning. As Fairbairn (1952) has put it, an infant seeks an object, not pleasure. Naturally the object is usually an object of pleasure but the aim is primarily to establish contact with an object. Here again no test has been carried out, and in the absence of one, most people's view will be determined by what they think very young infants are like, and on this most people have views, perhaps strong ones, even though they have never actually had any dealings with infants.

These areas of differences may be summarized as follows: (a) an important difference about the way in which one divides up the unconscious; (b) a difference about the relative roles played by sexuality and aggression in producing neurosis; (c) a basic difference about the biological as opposed to a purely psychological source of neurosis, consisting of biological tensions and failure to discharge; and lastly, (d) the rock-bottom functioning of the mind being determined always in part by object relations or sometimes wholly by a non-object-relational force.

In what perspective are we to put these? I cannot but think that, if there were no further differences of basic view, the difference about whether you divide the unconscious into a repressing and repressed area or whether you divide it into two components split off from one another by a horizontal cleft would hardly amount to a serious ground of contention. It would amount only to a normal difference of opinion which you would expect to find in the thought of two close colleagues. I would even say the same about the difference of stress put on sexual and aggressive factors, though the difference here would be greater—in any case, classical analysts would now accept the greater emphasis on aggression. Is the fundamental difference, then, the biological factor having to do with sexual discharge? This is a slightly complex question because Freud himself was in two minds about the matter. His whole psychoanalytical life was devoted to finding psychological explanations, but in his youth he believed in the possibility, in principle at least, that one day we should be able to explain psychological phenomena chemically, and, though he was never able to use this idea, he never gave it up. Hence he plainly attached special significance to the biological factor. It is reasonably clear that the order of priority of Freud's ideas was that he regarded the biological factor as paramount, and *therefore* that he could not assign to object relations a necessary psychological role in determining every human action. Those who believe in a strictly psychological explanation would not be adamant about excluding biological factors; what they would oppose would be the hypothesis that biological factors could play an exclusive part in determining every human action, because this would be incompatible with an object-relations theory. Hence the issue is not between partly biological and partly psychological explanations on the one hand and wholly psychological explanations on the other, but whether or not there can be purely biological explanations with no admixture of object relations.[6]

Thus it would seem that there is a basic cleavage that centers primarily on the question of object-relational explanations.[7] We can see that this cleavage is a difference in overall view of man: for Freud, man is a being whose object relations can be swamped by biological sexual drives; for Melanie Klein, man is a being whose sexuality is object-relational from the first cry to the death-rattle.

The four areas of difference, then, in ascending order of importance (cleavage of the unconscious; sex *vs.* aggression; purely biological explanations of human activity or partial; and objectless libido *vs.* object relations) constitute, not the (more or less)

[6] This divergence has practical consequences. The inclusion of the biological factor in the framework of explanation tends to prevent certain sorts of change and progress from being made, which are possible in the other view. Thus if the seeds of a severe disorder, more severe than an ordinary neurosis, are laid in the first years or even months of infancy by failure to discharge on the biological level, and if the phase of primary narcissism is not one of oceanic satisfaction but of narcissistic wound, then the implication for treatment in later years would be that this would be psychologically irreversible and therefore untreatable. A similar implication would be that the psychoanalysis of infants would be impossible. In the alternative view, the analysis of severe disorders rooted in the earliest phases of infancy and also the analysis of infants becomes a theoretical possibility, so in the end even a question of overall view may be capable of being settled by what can or cannot be done in practice.

[7] To avoid misunderstanding it must be emphasized that Freud included a vast quantity of object-relational explanation in his scheme, so the issue is not a straightforward one between object-relational explanation and non-object-relational, but between wholly object-relational and some non-object-relational explanation.

empirical theory, but the embedded ontology of classical and postclassical analysis.

DIFFERENCES OF *Weltanschauungen* IN FREUD AND MELANIE KLEIN

Now, a point of view usually fastens hold of embedded ontology and implications ascribed to it, and this is the *Weltanschauung*. It is a social event of significance when a scientific theory creates a new *Weltanschauung*. No doubt it sometimes happens that a revolution in outlook develops in a scientist's mind first, and that this provides an appropriate setting for his new empirical theories. But the order can also be the reverse. Both with Freud and with Melanie Klein, clinical discoveries came first; they were not founded upon, but heralded, a new overall view of man. This is our next concern.[8]

Female Sexuality

A fundamental difference between the nature of man and woman is apparent. First woman. For Freud a woman is, both in her own view of herself and in the view of a man, not intrinsically female but a castrated male. She necessarily passes through a stage of castration complex in the fourth year (Freud put it later, but classical analysts would now update it a couple of years), and this is held to be a normal development, not a pathological deviation. In her view of herself, she discovers the lack of the man's organ, and in fantasy feels she once possessed one and has been robbed of it; the man's unconscious fantasy is the same.[9] She achieves womanhood, in fantasy, i.e., feels no longer castrated, only when she has borne a child to replace the

[8] The most prominent feature of Freud's *Weltanschauung* is doubtless determinism. Since it is shared by Melanie Klein, I shall not be discussing it, but shall confine myself to features that are different.

[9] Let us not forget that in Jewish and Christian cosmogony woman had a phallic origin, being made from man's rib.

castrated organ. On the other hand, a man, for Freud, is intrinsically male. With Melanie Klein the situation is reversed.

At this point we meet Ernest Jones's contribution—the most important contribution he ever made to psychoanalytic theory (Jones, 1927, 1932). He disputed Freud's view of female sexuality and maintained that the phallic phase or castration complex in the woman was a pathological defense against recognition of her own type of organ and sexuality, for he held that the woman in early childhood is aware, though sometimes not consciously, of the vagina. In other words Jones took the somewhat unorthodox view that man is male, woman female, and denied that a woman is a kind of imperfect man. Jones's work, which came at the end of the twenties, afforded a highly significant transition between Freud and Melanie Klein. She, of course, made the idea of woman as female all-pervading.

This all-pervading character is literal: for her, man ceased to be intrinsically male. As a corollary to the theory of the depressive position, a man (or his penis) is, in unconscious fantasy, but an extension of the nipple. Hence, although, for Melanie Klein, woman is female, man is not intrinsically male but a female derivative. It is perhaps just conceivable that Jones had a point.

Here is a difference of *Weltanschauung*. It is a highly significant one for our times as well as for Freud's. If his Victorian age did in reality reflect the idea of woman as a poor specimen of manhood, this is an age when great numbers of *men* are not sure of their manhood.[10] And this may well be reflected in Melanie Klein's hypothesis, which corresponds approximately to Freud's attribution of penis envy to the female, that breast envy characterizes the male.

[10] I doubt if we shall have any real stability in social (or world) affairs until we are animated by a *Weltanschauung* in which men are understood as men and women as women. Freud's and Melanie Klein's cosmogonies are one-sided but may yet be given a perspective by social anthropology.

Primary Narcissism vs. Object Relations

No small difference of *Weltanschauung* permeates the dichotomy between the ideas of object relationship and primary narcissism.

The broad picture of primary narcissism is one of oceanic self-feeling—not even concern for one's self, for no contrasting other is recognized as such. The problem for the infant and for Freud's libido theory is how to burst the dam of narcissistic libido and attach one's feelings to another. If the goal is attained, this dam always exerts a regressive pull on the adult. So the picture—and it is a Victorian picture as well as a Freudian one—is that man is fundamentally selfish. Altruistic deviations are at worst a denial of the real selfishness and at best a reaction-formation, which, though going far more than skin-deep, is essentially a disguise of the inner selfishness. Freud's *Weltanschauung* is that, for the most part and with not very far-reaching exceptions, man is fundamentally a selfish pawn at the mercy of the pleasure principle.

For Melanie Klein object relations allow a possibility of a very different view of man. The very idea implies that one seeks a person (or part thereof) at all costs, even at the risk of sacrificing pleasure. It does not automatically carry with it that one will exercise concern, responsibility, or reparation, but it could carry them naturally enough. So the Kleinian *Weltanschauung* includes a measure of altruism as part of the nature of man, even from earliest childhood. This is not an uplift picture (Melanie Klein had no illusions about what people are like); it does not mean that man is predominantly altruistic. Indeed it is compatible with the possibility (and this is the actuality to date) that man is mainly selfish. It means that selfishness and altruism exist side by side, each a "genuine" phenomenon. It might even be that "normality" would involve a measure of about 50 per cent altruism and that psychopathology consists of dysfunctions of altruism. It is not necessary, however, to adopt such a speculation in order to obtain the Kleinian *Weltanschauung*.

An alternative way of depicting man as not all-pervadingly selfish avoids the strong Kleinian claim that infants can have concern, in the sense of sacrificing at their own expense. (The Kleinian view would, of course, be that this would be partly to assuage guilt and therefore not be wholly at their own expense, but that it could be wholly at their own expense in so far as giving something away is involved). For it has been put to me on the basis of observation that an infant who gives you something to eat wants to have it back (even if you are expected to eat it); in other words the situation is one, not of giving something up, but of *sharing* it. I have made an observation susceptible of a similar construction (Wisdom, 1963c). The question arises whether sharing can take place without the presupposition of willingness to give up one thing for the sake of another. I have also suggested (Wisdom, 1963c) that a place should be allowed among the primary processes for *exchange,* meaning exchange of parts of the personality; so that sharing would be a form of exchanging. Thus selfishness would be a dysfunction of free exchange of personality with others; and, on the other hand, extremes of self-sacrifice would be the opposite dysfunction, i.e., the giving up of something would be masochistic. Thus it is possible to base unselfishness not on the notion of giving up but on that of sharing/exchange.

The cash value of the difference of *Weltanschauung* may lie in this. When a person does something good, do you *have* to assume he had an ulterior motive (granted that this would be the reality in the majority of cases)? The point is much simpler than it seems when we become sophisticated philosophically, especially when influenced by "reductionist" philosophies. It is this. If you aid a drowning man, are you sorry for his plight, or do you want to win a life saving medal? The Kleinian *Weltanschauung* permits of distinguishing these; the Freudian sees the action only in terms of what you get out of it.

With regard to the object relationship *Weltanschauung,* justice demands a spreading of the credit. Melanie Klein is the greatest contributor to this area, but others added more than a mite. Balint (1935) was the first, so far as I know, to put the idea forward explicitly, though Melanie Klein may have already been using it. Fairbairn (1952) systematized it and made it fully explicit theoretically as Melanie Klein never did. Melanie Klein was not interested in such things as *Weltanschauungen,* nor was this Balint's aim, and Fairbairn would not have wished to blow up his ideas in a way that might have seemed pretentious; but the *Weltanschauung* is inherent in his writings and it is to him that the credit most properly belongs.

Here I must add a remark upon the curious nonrole played in psychoanalysis by D. H. Lawrence. One has the impression that he did not find it congenial (nor, I think, does C. P. Snow). Yet Lawrence (and Snow) have displayed an incomparable sense of human relationships. I would conjecture that Lawrence found classical analysis apparently unconnected with human beings (though incorrect, this would surely be understandable); might he not have taken a different view of post-classical, object-relaitonal analysis?

Love and Sex in Freud and Melanie Klein

A further difference of *Weltanschauung* arises over the relationship between love and sex.

Psychoanalysts have had curiously little to say on this subject,[11] considering that they, of all people, are in a position to know most about it. They have, it is true, contributed some unsuspected discoveries, such as the oral, anal, as well as genital forms, but these are usually placed in a context of sex *per se.* And Freud made a distinction between anaclitic and narcissistic object choice, but this does not impinge on our topic.

For Freud, love would seem to be no more than an overflow

[11] A notable paper, however, has been written by van den Haag (1964).

of libido induced by frustration or inhibition. That is to say, libidinal desire can, in the nature of things, never be adequately satisfied, and the unsatisfied residue becomes transformed into a sentiment toward a person, perhaps not unlike the process of sublimation, though without becoming desexualized. One should add that the reason why the libido can never be adequately satisfied does not lie in the inevitable frustrations of daily life but in the taboo on the primary object of libidinal desire, the mother —and, in Freud's theory, she would seem to be an object of libidinal desire and not initially an object of love. In short, love would be sublimated surplus libido.

Such a *Weltanschauung* is important, for it probably reflects the unvoiced view of a sizable proportion of mankind (I am not so sure that it reflects womankind).[12] It is certainly not so extreme a view as Schopenhauer's, namely, that love is a snare set by sex to ensure the survival of the race; but it has in common with Schopenhauer's view that love is a derivative and in some measure, one might say, a sham. (This is not [yet] to be read as a criticism, because it might after all be the truth.)

Connected with this is a curious point. In the classical view, if love is an overflow of excess libido, to increase erotic satisfactions should diminish the pulsation of love, and, as it were, take the lovingness out of love. Moreover, given his own personal experience of love, it is strange that Freud should have set the libido theory above it. But perhaps we can understand this in terms of the *Weltanschauung* of his times.

I cannot forbear remarking on the way a theory can blind a man to what he knows. For Ernest Jones had deep experience of love, and yet he applied the libido theory in such a way, I think, as to take the lovingness out of love. And something the same goes for Freud, who also knew great love. Child of the Victorian

[12] There are of course many degrees and forms of love with which I am not concerned: a relationship focusing mainly on common parentage; a relationship providing mainly a shot in the arm, etc. I am restricting myself to the case where top value is placed on a direct personal relationship regarded as creative for the parties concerned.

age and of the libido theory, he regarded sexual experience as the greatest pleasure known to man. Yet there are those who would think that a woman's smile may send shooting through a man physical sensations comparable in intensity to an orgasm (of course no way is known of measuring the two and comparing them). There is excuse for exaggerating the pleasure of orgasm, for it usually accompanies an interpersonal relation and may therefore get credit for pleasure that may really belong to that relationship; moreover there are several kinds of circumstances in which the interpersonal relation is minimal, so that the orgastic satisfaction is obtained more or less unadulterated and can be seen to be great, though hardly of another world. Freud's theory, rather than his experience, placed a faulty perspective upon the erotic.

To remark on D. H. Lawrence once again: *Lady Chatterley's Lover* may appear to be in the highest measure about sex, but fairly and squarely he places love at the center. Hence no contact between him and Freud.

The conception that emerges from Melanie Klein, though not specifically articulated, is different from libido-dominated love. The theory of the depressive position allows of (i) taking pleasure in or being gratified by the object, (ii) valuation of the object (rooted in the prior idealization of it from the paranoid-schizoid position) without considering the gratification it affords, (iii) an intimate connection between a love object and the possibility of its loss, plus a state of mourning (through ambivalence with the constant wish of damaging the love object), and (iv) the sense of concern for the object manifested in reparation. And these are all fundamental components, though not the only ones, in adult love.

One could say that Freud's libido theory was a theory of sex and Melanie Klein's theory of the depressive position a theory of love, though this characterization of Freud's must be enlarged to include implications for the nature of love and its dysfunctions. In Melanie Klein's theory, love or its component of valuation would be connected with (or perhaps expressed through) oral erotic pleasure in the object; whether she would have regarded the reparative component as expressible in oral erotic terms is uncertain but is likely. Thus love and sex would have a common focus. For Freud, on the other hand, since love was a by-product of libido, there would be nothing in the theory to bring them to a common focus or, in particular, to depict erotism as a vehicle of love.

If we consider love as distinct from erotism, we shall find a parallel result. Thus, if we consider, not love connected with fulfilled erotism, but love in any of the three or four ways that are normally connected with gnawing pain, such a state is covered by the theory of the depressive position, involving as it does loss of object, damage done to the object, and even threat of disruption to the self. In Freud's theory, however, unaccepted love should presumably evoke pain somewhat similar to that of frustrated libido: that is to say, the pain would stem wholly from psychical tension but not from loss of the love object as such.

It is true Freud did not let the matter rest there, for, nearly two decades after his postulation of the libido theory, he turned his attention to normal mourning (Freud, 1917). His central idea was that the grief-stricken person incorporates and identifies his ego with the lost object. Thus Freud did not disregard the factor of loss of love object. Nonetheless the pain involved would seem to arise not from the loss of the object but from the effect of that loss upon the libido. That is to say, the introjection of the lost object would be a defense against grief (to give the libido some outlet in fantasy), and thereby would presuppose the grief, and so the loss of object would not itself constitute grief.

In this connection it is worth remarking that Freud admitted great difficulty in pinning down the difference between normal grief and pathological depression; and he was right, for there was no factor in the libido theory that would discriminate between them.

Let us try to see what the Kleinian view might reasonably be.

The theory of the depressive position is in somewhat better shape than the libido theory with regard to the painful aspects of love, for it involves two factors: the depressive guilt at the ambivalent attack on the love object, and the depressive anxiety at the loss of that object. It is reasonable to suppose that emphasis on the former could lead in the direction of melancholia, while emphasis on the latter would characterize grief. But the Kleinian theory does not make this division sharp-cut. The loss of object in fantasy is held to be due to the ambivalent attack, so that there is always a melancholic tendency. The difference would have to be sought from the action of reparation: in melancholia, reparation is in fantasy impossible; in grief, reparation cannot be exercised, but the *capacity* to repair remains.

A Paradox of Love: Exchange of Selves

From love and sex we turn to certain features of love in itself, to inquire how far they fit the conceptions of Freud, Melanie Klein, and the expectations of society.

Let us first dwell upon a paradox of love. On the one hand it is "self-concerned" in the highest degree. It will stand no barriers in the sense that it involves a readiness to break down all opposition (that realities in fact exercise controls over this is not germane to the present point), and it may even be wholly selfish when insisting on obedience from the loved person. On the other hand it is also "self-demoting" in the highest degree. It knows no reserve about relegating the self to second place in relation to the other (again realities are a powerful modifying influence but not germane here). The paradox will be diminished, at any rate transplanted, if we make a paradoxical supposition that these two facets are always in some degree fused (varying from person to person and varying in one person at different times).[13]

[13] Small wonder if the resulting state rather defies phenomenographical dissection. Not only so, but intellectual comprehension is baffled by what is tantamount to an empirical working model of the Hegelian dialectic. For in the dialectic of subject and object, the subject (i) creates the object, (ii) dominates and remodels it, (iii) is dominated and remodeled by it, (iv) absorbs it,

Evidently the "self-concern" component of love with stress on the subject would fit in well enough with the libido theory. If this is all that the flux of libido permits, love is reduced to the formation of the object, dominating it, and absorbing it.[14] And this would seem to be all, for how could the "self-demoting" component with stress on the object emerge from the flux of libido? The theory of the depressive position, however, not only implies the "self-concern" components, for the infant creates the fantasy of the object (the breast) and dominates it (even annihilates it) in hate and absorbs it in love and hate, but also, through projective identification, can lose itself in it, direct its own aggression or tenderness back on itself and may become dominated (even annihilated) by it or re-created by it, and may through reparation re-create the object it has destroyed.[15]

But we still lack an explanation for one of these two components of love, the over-riding relegation of all else to second place, self-demotion, in relation to the prized object. We may explain it for the individual in terms of the depressive position thus: In the state of ambivalence, the desired object is attacked; this attack is not cancelled, but redressed by reparation. We thus have the combination of desiring a good object plus repairing the damage one does to it. That damage is therefore not apparent. Hence the object appears all good again; for the neutralization by reparation of the damage done by one's destructiveness relieves the desired object of all diminution of good quality. This state, being without blemish, therefore resembles the idealization

(v) loses itself in it, and finally (vi) fuses absolutely with it while retaining its own identity. This has—quite rightly—proved too much for logicians to swallow. It may be taken, however, as a model, not of logic but of love. Interestingly, McTaggart (1896)—and he had no supporter—interpreted Hegel's Absolute as love. I should not like to say McTaggart was wrong. Like Jones and Freud, McTaggart knew love, and possibly his theory, though less good than theirs, served him better. If he was right, this underlines the difficulty of giving an adequate characterization of love.

[14] I.e., the features (i), (ii), (iv) of the preceding footnote.

[15] I.e., the features (iii), (v) of the last footnote but one. (vi) would be satisfied if, on mastering ambivalence, the infant then feels fused with the object; this is not, however, a necessary consequence of the depressive position.

of the paranoid-schizoid position. But it is not the same, for in the paranoid-schizoid position the idealized object is kept wholly good by being split off from what is bad, while in the depressive position it is not kept good by a split but by neutralization of its bad part. I would suggest that the normal idealization of love arises in this way, through neutralization of the bad by reparation. The idealization of the paranoid-schizoid position, however, where goodness of quality, if achieved, is achieved by a split (and where there can even be a rudimentary form of giving shown toward the object), may be mistakable for love (or an unintegrated form of love), but differs in having an air of unreality, in having no trace of conquered ambivalence, and in suddenly giving place to hate. Thus love that is mainly rooted in the paranoid-schizoid position may resemble but be a travesty of love that stems mainly from the depressive position. The "self-concern" and "self-demoting" aspects would thus be signs of the extremes of the paranoid-schizoid position living on in us.

Not yet accounted for in the foregoing is the highly personal form of some relationships (which seems to be increasingly sought). Attraction, high valuation, care, selflessness, even self-demotion, lack some aspect of the personal. The distinction is based on two main features of mutual understanding, and a third consequential one. What are these?

Understanding a person may consist in knowing that he will be touched if you give him a bottle of whiskey and remember a particular brand he likes; you may be sympathetic to this feeling and wish to satisfy it. Some such understanding might well make innumerable marriages flourish. A further form of understanding might perhaps be characterized as feeling the other person's feelings. This is poles apart from sympathetic recognition of needs without feeling them (and of course from the high degree of co-operation involved in "You scratch my back if I scratch yours"). The distinction is unfortunately obscure, for sympathetic recognition must involve some sort of feeling; so the question is, how does sympathetic recognition fall short of feeling the feelings of the other person? If your wife has lost her cat, you may feel the feeling of loss, of a kind and intensity to be associated with such a loss. You might on the other hand feel mortified that you had not prevented the loss. Or you might feel a strong desire to find the cat. The first would be a case of feeling her feelings. The last two would not be, but they would be cases of feelings *complementary* to her feelings. To have the same feelings or complementary feelings mainly about the more important values of the other person would perhaps constitute the intimacy of personal relationship. How, then, might ordinary sympathy differ from this? I think the difference may lie in the specificity of the sympathy: a man who loves his wife may show one form of sympathy for her loss of a cat by feeling just that sort of loss, or he may show another form of it by feeling only the feeling of something gone wrong. Again, if he has a desire to make good the loss, in the one case he will set his heart on finding the cat and simply endure the loss with her if he can't find it; in the other, he will get her another cat.

We are led insensibly into the second feature of mutual understanding: to do with sharing experiences (which presupposes feeling the other person's feelings). I do not think "sharing" at all adequately describes the process; it sounds static, like two cameras receiving the same impression on their plates. The dynamic factor is that once a person's experience is shared by another—much as enjoyment of a concert may be heightened by the other's enjoyment, and perhaps better illustrated by a dance that cannot be done alone—his experience changes and grows; there is a positive feedback. In the jargon of our day, this is "transactional" (its dictionary use, however, is not expressive of the feedback). The feedback shows in a mingling of the personalities. If a new expression is wanted, I would prefer *personality-mingling*. What this consists of, I would conjecture, is a mutual *exchange* of aspects of the self. Reduced to humdrum terms, two people, when their love turns to sharing, are simply, like children with a ball, throwing parts of their personalities to and fro.

The third feature alluded to is the stable growth of a personality toward what he has in him to become. This would be consequential, but not a necessary consequence of the other two features, and it would be long-term, a goal of love rather than a characteristic denoted by it. Something like it could develop in the less mingling form of relationship simply as a boost effect, but hardly in its fullest form, especially as some forms of growth seem more like emergent properties of the couple than a property in a straightforward sense of an individual, so the idea does seem to belong to the present area.

What degree of fit is there between the Klein-Fairbairn *Weltanschauung* and the outlook of contemporary man with regard to love?

It has to be prefaced that no one knows what contemporary man thinks about love. It is only within living memory that it became possible to write and talk about sex. This revolution gathered momentum, and today there is little that cannot be said. And, although we are still pretty ignorant about the sexual behavior of mankind, a certain amount of information is coming on the market. It is quite otherwise with love. It has of course always been the subject of *mention*. But examined and discussed? With rare exceptions, no. The beginnings of a revolution are perhaps rumbling, for a few books have moved in this direction. But the development is fraught with difficulty. I would think it could cause even more social embarrassment than discussion of sex did before 1914.[16] For one thing, one is likely to give away more about one's self in discussing love between man and woman than in discussing sex. And, on quite a different footing, the sheer objective difficulty of specifying what one is talking about is genuinely great. There is the further objective difficulty, strangely enough, of discriminating between aspects of a complex experience. Nothing has been written on love approaching a

[16] It might be thought that there is a unique difficulty about going into matters of sex, springing from the infantile components of sexuality; but what about the infantile components of love?

parallel[17] to the Kinsey report, so one knows next to nothing about the range of variability in the phenomena experienced by man.

Subject to this state of ignorance, one has only impressions to go on. I have the impression that a notable, not perhaps large, proportion of people have a *social image* of love as a very personal form of personal relationship. It is not to be suggested that there were never individuals, or pairs, who viewed it thus in former times; certainly there were. What is in doubt is whether it was a group image of love that mankind entertained as an ideal or even as a possibility. More likely, when it occurred, say before 1914, it happened to pairs who had thought of love differently. Were they not more likely to have had a romantic conception of it—attraction, valuation, care, selflessness, heroism, perfection, with no thought of acceptance of blemishes let alone ambivalence—unaware of the mingling of personalities?

If some such mingling relationship was not widely sought in the last century, Freud's *Weltanschauung* was not altogether out of accord with the times. But it was not fully in accord either: it may have reflected the outlook of man, but hardly of woman. By contrast, the Klein-Fairbairn object-relationship *Weltanschauung* does seem to anticipate a growing outlook on the part of some men and women. If for the Victorians (though not for the libido theory) sex was a concession to love, for some contemporaries (and for Melanie Klein and Fairbairn) it is expression. And as regards love in itself, it seems plain that the object-relationship theory is fully capable of accommodating the idea of love as a mingling relationship.[18]

[17] The nearest is perhaps J. F. Cuber and P. B. Harroff, *The Significant Americans,* and even this work is in reality about something different, namely, the nature of marriage.

[18] A curious problem opens up here. If there is a demand for any form of love with sex as an expression of it, then marriage that is founded on suitability, division of labor, etc., but without love will tend to exclude sexuality and defeat part of its own purpose. True, enough sexuality might remain to ensure procreation. But most sexuality would have to be satisfied in extra-

SUMMARY OF DIFFERENCES OF *Weltanschauung*

To sum up these differences of *Weltanschauung* to be found in Freud and Melanie Klein, there were three fundamental cleavages: These concern the differences between men and women, whether man is throughout object-relational or basically narcissistic, and whether love is a by-product of sex or operates through it; to which was added a discussion of the evolutionary function of love and whether Freud's or Melanie Klein's ideas accounted for it better. Before trying to put the differences into perspective, a word is needed on the blur in the distinction between embedded ontology and *Weltanschauung*.

An empirical theory may contain ontological features amenable to test by observation. Thus relations of structure are, in a reasonable sense, ontological, e.g., that an atom contains electrons that have the relation of being satellites to the nucleus. Such ontological features form a conjunctive part of the total empirical hypothesis. But the embedded ontology I wish to distinguish is neither testable by observation nor is it a conjunctive part. It pervades empirical content. The point is that the structure of absolute space, for example, is a piece of ontology different in kind from the structure of the atom; but, though neither testable by observation, nor a part of Newton's empirical theory in the sense of being one of its empirical hypotheses, it is a structure ascribed to the world by the empirical theory.

Now the embedded ontology may be a component of a *Weltanschauung;* for as a result of endowing space with the quality of absoluteness, you will look upon the world with a certain set. So that, for instance, if anyone suggests that if a rigid body moves it might lose part of its length while in motion, you will (at first) treat this as a joke (a bad one) or a piece of lunacy. But although there is a close relation between embedded ontol-

marital love-relationships. It follows that the idea of sex as an expression of love requires marriage to be founded on love. But a huge body of opinion has always had it that (romantic) love and marriage are incompatible.

ogy and *Weltanschauung,* they are not the same: the one is solely about the world, even though not testable by observation; the other is a way of approaching the world and its make-up.

We can now inspect what has been distilled from the foregoing discussion.

The alternative divisions of the unconscious, horizontal for Freud, vertical for Melanie Klein, are pieces of ontology embedded in the theory. They could enter into a *Weltanschauung.* They do. They enter it when developing a psychoanalytic theory—you construct a theory on a model of repression or of splitting; they enter it when doing clinical work—you think of a patient in terms of repression or splitting. So a *Weltanschauung* evolves *vis-à-vis* the area of psychiatry. But we should not take the prefix *Welt* too literally when the focus is restricted to one ingredient in it. The ontology here hardly evokes an *Anschauung* that covers the entire world.

Similarly with the embedded ontology of pansexualism *versus* aggression.

The divergence of view between having some neuroses with purely biological roots and postulating some psychological roots for all neurosis, and the divergence between a partly impersonal psychology and a wholly object-relational psychology, also form a *Weltanschauung,* for a large difference on the nature of man opens out.

We then turned from matters where the ontology was more in evidence to matters where ontology is less prominent but *Weltanschauung* looms large.

The difference between man and woman is of course ontological, but the overall views of man that result overshadow it. Even this, however, seems less fraught with significance (for psychoanalytic controversy, though perhaps otherwise for society) than the other matters.

The narcissistic view of man *versus* the view that man is rooted in his relations to others implies an immeasurable difference. So does the idea of love as surplus libido *versus* the interpersonal that is larger than sex. Probably the question of the difference between man and woman can be subsumed under this.

CONCLUSION: BASIC CLEAVAGES OF *Weltanschauung*

The factors that make for differences of *Weltanschauung* may now be sieved out thus. For Freud's overall outlook, there were (i) the strong biological undertow, (ii) the psychic representation of it in the form of impersonal libido, (iii) the consequential view of love as a by-product of sex, and (iv) the intimately connected primary narcissism and fundamentally "selfish" nature of man. And it is plain that these are all aspects of the same thing, which might be summed up as "egocentric hedonistic dominance" (which places man in constant conflict with reality and with the perpetual need to make concessions to it). For Melanie Klein, man is (i) always seen psychologically, (ii) always object-relational, (iii) a love-giving animal, and (iv) essentially (however weakly) altruistic as well as selfish. And it is again plain that these are all aspects of one thing, which would be too mildly summed up as "pervasion by object-relationship," but perhaps more adequately by "man as idealist-destroyer-rebuilder in the matter of human relations."

I have expressed the view that basic controversy among scientists concerns, not empirical content, nor even embedded ontology in itself, but *Weltanschauung*. It is probable enough that opposition to Melanie Klein from classical psychoanalysts does not center on questions of content (e.g., whether there is a pregenital form of Oedipus complex) but on their view of man. For if they have risked their professional lives in the service of Freud's *Weltanschauung*, with the near martyrdom this often entailed, and if they have done this under the banner of science, rebellion, and emancipation, how could they acquiesce in a further development that rendered otiose a major element in the rebellion? And if, having entered personally into personal relations, they adopt a *Weltanschauung* repudiating them, are they not like a defecting suitor? Perhaps there is no fury like a *Weltanschauung* discarded?

The Problem of Assessing *Weltanschauungen*

Can a question of *Weltanschauung* be settled? Empirical testing by observation usually does not apply. In my view, the procedure would be to find an independent way of testing some empirical theory containing either object relations or primary narcissism as a consequence, and this would settle the other differences of *Weltanschauung* between Freud and Melanie Klein. Such a procedure might have to wait a long time, however, and perhaps indefinitely. Now it is just possible that the issue of object relation *versus* primary narcissism may be amenable to empirical testing, and I have indeed proposed certain tests elsewhere (Wisdom, 1967). But the question should not be left as a matter of temperament or loyalty.

The whole tenor of this paper has been to favour the Kleinian *Weltanschauung* as against Freud's, in trying to show that hers coheres, as his does not, with certain, perhaps not all, basic factors in our lives. Since questions of *Weltanschauung* are not as a rule amenable to being settled by the empirical methods of science, the issue is apt to evoke partisan reactions. It is pertinent, therefore, to explain my personal position. I have put forward my general argument not as a *parti pris* Kleinian, but because I think Melanie Klein's empirical theories and *Weltanschauung* constitute an improvement over Freud's, occasionally as a replacement, though usually as an addition.[19] I happen to think that nearly all Freud's empirical-type hypotheses are right, but that in perhaps four instances he was wrong. Thus with Jones, (i) I hold that Freud was wrong about the genesis of female sexuality; (ii) I consider that the non-object-relational libido

[19] Freud's achievement was so great that no criticism and no defect in his work can detract from it. Has Newton's reputation suffered in the least degree through the collapse of his greatest theory?

theory, including primary narcissism, (though it gave magnificent service for a quarter of a century or more) is unworkable; (iii) it also seems to me that by underplaying the role of aggression, Freud, in his theory of the sense of guilt, missed the most important mechanism; and (iv) I look on his instinct theory as a misfortune. This is not much out of his enormous contribution, though some of it is far reaching. I also happen to think that where Melanie Klein differed from Freud she was nearly always right, and that she sometimes wrongly agreed with Freud, notably over the theory of libido and that of instinct. And of her own numerous contributions, nearly all were right, though I hold that in perhaps three matters she was wrong. I would think (i) she was wrong in her theory of the source of masculinity, carrying with it a quite faulty understanding of the role of the father, as contrasted with that of the mother, in relation to the infant; (ii) that her adherence to libido theory was an inconsistency, and with it (iii), that her attachment to instinct theory was an unnecessary excrescence that tarnished the scientific nature of her work. This, if correct, will not dethrone her from her place next to the very few women to have contributed to science, such as Sonja Kowalewski in mathematics and Marie Curie in physics. My slight area of disagreement with Freud is the more radical. His theory is not amenable to minor adjustment, but Melanie Klein's could be modified to accommodate (ii) and (iii) without making any appreciable difference, though (i) would have some repercussions. In addition, both Freud and Melanie Klein seem to me to be wrong in their basic assumption about the relation of man as an individual to society; but this area lies outside the scope of the present enquiry.

Although I have supported Melanie Klein's *Weltanschauung* about object relations, this is not unqualified support. The last word has not been said on the subject; for it is possible that a non-object-relational factor may enter into combination with object relations. This is a fundamental problem to investigate.

To state my position makes things easier for the reader. But it seems especially desirable to state one's position when discussing positions that themselves cannot be established.

Conclusion

Some philosophers of science may be surprised at the detail gone into, for it is usual enough to confine discussion to a few general ideas, like the unconscious or the superego. But in the field of physics, for example, it is accepted as a matter of course that, while a philosopher of physics may discuss only a few general ideas, like causality, some go into problems of philosophy of physics involving considerable technical detail. In my view, the same is required in the philosophy of psychoanalysis.

This paper is an application of a theory of philosophy of science to psychoanalytic theory. Thus I have divided the theoretical work of Freud and of Melanie Klein into (i) clinical hypotheses, (ii) metapsychology or explanatory theories, (iii) embedded ontology (with the qualification that the explanatory theories, if not in fact explanatory in the sense of being empirically testable, would fall under embedded ontology), and (iv) *Weltanschauung*. It seems to me that we cannot clarify the scientific status of the theory of either Freud or Melanie Klein without these distinctions; and that to do so is essentially a piece of philosophy of science, even if it involves a new development within philosophy of science itself. I have dwelt only briefly with the clinical hypotheses and with the possibly explanatory theory, since it has been the subject of discussion elsewhere, and the distinction is to a small extent familiar. The embedded ontology I have gone into at greater length since it has not been discussed or even distinguished as such; but devoted most attention to the *Weltanschauung*, which also has been neither discussed nor distinguished as such, but which is even more in need of attention.

It seems clear that a clinician cannot handle research into clinical hypotheses without having his area demarcated from the rest. More importantly, a psychoanalyst who wishes to test his